JEWISH RHETORICS

JEWISH RHETORICS
History, Theory, Practice

MICHAEL BERNARD-DONALS
and
JANICE W. FERNHEIMER
editors

Brandeis University Press
WALTHAM, MASSACHUSETTS

Brandeis University Press
An imprint of University Press of New England
www.upne.com
© 2014 Brandeis University
All rights reserved
Manufactured in the United States of America
Designed by Christopher Kuntze
Typeset in Adobe Kepler and Neue Aachen Bold by Integrated Publishing Solutions.

For permission to reproduce any of the material in this book, contact Permissions, University Press of New England, One Court Street, Suite 250, Lebanon NH 03766; or visit www.upne.com

Selection on page 160 from *Understanding Comics* by Scott McCloud. Copyright © 1993, 1994 by Scott McCloud. Reprinted by permission of HarperCollins Publishers.

Unless otherwise noted, all translations in chapter 1 are from *The Book of Psalms: A Translation with Commentary,* translated by Robert Alter. Copyright © 2007 by Robert A. Alter. Used by permission of W. W. Norton & Company, Inc.

Library of Congress Cataloging-in-Publication Data

Jewish rhetorics: history, theory, practice / Michael Bernard-Donals and Janice W. Fernheimer, editors.
   pages cm
Includes bibliographical references and index.
ISBN 978-1-61168-639-5 (cloth: alk. paper) — ISBN 978-1-61168-640-1 (pbk.: alk. paper) — ISBN 978-1-61168-641-8 (ebook)
1. Hebrew language—Rhetoric. 2. Yiddish language—Rhetoric.
3. Hebrew literature—History and criticism. 4. Yiddish literature—History and criticism. 5. Jewish literature—History and criticism.
6. Jews—Identity. I. Bernard-Donals, Michael F., editor.
II. Fernheimer, Janice W., 1976– editor.
PJ4740.J49 2014
808'.04924—dc23   2014023651

5 4 3 2 1

Contents

Introduction   vii
    Michael Bernard-Donals and Janice W. Fernheimer

1. Taking a Stance toward God: Rhetoric in the Book of Psalms   1
    Davida Charney

2. The Rhetoric of Rabbinic Authority: Making the Transition from Priest to Sage   16
    Richard Hidary

3. Judah Messer Leon and the *Sefer Nofet Zufim*: Rethinking Rhetorical Delivery in the Early Age of Print   46
    Jim Ridolfo

4. "The Pretty Heiress from Our Old House": Figuring the Yiddish-Hebrew Relationship in Rhetorical Works by Itzik Manger and Ya'akov Fichman   58
    Hannah S. Pressman

5. The Jewish Rhetoric of the Twentieth Century: Chaïm Perelman, *Double Fidélité*, and the Pre-Holocaust Roots of the New Rhetoric Project   77
    David A. Frank

6. Socrates as Rabbi: The Story of the Aleph and the Alpha in a Postinformation Age   93
    Steven B. Katz

7. Maimonides's Contribution to a Theory of Self-Persuasion   112
    David Metzger

8. Rabbi Moses ben Nachman, Sophist? 131
Patricia Bizzell

9. Is Midrash Comics? A Fish Story about Graphic Narrative, Visual Rhetoric, and Rabbinic Hermeneutics 147
Susan Handelman

10. S. Yizhar's *Khirbet Khizeh* and the Rhetoric of Conflict 165
Shai Ginsburg

11. Esther's Book: A Rhetoric of Writing for Jewish Feminists 180
Susan Zaeske

12. "Shema Yisrael": Listening in Judaism and What It Has to Teach Us 198
Joy Arbor

13. Simulated *Shiur*? Post-It Notes of an ArtScroll Amateur 215
Jonathan Boyarin

14. Of Superheroes and Synecdoche: Holocaust Exceptionalism, Race, and the Rhetoric of Jewishness in America 231
Jennifer Glaser

15. "That Ceremonious Feeling of Growing Up": The Educational Practice of Bar Mitzvah in the Jewish Children's Folkshul 249
Eli Goldblatt

Acknowledgements 265
Contributors 267
Index 271

Introduction
Jewish Rhetorics: History, Theory, Practice

MICHAEL BERNARD-DONALS
and JANICE W. FERNHEIMER

In the past two decades, humanities scholars have paid a great deal of attention to ways of speaking and writing that are particular to members of ethnic minority groups and cultural enclaves who were previously underrepresented in historical and theoretical accounts. Many of these studies share a more or less stable definition of ethnicity and cultural membership, one that is careful not to take for granted a monolithic set of criteria for membership but that nonetheless refers to, in Werner Sollors's words, "an acquired... sense of belonging that replaces visible, concrete communities whose kinship symbolism may yet mobilize in order to appear more natural" ("The Invention of Ethnicity," xv). In other words these studies embrace an imagined community in Benedict Anderson's sense of the term: they create a sense of affiliation and a set of common historical or cultural memories or tropes that identify, far more than borders or even belonging itself can do, those who share an imaginary, if not a real, cultural or historical location.

It is this sense of ethnicity, identity, and cultural history as invented or imagined that leaves room for the inclusion of Jews—a group whose discursive practices, shared cultural assumptions, and rhetorical engagements with majority cultures around the globe would seem ripe for discussion—in a historical and conceptual consideration of a rhetorical project. As a marker of identity, the term "Jewishness" often has as much to do with an absence of a shared territorial origin as it does with a shared heritage of diaspora and assimilation.[1] In recent years, rhetoric and composition scholars have done significant work to complicate the definition of a rhetorical tradition, as evidenced by volumes dedicated to ethnic, non-Western, alternative, or cultural rhetorics (Gilyard and Nunley; Lipson and Binkley; Gilyard and Taylor; Mao and Young; Baillif). Yet few scholars have addressed Jewish rhetorics. To date, Andrea Greenbaum and Deborah Holdstein's *Judaic Perspectives in Rhetoric and Composition* is the only collection of essays dedicated to the topic.[2] There are any number of reasons for the still nascent state of the field of Jewish rhetorics, but—to speak only of the contemporary context—three seem most significant.

First, discussions of minority and ethnic rhetorics tend to conflate the categories of race and ethnicity, and Jews don't fit neatly into either. From the late nineteenth century until after the Second World War, Central and Eastern European Jews in the United States were interpreted by the mainstream (read: mostly white and Protestant) culture as nonwhites. This interpretation of American Jews began to change after the Second World War and the creation of the state of Israel, when Jews' rise to cultural and economic prominence in the United States led to a change in status to marginally white, thus depriving Jews of a unifying, racial marker of difference (see Ignatiev; Goldstein; Brodkin; Jacobson).

The complex and important role that language plays in shaping Jewish cultural identity offers a second reason why Jewish rhetorics often have been excluded from broader discussions in rhetorical studies. Again to speak only of the contemporary American context, since mainstream US culture identified Jewish culture as primarily one and the same as Ashkenazi Jewish culture, the nearly wholesale destruction of Yiddish and Eastern European culture more broadly during the Holocaust made it harder for Yiddish to be seen as a common tongue spoken by a majority of Jews.[3] Yeshiva and *ḥeder* cultures have also largely disappeared outside of Israel and religiously observant communities, whose members continue to offer such educational opportunities—though often only for Jewish males.[4] Yet these cultural educational practices offered access to systematic study of the Torah and Talmud, Judaism's principal rhetorical texts from which (mostly male) children learned modes of argument and reasoning. And although the number of Yiddish speakers significantly decreased after the Second World War, modern Hebrew speakers have been on the rise, especially since Eliezer Ben-Yehuda's careful efforts to revive Hebrew as a modern, spoken language in the nineteenth century. But Hebrew occupied an uncomfortable position with respect to the Western tradition that viewed it as exotic and other, although simultaneously foundational to Western culture. In the United States at least, the argument goes, since the acculturation that followed the Second World War, Jewish linguistic particularity has been largely if not wholly subsumed into mainstream culture, much as members of the original Reform movement in the mid-nineteenth century had hoped it would. Of course, this simplified narrative has focused mainly on the linguistic practices of mostly Ashkenazi Jews in the United States and has not addressed the important ways that other specifically Jewish linguistic practices—such as the speaking and preservation of Ladino for Sephardic Jews, and the use of Judeo-Arabic, Judeo-Farsi, and Hakatia—serve other Jewish communities and shape their cultural and rhetorical practices. Since Jewish peoples and practices have traveled far across geographic space and over historical time, the linguistic resources necessary to investigate them in a comprehensive way are more than most contemporary scholars have at their disposal.

The daunting historical and geographic scope of Jewish rhetorics combined with their uncertain place offers a third reason. The nature of diasporic existence has contributed to an overwhelming plurality of Jewish experiences in lands around the globe. Similar to the way Jewish peoplehood complicates the American bifurcation of race into white and black, this abundance of experience presents a challenge to one way of expanding the rhetorical tradition in either Western or non-Western directions. Depending on the historical period and geographic locale, Jewish rhetorics might fit in either, neither, or both categories of Western and non-Western. Attending to Jewish rhetorics' place in the curriculum contributes another layer of complexity. Should Jewish rhetorics be considered in conversation with other rhetorical traditions, or as a single though multifaceted tradition in its own right?

Yet the challenges presented by the richness and diversity of Jewish rhetorical traditions that have survived and thrived in the culture of diaspora in which Jews have lived for millennia certainly warrant greater attention. In fact, there are a number of Jewish rhetorics, all of which have at their core a significant body of rhetorical precedent for their modes of writing and argumentation, precedents that reside in biblical texts, the Talmud, Midrash, rabbinical responses (*responsa*) to contemporary questions about religious practice and social ethics, secular engagements with and petitions to local and national government bodies, and historical writing. These rhetorics originated in various parts of the world: in the Middle East, at times when Jews lived in their own communities and also when they lived among Christians and Muslims; in North Africa and Spain, as Jewish culture moved, thanks to the Jewish intellectual and professional groups affiliated with the caliphate between 750 and 1492 CE; in Europe, particularly Eastern Europe in the Pale of Settlement in what is now Poland, western Russia, Belarus, and Ukraine; and in the English- and Spanish-speaking countries of the Americas in the years just before and after the Holocaust. Perhaps the most prominent rhetorical tradition is what Sergey Dolgopolski calls "Talmud" (as opposed to the Talmudic texts themselves), a mode of argument that relies on religious and legal precedent but that also depends on the deftness and the originality of the rabbinic scholar.[5] Jewish and Greek (that is to say, "traditional") rhetorics have animated each other since the fourth century BCE in Alexandria,[6] just as Jewish and Islamic hermeneutic and rhetorical practices have reworked and reinterpreted Greco-Roman rhetoric since the beginning of the early modern period in the West.

Moreover, for the members of many Jewish communities, self-identity has been profoundly shaped by the experience of exile—with the exception of those Jews who have historically resided in Palestine. What could be called a Jewish rhetorical stance, which involves maintaining a resolute sense of engagement with one's fellows and one's community while remaining aware of one's own and the community's dislocation among the members of those communities, is an important alternative to a paradigm of rhetoric that has often seemed to insist on the reconciling of differences and the creation of consensus. This is particularly true given the rise of global culture, in which national borders have given way to other forms of organization. This book seeks to rectify the lack of attention to Jewish rhetorics by examining Jewish rhetorics' historical and theoretical foundations; their cultural variants and modes of cultural expression; their intersections with, and the ways they have influenced and been influenced by, Greco-Roman, Christian, Islamic, and contemporary rhetorical theory and practice; and their actual and potential effect on contemporary scholarship in rhetoric and on the ways we understand and teach language and writing.

But the book also attempts to define just what "rhetoric" means in a Jewish context, a task complicated by the fact that both "rhetoric" and "Jewish" are contested terms, no matter the historical or cultural context. The term "rhetoric" originally referred to a set of discursive practices and patterns of language designed to—in Aristotle's terms—discover the available means of persuasion in any given case. As it has come down to us from the Greeks, rhetoric involves a process of discursive invention whose aim is to make clear how to contend with our current circumstances and how to proceed, through deliberation, in our interactions with others in the future. In its forensic function, rhetoric is a means of determining, in lieu of scientific or other systems of thought, whether or not something has occurred, and thus it is linked to historical discourse. Thucydides's work provides a clear example of this kind of rhetorical practice: he prepared a history of the classical world based on eyewitness accounts, both oral and written, and his aim was to bring together, from various contradicting accounts, a unified sense of what had happened. Rhetoric's deliberative function, exemplified by Cicero's oratorical performances in the Roman Senate, is to determine the best course of action, drawing from common perceptions of the current state of affairs; individuals' and the community's perceptions of common sense and the prevailing cultural, legal, and moral precepts of the time; and the rhetor's own ideological and practical commitments. And in its epideictic function, rhetoric is meant to provide definitions for proper conduct, community membership, and national and cultural belonging by means of the paean, the sometimes poetic praising or blaming of individuals, cultural institutions, and national actions. Over time, rhetoric's purview has expanded and contracted, sometimes—as during the early modern period—being associated mainly with the range of figurative language available to writers for creative rather than for persuasive purposes, and sometimes—as during the contemporary period—encompassing the broad range of human symbolic expression, including not only written and oral discourse but also nonverbal, visual, mathematical, and scientific creation.

But rhetoric has always been tied to its historical and cultural circumstances, and so—its traditional connection with the West notwithstanding—there has never been a single rhetoric. Rather, there have always been multiple rhetorics that are particular to times, locations, purposes, cultural practices, and institutions. As a set of practices that influence and shape discursive strategies for communication, persuasion, and education, rhetorics may share some key features while diverging in ways that are culturally and geographically specific. As we discuss below in this introduction, this is of course also true for Jewish rhetorical practices, and many of the contributors to this book make clear just how these practices take on a life of their own in Jewish contexts, sometimes indebted to the classical rhetorical past (and the Western present), and sometimes sui generis, tied specifically to the contours of Jewish life in its various locations and iterations. To cite only a few salient examples, it is hard not to recognize, in the biblical context, the intimate relation between discursive utterance and divinity, particularly in the first chapter of Genesis, when the world of creation is essentially uttered into existence (Genesis 1:3), or in the naming of the animals according their characteristics (Genesis 2:20).[7] Here, language is in a certain sense incantatory, with the presence of the divine rendered through utterance—which provides a point of departure for Steven Katz's essay in this volume. Maimonides, on the other hand, refuses the immediacy of language, instead seeing a trace of the divine in human language. He believes that it is necessary for those educated in Torah to provide a link between the divine meaning of the text and its human iteration for the present. For Maimonides, interpretation has a central place in Jewish rhetorical practice, in which the everyday language of the Torah is understood to be related, formally, to divine language. It is the utterance as expressed—on the page or from the mouth of the speaker—that must be examined, rather than its hidden meaning. To provide a final example from the contemporary period, the Jewish philosophers Martin Buber and Emmanuel Levinas understand utterance to be an expression of one's relation to others, and any discourse (poetic, persuasive, or conversational) places the speaker in a position of vulnerability and openness to others. Thus, each discursive act is an ethical act and has the potential to do harm to one's interlocutor as much as it has the potential to draw that interlocutor into a community of selves.[8]

All three of these expressions of rhetoric could, we think, be easily brought into connection and conversation with rhetorical principles already well established in the Greco-Roman tradition. The idea that the thing is made manifest in the utterance, at least in its ideal form, could be said to be consistent with Platonic notions of rhetoric,[9] in which dialectical exchange makes visible the relation between word and thing; the idea that interpretation is necessary to bring the vulgar and the intended meaning of language—of a law or a scriptural text—into relation if not coordination is Augustinian and shares characteristics with the Western tradition of hermeneutics; and Buber's and Levinas's ethical rhetorical practice shares features with the Western notions of *kairos* (timeliness) and ethos, which speak to the sense of engagement with the present and to the drawing of communitarian boundaries, respectively. Yet we also understand the danger of considering these practices only through a Western lens. Each of these approaches to language and rhetoric—the biblical, the interpretive or Talmudic, and the ethical—are tied tightly to their Jewish contexts, and although there are historical and cultural connections to be drawn between the emergence of Jewish culture and the hegemony of other Mediterranean—and, later, European—cultural ideologies and cultural practices, the rhetorics that have developed in Jewish contexts have done so in response to the particularities of Jewish experiences, whether those experiences are principally religious, cultural, ethnic, or intellectual.

Of course, the definition of the term "Jewish" can be just as contested and complicated as that of "rhetoric." The relative inclusiveness of "Jewish" often differs depending on whether or not it is being defined by those inside the Jewish community, who often disagree with another and offer more stringent criteria for membership than do those outside the Jewish community, who often have defined membership by the presence of a single ancestor of Jewish birth, regardless of whether an individual continued to believe in, practice, or conform to Jewish religious ritual. Traditionally, Jews have defined Jews as those who have been born to an authenticated Jewish mother (one with Jewish heritage and ancestors) or those who have elected to become Jewish through Jewish religious observance and conversion. In the former circumstance, Jewish identity and status is conferred by birth, and in the latter situation, Jewish identity and status is conferred through practice and communal approval, typically in the form of a *bet din* (a religious court of three rabbis) that validates and legitimizes the transformation of status from non-Jew to Jew. Of course, there are myriad debates among different groups of Jews about which *bet din* is able to confer status and whether or not other Jewish communities will recognize the legitimacy of this status. These questions of identity and membership have interesting implications for the definition of a Jewish rhetorical tradition, and who might be considered a legitimate author of Jewish rhetoric.[10]

Perhaps one touchstone of both conversation about and distinction between Jewish and Western rhetorical practices is the notion of the canons of rhetoric. The canons of rhetoric that are familiar to scholars in rhetoric and composition from the Greco-Roman tradition include invention, arrangement, style, memory, and delivery, each of which receives greater or lesser attention depending on the particularities of a historical period (Ridolfo). Although these canons are a useful heuristic for both invention and analysis, we cannot ignore their deep roots in a tradition whose values differ significantly from and were often in direct competition with those of Jewish culture. As Deborah Holdstein points out in her essay "The Ironies of Ethos," even some of our most valorized rhetorical terms are not ideologically neutral. Although she is referring specifically to the Greek notion of ethos, her critique is still valid for a consideration of other terms or concepts. As scholars doing work in comparative rhetoric and history or in the theory of non-Western rhetorical traditions have long cautioned, there is not only something lost but also something dangerous in the attempt to understand and interpret all rhetorical practices through the Greco-Roman lens. Yet even if the specific term "rhetorical canon" might be located in this other tradition, the concept of "canon" remains useful for thinking about and theorizing modes of Jewish rhetorical practices on their own terms.

Instead of forcing the round pegs of Jewish rhetorics into the square holes of the Greco-Roman tradition, we suggest that it is more productive to consider what might count as Jewish rhetorical canons based on the values and concepts exemplified in Jewish rhetorical texts and actions. One Jewish canon might be that of attending to "to-ness" or relationship,[11] and this might be considered in terms of the relationship of the individual to the community or that of the insider group to an outsider group. Another might be the canon of hearing, first emphasized by Susan Handelman in *Slayers of Moses* in 1982 and Margaret Zulick in "The Active Force of Hearing" in 1992, and discussed at greater length by Joy Arbor in this volume. This concept refers to the moments when not simply speaking but also hearing and acting in response to what is spoken are emphasized, or when there are intentional gaps and silences to enable greater audience engagement and interpretation. Perhaps most significantly (and in contrast to the relatively passive role the audience plays in Aristotelian rhetoric), this canon emphasizes the importance of the audience in all rhetorical actions, for without audience acceptance and uncoerced adherence, rhetorical action cannot take place. A third canon might be called *hidush*. At first glance, this concept might seem to resemble Greco-Roman invention, because literally the Hebrew word is related to the root chet (ח), dalet (ד), and shin (ש) that form the word *hadash* (new), and in fact this Talmudic principle encourages students to so deeply engage with the text that they not only make it their own but also make it new through dialogue and interaction, both with the text and with a study partner. However, *hidush* differs from Greco-Roman invention in that, as Dolgopolski points out, it emerges not sui generis, but rather through the principles of exaction and engaged discussion, through the relationship formed by the interaction of tradition and invention. A fourth canon might be called *tzedek*, the principle of justice that underscores much of Jewish thought, narrative, law, and interpretation to determine the proper course of ethical action. This canon both exemplifies and grows out of the command "*tzedek tzedek tirdof*"—literally, "justice, justice, chase after," and usually translated as "justice, justice, shall you pursue" (Deut. 16:20). In fact, some of the canons, such as memory, might be shared by both the Jewish and Greco-Roman traditions, though arguably within the Jewish tradition memory is one of the most emphasized, especially as it connects to "toness" by helping forge bonds between individuals and communities while also preserving and protecting differences among individuals and communities (Yerushalmi). A sixth canon might be that of multiplicity, which underscores the nonadoption of the principle of noncontradiction—for, as we know from the Talmud, both "these and these" are the words of truth. Although this example refers specifically to the schools of Hillel and Shammai, whose members were often engaged in vigorous debate, it also reflects the privileging of multiple interpretations and the value of continuous interpretative generation. It reflects the both/and approach we often see in the rabbis' attempts to reconcile conflicting opinions and truths. It diverges greatly and significantly from the tendency of Western rhetoric to move toward consensus, resolution, and elimination.

These canons are both derived from and influenced by the values expressed in three main textual modes of classical Jewish rhetoric: Torah (*Tanakh*), which establishes the law and expresses narratives of individual, community, nation; Mishna and Gemarra, which together make up the Talmud, which interprets the laws articulated in the Torah; and Midrash, the practice of Jewish explication that fills in narrative gaps in both the Torah and the Talmud and consists of its own body of rabbinic commentary. It is helpful to think of each of these modes with respect to its relationship to Jewish law,[12] but it is also helpful to point out that although the textual canons of all three modes were eventually closed off to further additions, the continued learning, recitation, and generation of all three are alive and well in the Jewish rhetorical practice of Midrash. Although the "drashes" generated by contemporary individuals are not halachically binding in the way that those of earlier rabbis are, they continue to aid in human understanding and adaptation of laws, rituals, and cultural values. Not technically a canon, Midrash is nonetheless an important genre of Jewish rhetorical production. It remains the central task of this book to begin to identify both the relations between Jewish rhetorics and other (call them Western and non-Western) rhetorical practices and the unique features of Jewish discursive practices across the communities and historical periods in which Jews have found themselves, either at home, in diaspora or both. This point leads us to an important question.

History

Is there a distinctly Jewish rhetoric? It's a worthwhile question to ask and a difficult one to answer: with its several-thousand-year tradition of disquisition, argument, knowledge making, and philosophy, whatever a Jewish rhetoric might look like, it has a longer history than the Greco-Roman one that has served as the underpinning of most of what we think of as Western philosophy and rhetorical traditions. The Jewish and Hellenic worlds shared trade routes, cultural spaces, and texts beginning in the first millennium BCE. In the thousand years between the rise of Athens as a hub of literacy and philosophy and the partition of the Roman Empire, Jewish culture underwent a drastic shift as Jews went from the Babylonian exile, to the culture that emerged around the second Temple, to a longer (and, some might argue, permanent) exile that led to the diasporas throughout Europe and Western and Central Asia, and to the formation of the rabbinical tradition that gave birth to the Talmud. These cultural shifts were inevitably buffeted by the cultures (and the peoples) with which (and with whom) Jews, particularly Jewish thinkers and scholars, interacted. As a result, there is a question of just where Jewish ideas—in philosophy, metaphysics, rhetoric, and artistic traditions—leave off and where those propelled by the Greco-Roman tradition begin.[13] In the field of rhetoric this is a particularly difficult question, due in part to the difference between the ideal, if not the actual, understanding of rhetoric as tied to a civic culture in the Greco-Roman tradition and the ideal, if not also the actual, understanding of Jewish rhetoric as tied to a divine law.

In the Hellenic period, when rhetoric emerged as a systematic practice, the relationship between Jewish and Greek culture was complicated: although most Jews became Hellenized to some degree during the second and third centuries BCE, and although many Jews accepted some tenets of Greek thought, others decisively rejected it. Particularly with the expansion of Greek influence under Alexander, Hellenistic philosophical and scientific discussions became thoroughly incorporated into the Jewish world of the Mediterranean. Among the most visible signs of this interrelationship was the creation in Alexandria of the Greek translation of the Hebrew Bible (the Septuagint). This translation allowed the widespread dissemination of the Jewish biblical canon, at least among the literate classes, and was, according to Robert Seltzer, "one of the most important translations ever made, because through it the Bible first became an essential element of the Western tradition" (202). We would add that its rhetoric—with its hypotactic grammar, its tropes of exile and return, and the appeals to the divine most prominently exhibited in Psalms—became part of the Western tradition, even if its emphasis on the ritual importance of the Torah remained distinctly Jewish. Seltzer also notes the importance of the influence of Philo Judaeus, who brought biblical interpretation into conversation with Hellenistic philosophical thought. Philo's work includes a strong theory of biblical interpretation, which connects to the Platonic notion of the oneness of the divine beyond the capacity of human discourse, and which involves an early version of the notion of divine grace—a notion that, four hundred years later in Augustine, figures prominently in a theory of rhetoric that sees rhetoric as a logical instrument for the extralogical power of what resides beyond the materiality of the visible world.

By the beginning of the early modern period, in the midst of the Christian world and while Islamic religious, philosophical, and scientific thought advanced, Jewish culture had become widespread throughout Europe and the Middle East, and rabbis had become a religious authority in the absence of the priestly class, which had been lost after the destruction of the second Temple and the diaspora of the first millennium. It was during this period that the painstaking system of biblical commentary and legal discourse found in the Talmud—which assumed that the Torah was an unending process of interpretation that resulted in the constant iteration and reiteration of innovative and contemporaneous understandings of Jewish observance and of legal thought—became the predominant form of writing, a form that had its own tropes and logical patterns. A good deal of the writing in Jewish studies has taken up the question of the relation between Talmudic texts and their underlying similarities to prevailing modes of writing in the old

Roman and flourishing Middle Eastern cultures, and two of the chapters in this book (by Patricia Bizzell and David Metzger) trace, for example, the relation of Maimonides's and Nachmanides's writing to the rhetorical precedents established in Platonic or Aristotelian modes of argumentation. Writers like Dolgopolski have made the case that Talmudic logics—as distinguished from the Talmud—are a distinctly Jewish form of reasoning whose effects are visible in contemporary thought. Unique to the mode of argument in Talmud is the idea that at the heart of every disputation is both a logical and a temporal dislocation. The logical dislocation has its source—though source is not quite the right word—in a circumstance (or exigence, in rhetorical terms) about which no consensus can be obtained. Talmudic arguments are ultimately arguments that proceed by means of disagreements, and it is by means of this engagement—through the trope of exaction—that those involved become who they are: they are making something (and themselves) out of nothing. In doing so, the Talmudist orients herself to the radical past to open up the present. The act of invention that lies at the foundation of Talmud is caught between the radical past and the future, and the act orients the Talmudist, the person engaged in the art of Talmud, to a heterogeneous present. Dolgopolski writes: "Disagreement is by no means located in the single mind of th[e] Talmudist. Rather, it emerges as the Talmudist overcomes the limitations of his or her single-mindedness. . . . [T]he disagreement exceeds the limits of the Talmudist's own individuality and opens the Talmudist to the other—which, however, is experienced *as* the other, rather than embraced in any overarching spirit of understanding" (265). Both time, as *chronos*, and the individual, as subject, open to becoming in the present.

This notion of Talmud as both a distinctly Jewish mode of reasoning and writing and as opening onto a futurity rather than a biblical past has influenced what could be called a resurgence of Jewish rhetoric in the contemporary period, a period that—since the Holocaust—has recast Jewish thinking about the location of utterance, the contingency of thought, and rhetoric's need to be as much an instrument of dislocation of memory and community as a way of forging community and the establishment of a logical sense of reasoning dependent on a definable historical past and a firm sense of peoplehood. Susan Handelman's *Slayers of Moses* and *Fragments of Redemption* both went a long way toward making the connection between Jewish thought and new directions in contemporary theories of language and rhetoric. Although they were controversial among scholars of Jewish religious thought, they nonetheless presented a compelling picture of the relationship between a Jewish rhetorical past and a contemporary, and poststructural, discursive present. It's worth mentioning here the recent interest both in the work of Chaïm Perelman, long recognized as one of the principal figures in the revival of rhetoric in the twentieth century, and in the provocations of Jacques Derrida and Emmanuel Levinas, neither of whom is known as a rhetorical theorist but each of whom made clear the implications of the Jewish experience for how we treat language. As David Frank has written, Perelman's major works juxtaposed the Jewish sense of justice (*tzedek*) with its counterparts in the Greco-Roman and Christian cultures and pointed to Jewish patterns of reason and argumentation as countermodels to the Western tradition. The origins of Perelman's groundbreaking book, *The New Rhetoric* written with Lucie Olbrechts-Tyteca, can be traced, in part, to the Holocaust and to Perelman's post-Holocaust desire to demonstrate the need for both a state with a Jewish majority (Israel) and for a Jewish presence in nation-states in which Jews are a minority. Perelman's experience in Poland and prewar Belgium taught him to appreciate European cosmopolitan values and to fear the rise of antisemitism. It reflects a strong critique of the positivist underpinnings of twentieth-century rhetoric and juxtaposes that critique with a Talmudic understanding that requires both an engagement with a tradition that grounds our ability to reason together and a commitment to the emergence of a new way of thinking that is as surprising as it is useful to the forging of a new set of ethical relations.

The ethical turn also characterizes Derrida's and Levinas's understandings of rhetoric, which they see as tied to tropes of deterritorialization and diaspora. For both thinkers, the violence of the middle twentieth century was caused by the desire to eliminate the exception—the Jew—and the logic of elimination exemplified Western thought taken to its logical extreme. This extreme view understood rhetoric's job as helping forge consensus, eliminate disagreement, and create a community of knowledge and belief. For Perelman, finding an alternative to this view meant returning to the concept of justice (the first work he published after the war was an book titled *Justice*) and developing a middle way between Enlightenment reason and radical skepticism, in his own regressive philosophy (see Frank and Bolduc). Both Levinas and Derrida sought to extract from the Jewish tradition a sense of argument that did not depend on *doxa*, the opinions held by the majority, but on the sense of immediacy and connection that could be created only when the parties involved in communication recognized each other's radical otherness. For Levinas, this meant rejecting epistemology as first philosophy and replacing it with ethics; for Derrida, it meant highlighting the disruptive capacity of discourse. Both thinkers were clearly indebted to a Talmudic sense of reasoning in which the emergence of a new—a radically other—understanding should be understood as an event. According to this Talmudic sense of reasoning, we are at our best when unencumbered by the sense of community in which individuals disavow difference.

Theory

Among the many strands of Jewish thought that have found their way into contemporary theoretical accounts of rhetoric and discourse is the mystical body of work known collectively as Kabbalah. A notoriously difficult set of texts to understand, let alone to master, Kabbalah has nonetheless entered into the theoretical imaginary, if not the lexicon, of theorists who take an interest in the materiality of language and its relation to the extralogical or even divine power that resides behind language. Perhaps the most prominent twentieth-century thinker to incorporate explicit references to Kabbalah into his musings on language was Walter Benjamin, whose lifelong correspondence with Gershom Scholem—who devoted his life to the study of the body of texts at the heart of Jewish mysticism—heavily influenced his thought. Central for Benjamin was the Lurianic Kabbalah's account of creation, in which the divine spheres, which contained the materiality of the world, were shattered with Adam's transgression, scattering shards of materiality and divinity, chaotically commingled, throughout creation. The Jewish redemptive task, according to this understanding, was to gather the shards, one by one, and rejoin them together; *tikun olam*, the repair of the world, was an attempt to reorder the shards of the broken vessels. In a number of Benjamin's essays, collected together in works like *Illuminations* and *The Arcades Project*, the task of redemption is an explicitly discursive and rhetorical one. In "The Task of the Translator," a frequently cited essay, Benjamin clearly makes the connection to Kabbalah when he writes that there is, in each translation—which matches original language to target language—not some original authorial meaning but, rather, behind both the original and translation, something that might be called divine language, which can be understood as one of the shards of the scattered vessels. The work of translation—that is, the process and not the end result—is the work of redemption. In rhetorical terms, this suggests that in utterance, in translating what we understand into a language through which others may understand it too, we engage in everyday acts of redemption, in bringing to light something that resides behind both what we say and what others understand. It also suggests that all rhetorical acts must be seen as acts of translation, which is less a matter of trying to match what we say to what we mean than it is of making visible the necessary disjunction between the two, a disjunction that makes all the more visible the *ursprache*, the divine language, behind it.

As we wrote in the section on history, the effect of Jewish experiences in diaspora—in its many iterations over several millennia—cannot be overstated in describing what might be called a Jewish rhetorical stance. Many Jews' experiences as members of a community in perpetual exile—the modern state of Israel notwithstanding—may well provide a rhetorical model of apartness and vexed belonging that might profitably supplement if not supplant the overriding metaphors of ethnicity, culture, or religion that have tended to dominate discussions of Jewish identity. This is an argument that has been made most prominently by Derrida and Levinas, and it is an argument that is distinctly Jewish in character, one that focuses on the dangers of community; the formation of consensus; and the need to acknowledge the minority, the marginal, the other. Playing on the double meaning (host and guest) of the French word *hôte*, Levinas suggests that when one individual engages another in language either by giving an account or through traditional argument, he acts at once as host and guest. Derrida writes that the context in which a speaker resides is a double one, in which "the inhabitant [is] a guest (*hôte*) received in his own home, [which] would make of the owner a tenant, of the welcoming host (*hôte*) a welcomed guest (*hôte*)" (42). The location of utterance involves a double displacement: a conceptual or epistemological one and a physical one. When one individual enters into a discursive relation with another, she resides in a kind of no person's land, in which she is both at home and in exile—neither completely apart from, nor completely a part of, the community or the location in which she speaks.

In ethical terms, the individual is vulnerable because she is troubled by the presence of that other. In political terms, there is no place that she can comfortably call home, domicile, community, or nation. A Jewish rhetorical stance would involve an engagement with others that deterritorializes those involved in the discourse, not just the speaker and the listener but also the others who become involved in it. It would acknowledge that there will always be people, or a people (or a nation or homeland), in which social engagement takes place, but that the homeland or community—if understood as what fixes us with an identity—also runs the risk of becoming a site of exclusion.

This notion of engagement—as a moment that exceeds our control but that is nonetheless brought about (though betrayed) in the language of what is said—is related to the rhetorical term *kairos*. If engagement is a disruption of community, the "we" that poses a threat to the minority or the other, then this engagement, as kairotic or timely, might better be considered with a Jewish inflection. Thus it would become an acknowledgment that the moment of speaking—the call to rhetoric—is not so much something over which we have control as it is an aspect of language that we inhabit, that is simply there, and that affects us and our relation to others as we seek to engage them justly. This insight involves the sense that our reason and our material being (our bodies) cannot be separated from one another, and that our minds and our bodies cannot be separated from the materiality of others and of the objects in the world in which we live. We are, finally, responsible for ourselves because we are responsible for the others who make us what we are. So far in this introduction we have attempted to offer a brief history of the ways Jewish rhetorics intersect with Greco-Roman traditions and the ways they offer a different rhetorical and theoretical stance with its own goals, values, and ends. In what follows, we will lay out the ways this unique history and theory influences the realm of Jewish rhetorical practice, how those practices continue to evolve and take shape in the contemporary period, and why it is important for scholars in rhetoric, composition, and Jewish studies to consider the goals, values, and ends of Jewish rhetorics in their scholarship.

Practice

Given the complicated histories of Jewish rhetorics and the different theoretical approaches that might be derived from them, discussing Jewish rhetorical practices gives rise to some interesting challenges and opportunities. The composing of a Jewish rhetorical tradition is an act of "pan-historiography" as defined by Debra Hawhee and Christa Olson, because it encompasses "histories whose temporal scope extends well beyond the span of individual generations . . .[and] studies that leap across geographic space, tracking important activities, terms, movements, or practices as they travel with trade, with global expansion, or with religious zealotry" (90). Of course, Hawhee and Olson also caution that such expansive histories "always run the risk of slipping from wide-angle views of indeterminancy to totalizing narratives. Their very strengths, the ability to account for change over time and demonstrate the cumulative nature of rhetorical practice, can put them at risk" because of the danger in what the authors appropriately term the "the sweep," or the "tendency to homogenize whole eras, places, and controversies into manageable and misleadingly coherent terms" (96). In order to guard against the tendency to generate monolithic generalizations while allowing for the examination of what remains consistent and what changes over time, Hawhee and Olson recommend what they term a "time-slicing approach" to prevent "ahistoric skating" across historical epochs. Such an approach allows scholars working in and across the history of rhetoric to pair "fine-grained analysis of the complexities in those slices with comparisons across slices [and] helps ensure that . . . claims, though broad, are grounded" (96).

Working in these pan-historiographic terms, across several continents and thousands of years, the act of composing a Jewish rhetorical tradition becomes vaster than the confines of this volume allow. Samuel Edelman provided a brief and early attempt at Jewish rhetorical pan-historiography in his "Introduction to Jewish Rhetorics," which was published more than a decade ago in one of the first special issues of a journal dedicated to Jewish rhetorics. This collection builds on the important work he began, but we caution the reader that the volume does not offer a full pan-historiography of Jewish rhetorics. Rather, each chapter offers a "fine-grained analysis" specific to its textual, theoretical, and historical context.

We argue that the chapters participate in what LuMing Mao terms the "art of recontextualization," a practice that emphasizes "openness and interdependence" and "rejects any external principle or overarching context to determine the context of the other"; instead, recontextualizations rely "on terms of interdependence and interconnectivity to constitute and regulate representation of all discursive practices," thus allowing scholars to "bring both their own context and that of the other into critical view" ("Writing the Other," 46). Though this collection focuses on episodes of Jewish history, theory, and practice, we hope that it both participates in and stimulates "a necessary sense of dialogism," since each essay is a conversational opening that offers "an act of contextualization" that "remains incomplete and open-ended" and thus also "calls for and indeed begets a new one, and so on ad infinitum" (ibid.). Taken as a whole, we hope the collection participates in the art of recontextualizing the Jewish rhetorical tradition and, in so doing, offers a starting place for further scholarly conversations about its place in relation to other cultural rhetorical traditions as well as in the broader pan-historiographic history of rhetoric.

Although the authors in this collection do not provide a broad, pan-historiographic anthology of Jewish rhetorics that spans the more than three millennia Jewish rhetorics have been in existence, we argue that the fields of rhetoric, composition, and Jewish studies would strongly benefit from such a comprehensive text and urge other scholars to continue where we have left off. Building on earlier work in Jewish rhetorical studies by Isaac Rabinowitz, David Frank, Andrea Greenbaum and Deborah Holdstein, this collection was envisioned as taking yet another step on the path toward developing a full and robust history and theory of Jewish rhetorical traditions. We chose to focus both this introduction and the collection itself on the three areas that we envision as most important to constructing this robust pan-historiography of Jewish rhetorics: history, theory, and practice. As interrelated aspects of Jewish rhetorics, we hope the sections on history, theory, and practice will be useful when considered together in courses on both Jewish history and rhetorical history and theory and as key supplements to courses on and considerations of Jewish pedagogy and thought.

It should not be surprising that the broad scope of Jewish rhetorical history and theory are matched by equally diverse Jewish practices. The canons of to-ness, hearing, *hidush*, *tzedek*, memory, and multiplicity offer productive ways for thinking about the ways Jewish rhetoric is both practiced and taught. One way to locate Jewish rhetorical practices is to more deeply investigate topoi that generate and frame Jewish rhetoric. The canons offer productive ways for thinking about topoi that Jewish rhetorical practices take up in the contemporary period: memory and to-ness are some of the dominant trends in discourses about the Holocaust; to-ness, multiplicity, memory, and *tzedek* are at work in discourses about Israel or Palestine (some of these issues are taken up in Shai Ginsburg's chapter about *Khirbet Khizeh* in this volume); ritual and spiritual practices are part and parcel of the way individuals and communities form to-ness or a relationship with a greater Jewish community or peoplehood and point to the divine presence. Although we envision Jewish rhetorics as a cultural tradition, we cannot deny that they also participate in discourses concerning religious rhetoric or that the practices and rituals of contemporary Jewish communities offer great potential for rhetorical investigation. Another productive line of inquiry can be found in Jewish pedagogical strategies: as Jonathan Boyarin notes in his work with the ArtScroll and his nontraditional Talmudic study in this volume, the yeshiva in both its historical and contemporary form offers a way to examine what might constitute Jewish pedagogical practices, where they came from, how they are developing, and how they might influence contemporary writing practices in the classroom. Lauren Fitzgerald began to take up this question by using *chevruta*-style learning in a secular writing center environment, and Ephraim Kanarfogel, a professor of Jewish studies, has also attended to the historical roots of Jewish education in the medieval period. Adam Becker, a classicist, has investigated the intersections of Islamic, Christian, and rabbinic scholarship and their shared concern for the education and identity inculcation of young men. The intersection of ritual, education, and identity is a rich area that Eli Goldblatt's chapter on secular bar mitzvah in this volume addresses. As demonstrated by the interdisciplinary nature of the scholars who have contributed to this line of inquiry, Jewish pedagogy is a rich area for future investigation. We hope the section on Jewish practice in this volume will be useful to scholars in an equally wide range of disciplines, including rhetoric, composition and education, as well as Jewish, classical, and medieval studies.

Of course, as Michelle Baillif (revisiting earlier work by Victor Vitanza) points out in her introduction to *Theorizing Rhetorical Histories*, every writing of a history also must attend to what is not being written, and we would be remiss not to highlight how much this volume slants toward the Ashkenazi tradition. With the exception of two important pieces, David Metzger's chapter on Maimonides and Jim Ridolfo's chapter on Judah Messer Leon, this collection emphasizes practices, history, and theory that would be familiar to or that have been generated by Jews of Ashkenazi descent. This is not to say that there are not equally important and valuable contributions from the Sephardi and Mizrachi traditions. We are sure that there are, and we encourage whoever is reading the chapters in this volume to be very aware of both these gaps and the need to fill them with further research.

The essays we have included have more to do with the type of scholarly inquiry currently in progress and the still-nascent state of the field. The range is limited more by our own awareness of scholars currently working at the intersections of rhetoric, composition, and Jewish studies than by any deliberate exclusion of these other aspects of Jewish rhetorical traditions. By no means did we intend to further limit what Isaac Rabinowitz rightfully termed in 1985 a "comparatively neglected field of rhetorical study" that would "bounteously reward more intensive cultivation" (144). In fact, we hope this collection has the opposite effect, by whetting the scholarly appetite of people interested in and working across rhetoric, composition, and Jewish studies. Some work has been done on Sephardi rhetorics, notably Handelman's work on Rabbi Askenazi (who, despite his name, was a Sephardi rabbi from Algiers), Joseph Ringelbaum's extensive work on the educational practices of Shas, Charles Manikin's work on Aristotelian and humanist logic in Hebrew, and Arthur Lesley's work on Italian Jewish Renaissance conceptions of the Hebrew author. However, much remains to be done and to be framed as part of the Jewish rhetorical tradition.

Part of the reason little work on the rhetorical practices of Sephardi and Mizrachi Jews exists has to do with the unfamiliarity of Jewish studies scholars with methods of scholarship on rhetoric and composition. Another part also has to do with the lack of familiarity of scholars in rhetoric and composition with both Jewish rhetorical traditions and the languages necessary to study Sephardi and Mizrachi texts (Arabic and Hebrew, to mention only two). Excellent work can be done using translations, but the problem presented by a lack of linguistic access provides at least a partial reason for the gaps that remain.

Another important aspect that requires significant attention is the way gender and women influence Jewish rhetorics. With the exception of Susan Zaeske's important chapter on the Book of Esther and Jewish women's writing theories, this volume includes less material than we would have liked that consciously addresses the way gender affects the type of rhetorical actions and spaces available to women in Jewish rhetoric. Although scholars such as Andrea Lieber have made significant strides toward including women's voices in Jewish textual traditions, much work remains to be done before women's voices are fully incorporated into Jewish rhetorical theory, history, and practice.

INTRODUCTION xxvii

We hope this volume creates a place for both Jewish rhetorics and the act of recontextualization. To expand that place, we would like to return to the Jewish rhetorical canon of to-ness and argue that Jewish history and theory of rhetoric is not necessarily best served by continued isolation. It is necessary and worthwhile to further develop the pan-historiographic work begun by Edelman, but it may be even more important to realize the future he imagined, where "the rhetorics of the Greek, Chinese, Jewish, and other civilizations are taught comparatively and through that distinctively Jewish pattern of reasoning, *Kal-ve-Chomer* (juxtaposition)" (123). To this end, we hope that the essays in this volume will serve multiple purposes, begin to provide a way in to Jewish rhetorical history, theory, practice and also lay the groundwork for a deeper pan-historiography and encourage both further work in this tradition and scholarly conversation across traditions—be they cultural, ethnic, religious, Western, or non-Western. It is our hope that this volume will make room for the mutual interanimation of Jewish studies and rhetorical ideas, concepts, practices, and for rhetorical scholarship to engage in important conversations with Jewish canons, practices, and approaches to rhetoric. The intersection of such rich disciplines provides multiple points of entry for Jewish rhetorics to engage with and further our understanding of cultural rhetorical traditions and Jewish history, theory, and practices. The time is ripe for such investigations. As the great Jewish sage Hillel said, "If I am not for myself, who will be for me? If only for myself, who am I?" and "If not now, when?"

NOTES

1. Of course, Jewish Israelis provide the exception to this claim, at least since 1948.

2. Both Gilyard and Nunley's *Rhetoric and Ethnicity* and Gilyard and Taylor's *Conversations in Cultural Rhetoric and Composition Studies* do excellent work in beginning conversations in cultural rhetorics, but they do not include Jewish voices. Lipson and Binkley's *Rhetoric Before and Beyond the Greeks* and *Ancient Non-Greek Rhetorics* each include a chapter dedicated to Jewish rhetorics, but they are categorized as non-Greco-Roman and non-Western.

3. Yiddish is enjoying a renaissance, both as a spoken language used by ultra-Orthodox Jews in Israel and elsewhere to communicate about mundane matters, and in the academic realm in Israel, where Yiddish language and cultural studies are on the rise (Maltz). See also Rabinowitch, Goren, and Pressman; Benor.

4. *Ḥeder* describes the traditional educational system used for elementary education of Jewish boys in Eastern Europe. It is derived from the Hebrew word for room. See Zalkin.

5. In "Ancient Traditions, Modern Needs," Samuel Edelman suggests that "Jewish rhetoric can be roughly subdivided into periods corresponding to the development of major pieces of

Jewish sacred and secular literature" and divides Jewish rhetorical history into the following periods (114–15). First was the Biblical period, which emphasized rhetoric as narrative (115); the Talmudic or Hellenistic period, which was characterized in part by a shift from orality to interpretation (115). Second was the Medieval period, which was marked by vast textual and methodological production and innovation, with key texts and approaches including the Mishna Torah, rabbinic interpretations, legal codification of the Shulchan Aruch, poetry, *purimspiels*, the mystical approach reflected in the Zohar and Kabbalah (118), the development of Jewish vernacular languages such as Yiddish, and "the preservation of much of Greco-Roman thought, philosophy, rhetoric and science in the hands of Jewish (Hebrew) and Arab sources" (118). Third was the Renaissance period, which "is marked by greater Jewish pluralism, and at the same time, greater geographic separation embodied in the growing split between Ashkenasim and Sephardim (Western and Eastern approaches to Judaism) (119). Fourth was the Enlightenment, which was characterized by a paradoxical relationship between Jews and non-Jews: on the one hand, Jews were emancipated; and on the other hand, this new freedom brought greater separation rather than integration between Jews and non-Jews (119–20). And finally was the contemporary or modern period.

6. For a recent complication of the rhetorical tradition, see Graff, Walzer, and Atwill.

7. Yehoshua Gitay, one of the first scholars to seriously consider Jewish rhetorical practices, has written extensively on prophetic and other rhetorics in the Jewish Bible.

8. Early scholarship in Jewish rhetorics homes in on precisely this ethical relation and the importance of hearing and audience uptake in Jewish rhetorical practice. For a further discussion of the way Jewish ethical practices focus heavily on the constraints for speech, see Falk. For a more detailed consideration of hearing as part of the Jewish rhetorical situation, see Zulick.

9. Boyarin explores this connection explicitly as he compares the epistemological and textual practices in the Platonic dialogues and the Talmud Bavli.

10. For a more detailed discussion of the implications of Jewish identity for Jewish rhetoric, see Fernheimer.

11. Fernheimer introduced this notion, although not explicitly as a Jewish rhetorical canon, in *Talmidae Rhetoricae*.

12. We use the term "Jewish law" because we recognize that although all branches of Judaism agree that there are Jewish laws, they do not agree on which ones must be followed. The Orthodox and ultra-Orthodox communities refer to Jewish law as halacha, but other branches may not accept all of the tenets presupposed by some halacha. The halacha directing and prescribing behavior with respect to gender are some of the most disputed.

13. David Daube wrote perhaps one of the earliest essays to make a similar argument: "Rabbinic Methods of Interpretation and Hellenistic Rhetoric."

BIBLIOGRAPHY

Baillif, Michelle, ed. *Theorizing Histories of Rhetoric*. Carbondale: Southern Illinois University Press, 2013.

Becker, Adam. *Fear of God and the Beginning of Wisdom: The School of Nisibis and the Development of Scholastic Culture in Late Antique Mesopotamia*. Philadelphia: University of Pennsylvania Press, 2007.

Benjamin, Walter. *The Arcades Project*. Edited by Rolf Tiedemann. Translated by Howard Eiland and Kevin McLaughlin. Cambridge, MA: Belknap Press of Harvard University Press, 2002.

———. *Illuminations: Essays and Reflections*. Edited by Hannah Arendt. Translated by Harry Zohn. New York: Schocken, 2007.

———. "The Task of the Translator." In *The Translation Studies Reader*, edited by Lawrence Venuti, 75–83. London: Routledge, 2000.

Benor, Sarah Bunin. *Becoming Frum: How Newcomers Learn the Language and Culture of Orthodox Judaism*. New Brunswick, NJ: Rutgers University Press, 2012.

Boyarin, Daniel. *Socrates and the Fat Rabbis*. Chicago: University of Chicago Press, 2013.

Brodkin, Karen. *How the Jews Became White and What That Says about Race in America*. New Brunswick, NJ: Rutgers University Press, 1998.

Daube, David. "Rabbinic Methods of Interpretation and Hellenistic Rhetoric." *Hebrew Union College Annual* 22 (1949): 239–64.

Derrida, Jacques. *Adieu: to Emmanuel Levinas*. Translated by Pascale-Anne Brault and Michael Naas. Stanford, CA: Stanford University Press, 1999.

Dolgopolski, Sergey. *What Is Talmud? The Art of Disagreement*. New York: Fordham University Press, 2009.

Edelman, Samuel. "Ancient Traditions, Modern Needs: An Introduction to Jewish Rhetoric." *Journal of Communication and Religion* 26, no. 2 (2003): 113–25.

Falk, Erika. "Jewish Laws of Speech: Toward Multicultural Rhetoric." *Howard Journal of Communications* 10, no. 1 (1999): 15–28.

Fernheimer, Janice W. "*Talmidae Rhetoricae*: Drashing up Models and Methods for Jewish Rhetorical Studies." *College English* 72, no. 6 (2010): 577–89.

Fitzgerald, Lauren. "Torah Is Not Learned but in a Group: Collaborative Learning and Talmud Study." In *Judaic Perspectives in Rhetoric and Composition*, edited by Andrea Greenbaum and Deborah Holdstein, 23–40. Cresskill, NJ: Hampton, 2008.

Frank, David. "The Jewish Countermodel: Talmudic Argumentation, the New Rhetoric Project, and the Classical Tradition of Rhetoric." *Journal of Communication and Religion* 26, no. 2 (2003): 163–95.

Frank, David, and Michelle K. Bolduc. "Chaim Perelman's 'First Philosophies and Regressive Philosophy': Commentary and Translation." *Philosphy and Rhetoric* 36, no. 3 (2003): 177–88.

Gilyard, Keith, and Vorris Nunley, eds. *Rhetoric and Ethnicity*. Portsmouth, NH: Heinemann, 2004.

Gilyard, Keith, and Victor E. Taylor, eds. *Conversations in Cultural Rhetoric and Composition Studies*. Aurora, CO: Davies Group, 2004.

Gitay, Yehoshua. "Biblical Rhetoric: The Art of Religious Dialogue." *Journal for Semitics* 18 (2009): 34–56.

Goldstein, Eric L. *The Price of Whiteness: Jews, Race, and American Identity*. Princeton, NJ: Princeton University Press, 2007.

Graff, Richard, Arthur E. Walzer, and Janet M. Atwill, eds. *The Viability of the Rhetorical Tradition*. Albany: State University of New York Press, 2005.

Greenbaum, Andrea, and Deborah Holdstein, eds. *Judaic Perspectives in Rhetoric and Composition*. Cresskill, NJ: Hampton, 2008.

Handelman, Susan A. *Fragments of Redemption: Jewish Thought and Literary Theory in Benjamin, Scholem, and Levinas*. Bloomington: Indiana University Press, 1991.

———. *Slayers of Moses: The Emergence of Rabbinic Interpretation in Modern Literary Theory*. Albany: State University of New York Press, 1982.

Hawhee, Debra and Christa Olson. "Pan-Historiography: The Challenges of Writing History across Time and Space." In *Theorizing Histories of Rhetoric*, edited by Michelle Ballif, 90–105. Carbondale: Southern Illinois University Press, 2013.

Holstein, Deborah H. "The Ironies of Ethos." *JAC* 20 (Fall 2000): 942–48.

Ignatiev, Noel. *How the Irish Became White*. New York: Routledge, 2008.

Jacobson, Matthew Frye. *Whiteness of a Different Color: European Immigrants and the Alchemy of Race*. Cambridge (MA): Harvard University Press, 1999.

Kanarfogel, Ephraim. *The Intellectual History and Rabbinic Culture of Medieval Ashkenaz*. Detroit, MI: Wayne State University Press, 2012.

———. *Jewish Education and Society in the High Middle Ages*. Detroit, MI: Wayne State University Press, 2007.

———. *"Peering through the Lattices": Mystical Magical and Pietistic Dimensions in the Tosafist Period*. Detroit, MI: Wayne State University Press, 2000.

Lieber, Andrea. "A Virtual *Veibershul*: Blogging and the Blurring of Public and Private among Orthodox Jewish Women." *College English* 72, no. 6 (2010): 621–37.

Lipson, Carol S., and Roberta Binkley, eds. *Ancient Non-Greek Rhetorics*. West Lafayette, IN: Parlor, 2009.

———. *Rhetoric Before and Beyond the Greeks*. Albany: State University of New York Press, 2004.

Maltz, Judy. "Yiddish Is Dead. Long Live Yiddish!" *Haaretz*, 21 December 2012.

Mao, LuMing. *Reading Chinese Fortune Cookie: The Making of Chinese American Rhetoric*. Logan: Utah State University Press, 2006.

———. "Writing the Other into Histories of Rhetorics: The Art of Recontextualization." In *Theorizing Histories of Rhetoric*, edited by Debra Hawhee and Christa Olson, 41–58. Carbondale: Southern Illinois University Press, 2013.

Mao, LuMing, and Morris Young. *Representations: Doing Asian American Rhetoric*. Denver: University Press of Colorado, 2008.

Perelman, Chaïm. *Justice*. New York: Random House, 1967.

Perelman, Chaïm, and Lucie Olbrechts-Tyteca. *The New Rhetoric: A Treatise on Argumentation*. Translated by John Wilkinson and Purcell Weaver. Notre Dame, IN: University of Notre Dame Press, 1969.

Rabinowitz, Isaac. *Pre-Modern Jewish Study of Rhetoric: An Introductory Bibliography*. Berkeley: University of California Press, 1985.

Rabinowitch, Lara, Shiri Goren, and Hannah S. Pressman, eds. *Choosing Yiddish: New Frontiers of Language and Culture*. Detroit, MI: Wayne State University Press, 2013.

Ridolfo. James. "Rhetorical Delivery as Strategy: Rebuilding the Fifth Canon from Practitioner Stories." *Rhetoric Review* 31, no. 2 (2012): 117–29.

Seltzer, Robert M. *Jewish People, Jewish Thought: The Jewish Experience in History*. Upper Saddle River, NJ: Prentice Hall, 1980.

Sollors, Werner, "The Invention of Ethnicity." In *The Invention of Ethnicity,* edited by Werner Sollors, ix–xx. New York: Oxford University Press, 1989.

Yerushalmi, Yosef Hayim. *Zakhor: Jewish History and Jewish Memory*. Seattle: University of Washington Press, 1983.

Zalkin, Mordechai. "Heder." *The YIVO Encyclopedia of Jews in Eastern Europe*. www.yivoencyclopedia.org/article.aspx/Heder. Accessed 23 November 2013.

Zulick, Margaret. "The Active Force of Hearing: The Ancient Hebrew Language of Persuasion." *Rhetorica* 10, no. 4 (1992): 367–80.

JEWISH RHETORICS

1

Taking a Stance toward God
Rhetoric in the Book of Psalms

DAVIDA CHARNEY

Any discussion of Jewish rhetoric must include the Hebrew Bible. The greatest figures of the Hebrew Bible, including Abraham, Moses, Jeremiah, and Job, are celebrated for arguing—not so much with other people, but with God. David Frank writes that "the God of the Hebrew Bible is, by nature, argumentative" and that "agonistic speech is the beginning of Jewish theology" (73).

Of all the parts of the Hebrew Bible that might spring to mind in association with argument, the Book of Psalms is probably among the last. "'The Lord is my shepherd'; 'by the rivers of Babylon'; 'out of the mouth of babes' (sic); 'the valley of the shadow of death'—that's probably about the extent of what the average post-religious reader carries around from the Book of Psalms," as Christopher Tayler notes in his *Guardian* review of Robert Alter's recent translation of the psalms. Readers who frequent a church or synagogue can do a bit better than that, having become familiar with the hymnic hallelujahs that make up parts of the liturgy. But they may be surprised to learn that only about a fifth of the 150 poems in the Book of Psalms are straightforward hymns of praise or other expressions to be expected from a religious assembly.

In fact, more than a third of the psalms have a first-person speaker who directly addresses God to give thanks, ask for something, or lament. The first-person speakers in the psalms are beset by opponents, whether other Israelites or aliens—they are the victims of false accusations, threats from neighborhood bullies, and slanders from gossips. They are caught in the trials of daily life—they are aging or sick; they face temptation, see the wicked prosper, and lose faith in God's abiding presence. The problems have political, legal, and philosophical implications, but they are primarily personal and social. The speakers deal with their problems by arguing with God, attempting to persuade God to intervene in their lives to resolve the crisis in which they find themselves. They ask for vindication, for their opponents to be swept away, for divine reassurance. As speakers seeking to persuade a hearer to enact a proposed solution to a serious problem, the psalmists are engaging in deliberative rhetoric.

When Israelites engage with God in the psalms, they know that the parties to the dispute are unequal in terms of the power needed to resolve the issue. But the plausibility of their arguments rests on three major assumptions. The speakers assume that both humans and the divine are capable of persuasion and open to argument. God's willingness to argue rather than just lay down the law bespeaks an extraordinary generosity toward humanity, for "it is sometimes a valued honor to be a person with whom another will enter into discussion," as Chaïm Perelman and Lucie Olbrechts-Tyteca point out (16). The speakers also assume that their covenantal relationship to God binds both sides to promoting such key cultural values as צדק (justice) and חסד (lovingkindness). In most psalms, the primary reason for God to intervene is that these values are at stake. Finally, the speakers assume that, like humans, God may decline to respond to even the most eloquent and righteous speaker or may answer in an undesired manner. It is this feature that distinguishes the psalms from magical incantations (possibly including cultic ritual sacrifices) that need only be pronounced or performed correctly to be effective.[1] The speakers of the psalms are inclined to be persistent: if God does not respond to one appeal, the speakers continue to cry out, hoping that the desired response will eventually come. Psalms are designed to keep the Israelite community engaged in divine discourse even when the hoped-for response is not forthcoming.

Although God is the primary audience, speakers in the psalms also seem to shape their texts to influence public opinion. In ancient Israel, trouble was quickly taken as a sign of divine displeasure, so the afflicted were also subject to isolation. As such, the speaker in a psalm also seeks to be reabsorbed into the community. Thus, the speakers face complex rhetorical situations.

By viewing the psalms through the lens of contemporary rhetorical theory, it becomes evident that the shape of a psalm offers important clues to the speaker's assessment of the rhetorical situation or *kairos*, the speaker's current stance vis-à-vis God and the community, and his or her desired standing. My goal in this chapter is to illustrate the range of rhetorical strategies adopted by speakers in the psalms by sketching the common stances that recur throughout the Book of Psalms. These stances, several of which I'll discuss here, are maintaining the status quo of a trusting relationship between God and the speaker, establishing the right of innocent Israelites to redress from trouble, denouncing others with competing claims for God's favor, appealing to God's self-interest in saving faithful Israelites, modeling the appropriate stance toward God for other Israelites, and convincing one's self to remain faithful.

Kairos and the Psalms

According to rhetorical theorists such as Lloyd Bitzer, in order for a situation to be a rhetorical situation, a speaker has to be experiencing a sense of exigence or urgency that can be productively addressed with language.[2] The speaker fashions the language into a spoken or written text and delivers it in such a way as to influence a particular set of hearers—those who have some ability to affect the situation and perhaps ameliorate its urgency. The art of the rhetor lies in making the most appropriate choices from among the available means of persuasion. The rhetor assesses the immediate situation, including the current stance of any possible hearers, and shapes the text to make it most likely to persuade—to change the beliefs, attitudes, or actions of—the intended hearers. These considerations influence the choice of claims, the amount and kinds of supporting evidence, the style, the forms of address, and even the length of the text. Rather than giving equal space to each point, speakers devote greater amplitude to points the audience will consider controversial and therefore most in need of elaboration and supporting appeals.

The most common move for a speaker in the psalms is to assume the mantle of innocence. In this, Israelites were quite unlike their neighbors in the ancient Near East, according to the scholars Dale Patrick and Ken Diable. When the personal god of an Akkadian or Sumerian was unresponsive in a time of trouble, the petitioner would perform a ceremony and write a prayer-letter to persuade a higher god to intervene on his or her behalf. The prayer-letters are similar in structure to the Hebrew psalms, describe similar troubles, and express similar dismay. However, the Mesopotamian petitioner commonly used the letter to confess to or plead ignorance of the sinful or neglectful behavior that had angered the god. Patrick and Diable write: "Quite the converse is true of the individual lament in the Hebrew

Bible; only rarely does the psalmist admit guilt; in fact, the general stance of the psalmist is that of an innocent sufferer" (21).

Presumably Israelites who felt guilty and sought forgiveness made the sacrifices and performed the rituals for expiating sins or resuming a state of ritual purity that are detailed at length in the Torah. Perhaps these do not survive in the Hebrew Bible because the occasions were considered unworthy of the intricate poetry developed in the psalms. Perhaps the situations that called for high art were precisely those in which none of the rituals of expiation applied, because the trouble was inexplicable. It is these situations that call for a direct challenge, persuading God to change in attitude or action, because God is allowing an innocent person to suffer for no reason. The present-day muting of this kind of challenge is precisely why the theologian Walter Brueggemann has argued forcefully for restoring the individual laments to the Christian liturgy, because they allow for a "redistribution of power" and "put God at risk" (59).

The underlying assumption in every lament is that God responds to Israelites because they are bound together by covenant. If an innocent and faithful Israelite is in trouble and God fails to respond, then God's faithfulness and/or commitment to justice come into question. To use Stephen Toulmin's terms, the covenant *warrants* the claim that God should respond to the speaker's call. A culture's strongest warrants are so blindingly obvious that they are often left unmentioned. Why remind a hearer—particularly an omniscient one—of what should be obvious? However, reminders are sometimes needed, Perelman and Olbrechts-Tyteca emphasize, not because they change a belief or value but because they raise its salience or *presence* in the hearer's conscious attention just at the moment when it is needed to support a claim.

Thus, as part of an extended argument to persuade God to take action, a frequent move is an explicit reminder of the terms of the deal, as in Ps. 22:5–6, Ps. 44:2–4, and Ps. 74:2.

REMINDER OF COVENANT

Ps. 22:5–6   In You did our fathers trust, they trusted and You set them free. To you they cried out, and escaped, in You they trusted and were not put to shame.[3]

Ps. 44:2–4   God, with our own ears we have heard, our fathers have recounted to us a deed that You did in their days, in days of yore. You, Your hand dispossessed nations—and You planted them. You smashed peoples and sent them away. For not by their sword they took hold of the land, and it was not their arm that made them victorious but Your right hand and Your arm, and the light of Your face when You favored them.

Ps. 74:2   Remember the community You made Yours long ago, Your very own tribe that You redeemed, Mount Zion, where you dwell.[4]

In each of these cases, the speaker goes on to contrast the normal or ideal situation that occurred before the current crisis, in which the community or the individual is withering under some kind of attack—whether military, legal, political, or social. But the specific shape that the psalm takes from here on depends on the speaker's current standing vis-à-vis God.

Establishing the Right of Innocents to Redress

The psalmists clearly recognized that it is not enough to wave the covenant in God's face without some evidence that the speakers are holding up their end of the bargain. Perhaps God is ready to act for faithful and innocent Israelites but doubts that the speaker is someone to whom the covenant would apply. Speakers address these concerns in three common ways: making assertions; calling in outside testimony; and referring to God's knowledge of the speaker, either citing tests that God has conducted or God's previous interactions with the speaker.

Speakers often make positive assertions of being faithful and innocent, but they also make negative claims of having avoided evil, as in Ps. 17:4, Ps. 26:4–5, and Ps. 44:18–20.

ASSERTION OF AVOIDING EVIL

Ps. 17:4   As for human acts—by the word of Your lips! I have kept from the tracks of the brute.

Ps. 26:4–5   I have not sat with lying folk, nor with furtive men have dealt. I despised the assembly of evildoers, nor with the wicked have I sat.

Ps. 44:18–20   All this befell us, yet we did not forget You and we did not betray Your pact. Our heart has not failed, nor have our footsteps strayed from Your path, though You thrust us down to the sea monster's place and with death's darkness covered us over.

Another way to support a claim to innocence is to present testimony from others. In ancient Israelite culture, this may have been difficult because Israelites who were in visible trouble were often shunned. Rather than citing character witnesses, the speakers in the psalms sometimes refer to being mocked or taunted by their neighbors. But when they are mocked for crying out to God, they can turn that to their advantage, as in Ps. 22:9 and Ps. 42:11, where they even use direct reported address to quote the mockers.

TESTIMONY FROM EXTERNAL WITNESSES

Ps. 22:9   All who see me will mock me, will open the lip, wag the head: "Rely on LORD; He will deliver him, He will rescue him for He delights in him."[5]

Ps. 42:11   Crushing my bones, my foes revile me, taunting me always with, "Where is your God?"[6]

Seen as part of an argument supporting the speaker's own character, a taunt serves multiple purposes. First, it conveys the sting of humiliation, evoking the hearers' compassion. At the same time, the taunt is evidence that the speaker has trusted in God openly—so openly that his opponents make fun of him for it. If the mockers' taunts are to be believed, the ethos or character of the speaker is validated; he is the type of person to whom God should respond. Quoting the mockery even serves a third purpose, raising the threat that God's reputation is at stake: if God does not reply and rescue the speaker, then God may also be open to the mockery of the wicked or the nonbelievers.

Apart from adducing human testimony, including their own, speakers also appeal to God's knowledge of their case, portraying God in vivid terms as the midwife to their birth in Ps. 22:10–11, or as the tester of the speaker's character in Ps. 17:3, presumably when the speaker was struggling with his conscience.

GOD'S PREVIOUS KNOWLEDGE AND TESTING

Ps. 22:10–11   For You drew me out from the womb, made me safe at my mother's breasts. Upon You I was cast from birth; from my mother's belly You were my God.

Ps. 17:3	You have probed my heart, come upon me by night, You have tried me, and found no wrong in me. I barred my mouth to let nothing pass.
Ps. 139:1–5	LORD, You searched me and You know. It is You Who know when I sit and I rise. You fathom my thoughts from afar. My path and my lair You winnow and with all my ways are familiar. For there is no word on my tongue but that You, O LORD, wholly know it. From behind and in front, You shaped me, and You set Your palm upon me.

In three psalms that I have treated more fully elsewhere ("Maintaining Innocence before a Divine Hearer")—Ps. 22, Ps. 17, and Ps. 7—the question of the speaker's innocence dominates the entire text, both in terms of content and expression. The speaker in Ps. 22 devotes an unusually lengthy opening to an extended defense of his innocence with all of the strategies described above. In Ps. 17, in addition to claiming to be innocent and providing evidence to support that claim, the speaker closely aligns himself with God morally and even in figurative bodily images, setting himself in a position superior to both opponents and other mortals.

In one of the most interesting innocence psalms, Ps. 7, the speaker dramatically shortens the usual claims to worthiness. Instead, he takes an oath called a conditional self-curse, calling down God's retribution then and there if he did what he is accused of doing. The underlying sense of uncertainty introduced by the conditional character of the self-curse continues throughout the psalm, with the speaker calling for the appropriate degree of justice.

Ps. 7:9	Grant me justice LORD, as befits my righteousness and as befits my innocence that is in me.

The psalmists, who presumably wrote and performed most of the psalms on behalf of individual Israelites,[7] seem in this case to have subtly positioned the speaker in a very precarious position, leaving it to God to sort out the merits of the case. In all these innocence psalms, however, speakers treat their innocence not as obvious but as precarious, a point in need of articulation and support: the better the case that the speaker makes for being innocent, the better his ground for challenging God's neglect as a case of injustice.

Denouncing Others with Competing Claims

In a number of individual psalms—Ps. 35 is a particularly good example—the speakers are not concerned so much with defending their own characters as with besmirching the characters of their opponents. The opponents are uniformly described as enemies of the speaker; they are contemplating or carrying out plots, lying and making false accusations, or carrying out physical assaults. What is most interesting about these psalms is the explicit value they place on equity and reciprocity. For Israelites, justice means repaying a person according to his or her deeds. Thus the merits of the speaker and his or her righteous allies (the poor, the weak, the righteous) are directly mirrored by the faults of the opponents (the greedy, the arrogant, the wicked). The desired fate of the speaker (divine rescue, sustenance, public triumph) is mirrored by the desired fate of the opponent (divine punishment, destruction, public humiliation).

Disputes between speakers and opponents are described in very little detail, presumably allowing the same psalms to be used on a variety of occasions. However, a few psalms hint at particulars, such as false accusations of theft (Ps. 69:5 and Ps. 35:11) or the betrayal of a treaty (Ps. 7:4–6).

FALSE ACCUSATION

Ps. 69:5   More numerous than the hairs of my head are my unprovoked foes. My destroyers grow strong, my lying foes. What I have not stolen should I then give back?

Ps. 35:11   Outrageous witnesses rose, of things I knew not they asked me.

In denunciatory psalms, the speaker's assertions of innocence are not simply presented as reasons for God to respond, as they were in the innocence psalms. Instead, these assertions are part of the description of the opponent's attack and are designed to characterize the opponent's hostility as unprovoked, as in Ps. 59:3–5 and Ps. 35:6–8. The assumption is that had the speaker been guilty of any provocation, then the opponent's attack would be reasonable and unobjectionable.

CHARACTERIZATION OF ATTACK AS UNPROVOKED

Ps. 59:3–5   Save me from the wrongdoers, and from men of bloodshed rescue me. For, look, they lie in wait for my life, the powerful

	scheme against me—not for my wrong nor my offense, O LORD. For no misdeed they rush, aim their bows. Rise toward me and see!
Ps. 35:6–8	May their way be darkness and slippery paths, with the LORD's messenger chasing them. For unprovoked they set their net-trap for me, unprovoked they dug a pit for my life. Let disaster come upon him unwitting and the net that he set entrap him. May he fall into it in disaster.

As indicated by these examples, the Israelites' view of justice is clearly reminiscent of the Torah-based principle of talion, "an eye for an eye" (Exodus 21:23–24). In particular, it is acceptable in Ps. 35:6–8 for the opponents to slip and fall in darkness because that is exactly what they were plotting for the speaker. The equivalence principle is also quite clear in the language of payment in Ps. 28:4–6.

CALLING FOR PAYBACK

Ps. 28:4–6	Pay them back for their acts and for the evil of their schemings. Their handiwork give them back in kind. Pay back what is coming to them. For they understand not the acts of the LORD and His handiwork they would destroy and not build.

The characters of the speaker and opponents are also presented as mirror images in another way, when speakers claim to have acted generously toward the very opponents who then attack them in Ps. 109:4–5 and Ps. 35:12–15.

RETURNING EVIL FOR GOOD

Ps. 109:4–5	In return for my love they accuse me, though my prayer is for them. And they offer me evil in return for good and hatred in return for my love.
Ps. 35:12–15	They paid me back evil for good—bereavement for my very self. And I, when they were ill, my garment was sackcloth, I afflicted myself with fasting. May my own prayer come back to my bosom. As for a friend, for a brother, I went about as though mourning a mother, in gloom I was bent. Yet when I limped, they rejoiced, and they gathered, they gathered

against me, like strangers, and I did not know. Their mouths gaped and they were not still.

From the speakers' perspective, the world of the Israelites seems black and white. However, there is evidence that this is not the whole story. In most cases, the opponents are almost certainly other Israelites. So through a rhetorical perspective, it is possible to imagine the disputes as situations in which different parties, each equally aggrieved, simultaneously petition God for rescue, each in beautiful and impassioned poetic language, each defending his or her own character and besmirching the other's. It is probably for this reason that the most common accusations against an opponent are plotting in secret, lying, and boastful, arrogant speech that the opponent hopes will go undetected by God. Only the speaker, the ostensible victim, seems to realize the truth and read the opponent's heart. By implication, the public and even God might not realize the opponent's true character. By accusing an opponent of habitual lying, a speaker may hope to undermine the success of a psalm that the opponent might offer.

OPPONENTS AS DECEITFUL

Ps. 55:22   His mouth was smoother than butter—and battle in his heart. His words were softer than oil, yet they were drawn swords.

Ps. 64:6–7   They encourage themselves with evil words. They recount how traps should be laid. They say, "Who will see them? Let them search out foul deeds! We have hidden them from the utmost search, in a man's inward self, and deep is the heart."

In a few cases, the speaker's sense of grievance is so strong that he or she is apparently indistinguishable from the opponent. In Ps. 109, one of a set of so-called "imprecatory psalms," a speaker spends the bulk of the psalm uttering blood-curdling curses against an opponent and the opponent's family, goods, and descendants. Amazingly, however, one of the faults that the speaker lays at the opponent's door is itself a love of cursing.

Ps. 109:17–19   He loved a curse, may it come upon him, he desired not blessing—may it stay far from him. He donned a curse as his garb—may it enter his innards like water and like oil in his bones. May it be like a garment he wraps round him and like a belt he girds at all times.

As in Ps. 7, the innocence psalm in which the speaker seems to undermine his own innocence, the speaker in Ps. 109 may have been positioned by the psalmists to overdo it, leaving it up to God to sort out which of the two parties was worse.

Appealing to God's Self-Interest

The Hebrew word for the psalms, *tehilim*, means praises, and the psalms certainly live up to their name in containing unending praise of God. All this praise is in itself an appeal to God's better nature: if God claims the attributes of upholding truth, justice, and compassion, then it is fair to expect God to live up to these attributes. But the psalms also suggest that God wants to be praised in public discourse. Accordingly, numerous speakers make the case that God should rescue them because their deaths would deprive God of their praise.

ENSURING CONTINUATION OF PRAISE

Ps. 6:6   For death holds no mention of You. In Sheol, who can acclaim You?

Ps. 30:10   What profit in my blood, in my going down deathward? Will dust acclaim You, will it tell Your truth?

Ps. 88:11–13   Will You do wonders for the dead? Will the shades arise and acclaim you? Selah Will Your kindness be told in the grave, Your faithfulness in perdition? Will Your wonder be known in the darkness, Your bounty in the land of oblivion?

The argument that God should intervene for the sake of continued praise receives its fullest elaboration in Ps. 71, in which the speaker attests to his previous role as a model for others to praise God, a function that cannot continue unless God rescues the speaker and renews his strength.

Ps. 71:17–19   God, You have taught me since my youth and till now I have told Your wonders. And even in hoary old age, O God, do not forsake me. Till I tell of your mighty arm to the next generation, to all those who will come, Your power, and Your bounty, O God, to the heights, as You have done great things, O God, who is like You?

Serving as a Model for Others

In three psalms, Ps. 4, Ps. 62, and Ps. 82, the persuasive skills of the first-person speaker are directed not at God but at an immediate audience of listeners who may be straying from a faithful path.[8] In Ps. 4, the extreme rivals seem to be apostates who are apparently worshiping other gods and prospering materially despite that fact. In Ps. 62, the hearers seem to be slipping in their behavior within the community—harming other people rather than worshiping other gods. In the unusual Ps. 82, God is the speaker who addresses an assembly of other deities, rebuking them for their failure to uphold justice and threatening them with destruction just like mortal princes.

In all three psalms, the speaker's rhetorical strategy is to establish his authority, rebuke the strayers directly, offer them steps to take toward recovery, and affirm the value of faithfulness. The persuasive power derives from the considerable space devoted to addressing and referring to the strayers, phrasing rebukes as rhetorical questions (for example, "how long will you go on?") and giving a sequence of imperatives to describe steps on a path back to good behavior. In Ps. 4 and Ps. 62, the speakers also use strategies of identification that seem to come right out of the books of Kenneth Burke or Chaïm Perelman: they associate themselves with values that the hearers also cherish and offer the hearers ways to distance or dissociate themselves from hard-core evildoers.

Conclusion

Individuals offering a psalm may have had a variety of goals, such as seeking to stay on good terms with God, offering thanksgiving, and calling for justice. The psalmists do not see it as presumptuous to challenge God because, as Harold Fisch puts it in the case of Job, "the challenge is itself made possible only by the having been fashioned by a creator God in such a way as to be able to ask such questions" (32). Unlike Job, however, the psalmists do not seem to have waited for a response to come in the form of discourse. It is possible that they simply used future events to interpret the success or failure of a psalm (perhaps accompanied by a sacrificial rite): eventually an illness may pass or an opponent's anger may be appeased.

After offering a lament, individuals who perceive their situation to have improved may go on to perform psalms of thanksgiving, some of which include a recapitulation of the now-resolved crisis. Those whose problems persist may be encouraged to continue lamenting. Habituating Israelites to continue arguing and struggling with God, regardless of the outcome in any given case, rehearses the cultural commitment to justice, keeps alive the expectation of eventual deliverance, and wards off apostasy.

Like others who practice rhetoric, the psalmists recognize that arguments do not carry the force of formal logic, cannot guarantee a just or valid outcome, and—no matter how well conceived—cannot compel the hearers to assent.

This study indicates the promise of closer study of religious and sacred texts, whether in the Judaic or other traditions. This study suggests that the civic public arena is not the only one conducive for the discovery and honing of persuasive strategies. The psalmists in ancient Israel may have done so in a predominantly religious or cultic context, raising the question of how other ancient cultures regarded discourse with the divine, if they had any. Are the psalmists unique in their willingness to make face-threats to God and challenge divine injustice?

In the case of archaic Greece, Jeffrey Walker has already argued for the centrality of persuasive discourse in poetic form: "Insofar as epideictic is the 'primary' or central form of rhetoric, and poetry is the original and ultimate form of epideictic (or is understood as such), poetry is also the original and ultimate form of rhetoric" (41). The poetic texts that Walker examines in making this case, however, are primarily secular, written to celebrate athletic achievements or to entertain in symposia; he does not consider how poets conceived of and addressed a divine audience.

The classicist William Furley notes that Greek religious hymns were not as well preserved and transmitted as civic and literary texts and have therefore received "less than their due attention from modern scholars" (29). The neglect of the hymns, he argues, has led to exaggerated emphasis on the rituals of sacrifice as compared to the Greeks' conception of the sacred. In fact, Furley's description of the general construction of the hymns points to their important similarities with the psalms, particularly the overall goal of attracting the favorable attention of the god: "The entire strategy behind hymn-composition and performance was to attract the attention of the divinity addressed in a favorable way; ritual and choral worship combined to flatter, woo, charm and persuade a single god or a group of gods that the worshipper(s) was deserving of sympathy and aid" (32). The types of hymns bear at least some resemblance to the psalms, according to a listing by Menander in the classical period—most pertinently the petitions that included separate designations for positive requests ("precatory" hymns) and requests for averting something ("deprecatory" hymns) (Walker 307). Any surviving texts of these types especially warrant further rhetorical analysis.

Apart from comparisons with ancient Greece, this study indicates that the psalms warrant further study from scholars in Jewish and biblical studies because they offer important clues to the evolution of Judaic culture and theology.

NOTES

1. For a sketch of how the psalms might have operated in the sacrificial rituals of the Temple, see Charney, "Performativity and Persuasion in the Hebrew Book of Psalms."
2. Bitzer conceived of the exigence as a feature of the real world external to the speaker, but other scholars such as Scott Consigny argue that individuals may also use rhetoric to create exigence. For a recent update on the concept of rhetorical situation, see Kathleen McConnell.
3. Unless otherwise noted, all translations are from Robert Alter.
4. The translation is from the Jewish Publication Society's *JPS Hebrew-English Tanakh*.
5. The translation is from Hillel Goldberg, 69.
6. The translation is from *JPS Hebrew-English Tanakh*.
7. William Morrow suggests that the psalmists were a heterogeneous group: "the expert poets involved in composing lament, certainly in the stage of oral tradition, could have been skilled lay persons as well as identifiable functionaries of the religion of the large group such as temple singers or prophets" (68). He suggests that they may have composed and performed some psalms in "liturgical services conducted on an *ad hoc* basis for individuals in need" (70).
8. I give a fuller account of two of these psalms in "Keeping the Faithful."

BIBLIOGRAPHY

Alter, Robert. *The Book of Psalms: A Translation with Commentary*. New York: W. W. Norton, 2007.
Bitzer, Lloyd. "The Rhetorical Situation." *Philosophy and Rhetoric* 1, no. 1 (1968): 1–14.
Brueggemann, Walter. "The Costly Loss of Lament." *Journal for the Study of the Old Testament* 36, no. 10 (1986): 57–71.
Burke, Kenneth. "The Rhetorical Situation." In *Communication: Ethical and Moral Issues*, edited by Lee Thayer, 263–74. New York: Routledge, 1973.
Charney, Davida. "Keeping the Faithful: Persuasive Strategies in Psalms 4 and 62." *Journal of Hebrew Scriptures* 12, no. 16 (2012): 1–13.
———. "Maintaining Innocence before a Divine Hearer: Deliberative Rhetoric in Ps. 22, Ps. 17, and Ps. 7." *Biblical Interpretation* 21, no. 1 (2013): 33–63.
———. "Performativity and Persuasion in the Hebrew Book of Psalms: A Rhetorical Analysis of Psalms 22 and 116." *Rhetoric Society Quarterly* 40, no. 3 (2010): 247–68.

Consigny, Scott. "Rhetoric and Its Situations." *Philosophy and Rhetoric* 7, no. 3 (1974): 175–86.

Fisch, Harold. *Poetry with a Purpose: Biblical Poetics and Interpretation*. Bloomington: Indiana University Press, 1988.

Frank, David A. "Arguing with God, Talmudic Discourse, and the Jewish Countermodel: Implications for the Study of Argumentation." *Argumentation and Advocacy* 41 (fall 2004): 71–86.

Furley, William D. "Praise and Persuasion in Greek Hymns." *Journal of Hellenic Studies* 115 (1995): 29–46.

Goldberg, Hillel. "Psalm 22: The Retrieval of Faith." *Tradition* 24, no. 2 (1989): 66–77.

Jewish Publication Society. *JPS Hebrew-English Tanakh*. 2nd ed. Philadelphia: Jewish Publication Society, 1999.

McConnell, Kathleen F. "In Appreciation of the Kind of Rhetoric We Learn in School: An Institutional Perspective on the Rhetorical Situation and on Education." *Quarterly Journal of Speech* 96, no. 3 (2010): 278–99.

Morrow, William S. *Protest against God: The Eclipse of a Biblical Tradition*. Sheffield, UK: Sheffield Phoenix Press, 2006.

Patrick, Dale, and Ken Diable. "Persuading the One and Only God to Intervene." In *My Words are Lovely: Studies in the Rhetoric of the Psalms*, edited by Robert Foster and David M. Howard Jr., 19–32. New York: T. and T. Clark, 2008.

Perelman, Chaïm, and Lucie Olbrechts-Tyteca. *The New Rhetoric: A Treatise on Argumentation*. Translated by John Wilkinson and Purcell Weaver. Notre Dame, IN: University of Notre Dame Press, 1969.

Tayler, Christopher. "In the Vale of Death's Shadow." *Guardian*, 21 December 2007.

Toulmin, Stephen Edelston. *The Uses of Argument*. Cambridge: Cambridge University Press, 1958.

Walker, Jeffrey. *Rhetoric and Poetics in Antiquity*. New York: Oxford University Press, 2000.

2

The Rhetoric of Rabbinic Authority
Making the Transition from Priest to Sage

RICHARD HIDARY

From biblical times through the second Temple period, the role of Jewish religious leaders was performed primarily by the priests, who were entrusted with mediating between God and the people.[1] During the first century CE, however, a significant shift occurred with the transfer of authority from the priests to the rabbis.[2] Since then, rabbis have remained the religious leaders of all medieval and modern varieties of Judaism. Historians have analyzed in great detail the political and social factors that brought about this shift. This chapter will review these historical factors but will then focus on the internal dynamics of the Talmudic discourse that document this shift. More specifically, the chapter will trace the rhetoric that the rabbis of the Talmud used to effect this change and persuade their adherents of the authenticity of their new position and teaching. Unlike the Jews during the second Temple period, who had at least some temporal authority (both that granted to them by the Romans and that derived from the Temple), the rabbis could gain followers only through persuasion, and in that sense their rhetoric is one of their defining qualities.

More than simply a change in titles, the rabbi represents a fundamentally different form of authority than that of the priest. Whereas the legitimacy of the priests derives from their lineage, that of the rabbis was a function of their knowledge.[3] Even an illiterate priest could fulfill his role as long as he was capable of performing the Temple rites, which were widely believed to be the primary way for people to relate to God. For the rabbis, however, Torah replaces the Temple as the central institution of worship and it is halacha rather than Temple ritual that forms the path of divine service. The rabbis' authority derives from their role as interpreters of Torah and teachers of halacha. Rabbis do not serve as intermediaries between man and God as priests do; rather, all Jews can and should have equal access to Torah and can worship God directly through prayer and halacha—even if it is the rabbis who are authorized to explain the Torah and define the parameters of that worship.[4] Rather than being Temple officiates, the rabbis gained their authority by serving as teachers, judges, and preachers—all roles that require effective rhetorical skill.[5]

Although in modern synagogues priests receive only token symbolic honors,[6] we can get some sense of how important the priesthood was just before the Hasmonean revolt from the extraordinary praise of the high priest Simon II (circa 219–196 BCE), near the end of the book of Sirach. After recounting some of Simon's accomplishments, Sirach describes the scene of the high priest leaving the holiest precinct of the Temple: "How glorious he was, surrounded by the people, as he came out of the house of the curtain. Like the morning star among the clouds, like the full moon at the festal season; like the sun shining on the temple of the Most High, like the rainbow gleaming in splendid clouds."[7] Sirach continues to describe the glory of the other priests and the Temple services in glowing terms.[8]

Indeed, even the group of people who broke away from the Jerusalem Temple to form the Dead Sea Sect followed a priest known as the Teacher of Righteousness as their supreme leader and maintained a central role for priests throughout their leadership hierarchy.[9] Other groups, such as the Elephantine community and the Samaritans, also remained Temple based.[10] Early Christians similarly assumed that Judaism could not exist without the Temple, and they therefore concluded that God's covenant with Israel in the flesh had been abrogated.[11] The shift away from a Temple-based religion with priests and sacrifices at its center and toward a text-based religion with rabbis and Torah at its center is therefore fundamental to the definition of postdestruction Judaism.

Historians point to at least three political factors in the gradual decline of the priesthood and the rise of the rabbis.[12] First, the destruction of the Temple in 70 CE left the priests bereft of their primary power center. Second, many priests and their supporters perished during the Roman revolt leading up to the Temple's destruction. The Saducean party, made up mostly of priests and members of the aristocracy, zealously fought against the Romans—as did the members of the Dead Sea Sect. The Pharisees, in contrast, sought peace with the Romans and probably fared better in the war. The Pharisees were not only the party of the masses,[13] but they were also the predecessors of the rabbis. The third factor, then, in the ascendancy of the rabbis over the priests is the success of the Pharisees or rabbis in negotiating with the Romans and forming a Judaism that could survive without the Temple.[14]

The last of these factors is recorded in one of the major foundation stories of the rabbinic movement. The story, as told in Avot d'Rabbi Natan, begins with Vespasian asking those besieged in Jerusalem to surrender rather than see their Temple burnt down. The fighters reject his offer. Rabban Yoḥanan ben Zakkai then repeats the request, which is again rejected. Meanwhile, Vespasian's spies within the walls have noted Rabban Yoḥanan ben Zakkai's efforts and recorded that he was among the friends of the emperor. After realizing that diplomacy would not work, Rabban Yoḥanan ben Zakkai feigns his death in order to sneak out of the walls of Jerusalem in a coffin. The narrative continues:

> They took him out and carried him until they reached Vespasian. They opened the coffin and he stood before him. He [Vespasian] said to him, "Are you Yoḥanan ben Zakkai? Ask, what shall I give you?" He said to him, "I ask nothing of you except that I may go to Yavneh and study with my disciples, and institute prayer there, and perform all the commandments." He said to him, "Go and do everything that you wish."[15]

Jeffrey Rubenstein notes that this story is mentioned as a commentary to Mishna Avot 1:2: "The world stands on three things: on the Torah, on the Temple service and on deeds of loving-kindness." Anticipating the imminent destruction of the Temple, and hence one of the pillars of the world, Rabban Yoḥanan requests Yavneh as a replacement for the Temple.[16] The accuracy of this narrative is doubtful, considering that Josephus relates a very similar story about his own meeting with Vespasian.[17] Nevertheless, this narrative does reflect the way the rabbis saw their own beginnings.

In addition to the above political factors, the success of the rabbis was partly due to their ability to inherit the popularity of the Pharisees. Josephus explains that the Pharisees gained their influence, at least in part, through their belief in the immortality of the soul and in reward and punishment after death.[18] Josephus also reports that the Pharisees taught many oral traditions from their fathers even though they were not written in the Torah.[19] The rabbis, in turn, transmitted all of their teachings as part of an oral Torah that was given at Sinai and therefore of equal authority to the written Torah.[20] This not only infused their laws with legitimacy but also gave them flexibility to legislate for the needs of the times even when that meant deviating from the plain meaning of the Torah.

Taking advantage of their political ascendancy at Yavneh, the early rabbis took steps to quash the Sadducees and avoid further sectarianism. They declared anyone who did not believe in the resurrection of the dead to be a heretic and also introduced into the daily liturgy a prayer cursing heretics. This effectively forced Sadducees and other deviant groups out of the synagogues.[21] At the same time, the rabbis decided to be tolerant and inclusive of more moderate dissenters by recording their opinions in the Mishna,[22] declaring that "these and these are the words of the living God,"[23] and thereby creating a "grand coalition."[24]

However, the above political factors and legislative efforts, as important as they are for the historical record, do not sufficiently explain the social and communal components of the shift away from the authority of the priesthood. After all, the Temple, sacrifices, priests, and purity were too far entrenched in Jewish law and in the minds of the people to be so easily discarded. Therefore, I would like to present a collection of rabbinic traditions that document the legal and theological teachings that the rabbis imparted as they led their followers through this transition. Specifically, I would like to explore three questions: What are the rhetorical tropes that the rabbis used to convince their followers of the legitimacy of this shift? What are the legal innovations that the rabbis enacted to effect this change in roles? And what happened to all of the laws of purity and sacrifice that were the focus of the priests and the Temple? To the extent that the traditions we are about to review date to the late second Temple and early rabbinic periods—and I think many of them do—these rabbinic traditions contribute to the historical record. But equally important is what these traditions tell us about the worldview of the rabbis who recorded them and of the people who followed them. The following texts will demonstrate how rabbinic rhetoric, sometimes explicitly and sometimes subtly, played a fundamental role in the continuity and definition of all subsequent Judaism.

I have separated these traditions into four categories based on the type of rhetoric they use. In the first category, the rabbis use a rhetoric of comparison to present rabbis and Torah learning as more important than the priests and priesthood. The second category includes texts that use the language of legal fiction to convince rabbinic adherents that their following various commandments can be considered equal to the offering of sacrifices.

In the third category, the rabbis adopt a rhetoric of substitution to replace the role of the priest with that of the rabbi, or that of a Temple rite with a non-Temple equivalent.[25] The fourth category includes traditions that extend certain Temple rituals and priestly purity laws beyond the Temple and the priesthood, enabling the rabbis to absorb what was once the realm of the priests into their own halachic world. Only by combining the historical chain of events with this internal perspective of the rhetorical and legal strategies that the rabbis used to effect this change will we be able to gain a fuller understanding of the shift from priests to rabbis.

Rhetoric of Comparison: Rabbis versus Priests

The following texts use a rhetoric of comparison, a very common technique in Greco-Roman declamation.[26] The exercise in comparison (*synkrisis*) was one of the stages in the *progymnasmata* in which the student would evaluate the relative worth of two people or things. Hermogenes writes that this type of argumentation would often take the apparently lesser value and show it to be equal to the apparently greater one. For example, an orator might argue that Odysseus, although generally considered lesser than Heracles, was actually equal to him.[27]

The first text in this section explicitly states that rabbis are at least as important as priests. Discussing a case in which there are limited resources and only one poor person can be fed[28] or ransomed from captives, Mishna Horayot 3:8 provides a hierarchy for deciding who takes priority:

> A priest precedes a Levite, a Levite precedes an Israelite, an Israelite precedes a *mamzer*,[29] a *mamzer* precedes a *natin*,[30] a *natin* precedes a convert, a convert precedes a freed slave.
>
> When is this so? When they are all equal. However, if the *mamzer* was a scholar and the high priest was an ignoramus,[31] then the *mamzer* scholar precedes the high priest ignoramus.

The first half of the Mishna lists the ancient hierarchy based solely on lineage and with the priest at the head. The second half, however, limits this hierarchy to a situation when they are equally knowledgeable of Torah. In doing so, the Mishna almost completely undoes the primary status of priests and places the rabbinic scholar at the head.[32]

The next two texts compare priesthood with Torah. Mishna Avot 6:5 teaches: "Torah is greater than priesthood and kingship for kingship is acquired through thirty qualifications, priesthood through twenty-four, but Torah is acquired through forty-eight things." Although this late Mishna[33] praises Torah for being the most difficult to acquire, the following Tanaitic midrash praises the crown of Torah above all for its being the most accessible:

> There are three crowns: the crown of Torah, the crown of priesthood, and the crown of kingship. Aaron merited and received the crown of priesthood. David merited and received the crown of kingship. But the crown of Torah remains.... Anyone who merits the Torah it is as if all three remain and he has merited all of them; and anyone who does not merit Torah it is as if all three remain and he has not merited any one of them.[34]

This text points out the fundamental difference between Torah, which granted democratic and equal access to all people, and priesthood, which is limited to Aaron's lineage. Second, this midrash establishes Torah as the sine qua non for receiving God's glory, without which even priesthood is meaningless.

Bavli Berakhot 32b states: "Prayer is greater than sacrifices."[35] Similarly, the last two texts in this category compare sacrifices with good deeds and find the latter to be at least as effective as the former for achieving atonement:

> One time, Rabban Yoḥanan ben Zakkai was leaving Jerusalem and R. Joshua was walking behind him and he saw the Temple destroyed. R. Joshua said: "Woe is to us that the Temple is destroyed, the place that atoned for the sins of Israel." Rabban Yoḥanan ben Zakkai responded, "My son, we have a means of atonement equivalent to it (*kemotah*). What is it? It is acts of loving-kindness, as the verse states, 'For I desire goodness, not sacrifice' (Hosea 6:6)."[36]

Rabban Yoḥanan ben Zakkai uses a language of comparison: "equivalent to."[37] This text is especially interesting because it includes a dialogue in which Rabbi Joshua presents the more predictable reaction to the destruction—namely, that there is no longer any possibility for atonement. He acts as a foil to highlight the radical innovation of Rabban Yoḥanan ben Zakkai: acts of kindness are equivalent to sacrifices. A late midrash expounds on why righteousness is even better than sacrifices:

> "To do what is right and just is more desired by the Lord than sacrifice" (Proverbs 21:3). "Like a sacrifice" is not written, but rather "more than a sacrifice." How so? Sacrifices are only practiced at the time of the Temple but righteousness and justice are practiced at the time of the Temple and beyond the Temple.

Another reason, sacrifices only atone for inadvertent sins while righteousness and justice atone both for inadvertent and intended sins.

Another reason, sacrifices are only practiced on earth but righteousness and justice are practiced both in the heavens and on earth.

Another reason, sacrifices are only practiced in this world while righteousness and justice are practiced both in this world and in the next.[38]

There are many statements of this type, but this should suffice to show that both Tannaitic and, to an even greater degree, Amoraic sources use a rhetoric of comparison in order to argue that rabbis, the Torah that they teach, and the righteousness that they preach are as important as the priests and their sacrifices—or even more important.[39]

Rhetoric of Legal Fiction: Torah and Prayer Are Considered Like Sacrifices

The texts in the next set use the language of legal fiction. Like a comparison, a legal fiction relates two different things. However, a legal fiction does not weigh their relative values but rather considers one thing as if it were the same as another. So, instead of downplaying the importance of priests, these texts maintain that priests and Temple rites are central but that rabbis and halacha are functionally equivalent. In these texts, the rabbis take over the role of the priests and various halachic rituals are analogized to Temple rites and can therefore replace them.[40]

Legal fictions are common to both Roman and rabbinic jurisprudence and furthermore are distinctive to only those systems among the various legal systems of the ancient Near East and Hellenistic world.[41] A legal fiction is a persuasive rhetorical device that helps convince both the judge and the audience that a certain ruling or judgment, although seemingly unprecedented, is actually proper and required in the legal system.[42]

The rabbis use a legal fiction in order to promote Torah study by considering it just like a sacrifice:

> When Scholars study Torah in any place, I consider it as if (*ke-illu*) they have burned incense to Me.... When scholars study Torah at night, Scripture considers it as if (*ke-illu*) they are involved in the sacrificial service.... Scholars who study the laws of the sacrificial service, Scripture considers it as if (*ke-illu*) the Temple was built in their days.... Anyone who studies Torah, it is as if (*ke-illu*) he has sacrificed a burnt offering, a meal offering, a sin offering, and a guilt offering.[43]

Since the study of Torah achieves the same goal as sacrifices do, the former can replace the latter.[44] Going a step further, several statements liken a Torah scholar to a priest and an altar: "Anyone who brings a present to a Torah scholar it is as if (*ke-illu*) he gives a first-fruit offering."[45] Even more strikingly, "one who wishes to perform a wine libation upon the altar should fill the throat of a Torah scholar with wine."[46] The body of the rabbi is considered as if it were an altar that can receive a wine libation.

In a similar vein, Rabbi Sheshet used to recite this prayer when he fasted:

> Master of the Universe! It is revealed to You that when the Temple was standing, a person who sinned would bring a sacrifice from which they only sacrificed its fat and its blood and that would atone for him. Now, I sat in fasting and my fat and blood have diminished. May it be Your will that my fat and blood that diminished should be as if (*ke-illu*) I have sacrificed it to You on the altar and You will accept me.[47]

Rabbi Sheshet thus makes an analogy between the fat and blood of an animal sacrifice and the fat and blood of his own body. Although he almost literally sacrifices his own body, he still uses a legal fiction to complete the transformation of his action into an animal sacrifice in the Temple. Not only fasting but also eating is considered like a sacrifice:

> R. Shimon says: three people who ate at one table but did not say upon it words of Torah, it is as if (*ke-illu*) they ate from sacrifices offered to the dead,[48] as it says, "Yea, all tables are covered with vomit and filth so that no space is left" (Isaiah 28:8). However, three people who ate at one table and did say upon it word of Torah, it is as if (*ke-illu*) they ate from the table of the Omnipresent, blessed be He, as it says, "And he said to me, 'This is the table that stands before the Lord'" (Ezekiel 41:22).[49]

The food at one's table is like a sacrifice. Whether it will be considered a proper sacrifice to God or an abominable pagan sacrifice depends on whether or not the diners sanctify the meal by sharing words of Torah during the meal. The Sifra similarly uses a legal fiction to liken giving food to the poor to offering sacrifices:

> Anyone who makes available forgotten sheaves, the corners of the field, or the poor man's tithe, Scripture considers it as if (*ke-illu*) the Temple is standing and he offers sacrifices in it.[50]

The four species that are taken on Sukkoth are also likened to a sacrifice:

> Anyone who takes a *lulav* in its binding and willow-branch with its wreathing, Scripture considers it as if (*ke-illu*) he built an altar and offered upon it a sacrifice,

as it is written, "Bind the festal offering with cords to the horns of the altar" (Ps. 118:27).[51]

Yakov Nagen provides evidence that this conceptual link between the *lulav* and sacrifices is also manifest in the detailed requirements for the *lulav*. A stolen *lulav* is invalid for use, just as a stolen animal may not be sacrificed; both must be owned by the person fulfilling the commandment, and both must be free from blemish. The *lulav* is waved in a manner similar to that used with a meal-offering, and the *lulav* and sacrifices are both accompanied by the recitation of hallel. Through these equations, the *lulav* prompts God to show favor just as sacrifices do.[52]

Another set of traditions replaces sacrifices with prayer: "One who prays in a synagogue it is as if (*ke-illu*) he has sacrificed a pure meal offering."[53] Similarly, "one who relieves himself, washes his hands, dons phylacteries, recites *shema* and prays, Scripture considers it as if (*ke-illu*) he built an altar and offered a sacrifice upon it, as it is written: 'I wash my hands in innocence and walk around Your altar, O Lord' (Psalms 26:6)."[54] The same idea is expressed elsewhere without recourse to a legal fiction: "Prayer takes the place of sacrifice."[55] Indeed, there is a whole set of traditions that replace the Temple and its activity with non-Temple equivalents but that do not use legal fictions. This brings us to the third category.

Rhetoric of Substitution: Rabbis and Halacha Replace Priests and Temple Rites

This category is similar to the previous one in that a non-Temple ritual is considered to be equivalent to a Temple parallel. However, this category does not use the language of legal fiction but rather explicitly states that one can substitute for the other. We cited above Mishna Avot 3:3 to the effect that the food at one's table is like a sacrifice. An early Amoraic statement expresses the same idea using the language of substitution:

> "The wooden altar was three cubits high and two cubits long and had inner corners and its length and its walls were of wood. And he said to me, 'This is the table that stands before the Lord'" (Ezekiel 41:22). It begins with "altar" and ends with "table"? R. Yoḥanan and R. Eleazar both say: "As long as the Temple was standing, the altar would atone for Israel. Now, a person's table atones for him."[56]

Picking up on the change of the referent in the verse from "altar" to "table," these two Amoraim explain that the verse thereby equates altar and table.

Once the Temple is destroyed, the table at one's home substitutes for the Temple altar to attain atonement.

Along the same lines, rabbinic literature teaches that the synagogue, to some extent, replaces the Temple: "'I have become for them a small Temple' (Ezekiel 11:13): R. Isaac said, 'These are the synagogues and study houses in Babylonia.'"[57] God's presence previously resided in the Temple, but it now abides in the synagogue: "Anytime ten people enter a synagogue, the Divine Presence is with them."[58] Mishna Megilah 3:3 applies to the synagogue the same rules that govern the sanctity of the Temple: "One may not use [a destroyed synagogue] as a shortcut, for it is stated, 'I will destroy your sanctuaries' (Leviticus 26:31), they are sacred even when destroyed." Mishna Berakhot 9:5 teaches the same law regarding the Temple: "One may not use it as a shortcut." The sanctity of the Temple is transferred to the synagogue, which similarly may not be used for personal benefit.[59] Even the architecture of the synagogue is modeled on that of the Temple: "One only builds the doors of synagogues on the east for so have we found in the Sanctuary that it was open to the east, as it is stated, 'Those who were to camp before the Tabernacle, in front—before the Tent of Meeting, on the east'" (Numbers 3:38).[60]

Steven Fine shows that the description of the great synagogue of Alexandria in Tosefta Sukkah 4:6 similarly borrows from Tannaitic descriptions of the Temple.[61] Indeed, the archeological evidence of synagogue dedicatory inscriptions and architecture confirms that the synagogue was considered holy space.[62] Fine concludes: "For the early Rabbinic Sages, synagogues were the institutional focal point for the reconstruction of Judaism. In their hands the meeting house in which Scripture was studied before 70 CE became an institution infused with Temple qualities. It became the sacred place of the time when the Temple did not exist."[63]

Other commandments like eating in a sukkah are also infused with cultic significance: "Just as the name of Heaven applies to the pilgrimage sacrifice so too does it apply to a *sukkah*."[64] Some of the laws of sukkah derive, in both content and language, from Temple-based laws. For example, the rules about eating meals in the sukkah are modeled after the rules for offering sacrifices on Sukkoth. Mishna Sukkah 2:6 teaches that Rabbi Eliezer requires two meals to be eaten in the sukkah on each of the seven days of the festival; the sages require only one meal on the first night of the festival. Compare the following two laws from the Mishna regarding making up for a missed meal:

Mishna Sukkah 2:6	Mishna Ḥagigah 1:6
R. Eliezer said further: One who did not eat on the first night of the festival can make it up on the night of the last day of the festival. The sages say that there is no makeup for this. On this it was stated: "A twisted thing that cannot be made straight, a lack that cannot be made good" (Ecclesiastes 1:15).	One who did not offer the festival sacrifices on the first day of the [Sukkoth] festival can offer them throughout the festival and on the last day of the festival. If the festival passed and he did not offer it, he is not obligated to pay for it. On this it was stated: "A twisted thing that cannot be made straight, a lack that cannot be made good" (Ecclesiastes 1:15).

As Nagen shows, Mishna Sukkah is modeled both in language and structure on Mishna Ḥagigah.[65] Rabbi Eliezer's opinion that one can make up for a missed meal on the eighth day of Shemini Aseret parallels the law in Hagigah that one may make up a missed sacrifice during the rest of the festival, including on Shemini Aseret. The opinion of the sages that there is no possibility of making up the required meal on the first night parallels the language of the second clause in Mishna Ḥagigah that there is no possibility of making up a missed sacrifice after the festival. Even though Mishna Sukkah 2:6 records two differing opinions, it is able to artistically replicate the two clauses of Mishna Ḥagigah. The author of this Mishna obviously thought of the sukkah meals as parallels to and even replacements for the festival sacrifices.

The Talmud Yerushalmi makes the equation between sukkah meals and the Temple explicit in its inquiry as to the source for Rabbi Eliezer's requirement for two meals in the sukkah per day:

> What is the source of R. Eliezer? It is stated here: You shall dwell [in Sukkoth for seven days]" (Leviticus 23:42), and it is stated there, "You shall dwell at the entrance of the Tent of Meeting day and night [for seven days]" (Leviticus 8:35). Just as regarding "dwell" stated there the verse requires nights like days, so too regarding "dwell" stated here the verse considers the nights like the days.[66]

Rabbi Eliezer derives the requirement to eat a meal in the sukkah in the night and the day of each of the seven days of the festival from the requirement of the sons of Aaron to remain at the Tent of Meeting night and day for seven days. Nagen further demonstrates how the detailed laws governing the height of the roof of a sukkah and the constitution of its walls, and even the symbolism associated with the sukkah, are all inspired by and derived from biblical descriptions of the Tabernacle. In this way, the rabbis transform the sukkah into a holy space parallel to that of the Temple.[67]

Mishna Horayot 3:8, cited above, teaches that rabbis are ransomed before priests. The next text also shows sages to be more important than priests but does so without ever mentioning the latter. Mishna Avot 1:1 provides the chain of transmission of the Torah: "Moses received the Torah from Sinai and transmitted it to Joshua, and Joshua to the elders, and the elders to the prophets, and the prophets transmitted it to the men of the Great Assembly." Priests, however, are curiously absent, even though Deuteronomy 31:9 explicitly reports that Moses handed the Torah over to the priests and the elders, along with a commandment to read it to the people every seven years.[68] Instead, the first two chapters of Mishna Avot continue to list all of the sages who represent the culmination of the chain. Many scholars find in this omission a conscious effort to subdue the historical importance of the priesthood in favor of the centrality of the Torah sage.[69] The priests have been replaced by the elders and sages of the Great Assembly.

Not only are priests replaced in their role as transmitters of the Torah, but the midrash also transfers their role as judges to the rabbis. Deuteronomy 17:8–9 describes the nation's highest court in Jerusalem: "If a case is too baffling for you to decide, be it a controversy over homicide, civil law, or assault—matters of dispute in your courts—you shall promptly repair to the place that the Lord your God will have chosen, and appear before the levitical priests, or the magistrate in charge at the time, and present your problem."[70] This verse seems to require that a court have some priestly members sitting on it.[71] Similarly, the Damascus Document and the Temple Scroll both require that some members of a court should be priests and Levites.[72] In contrast to this, Sifre Deuteronomy 153 asks whether the inclusion of priests on a court is obligatory and concludes that it is not:

> "To the levitical priests" (Deuteronomy 17:9). There is a commandment for a court to have priests and Levites on it. Can it be that this is a commandment and if they are lacking it is invalid? The verse comes to teach, "or to the magistrate," even if there are no priests or Levites it is still valid.

The judicial role of the priests can now be dispensed with. The same midrash also comments on the types of cases that fall under the jurisdiction of the high court. Whereas the verses in Deuteronomy list only civil and criminal laws, Sifre Deuteronomy 152 extends the court's jurisdiction to include all areas of halacha including afflictions of the body, of clothing, and of houses, as well as the laws relating to sanctified property and the suspected adulteress. Even though the Torah specifically assigns judgments in each of these areas of law to the priests,[73] this midrash now teaches that the court of sages shall judge these cases—even if there are no priests on the court.[74]

Although Deuteronomy 17:8 specifies that the high court must sit in the Jerusalem Temple, Sifre Deuteronomy 153 extends the law to include the court at Yavneh. The midrash thus expands the original law in three directions: the high court need not include any priests, has jurisdiction over purity and other laws otherwise exclusive to the priests, and can meet in Yavneh rather than only in the Temple. Taken together, these reinterpretations succeed in transferring judicial authority from the priests in the Temple to the rabbis at Yavneh.[75]

Moshe Halbertal analyzes the ways in which afflictions, charity, and prayer serve as substitutes for sacrifices. He distinguishes between two mechanisms through which this transference occurs.[76] In the weaker sense, these replacements serve to achieve the same goal as sacrifices, although through different means. For example, whereas sacrifice atones by giving an animal as a scapegoat that substitutes for oneself, suffering atones by standing in for the actual punishment that halacha requires for a sin.[77] In the stronger sense, these replacements are themselves forms of sacrifice. For example, when one gives money to the poor, there is a sense in which one gives that money to God, who is ultimately responsible for feeding the poor.[78] Similarly, various midrashim describe the utterances of prayer as being themselves offerings to God.[79]

To sum up this set of texts, these traditions seem to be coping mechanisms for continuing to survive as a nation and to have access to holiness, atonement, and communion with God without the Temple. In addition, these texts also have the effect of making the role of the priests almost obsolete and of increasing the significance of the rabbis in their stead.

Rhetoric of Appropriation: Temple and Priestly Laws Are Extended

The last set of texts is in many ways the most interesting because they do not replace the Temple activity and the priesthood, but rather continue them by extending them outside the Temple and requiring laypeople to act like priests. Instead of replacing Temple rites with a completely different activity such as prayer or acts of kindness, in this category of texts the rabbis appropriate the Temple rite or priestly law and make it their own. Precisely because these Temple rites have so much significance attributed to them, they are expanded beyond the Temple and, paradoxically, are thereby disassociated with the Temple and absorbed into the realm of rabbinic halacha.

The most explicit examples of this are the enactments of Rabban Yoḥanan ben Zakkai to extend rituals once performed exclusively in the Temple. The original law before the Temple's destruction dictated that if Rosh Hashanah fell on the Sabbath, the shofar would be blown only in the Temple. Once the Temple was destroyed, "Rabban Yoḥanan ben Zakkai made an enactment that they should blow [on the Sabbath] in every place that has a court."[80] This move, however, was not without controversy:

> Once when Rosh Hashanah fell out on Shabbat, Rabban Yoḥanan ben Zakai told the sons of Betera, "Let us blow." They said, "Let us discuss." He said, "Let us blow first and then discuss." After they blew, the sons of Betera said, "Let us discuss." Rabban Yoḥanan ben Zakai said, "The horn has already been sounded at Yavneh and we may not reverse it after it has been practiced."[81]

Rabban Yoḥanan ben Zakkai needed to resort to politics, negotiation, and even some shrewd maneuvering to achieve his goal of making the transition from Temple to synagogue as smooth as possible.

Similarly, the original law was that the four species were taken for only one day outside the Temple, and only in the Temple were they taken for all seven days of the Festival of Booths. The destruction of the Temple meant that nobody could perform the commandment of the four species on the last six days of the holiday. Therefore, "Rabban Yoḥanan ben Zakkai made an enactment that the *lulav* should be taken throughout the land all seven days in remembrance of the Temple."[82] Shofar and *lulav* are thus extended into the non-Temple realm and become appropriated into the rabbinic system.

We have already seen above how the rabbis likened taking the four species to offering a sacrifice. Nagen insightfully points out that Rabban Yoḥanan ben Zakkai's extension of the four species may be the cause for their taking on sacrificial symbolism. Taking the four species as practiced in the Temple was integrated into the general service alongside the sacrifices. Once it was removed from the Temple, it became the center of the service, so the rabbis gave the *lulav* significance as a sacrifice in its own right.[83]

A parallel phenomenon exists in the evolution of the Passover celebration. During Temple times, the Passover sacrifice was the center of the festival rite. Other rituals such as eating unleavened bread and bitter herbs, reciting hallel, and having a banquet were ancillary outgrowths of eating the Passover sacrifice. Numbers 9:1 decrees: "They shall eat it [the Passover sacrifice] with unleavened bread and bitter herbs." Although Exodus 12:18 mentions eating unleavened bread for all seven days as a counterpoint to not eating leaven for seven days, there is no specific obligation to eat unleavened bread alone on the first night.[84] The Mishna, however, appropriates the eating of unleavened bread on the first night, originally only part of the sacrifice, and extends it as a requirement independent of the sacrifice:

> They served him unleavened bread and lettuce (used for bitter herbs) and *ḥaroset*, even though the *ḥaroset* is not a commandment. R. Eleazar ben R. Sadok says, "It is a commandment." And in the Temple they serve him the carcass of the Passover offering.[85]

Since *ḥaroset* is singled out as not being required, we can infer that unleavened bread and bitter herbs are required independently of the sacrifice.[86] The midrash delineates the exegetical derivation for this extension:

> "[You shall eat unleavened bread] until the twenty-first day of the month at evening" (Exodus 12:18). Can it be that you are required to eat unleavened bread all seven days?
> Therefore the verse teaches "[For seven days you shall eat unleavened bread] with it [the sacrifice] (Deuteronomy 16:3)." You are required [to eat unleavened bread] only with [the sacrifice] but you are not required to eat unleavened bread all seven days....
> Can it be that I only know [that you are required to eat unleavened bread] when you have the Passover sacrifice? How do I know [that you are required to eat unleavened bread] even when you do not have the Passover sacrifice?
> Therefore the verse teaches "[For seven days] you shall eat unleavened bread" (Deuteronomy 16:3). Scripture sets it as an obligation.
> I only know [that you are required to eat unleavened bread] when the Temple is standing. How do I know [that you are required to eat unleavened bread] even when the Temple is not standing?
> Therefore the verse teaches "At evening you shall eat unleavened bread" (Exodus 12:18).
> I only know [that you are required to eat unleavened bread] in the Land of Israel. How do I know [that you are required to eat unleavened bread] even outside of the Land of Israel?

Therefore the verse teaches "In all your settlements [you shall eat unleavened bread]" (Exodus 12:20).[87]

The rabbis are thus able to ignore the absence of the sacrifice and extend the obligation to eat unleavened bread even without the Temple and even in the diaspora.[88] Besides the obligation to eat unleavened bread and bitter herbs, the rabbinic seder also extends the recitation of hallel, the drinking of wine (already mentioned in Jubilees),[89] and the retelling of the Exodus story.[90] The rabbis not only adopt these originally sacrifice-based rites but also adapt them by requiring that the Exodus story should be told through rabbinic midrash and by framing the seder within a structure of fixed blessings.[91]

The last few texts deal with the spread of ritual purity, once the almost exclusive domain of the priests, to various groups of nonpriests. According to biblical law, anyone who enters the holy precincts or eats sacred food must be in a state of ritual purity. Priests who regularly entered the Temple and partook of sacrifices and first-fruits and heave offerings had to regularly maintain their purity.[92] Laypeople, however, had to become pure only when partaking of the Passover sacrifice and other occasional sacrifices.[93] During the second Temple period, however, various groups that were not exclusively priests took it upon themselves to live in a state of purity at all times. The purity laws were observed very stringently by the members of the Dead Sea Sect[94] as well as by anyone who took upon himself or herself the pledges of living as a *ḥaver*, including a commitment to eat even profane food in purity.[95] There is much evidence to suggest further that the Pharisees and the rabbis took on various aspects of priestly purity laws and encouraged the eating of all food in a state of purity.[96] Thus, Mark 7:1–4 explains that the Pharisees complained about Jesus's disciples eating with unwashed hands since Pharisees always performed this ceremonial washing before eating. The Talmud uses striking rhetoric to bring home the importance of this ritual washing before the meal: "Anyone who eats bread without washing hands, it is as if he had sexual relations with a prostitute."[97] Another text grants this act biblical authority: "'You shall sanctify yourselves' (Leviticus 20:7)—this refers to the first washing before the meal."[98]

Similarly, Mishna Chullin 2:5 teaches: "One who slaughters a domestic animal, a wild animal, or fowl and blood did not come out, they are kosher and they are eaten with dirty hands since they have not been made susceptible to impurity by blood." To contract impurity, food must first become wet with water, blood, or certain other liquids.[99] This Mishna teaches that if an animal or bird does not bleed at the time of its slaughter, then the carcass is not susceptible to contracting impurity. Therefore, one may eat it without washing one's hands. One can infer from this that the Mishna would require washing hands for all cases when the animal does bleed at the time of slaughter, for fear that impurity on the hands would transfer to the meat. Since this Mishna includes wild animals, which may not be sacrificed, it is clear that hand washing would be required even for nonsacrificial meat.

Why did nonpriests eat in purity? Perhaps in order to fulfill Isaiah's vision of a future when the whole nation will become priests: "You shall be called priests of God and termed servants of our God."[100] But setting apocalypticism aside, it seems that many Jews were simply impressed with the power of the priesthood and believed that purity was an intrinsic good. Whatever the motivation, one resulting effect is that the purity laws were no longer the exclusive domain of the priests. This represents a different type of transition from priests to rabbis than the examples in the previous categories. Whereas previously we saw the Temple and priestly activities downplayed and replaced with nonpriestly equivalents, here the Temple practices and priestly laws are extended and adopted by nonpriests.

This adoption of ritual purity extends a significant step further when the rabbis make use of purity obligations in order to legislate other matters not directly connected to purity.[101] For example, Mishna Pesahim 10:9 decrees: "The Passover sacrifice after midnight makes the hands impure. A sacrifice that was slaughtered without proper intention or that was left over after its time limit makes the hands impure." These improper sacrifices and leftovers are already prohibited biblically.[102] Nevertheless, the sages of the Mishna added a fence around the biblical prohibition against eating these sacrifices by declaring that doing so will also cause impurity. It seems that a biblical prohibition was not enough to stop many priests from slaughtering animals improperly or being lazy in their consumption of the sacrifices. A threat of impurity, even the minor impurity of unclean hands that can easily be washed, was more effective at keeping them from sinning.[103] The sages piggybacked on the very deeply entrenched fear of impurity to achieve their legislative goals.

Similarly, Mishna Zavim 5:12 decrees that biblical scrolls cause food impurity. According to the Talmud Bavli, this is a rabbinic enactment to protect the scrolls. Priests would store their pure heave offerings together with the Torah scrolls, figuring that both were holy.[104] However, mice would come to eat the food and would damage the scrolls as well. The rabbis decreed that the scrolls cause impurity so that the priests would keep their food separate from the scrolls. The rabbis could have simply prohibited the storing of food with scrolls, but that prohibition would not be nearly as effective as threatening the priests with impurity.[105] In these examples and others like them,[106] the rabbis extended purity laws to areas that are completely unrelated to purity as a way of effectively legislating against problematic behavior. Instead of suppressing purity laws as part of their struggle with the priesthood, they made the realm of purity their own and used it to bolster their authority.

Since this study is phenomenological and not chronological,[107] I have not been careful to distinguish between early and late sources. In fact, all four rhetorical categories include early and late traditions from the Tannaim and Amoraim, suggesting that the rabbis used all of these strategies simultaneously. If I had to choose one category as the earliest, it might be the fourth category, which includes practices of ritual purity that date back even before the Temple's destruction, to the Pharisees and Shammai and Hillel. The enactments of Rabban Yoaḥanan b. Zakkai and similar extensions of Temple rites would then be the most readily implementable strategy. Indeed, Baruch Bokser writes: "An individual or group that suffers a traumatic loss must eventually confront and adjust to the new circumstances. But as long as the pain of loss is acute, one cannot openly alter one's relationship to the lost object or transcend it. To face the future, one needs to feel and demonstrate a continuity with the past."[108] The fourth category seems best suited to demonstrate continuity; instead of introducing a new ritual as a substitute for a Temple ritual, the Temple ritual is simply extended and changed in subtle ways. However, even if the fourth category was the earliest to be used, the others were surely not far behind, and all four eventually coincided and mutually reinforced each other.

These four rhetorical categories reflect diverse and overlapping approaches to the relationship between the world of the priests and that of rabbis. The four can perhaps be roughly paired with Kenneth Burke's four master tropes: metaphor, metonymy, synecdoche, and irony.[109] Burke contends that all discourse relies on these four ways of relating ideas to each other in order to discover and describe the world.[110] Metaphor is thus not simply a poetic flourish. Rather, as Sabine Maasen and Peter Weingart write, "metaphors serve to redescribe a phenomenon of a primary system in terms of a secondary system and by doing so, interact with each other. This interaction might presuppose an initial similarity or comparability of phenomena and their associative meanings.... However, it is the metaphor that actively evokes this process that ultimately will lead to a mutual transfer of meanings of aspects of them."[111]

Burke's four tropes are not distinctly independent methods; rather, each occupies part of spectrum of how closely related the two elements of comparison are to each other. Metaphor compares two different ideas, presenting one from the perspective of the other. Metonymy reduces a more complex realm to a less complex one or conveys the incorporeal in terms of the corporeal. In synecdoche, one thing is represented by its part or the part is represented by the whole, so that the two elements are cut from the same cloth. If we substitute cause for effect, genus for species, container for contained, sign for signified, or vice versa, we correlate not two distinct entities but two aspects of one phenomenon. Burke notes that metonymy is a "special application" of synecdoche, which moves only in the direction of reduction. Irony emerges when two terms are dialectically dependent on one another and thus neither can exist without the other—even though, or precisely because, they are in opposition to each other.

Mapping Burke's four tropes onto our four rhetorical strategies, even if only loosely, may help heuristically in unpacking the thought processes by which the rabbis transfer authority from the priests to their own houses of study. Like metaphor, the rhetoric of comparison views and judges one idea from the perspective of another. Instead of leaving each of the categories of priest, king, sage, and so forth in its distinct role and realm, these statements pit one against the other. The priest is now judged from the perspective of the rabbi, using the currency of Torah knowledge, and is found wanting.

In the rhetoric of legal fiction, the realms of Torah and Temple are brought into closer relationship by defining the value of the former in terms of the value of the latter. As in metonymy, the more ephemeral study of Torah is reduced to the more concrete offering of animal sacrifices. In metonymy—unlike in the rhetoric of comparison, where the priest is judged from the perspective of the rabbi—sacrifice remains the ultimate value, and Torah is what is praised and appraised in terms of priestly currency.

In a particularly striking example of metonymy discussed above, Rabbi Sheshet requests that the fat and blood that have diminished from his body while fasting should be substituted for a complete animal sacrifice.[112] If we remember that animal sacrifice is itself a substitute for human sacrifice,[113] then his metonymy actually succeeds in recovering the quintessential act of sacrifice as self-sacrifice.[114] In this sense, Rabbi Sheshet not only metonymically reduces the sacrifice of his own flesh to animal sacrifice, but also synecdotally uses part of his body to represent its whole.

Regarding the next trope, Burke writes: "The 'noblest synecdoche,' the perfect paradigm or prototype for all lesser usages, is found in metaphysical doctrines proclaiming the identity of 'microcosm' and 'macrocosm.'"[115] We find an example in the rhetoric of substitution, wherein the synagogue is called a small Temple. It then follows that the various activities performed in the synagogue will also represent parallel activities in the Temple. The sukkah is similarly regarded as a microcosm for the Temple.

Finally, the rabbinic appropriation of Temple and priestly laws into the halachic system parallels Burke's definition of irony since rabbinic authority both rejects and depends on the authority of the priest. The ability of the rabbis to legislate purity laws effectively weakened purity's hold on the populace and made it possible for the rabbis to control and use that power for their own halachic ends. By extending sacrificial rites beyond the Temple's boundaries, the rabbis succeeded in establishing their own realm of halacha as the legitimate extension of the Temple's sanctity. The rabbis could not have come into being without appropriating priestly rites, just as so many Temple-based values and rituals would not have endured without the rabbis. Priests and rabbis are dialectically dependent on each other.

In sum, the shift from priests to rabbis did not happen overnight during the summer of 70 CE. Rather, it occurred through a long and complex series of replacing, adopting, and extending various elements of the priesthood into the world of the house of study. The status of the priesthood would have been too well entrenched for the early rabbinic leaders to simply ignore or combat. Instead, through effective rhetoric and bold legislation, they turned the strength of the priesthood to their own advantage. The four rhetorical strategies found in the Talmud, like Burke's four tropes, range from rabbis contrasting themselves with priests to the two groups being intertwined and mutually defining. In saying that scholars are more important than priests, the rabbis acknowledge that priests are at the top of the lineage hierarchy;

however, they simply add another dimension that is not based on lineage but on knowledge. When they say that prayer, good deeds, or Torah study replace sacrifices—whether using the rhetoric of legal fiction or that of substitution—they admit that sacrifices are the central means of atonement. They simply argue by analogy that one can also achieve the effect of sacrifices by other means.

Perhaps their boldest but also most subtle move is to adopt the priestly system of purity and adapt it to their own needs. The rabbis become the experts in purity matters, adopt priestly behavior, and thoroughly co-opt the purity system. The very codification of sacrificial and purity laws in the Mishna not only enshrines but also rabbinizes the priests. The great effort and foresight of the rabbis in leading their followers through this traumatic period and difficult transition made it possible for Judaism to survive and thrive in subsequent centuries. Although Roman orators used the art of rhetoric in courts, politics, and—increasingly during the second sophistic period—for entertainment, the rabbis as a minority culture turned to rhetoric for their very survival. The Romans ruled through power, but the rabbis could resort to little more than persuasion—a tactic that in hindsight may have proved to be even more effective.

NOTES

I would like to thank A. J. Berkowitz, Binyamin Goldstein, Aaron Koller, Isaac Sassoon, and the editors of this volume, Michael Bernard-Donals and Janice W. Fernheimer, for their helpful comments and suggestions.

1. Martha Himmelfarb, *A Kingdom of Priests*, 1. Prophets also served as religious leaders and often provided a counterbalance to the priesthood, but their role was not nearly as effective on the popular level.

2. It must be emphasized that the roots of a nonpriestly mind-set were already in place before the second Temple period and had seeds even in the Torah itself. See Martha Himmelfarb, "'Found Written in the Book of Moses'"; and Reuven Kimelman, "From Priest to Rabbi to . . ." Similarly, priestly sects probably continued in some form after 70 CE (see Jodi Magness, "Sectarianism before and after 70 CE"; Martin Goodman, "Sadducees and Essenes after 70 C.E."). Nevertheless, the destruction of the Temple was clearly a catalyst for significant transition. Although nonpriests certainly held leadership positions before the destruction, as shown by the activities of the *soferim* and *zugot*, the introduction of the title "rabbi" in this century reflects the dramatic rise in prominence of the sages. Scholars debate whether the title was used before or only after the destruction, but all agree that it was not used before the first century (see Hershel Shanks, "Is the Title 'Rabbi' Anachronistic in the Gospels?"; Solomon Zeitlin, "A Reply"; Hershel Shanks, "Origins of the Title 'Rabbi'"; Solomon Zeitlin, "The Title Rabbi in the Gospels Is Anachronistic"; James Donaldson, "The Title Rabbi in the Gospels").

3. Himmelfarb, *A Kingdom of Priests*, 166.

4. See Cana Werman, "The Price of Mediation."

5. It is important to note that during Talmudic times the rabbis did not yet enjoy universal recognition by the Jewish populace (see Lee Levine, *The Ancient Synagogue*, 466–98). Nevertheless, it was primarily through rhetorical persuasion that they succeeded in maintaining their core constituency and gradually increasing their membership over time.

6. The custom of calling a priest to the Torah before a Levite traces back to Mishna Gittin 5:8.

7. Sirach 50:5–7 (New Standard Revised Version).

8. See Peter Schäfer, "Rabbis and Priests," 155–57; Martha Himmelfarb, "The Wisdom of the Scribe, the Wisdom of the Priest, and the Wisdom of the King according to Ben Sira"; Himmelfarb, *A Kingdom of Priests*, 30–45.

9. See Joseph Angel, *Otherworldly and Eschatological Priesthood in the Dead Sea Scrolls*, 1–14, 44–45; Heinz-Josef Fabry, "Priests at Qumran"; Robert Kugler, "Priests"; Albert Baumgarten, *Studies in Qumran Law*.

10. See Baruch Bokser, *The Origins of the Seder*, 7.

11. Ibid., 89.

12. See note 2.

13. Josephus, *Antiquities of the Jews*, 18.15, and *The Jewish War*, 2.162. See also Shaye Cohen, *From the Maccabees to the Mishnah*, 139–40.

14. See Richard Hidary, *Dispute for the Sake of Heaven*, 34. See also G. E. Lier, "Another Look at the Role of Priests and Rabbis after the Destruction of the Second Temple."

15. Avot d'Rabbi Natan A, 4. The translation is from Jeffrey Rubenstein, *Rabbinic Stories*, 50. See the parallel version at Bavli Gittin 56b and Lamentations Rabbah 1:5. For an analysis, see Jeffrey Rubenstein, *Talmudic Stories*, 139–73.

16. On the activity of the rabbis at Yavneh, see Gedalia Alon, *The Jews in Their Land in the Talmudic Age*, 253–87.

17. Josephus, *The Jewish War*, 3.399–408. See also Rubenstein, *Talmudic Stories*, 345 note 2.

18. Josephus, *Antiquities of the Jews*, 18.14–15.

19. Ibid., 13.297.

20. See Sifra Behukotai 2; Sifre Deuteronomy 351; Yerushalmi Peah 2:1 (17a); and Bavli Megilah 19b.

21. See Reuven Kimelman, "*Birkat Ha-Minim* and the Lack of Evidence for an Anti-Christian Jewish Prayer in Late Antiquity"; Hidary, *Dispute for the Sake of Heaven*, 34–35.

22. Tosefta Eduyot 1:1. It is significant that the sages agreed to record the teachings of the House of Shammai even though many of their laws agree with those of the sectarians. See Vered Noam, "Beth Shammai veha-halakha ha-kitatit"; idem, "Traces of Sectarian Halakha in the Rabbinic World."

23. Yerushalmi Yevamot 1:6 (3b) and Bavli Eruvin 13b.

24. Shaye Cohen, "The Significance of Yavneh," 42.

25. Baruch Bokser identifies only the first and third of these categories ("Rabbinic Responses to Catastrophe," 47–53).

26. See Christopher Forbes, "Paul and Rhetorical Comparison."

27. See George A. Kennedy, *Progymnasmata*, 83–84.

28. See Isaac Sassoon, *The Status of Women in Jewish Tradition*, 127–35.

29. Someone born of adultery or incest (see Deuteronomy 23:3).

30. Servants under the Levites in the Temple mentioned in Ezra 8:17, 20, et al. Bavli Yevamot 28b associates them with the Gibeonites of Joshua 9 and of 2 Samuel 21, and therefore views them as not of Israelite ethnicity.

31. The idea of a high priest who is an ignoramus may not be only theoretical. During the second Temple period, many of the high priests were Sadducees and thus not knowledgeable in Pharisaic law; some of them were even illiterate. Mishna Yoma 1:6 thus states that the sages would have to read to the high priest if he could not do so himself.

32. See also Tosefta Horayot 2:8–10.

33. The sixth chapter of Mishna Avot is a late appendage and not part of the original Mishna (see Hanoch Albeck, *Six Orders of Mishnah*, Nezikin, 2:351).

34. Sifre Numbers 119. See parallel texts at Avot d'Rabbi Natan A, 41, and Ecclesiastes Rabbah 7.

35. This theme is elaborated at Tanhuma *Ki Tavo*, 1. See also Bokser, "Rabbinic Responses to Catastrophe," 53–57.

36. Avot d'Rabbi Natan A 4. See also Bavli Berakhot 17a. For a further analysis, see Moshe Halbertal, *On Sacrifice*, 38–41.

37. The version at Avot d'Rabbi Natan B 8 reads "in its place (*tahteha*)" rather than "equivalent to it (*kemotah*)." That version thus employs a rhetoric of substitution rather than of comparison. See note 57 for a parallel statement that also uses a rhetoric of substitution.

38. Deuteronomy Rabbah 5, 3. See also Bavli Sukkah 49b and Yerushalmi Berakhot 2, 1 (4b).

39. For more examples, see Menachem Kasher, *Torah Shelemah*, 270–71; Ben Zion Rosenfeld, "Sage and Temple in Rabbinic Thought after the Destruction of the Second Temple." For further discussion, see Bokser, "Rabbinic Responses to Catastrophe," 47–50.

40. On analogies as a rhetorical device, see Chaïm Perelman and Lucie Olbrechts-Tyteca, *The New Rhetoric*, 371–98.

41. Pierre Olivier, *Legal Fictions in Practice and Legal Science*, 3–5. For a comparison between the use of legal fictions in both systems, see Leib Moscovitz, "Legal Fictions in Rabbinic Law and Roman Law."

42. See Lon Fuller, *Legal Fictions*, 54. The texts in this section are not technically legal but rather homiletic. Nevertheless, they use the language of legal fiction as a persuasive device just as legal arguments do.

43. Bavli Menachot 110a.

44. See also Avot d'Rabbi Natan A 4: "A sage who sits and preaches, Scripture considers it as if he has sacrificed fat and blood upon the altar." Along the same lines, Bavli Berakhot 33a states: "Anyone who has knowledge, it is as if the Temple was built in his days."

45. Bavli Ketubot 105b. Normally, the first-fruit offering would be given to a priest at the Temple (Deuteronomy 26:3). See also Bavli Berakhot 10b.

46. Bavli Yoma 71a.

47. Bavli Berakhot 17a. For further analyses, see Halbertal, *On Sacrifice*, 49.

48. The phrase *zivhe metim* appears in Psalms 106:28.

49. Mishna Avot 3:3. For a discussion, see Rosenfeld, "Sage and Temple in Rabbinic Thought," 455–56.

50. Sifra, Emor, *parasha* 10, 13:12.

51. Bavli Sukkah 45a.

52. Yakov Nagen, *Water, Creation and Immanence*, 83–122.

53. Yerushalmi Berakhot 4:1, 8d.

54. Bavli Berakhot 15a. On the importance of ritual hand washing, see below in this chapter. For more examples of legal fictions likening various actions to offering sacrifices, see Kasher, *Torah Shelemah*, 269–70.

55. Bavli Berakhot 26a. For an example of Roman law formulating a rule using a legal fiction while a parallel in rabbinic law does not, see Moscovitz, "Legal Fictions," 120–21.

56. Bavli Menaḥot 97a and Bavli Ḥagigah 27a. This statement also appears in Bavli Berakhot 17a, in the context of giving food to the poor at one's table. In that context, it has the same message as the teaching of Rabbi Yoḥanan b. Zakkai in Avot d'Rabbi Natan A 4, cited above: acts of kindness atone just as the Temple service does. However, there is no mention of feeding the poor in the other two Bavli contexts. Therefore, the original Amoraic statement seems to be comparing, or rather substituting, food on one's table with actual sacrifices. This statement thus seems to expand on the view propounded in Mishna Avot 3:3, which also cites Ezekiel 41:22. See also Kimelman, "From Priest to Rabbi to . . .," 110–11.

57. Bavli Megilah 29a. It is worth noting that this statement is Amoraic (200–500 CE) and thus is after the shift from priests to rabbis. In fact, Cohen writes that "the concern that the destruction of the Temple makes atonement unattainable is not documented in any Tannaitic document. Nor do the Tannaim equate the synagogue with the temple" ("The Significance of Yavneh," 46 note 50). Even if Cohen is correct that the Tannaim did not consider the synagogue as a replacement for the Temple, it is nevertheless significant that the Amoraim still felt the loss of the Temple strongly enough that they needed to find a substitute even centuries after its destruction. However, there is abundant evidence that the Tannaim also considered their synagogues to be partial replacements for the Temple, as we will see below.

58. Mekhilta d'Rabbi Ishmael, Jethro, Baḥodesh 11. For an analysis, see Steven Fine, *This Holy Place*, 53–55. See also citations from Pesikta de-Rav Kahana, *ba-yom ha-shemini* 8, at Fine, ibid., 65.

59. See also Fine, *This Holy Place*, 41–43. A similar use of the laws of the Temple for the place of prayer is found in the Damascus Document 11:22: "And all who enter the house of prostration, let him not come in a state of impurity but with laundered garments" (see ibid., 32).

60. Tosefta Megilah 3:22. See Fine, *This Holy Place*, 46.

61. Fine, *This Holy Place*, 43–45.

62. Ibid., 95–126. See also Himmelfarb, *A Kingdom of Priests*, 170–73.

63. Steven Fine, "From Meeting House to Sacred Realm," 27. See also Erich Gruen, *Diaspora*, 118–21.

64. Bavli Sukkah 9a and Bavli Betsah 30b.

65. Nagen, *Water, Creation and Immanence*, 32–34.

66. Yerushalmi Sukkah 2:7 (52a). For parallels, see Sifra, Emor, *parasha* 12, 17:6, and Bavli Sukkah 43a.

67. Nagen, *Water, Creation and Immanence*, 35–69. See also Jeffrey Rubenstein, *The History of Sukkot in the Second Temple and Rabbinic Periods*, 239–71; Jeffrey Rubenstein, "The Symbolism of the Sukkah"; Jeffrey Rubenstein, "The Symbolism of the Sukkah (Part 2)."

68. It is true that Mishna Avot 1:2 next names Simon the Just, who was a high priest; however, he is not identified by that title but rather as having been a member of the Great Assembly. The omission of priests is made even more glaring by the presence of Joshua, who is described as an attendant to Moses (Exodus 33:11) and his political and military successor (Deuteronomy 31:7), but not explicitly as a recipient of the Torah. Avot d'Rabbi Natan B 1, interestingly, does include Eli the high priest, who transmitted the Torah to Samuel.

69. Schäfer, "Rabbis and Priests," 166–72; and Steven Fraade, *From Tradition to Commentary*, 70–71.

70. The translation is from the Jewish Publication Society's *Tanakh*.

71. The central role of priests as judges is reiterated in Deuteronomy 19:17 and 21:5. Many passages in the Bible assume that priests dealt with more than just the cult. Leviticus 10:11 commands the priests to teach the people all of the laws, and Deuteronomy 17:18 and 31:9 place the priests in charge of keeping the scroll of the Torah safe. Ezekiel 44:24 attributes the adjudication of both ritual and civil laws to the levitical priests. In later times, 1 Chronicles 23:4 counts 6,000 Levites as officers and judges. It may have been the common court practice to have priests and lay judges together, as seen in 2 Chronicles 19:8–11, where Jehoshaphat makes a court in Jerusalem consisting of priests, Levites, and laymen.

72. See Hidary, *Dispute for the Sake of Heaven*, 311 note 46.

73. See Leviticus 13–14, 27:8, and Numbers 5:15, respectively.

74. Mishna Negaim 3:1 and Sifra Tazria Parashat Negaim 1:8–10 legislate that even if the sage decides a case, a priest must be present to officially issue the verdict. See also Steven Fraade, "Shifting from Priestly to Non-Priestly Legal Authority."

75. See also Hidary, *Dispute for the Sake of Heaven*, 297–325.

76. Halbertal, *On Sacrifice*, 47–48.

77. Ibid., 41–47.

78. Ibid., 38–41.

79. Ibid., 49–51.

80. Ibid., 41.

81. Bavli Rosh Hashanah 29b.

82. Mishna Rosh Hahsnah 4:3. For a parallel text, see Sifra, Emor, *parasha* 12, 16:9. It is noteworthy that Josephus describes the *lulav* as exclusively a cultic practice (see Rubenstein, *The History of Sukkot*, 75–84).

83. We also saw above how God's presence is said to dwell in the sukkah, which thereby serves as a substitute for the Temple. At the same time, the sukkah of the rabbis can also be considered an extension of the sukkah as a ritual connected to the Temple. One opinion among scholars derives the origin of the sukkah in the temporary tents set up in Jerusalem to accommodate the multitude of pilgrims (see Rubenstein, *The History of Sukkot*, 25–29). The Dead Sea Scrolls also associate sitting in the sukkah with the Temple service (see ibid., 64–68). If the sukkah during Temple times was only practiced near the Temple, then the rabbinic requirement to set up sukkoth everywhere would be a significant extension of the law to non-Temple settings. However, other scholars trace the origin of the sukkah to tents set up by farmers during the harvest season. Indeed, Philo mentions the building of sukkoth in the diaspora (see ibid., 69–73).

84. See also Deuteronomy 16:3, where the obligation to eat unleavened bread all seven days is dependent on the sacrifice.

85. Mishna Pesaḥim 10:3, following ms. Kaufman. For a parallel text, see Tosefta Pesahim 10:9.

86. Bokser, *The Origins of the Seder*, 39–40.

87. Mekhilta d'Rabbi Shimon b. Yohai 12:18.

88. See Joseph Dov Soloveitchik, *Halakhic Man*, 26–28.

89. See Bokser, *The Origins of the Seder*, 19.

90. Exodus 13:8 instructs one to tell his children about the Exodus from Egypt in the context of eating unleavened bread for seven days, but not specifically on the first night.

91. See Bokser, *The Origins of the Seder*, 67–75.

92. Leviticus 22:3–9; Numbers 18:11, 13, and 19:13.

93. Numbers 9:6; Deuteronomy 15:22 and 26:14. Rabbinic law also requires that laypeople eat their second tithe in purity (Mishna Ma'aser Sheni 2:10). Even though a few biblical verses suggest the possibility that purity laws must be kept outside the Temple, Tannaitic law systematically interprets all such verses as applying only to the Temple (see Vered Noam, "Shuv li-thuman shel hilkhot tahara").

94. Hannah Harrington, "Ritual Purity"; Himmelfarb, *A Kingdom of Priests*, 85–114.

95. Tosefta Demai 2:2.

96. See David Amit and Yonatan Adler, "The Observance of Ritual Purity after 70 C.E."; Hannah Harrington, "Did the Pharisees Eat Ordinary Food in a State of Ritual Purity?"; Jacob Neusner, *From Politics to Piety*; Gedalia Alon, *Jews, Judaism and the Classical World*, 190–234. For a counterargument, see Hanah Birenboim, "'A Kingdom of Priests'"; John Pioirier, "Why Did the Pharisees Wash Their Hands?"; E. P. Sanders, *Jewish Law from Jesus to the Mishnah*.

97. Bavli Berakhot 53b.

98. Bavli Sotah 4b. The seriousness attached to this law is already evident in Mishna Eduyot 5:6, in which one sage is reported to have been excommunicated for casting doubt on the importance of the cleanness of hands.

99. Leviticus 11:34 and Mishna Makhshirin 6:4.

100. Isaiah 61:6. This vision reverses Isaiah 24:2 and Hosea 4:9, in which all the people were punished together with the priests, but it builds on Exodus 19:6, in which the whole nation is called a kingdom of priests. See also Himmelfarb, *A Kingdom of Priests*, 2–3.

101. On the tendency of the rabbis to legislate in an area of halacha under their control to alleviate a completely unrelated problem, see Saul Lieberman, *Hellenism in Jewish Palestine*, 139–40.

102. Exodus 12:10 and Leviticus 7:17–18.

103. See Tosafot s.v. "*mishum*" to Bavli Pesaḥim 85a, who comment: "Even for wicked people, impurity is grave."

104. Bavli Shabbat 14a. For possible parallels to this practice at Qumran, see Jodi Magness, "Scrolls and Hand Impurity."

105. Mishna Yadayim 3:4–5 and Mishna Kelim 15:6 teach further that scriptural scrolls cause hand impurity, which is different from, though perhaps related to, food impurity. Solomon Zeitlin suggests that the Pharisees decreed that scripture defiles hands in order to prevent the priests from reading it (*The Rise and Fall of the Judean State*, 174–75). This was part of a polemic against the Sadducees, who were mainly priests and who followed only scriptural law and rejected Pharisaic oral tradition. If a priest consulted a Torah scroll, then he would be penalized by being unable to eat from heave offerings or sacrifices. If this interpretation is correct, it would mean a most extraordinary appropriation of the priestly purity laws. The Pharisees and rabbis were in such control of the purity system, which they had co-opted from the priests, that they were able to turn it against the priests. See also Martin Goodman, "Sacred Scripture and 'Defiling the Hands,'" 103–7; Shamma Friedman, "The Holy Scriptures Defile the Hands"; Menahem Haran, *The Biblical Collection*, 201–76; Chaim Milikowsky, "Reflections on Hand-Washing, Hand Purity, and Holy Scripture in Rabbinic Literature."

106. See Mishna Kelim 15:6 and Tosefta Shabbat 1:14.

107. For a chronological presentation of many of these texts, see Rosenfeld, "Sage and Temple in Rabbinic Thought"; and Bokser, "Rabbinic Responses to Catastrophe," 57.

108. Bokser, *The Origins of the Seder*, 90.

109. Kenneth Burke, "Four Master Tropes." On the first three tropes in Roman rhetoric, see Quintilian, *Institutes of Oratory*, 8.6.1–28.

110. On the fundamental role of metaphor in our understanding of experience, see George Lakoff and Mark Johnson, *Metaphors We Live By*.

111. Sabine Maasen and Peter Weingart, *Metaphors and the Dynamics of Knowledge*, 35.

112. Bavli Berakhot 17a.

113. See Genesis 22; Halbertal, *On Sacrifice*, 25.

114. This example follows Burke's description of the stages leading from literal to metaphorical to metonymic: "Language develops by metaphorical extension, in borrowing words from the realm of the corporal, visible, tangible and applying them by analogy to the realm of the incorporeal, invisible, intangible; then in the course of time, the original corporeal reference is forgotten, and only the incorporeal, metaphorical extension survives; and finally, poets regain the original relation, in reverse, by a 'metaphorical extension' back from the intangible into a tangible equivalent; and this 'archaicizing' device we call 'metonymy'" ("Four Master Tropes," 425, omitting Burke's parenthetical remarks).

115. Ibid., 427.

BIBLIOGRAPHY

Albeck, Hanoch. *Six Orders of Mishnah*. 6 vols. Jerusalem: Mossad Bialik, 1959.

Alon, Gedalia. *The Jews in Their Land in the Talmudic Age (70–640 C.E.)*. Translated by Gershon Levi. Vol. 1. Jerusalem: Magnes, 1984.

———. *Jews, Judaism and the Classical World: Studies in Jewish History in the Times of the Second Temple and Talmud*. Jerusalem: Magnes, 1977.

Amit, David, and Yonatan Adler. "The Observance of Ritual Purity after 70 C.E.: A Reevaluation of the Evidence in Light of Recent Archaeological Discoveries." In *"Follow the Wise": Studies in Jewish History and Culture in Honor of Lee I. Levine*, edited by Jodi Magness, Seth Schwartz, Zeev Weiss, and Oded Irshai, 121–43. Winona Lake, IN: Eisenbrauns, 2010.

Angel, Joseph. *Otherworldly and Eschatological Priesthood in the Dead Sea Scrolls*. Leiden: Brill, 2010.

Baumgarten, Albert. *Studies in Qumran Law*. Leiden: Brill, 1977.

Birenboim, Hanah. "'A Kingdom of Priests': Did the Pharisees Try to Live Like Priests?" In *Was 70 CE a Watershed in Jewish History? On Jews and Judaism before and after the Destruction of the Second Temple*, edited by Daniel Schwartz and Zeev Weiss, 59–68. Leiden: Brill, 2012.

Bokser, Baruch. *The Origins of the Seder: The Passover Rite and Early Rabbinic Judaism*. Berkeley: University of California Press, 1984.

———. "Rabbinic Responses to Catastrophe: From Continuity to Discontinuity." *Proceedings of the American Academy for Jewish Research* 50 (1983): 37–61.

Burke, Kenneth. "Four Master Tropes." *Kenyon Review* 3, no. 4 (1941): 421–38.

Cohen, Shaye. *From the Maccabees to the Mishnah*. 2nd ed. Louisville, KY: Westminster John Knox, 2006.

———. "The Significance of Yavneh: Pharisees, Rabbis, and the End of Jewish Sectarianism." *Hebrew Union College Annual* 55 (1984): 27–53.

Donaldson, James. "The Title Rabbi in the Gospels: Some Reflections on the Evidence of the Synoptics." *Jewish Quarterly Review* 63 (1973): 287–91.

Fabry, Heinz-Josef. "Priests at Qumran: A Reassessment." In *The Dead Sea Scrolls: Texts and Context*, edited by Charlotte Hempel, 243–62. Leiden: Brill, 2010.

Fine, Steven. "From Meeting House to Sacred Realm: Holiness and the Ancient Synagogue." In *Sacred Realm: The Emergence of the Synagogue in the Ancient World*, edited by Steven Fine, 21–47. New York: Oxford University Press, 1996.

———. *This Holy Place: On the Sanctity of the Synagogue during the Greco-Roman Period*. Notre Dame, IN: University of Notre Dame Press, 1997.

Forbes, Christopher. "Paul and Rhetorical Comparison." In *Paul in the Greco-Roman World: A Handbook*, edited by J. Paul Sampley, 134–71. Harrisburg, PA: Trinity Press International, 2003.

Fraade, Steven. *From Tradition to Commentary: Torah and Its Interpretation in the Midrash Sifre to Deuteronomy*. Albany: State University of New York Press, 1991.

———. "Shifting from Priestly to Non-Priestly Legal Authority: A Comparison of the Damascus Document and the Midrash Sifra." *Dead Sea Discoveries* 6, no. 2 (1999): 109–25.

Friedman, Shamma. "The Holy Scriptures Defile the Hands: The Transformation of a Biblical Concept in Rabbinic Theology." In *Minhah le-Nahum: Biblical and Other Studies Presented to Nahum M. Sarna in Honour of His Seventieth Birthday*, edited by Marc Brettler and Michael Fishbane, 117–32. Sheffield, UK: Journal for the Study of Old Testament, 1993.

Fuller, Lon. *Legal Fictions*. Stanford, CA: Stanford University Press, 1967.

Goodman, Martin. "Sacred Scripture and 'Defiling the Hands.'" *Journal of Theological Studies* 40, no. 1 (1990): 99–107.

———. "Sadducees and Essenes after 70 C.E." In *Crossing the Boundaries: Essays in Biblical Interpretation in Honour of Michael D. Goulder*, Stanley E. Porter, Paul Joyce, and David E. Orton, 347–56. Leiden: Brill, 1994.

Gruen, Erich. *Diaspora: Jews amidst Greeks and Romans*. Cambridge, MA: Harvard University Press, 2002.

Halbertal, Moshe. *On Sacrifice*. Princeton, NJ: Princeton University Press, 2012.

Haran, Menahem. *The Biblical Collection: Its Consolidation to the End of the Second Temple Times and Changes of Form to the End of the Middle Ages* [Hebrew]. Jerusalem: Magnes, 1996.

Harrington, Hannah. "Did the Pharisees Eat Ordinary Food in a State of Ritual Purity?" *Journal for the Study of Judaism in the Persian, Hellenistic and Roman Period* 26, no. 1 (1995): 42–54.

———. "Ritual Purity." In *The Dead Sea Scrolls and Contemporary Culture*, edited by Adolfo Roitman, Lawrence Schiffman, and Shani Tzoref, 329–47. Leiden: Brill, 2011.

Hidary, Richard. *Dispute for the Sake of Heaven: Legal Pluralism in the Talmud*. Providence, RI: Brown University Press, 2010.

Himmelfarb, Martha. "'Found Written in the Book of Moses': Priests in the Era of Torah." In *Was 70 CE a Watershed in Jewish History? On Jews and Judaism before and after the Destruction of the Second Temple*, edited by Daniel Schwartz and Zeev Weiss, 24–41. Leiden: Brill, 2012.

———. *A Kingdom of Priests: Ancestry and Merit in Ancient Judaism*. Philadelphia: University of Pennsylvania Press, 2006.

———. "The Wisdom of the Scribe, the Wisdom of the Priest, and the Wisdom of the King according to Ben Sira." In *For a Later Generation: The Transfomation of Tradition in Israel, Early Judaism, and Early Christianity*, edited by Randall A. Argall, Beverly A. Bow, and Rodney A. Werline, 88–99. Harrisburg, PA: Trinity Press International, 2000.

Josephus, Flavius. *Antiquities of the Jews*. Translated by Brian McGing. London: Wordsworth Editions, 1987.

———. *The Jewish War*. Translated by Betty Radice. London: Penguin Classics, 1984.

Kasher, Menachem. *Torah Shelemah*. Vol. 25. Jerusalem: Bet Torah Shelomo, 1992.

Kennedy, George A. *Progymnasmata: Greek Textbooks of Prose Composition and Rhetoric*. Leiden: Brill, 2003.

Kimelman, Reuven. "*Birkat Ha-Minim* and the Lack of Evidence for an Anti-Christian Jewish Prayer in Late Antiquity." In *Jewish and Christian Self-Definition*, vol. 2: *Aspects of Judaism in the Graeco-Roman Period*, edited by E. P. Sanders, 226–44, 391–403. Philadelphia: Fortress, 1981.

———. "From Priest to Rabbi to . . . : The Crystallization of Rabbinic Judaism." In *The Solomon Goldman Lectures: Perspectives in Jewish Learning*, edited by Nathaniel Stampfer, 4:95–111. Chicago: Spertus College of Judaica Press, 1985.

Kugler, Robert. "Priests." In *Encyclopedia of the Dead Sea Scrolls*, edited by Lawrence Schiffman and James VanderKam, 2:688–93. New York: Oxford University Press, 2000.

Lakoff, George, and Mark Johnson. *Metaphors We Live By*. Chicago: University of Chicago Press, 2003.

Levine, Lee. *The Ancient Synagogue: The First Thousand Years*. New Haven, CT: Yale University Press, 2005.

Lieberman, Saul. *Hellenism in Jewish Palestine*. New York: Jewish Theological Seminary Press, 1962.

Lier, G. E. "Another Look at the Role of Priests and Rabbis after the Destruction of the Second Temple." *Journal for Semitics* 16, no. 1 (2007): 87–112.

Maasen, Sabine, and Peter Weingart. *Metaphors and the Dynamics of Knowledge*. New York: Routledge, 2000.

Magness, Jodi. "Scrolls and Hand Impurity." In *The Dead Sea Scrolls: Texts and Context*, edited by Charlotte Hempel, 89–97. Leiden: Brill, 2010.

———. "Sectarianism before and after 70 CE." In *Was 70 CE a Watershed in Jewish History? On Jews and Judaism before and after the Destruction of the Second Temple*, edited by Daniel Schwartz and Zeev Weiss, 69–89. Leiden: Brill, 2012.

Milikowsky, Chaim. "Reflections on Hand-Washing, Hand Purity, and Holy Scripture in Rabbinic Literature." In *Purity and Holiness: The Heritage of Leviticus*, edited by Marcel Poorthius and Joshua Schwartz, 149–62. Leiden: Brill, 2000.

Moscovitz, Leib. "Legal Fictions in Rabbinic Law and Roman Law: Some Comparative Observations." In *Rabbinic Law in Its Roman and Near Eastern Context*, edited by Catherine Hezser, 105–32. Tübingen, Germany: Mohr Siebeck, 2003.

Nagen, Yakov. *Water, Creation and Immanence: The Philosophy of the Festival of Sukkot*. Otniel, Israel: Gilui, Yeshivat Otniel, 2008.

Neusner, Jacob. *From Politics to Piety: The Emergence of Pharisaic Judaism*. New York: Ktav, 1979.

Noam, Vered. "Beth Shammai veha-halakha ha-kitatit." *Madaʿe ha-Yahadut* 41 (2002): 45–67.

———. "Shuv li-tḥuman shel hilkhot tahara." *Zion* 72, no. 2 (2007): 127–60.

———. "Traces of Sectarian Halakha in the Rabbinic World." In *Rabbinic Perspectives: Rabbinic Literature and the Dead Sea Scrolls, Proceedings of the Eighth International Symposium of the Orion Center*, edited by Steven D. Fraade et al., 67–85. Leiden: Brill, 2006.

Olivier, Pierre. *Legal Fictions in Practice and Legal Science*. Rotterdam, the Netherlands: Rotterdam University Press, 1975.

Perelman, Chaïm, and Lucie Olbrechts-Tyteca. *The New Rhetoric: A Treatise on Argumentation*. Translated by John Wilkinson and Purcell Weaver. Notre Dame, IN: University of Notre Dame Press, 1969.

Pioirier, John. "Why Did the Pharisees Wash Their Hands?" *Journal of Jewish Studies* 47, no. 2 (1996): 217–33.

Quintilian. *Institutes of Oratory: Or, Education of an Orator in Twelve Books*. Translated by John Selby Watson. London: George Bell and Sons, 1892.

Rosenfeld, Ben Zion. "Sage and Temple in Rabbinic Thought after the Destruction of the Second Temple." *Journal for the Study of Judaism* 28 (1997): 437–64.

Rubenstein, Jeffrey. *The History of Sukkot in the Second Temple and Rabbinic Periods*. Atlanta (GA): Scholars, 1995.

———. *Rabbinic Stories*. New York: Paulist, 2002.

———. "The Symbolism of the Sukkah." *Judaism* 43, no. 4 (1994): 371–87.

———. "The Symbolism of the Sukkah (Part 2)." *Judaism* 45, no. 4 (1996): 387–98.

———. *Talmudic Stories: Narrative Art, Composition, and Culture*. Baltimore (MD): Johns Hopkins University Press, 1999.

Sanders, E. P. *Jewish Law from Jesus to the Mishnah: Five Studies*. London: Trinity Press International, 1990.

Sassoon, Isaac. *The Status of Women in Jewish Tradition*. Cambridge: Cambridge University Press, 2011.

Schäfer, Peter. "Rabbis and Priests, or How to Do Away with the Glorious Past of the Sons of Aaron." In *Antiquity in Antiquity: Jewish and Christian Pasts in the Greco-Roman World*, edited by Gregg Gardner and Kevin Osterloh, 155–72. Tübingen, Germany: Mohr Siebeck, 2008.

Shanks, Hershel. "Is the Title 'Rabbi' Anachronistic in the Gospels?" *Jewish Quarterly Review* 53 (1963): 337–45.

———. "Origins of the Title 'Rabbi.'" *Jewish Quarterly Review* 59 (1968): 152–57.

Soloveitchik, Joseph Dov. *Halakhic Man*. Translated by Lawrence Kaplan. Philadelphia: Jewish Publication Society, 1983.

Werman, Cana. "The Price of Mediation: The Role of Priests in the Priestly Halakhah." In *The Dead Sea Scrolls and Contemporary Culture*, edited by Adolfo Roitman, Lawrence Schiffman, and Shani Tzoref, 377–406. Leiden: Brill, 2011.

Zeitlin, Solomon. "A Reply." *Jewish Quarterly Review* 53 (1963): 345–49.

———. *The Rise and Fall of the Judean State: A Political, Social and Religious History of the Second Commonwealth*. Vol. 3. Philadelphia: Jewish Publication Society of America, 1978.

———. "The Title Rabbi in the Gospels is Anachronistic." *Jewish Quarterly Review* 59 (1968): 158–60.

3

Judah Messer Leon and the *Sefer Nofet Zuphim*
Rethinking Rhetorical Delivery in the Early Age of Print

JIM RIDOLFO

Introduction

The life and work of the Italian rabbi, philosopher, and rhetorician Judah ben Yehiel Messer Leon (1420 or 1425 to 1498 CE)[1] is significant not only because he was the first to pen a Hebraic treatment of Greek and Roman rhetorics—the *Sefer Nofet Zufim*, or *The Book of the Honeycomb's Flow*—but also because of his polemical role in numerous Jewish theological and educational debates, his unusual social position as a Jew in fifteenth-century Italian society, and his role in the transmission of Islamic rhetorics from North Africa to Europe. Although these achievements alone will firmly secure his place in the canon of Jewish rhetoricians, this chapter focuses on what I argue is a less visible and more specific contribution that he made to the history of Jewish rhetorical theory. In this chapter, I introduce Messer Leon as an unlikely theorist of rhetorical delivery. Unlikely, because he wrote very little on the subject in his major rhetorical work—but I argue that in practice, there is evidence that Messer Leon's delicate political and cultural situation necessitated that he strategically obscure what he knew or didn't know about the delivery of his writing and, in turn, enact a *hupokrisis*, or what Carl Holmberg describes as a delivery characterized by a concealing of motives and what Carolyn Miller calls "a dissimulation of means as much as ends" (20).

Background

In Italy the fifteenth century was a time of demographic and political change for the Jewish cultural and religious landscape. According to Arthur Lesley, during this era Jewish immigrants from "France, Provence, Germany, Spain, the Levant, and southern Italy" settled north of Rome, and "each group had its distinctive daily language, communal practices, school traditions, religious and legal authorities, and the competition between claimants for communal and intellectual authority called into the question the legitimacy of all leadership" ("Review" 105–6). Lesley explains how this immigration and diversification of Italian Jewish life led to considerable philosophical and religious disagreements: "Jews from Spain, Provence, and Italy would recognize [the] Maimonidean legal code, Maimonidean or Averroistic scholasticism, and Kabbalah. Jews from Germany and France had a different authoritative legal code and a different pietistic and mystical tradition. Experts on a particular body of texts would not be recognized as authorities by those who came from competing traditions" (ibid. 106).

As Gianfranco Miletto explains, this complex and evolving Jewish political and religious landscape, combined with the pressures of living as members of a minority group in a civil and religious society dominated by Catholics, motivated scholars such as Messer Leon to respond to changes with new models and theories of education, including the study and practice of Greek- and Roman-influenced rhetoric: "Rhetoric became a means for advancing the authority of the Rabbis inside the [Italian Jewish] community, and at the same time it facilitated a kind of cultural equality, putting the Rabbis on the same level as Christian scholars. . . . The great merit of Messer Leon lies in having recognized the cultural-social function of rhetoric for both intracommunal relations and the external relations with the Christians" (133).

Messer Leon was in a unique position to mediate external relations with Christians. The middle of the fifteenth century was a time of great freedom for Italian Jews. Wout Van Bekkum argues that Jews in major cities such as Messer Leon's Mantua were able "to have social contacts with Italian society at large without abandoning their Jewish tradition and faith totally—a true form of acculturation," and that this made "Renaissance Italy . . . a remarkable exception in Jewish existence" (240). Max Margolis and Alexander Marx echo Van Bekkum to emphasize that there was also greater freedom to mediate external relations between Jews and Christians: "Despite papal bulls and canonical discrimination, Jews in Italy freely associated with Christians" (481). Messer Leon is representative of this atmosphere of limited acceptance. He was the first Italian Jew to receive the honor of being able to confer doctoral status on students. This honor allowed him to wear a red hood in public, the mainstream medieval Italian dress for medical practitioners. As a bridge between Jewish and mainstream Catholic cultures, he was placed in a delicate rhetorical situation, and some of the more traditional members of the Italian Jewish community "accused [him] of assimilation because he adopted the custom" of wearing the hood (Bonfil, *Jewish Life* 103).

Although Messer Leon engaged with the dominant Catholic culture, he also sought to reform Jewish education in Italy to advance "a new combination of secular classical learning and scriptural exegesis for the education of Jewish professionals in Italy" (Murphy 161). As a consequence, a considerable portion of his scholarly and political efforts went into educational reforms. Lesley explains that Messer Leon's books of logic, rhetoric, and grammar were written for "yeshiva students in the 1450s" ("Sefer" 314). Lesley speculates that the *Nofet Zufim* was also written for this audience of yeshiva students (ibid.). According to Miletto, "whoever was educated at his school [yeshiva] distinguished himself by his encyclopedic knowledge, his skills in oratory, and the stylistic elegance of his writings" (133).

Controversies

Like his wearing of the red hood, Messer Leon's educational reforms were controversial among Italy's diverse Jewish communities. However, even more controversial were his political attempts to reform the structure of rabbinical authority in Italy. According to Robert Bonfil, "some fierce and agitated polemics have survived in which Messer Leon tried to impose his rabbinic authority on his fellow Jews in sensitive areas of every-day custom as well as intellectual activity," and Messer Leon circulated polemics advocating for a new religious legalism. His vision for a new legalism came from the rising religious influence of the Ashkenazim in the north of Italy, where he looked for guidance on religion and halacha (introduction vi–vii). According to Hava Tirosh-Samuelson, Messer Leon campaigned "to ensure that Jewish philosophers would devote their energies to logic" ("Jewish Philosophy" 515). For example, in the Ashkenazi tradition there was a prohibition against studying the Jewish philosopher Gersonides's commentary on the Pentateuch, and Messer Leon attempted to extend this prohibition to all Italian Jews through a ban on that commentary (Bonfil, introduction vii). Messer Leon attacked Gersonides's "denial of God's knowledge of particulars" (Tirosh-

Samuelson, "Messer Leon" 347) and even attempted to censor Gersonides's commentary on the very same printing press that published the *Nofet Zufim* (Amram 31), threatening to use his extensive political and religious influence to excommunicate through *herem* anyone who published or studied the works of Gersonides (Tirosh-Samuelson, "Jewish Philosophy" 515; Bonfil, *Jewish Life* 255).

Lesley contends that Gersonides's commentary found support among many Italian Jews ("Sefer" 314). In practice, Messer Leon tried to promote a number of texts in place of the commentary, including "the publication of Jacob ben Asher's Turim, which Ashkenazi Jews accepted as authoritative" (ibid.). In addition, he "wrote his own commentaries on Yediach Bedersi's Bechinat Olam (The Examination of the Universe) and on Maimonides' Guide of the Perplexed" (Tirosh-Samuelson, "Jewish Philosophy" 451). However, Tirosh-Samuelson suggests that ultimately the influx of immigrants from Spain and Provence may have hampered his efforts to counter the influence of Gersonides and advance his own religious agenda ("Jewish Philosophy" 515).

Sefer Nofet Zufim

The *herem* against the study of Gersonides makes it clear that Messer Leon was interested in the primacy of his texts over others. His magnum opus, therefore, deserves particular attention for its unique delivery.[2] The *Nofet Zufim*, first published in 1475–76 in Mantua,[3] distinguishes Messer Leon as the first Jewish scholar to "compose a Hebrew treatise on rhetoric based upon the Bible rather than on Greek and Latin sources" (Van Bekkum 229) and is the philosophical foundation of his educational reforms and the logic of his political controversies. In addition to its significant content, the book is also historically important because it was the first Hebrew book that was printed during the life of its author. In the *Nofet Zufim*, Messer Leon draws on the Hebrew Bible to "show that in the realm of style and oratory the prophets and Biblical historians must be acknowledged as the supreme masters" (Zinberg 40). By essentially reframing the classical rhetorical texts of Greece and Rome within the context of the Hebrew Bible, Messer Leon attempts to show that all Greek and Roman rhetorical wisdom may be found in the Hebrew Bible. According to Tirosh-Samuelson, quotations "are either cited verbatim or else paraphrased, and their concepts, arguments, and rhetorical vocabulary are rendered in Hebrew for the sake of proving that classical rhetoric, along with the rest of human wisdom, already existed in the divinely revealed Hebrew Bible" ("The Book of the Honeycomb's Flow" 235).

Although texts like Aristotle's *Rhetoric* had been studied and preserved by Islamic scholars such as al-Farabi and Averroes in the tenth and twelfth century, Aristotle's works were not translated into Latin until the fifteenth century (Tirosh-Samuelson, "Jewish Philosophy" 514). Consequently, Messer Leon is part of the first generation of Italian Jewish philosophers to study and engage with the works of Aristotle and the commentator Averroes. Messer Leon was "the person most responsible for the revival of Aristotelianism among Italian Jews," and he argued that Italian Jews should study scholastic logic in conjunction with yeshiva learning (ibid.).

Scholars of Messer Leon disagree about what role he played in the publication of the *Nofet Zufim*. Bonfil argues that Messer Leon had a role (introduction xi–xii), while Isaac Rabinowitz contends that he had no direct knowledge that his work was being published by Abraham Conat, the owner of the press. Rabinowitz argues that because Conat made considerable printing errors, Messer Leon, who was still in Mantua at the time, would not have allowed such a volume to go to press: "It is certain . . . that JML [Judah Messer Leon] . . . played no part whatever in its production as a printed book: [for] he neither edited it nor corrected it in proof (introduction, xxx–xxxi). However, other scholars such as Bonfil and Tirosh-Samuelson disagree.[4] In a review of Rabinowitz's book, Tirosh-Samuelson argues that it is still possible that Messer Leon did have a role in the publication of the *Nofet Zufim*, and that if he did, this role was in part political: "Little attempt is made [by Rabinowitz] to relate Messer Leon's political activities to his decision to publish a manual on rhetoric. No mention is made, for example, of the tension within the Italian Jewish community, of Messer Leon's leaning towards the Ashkenazic legal system, especially rabbinic ordination, or of the impact of the newly-invented printing press on Jewish learning, all of which are relevant to his decision to publish Nophet Suphim" ("The Book of the Honeycomb's Flow" 237–38).

Although there is no concrete evidence about what knowledge Messer Leon had of Conat's intentions to print the *Nofet Zufim*, there is evidence that Messer Leon at least understood the power of the printing press when he advocated censoring Gersonides's commentary. Bonfil contends that

Messer Leon's censorship efforts show that he was conscious of the political power of the printing press and, I would argue, points to an understanding of how the printing press could be politically and religiously influential in Jewish Italy: "The prohibition [was] directed principally towards the Ashkenazi communities, on reading Gersonides' commentary on the Pentateuch. In these struggles Messer Leon appears at first sight to be strongly rooted in medieval trends of thought, but at the same time, conscious of the possibilities that printing offered of spreading new ideas and influencing people" (Bonfil, introduction vii). This consciousness about printing may have extended to other kinds of copied texts. Based on his reading of Rabinowitz, Murphy argues that Messer Leon selectively circulated some "works publically [sic] while he reserved six of his other writings for private use by smaller circles" (161).

To summarize, although there is no evidence that Messer Leon had a hand in the publication of his manuscript on the first Hebrew printing press, it is possible that he was living in Mantua at the time of publication or was aware that his manuscript had been published and was being sold in Mantua. This detail, as I will show in the next section, has relevance for the contemporary theorizing of rhetorical delivery.[5] The impact that the *Nofet Zufim*'s publication may have had on his pressing political debates is also unclear. In this sense, the story of Messer Leon is ideal for rhetorical scholars of delivery who are also interested in studying current rhetorical practice. Although we know that Messer Leon was ultimately unsuccessful in his political aspirations, it is not apparent what role the print circulation of the *Nofet Zufim* played in his activities. It is known, however, that Messer Leon was at least conscious of the possibilities of this new medium when he attempted to censor the work of Gersonides. These facts grant him the rather dubious distinction of being both the first living author to be published on the Hebrew printing press and one of its earliest censors.

Sefer Nofet Zufim and Rhetorical Delivery

Messer Leon's promulgation of political decrees, selective circulation of some works and public circulation of others, and efforts to censor Gersonides are known, but little is known or has been written about Messer Leon's thinking on delivery. The *Nofet Zufim* contains only a cursory treatment of delivery, similar in scope to the classical works he considers in the book. There are, however, some small exceptions. In chapter 12 of the *Nofet Zufim*, Messer Leon says that delivery has been awarded by God, "the strong rod and the beautiful staff [Jer. 48:17]" (*The Book of Honeycomb's Flow* 127). Although acknowledging the strength and beauty of the fifth canon, Messer Leon says little about written delivery and nothing about the printing press.[6] On the former, he paraphrases Aristotle when he says: "And you should realize that while suggestion-of-countenance is not needed in written rhetorical pieces, it is certainly a necessity in discourses pronounced face-to-face," which he considers an advantage in political speeches, since where "there is debate the speaker really needs the help of all the devices which yield persuasion in order to bring off the victory" (ibid. 121). Beyond this brief distinction between written and oral delivery, there is no additional discussion of the fifth canon.

Messer Leon's work on delivery can thus be bifurcated into a book of rhetoric with little mention of delivery and a life of rhetorical practice in which interesting examples of novel rhetorical delivery, especially written and printed, surface in a number of discrete instances such as the printing of the *Nofet Zufim*, efforts to censor Gersonides, the selective circulation of some political material and not others, and the promulgation of decrees. I argue that this separation between Messer Leon's written theory and unarticulated practice points to what Miller describes as the two opposing impulses of rhetoric: "an impulse toward self-aggrandizement and another toward self-denial." Miller describes this principle of concealment as the "conviction that the means by which intentions are concealed must also remain undetectable" (20). Citing Baldassare Castiglione's concept of *sprezzatura* from the *Book of the Courtier*—the "art is hidden and whatever is said and done seems without effort or forethought"—Miller contends that this theme of concealment is based on the assumption that human relations are adversarial and "the belief that suspicion on our part, and spontaneity and sincerity on the part of our interlocutors[,] can protect us against deceptive concealment motivated by adversarial relations rests upon another assumption: that language can be mimetic" (26). It is also the case that the act of delivery itself may obscure. Holmberg considers Aristotelian oral delivery, *hupokrisis*, as the "concealing of motives by a translation of the Greek *hupo-* as under and *krisis* as judgment," and posits delivery as the "concealing of motive." Holmberg introduces the idea of a "hidden delivery" that is "not just pronunciation or presentation" or an "empirically verifiable or physical parameter of speech or writing" (138).

In the case of the *Nofet Zufim*, Bonfil speculates that the newness of the print medium itself held particular rhetorical importance. He theorizes that "even if one only considers its physical appearance, one can easily imagine the delighted excitement of contemporaries presented with what seemed to be a codex written simultaneously by 'many *calami* [quills] and not at all miraculously,' as the printer enthusiastically boasted in the colophon" (introduction v). It is somewhat curious, then, that there is no record of Messer Leon's reflection on this unique form of delivery. Given the political and religious controversies regarding him in the Jewish communities of Italy, and his unique situation as a bridge between Jewish and Christian societies, he would probably not be in a position to reveal or reflect on his personal strategies of delivery and circulation. His *sprezzatura*, then, can be read as a necessary condition of myriad difficult cultural and political situations. If Messer Leon were to make visible his strategies of delivery, he would probably lose the ability to make the circulation of his work seem "without effort or forethought" and, as a consequence, decrease his own rhetorical effectiveness.

A Jewish Rhetoric?

Is there a take-away lesson for scholars of Jewish rhetorics? As a little-known rhetorician with very little presence in contemporary literature on the history of rhetoric, Messer Leon's life and major works are no doubt significant for scholars interested in building a corpus of Jewish rhetorical traditions. The *Nofet Zufim* is certainly significant as a point of contact between the Islamic rhetoricians who preserved and transmitted Aristotle to Europe and Messer Leon, who adapted scholastic rhetoric to educate Jewish yeshiva students and attempted in the *Nofet Zufim* to reconcile Jewish religious learning with classical sources. However, for scholars of Jewish rhetorics, the probability of Messer Leon's *sprezzatura* provides insight into a key problem in the study of medieval Jewish rhetorics. As Patricia Bizzell argues, "real-world contestants are seldom so equal in power" as was the case in the Barcelona disputations (12). In such asymmetrical situations, it is less likely for rhetoricians on the margins to leave behind many traces or, as Miller puts it, to "name the tools" of their trade. I argue that Messer Leon's example provides an important question for the study of Jewish rhetorics and prompts researchers to examine the power relations between Jewish rhetoricians and larger societies. This, I argue, is an important precursor to asking the next question: does the rhetorician have any incentive to, as Miller prompts us to consider, name the tools of his or her trade? In the case of Messer Leon, the historical evidence suggests that he had no incentive to do so.

For researchers naming the rhetorician's tools, there is also the need to contextualize the rhetorical context so as to not essentialize rhetorical practices as exclusively Jewish. For example, to call Messer Leon's practice "Jewish" would be problematic, especially when reasoning from abduction or the absence of a record. Such essentializing would be particularly dangerous given the common antisemitic tropes that fixate on control of the media (see Michael 210). For scholars in rhetorical delivery, there is also much to be learned from Messer Leon's case study. In "Rhetorical Delivery as Strategy," I argue that "practitioner stories can challenge and expand existing theoretical frameworks of rhetorical delivery to include insights from practitioners' knowledge" (117). In the past several decades, scholars in rhetorical studies have moved from Aristotelian oral delivery to a broader, more expansive understanding of rhetorical delivery that includes a wide variety of print and digital media (Connors; Dragga; Welch; Helsley; Skinner-Linnenberg; Trimbur; Rude; DeVoss and Porter; Ridolfo and DeVoss; Porter, McCorkle). As we expand our definition of delivery to include more diverse media, scholars of rhetorical studies need to collect and consider practitioner case examples that may help build new theories of rhetorical delivery. Messer Leon's case is significant for scholars of rhetorical delivery because it provides an example that foregrounds a new means of rhetorical production and distribution. Such an example is particularly valuable to consider given the introduction in the past twenty years of new digital means of distribution such as the Web and electronic social networking. Messer Leon's example prompts scholars of rhetorical delivery to ask: if no record of activity or naming of the tools remains from the life and time of Messer Leon, what will remain from this time, this moment of technological change?

NOTES

1. Who was Judah Messer Leon? Mauro Zonta provides a short summary of the life of the rabbi, doctor, and teacher: "Judah ben Yehiel Messer Leon (c. 1425–1498) worked in some of the main cultural centres of fifteenth century Italy as a physician, philosopher and teacher of philosophy. He wrote various works on Hebrew grammar, rhetoric and Biblical exegesis. Possibly born in Montecchio Maggiore (now in the Italian province of Vicenza), tradition has it that he was given the title 'messer' [master] by the Emperor Fredrich III in 1450, as a reward for his work as a physician. In the years around 1450, he directed a Jewish academy (yeshivah)

in Ancona. In this academy, which was to follow him in his various places of residence, he lectured on Jewish traditional texts as well as on non-Jewish texts. He taught various subjects—especially Aristotelian logic and physics" (*Hebrew Scholasticism in the Fifteenth Century*, 209).

2. The *Nofet Zufim*, its rhetorical contents, and its place in Italian Jewish intellectual life in the fifteenth and sixteenth centuries also deserve additional scholarly attention. For discussions of the content of the *Nofet Zufim*, see, for example, Isaac Rabinowitz's edition of Judah Messer Leon, *The Book of the Honeycomb's Flow*; Robert Bonfil, introduction; Zonta *Hebrew Scholasticism in the Fifteenth Century*, chap. 4; Hava Tirosh-Samuelson, "Jewish Philosophy on the Eve of Modernity"; Arthur Lesley, "Sefer Nofet Tsufim and the Study of Rhetoric." These items cite additional relevant works.

3. Isaac Rabinowitz argues that Messer Leon was probably still in Mantua when the *Nofet Zufim* was being printed: "Although the *edito princeps* of the N.S. [*Nofet Zufim*] does not indicate the year and place of its printing, we know from those of Conat's imprints which do bear such indications that the place was definitely Mantua, and that the year, which cannot be later than early in 1476, was most probably 1475. Thus the probability is very great that JML [Judah Messer Leon] must still have been residing in Mantua when Conat first began to print the N.S." (introduction, xxx).

4. Tirosh-Samuelson implies that Messer Leon had a part in the decision to publish his manuscript and that the decision was not necessarily made by Conat. Her opinion is not shared by Lesley, who agrees with Rabinowitz that Messer Leon probably had nothing directly to do with the editorial process; however, Lesley does distinguish between Messer Leon's potential motives for writing the *Nofet Zufim* and his lack of involvement in the editorial process for the printed volume: "[Rabinowitz] concludes that Messer Leon 'almost certainly had no hand in the editorial operations' that determined the form of the printed text. As a result of this new consideration, the date and motives for the printing of the book must be separated from the date and motives for its composition" ("Sefer," 314).

5. The *Nofet Zufim* is also an important work for the study of cultural rhetorics and has much to offer to conversations in cultural rhetorics regarding the retransmission of Greek and Roman rhetorics from North Africa to Europe. This migration points to another aspect of Jewish delivery that has yet to be fully studied in rhetorical theory: the north-south migration via travelers on foot of Jewish texts and ideas from Timbuktu and the trans-Saharan trade routes, and the east-west movement of Jewish texts and ideas along the Silk Road from Europe to Kaifeng and beyond.

6. It is not likely that Messer Leon composed the *Nofet Zufim* with any knowledge that it would one day be published on Conat's future printing press. As James Murphy points out, the manuscript was completed as late as 1471. This would mean that there were at least several years between the completion of the manuscript by Messer Leon and Conat's printing activities. Furthermore, there is no definitive evidence that Messer Leon had any contact with Conat about his manuscript, and no evidence of his reaction to the printing of his manuscript. Lesley concludes that "the printer Abraham Conat took advantage of the availability of the text, without authorization, to offer for sale a Hebrew counterpart, by an eminent local scholar" ("Sefer" 314). However, Rabinowitz thinks that Messer Leon probably knew what Conat was doing: "He undoubtedly knew that Conat had made a manuscript copy of his book, and he may have known of Conat's intention, through the newly available printing process, to issue the work in multiple copies" (introduction xxx). But Lesley warns that "the scarcity of documents indicates caution" when trying to reach any conclusions about what Messer Leon

did or did not do ("Review" 106), and that there is "a need for additional evidence on the subject" ("Sefer," 314).

BIBLIOGRAPHY

Amram, David W. *The Makers of Hebrew Books in Italy*. London: Holland, 1988.
Bizzell, Patricia. "Rationality as Rhetorical Strategy at the Barcelona Disputation, 1263: A Cautionary Tale." *College Composition and Communication* 58, no. 1 (2006): 12–29.
Bonfil, Robert. *Jewish Life in Renaissance Italy*. Translated by Anthony Oldcorn. Berkeley: University of California Press, 1994.
———. Introduction to Judah Messer Leon, *Nofet Zufim: On Hebrew Rhetoric*, 1–68. Jerusalem: Magnes, 1981.
Connors, Robert J. "Actio: A Rhetoric of Manuscripts." *Rhetoric Review* 2, no. 1 (1983): 64–73.
DeVoss, Danielle Nicole, and James E. Porter. "Why Napster Matters to Writing: Filesharing as a New Ethic of Digital Delivery." *Computers and Composition* 26, no. 4 (2009): 207–24.
Dragga, Sam. "The Ethics of Delivery." In *Rhetorical Memory and Delivery: Classical Concepts for Contemporary Composition and Communication*, edited by John Frederick Reynolds, 79–95. Hillsdale, NJ: Lawrence Erlbaum, 1993.
Helsley, Sheri L. "A Special Afterword to Graduate Students in Rhetoric." In *Rhetorical Memory and Delivery: Classical Concepts for Contemporary Composition and Communication*, edited by John Frederick Reynolds, 157–69. Hillsdale, NJ: Lawrence Erlbaum, 1993.
Holmberg, Carl B. "Some Available Conceptions of Rhetorical Experience." *Rhetoric Society Quarterly* 10, no. 3 (1980): 135–142.
Leon, Judah Messer. *Nofet Zufim: On Hebrew Rhetoric*. Jerusalem: Magnes, 1981.
———. *The Book of Honeycomb's Flow: Sepher Nophet Suphim*. Edited and translated by Isaac Rabinowitz. Ithaca, NY: Cornell University Press, 1983.
Lesley, Arthur M. "Review." *Rhetorica* 1 (1983): 101–8.
———. "Sefer Nofet Tsufim and the Study of Rhetoric." *Prooftexts* 4 (1984): 312–16.
Margolis, Max L., and Alexander Marx. *A History of the Jewish People*. Philadelphia: Jewish Publication Society of America, 1927.
Michael, Robert. *A Concise History of American Antisemitism*. Lanham, MD: Rowman and Littlefield, 2005.
Miletto, Gianfranco. "The Teaching Program of David Ben Abraham and His Son Abraham Provenzali in Its Historical-Cultural Context." In *Cultural Intermediaries: Jewish Intellectuals in Early Modern Italy*, edited by David B. Ruderman and Giuseppe Veltri, 127–48. Philadelphia: University of Pennsylvania Press, 2004.
Miller, Carolyn R. "Should We Name the Tools? Concealing and Revealing the Art of Rhetoric." In *The Public Work of Rhetoric*, edited by John M. Ackerman and David J. Coogan, 19–38. Columbia: University of South Carolina Press, 2010.
Murphy, James J. *A Short History of Writing Instruction*. 2nd ed. Mahwah, NJ: Lawrence Erlbaum, 2001.
Porter, James E. "Recovering Delivery for Digital Rhetoric." *Computers and Composition* 26, no. 4 (2009): 207–24.
Rabinowitz, Isaac. Introduction to Judah Messer Leon, *The Book of Honeycomb's Flow: Sepher Nophet Suphim*, edited and translated by Isaac Rabinowitz, iii–lxx. Ithaca, NY: Cornell University Press, 1983.

Ridolfo, Jim. "Rhetorical Delivery as Strategy: Researching the Fifth Canon through Practitioner Stories." *Rhetoric Review* 31, no. 2 (2012): 117–29.

Ridolfo, Jim, and Dànielle Nicole DeVoss. "Composing for Recomposition: Rhetorical Velocity and Delivery." *Kairos* 13, no. 2 (2009). www.technorhetoric.net/13.2/topoi/ridolfo _devoss. Accessed 25 January 2014.

Rude, Carolyn. "Toward an Expanded Concept of Rhetorical Delivery: The Uses of Reports in Public Policy Debates." *Technical Communication Quarterly* 13, no. 3 (2004): 271–88.

Skinner-Linnenberg, Virginia. *Dramatizing Writing: Reincorporating Delivery in the Classroom*. New York: Routledge, 1997.

Tirosh-Samuelson, Hava. "The Book of the Honeycomb's Flow: Sepher Nofet Suphim." *Renaissance Quarterly* 37 (summer 1984): 234–38.

——. "Jewish Philosophy on the Eve of Modernity." In *History of Jewish Philosophy*, edited by Daniel H. Frank and Oliver Leaman, 438–515. London: Routledge, 1997.

——. "Messer Leon, Judah." In *Routledge Encyclopedia of Philosophy*, 331–36. London: Routledge, 1998.

Trimbur, John. "Composition and the Circulation of Writing." *College Composition and Communication* 52, no. 2 (2000): 188–219.

Van Bekkum, Wout Jac. "Jewish Intellectual Culture in Renaissance Context." In *Medieval and Renaissance Humanism: Rhetoric, Representation, and Reform*, edited by Stephen Gersh and Bert Roest, 227–41. Boston: Brill, 2003.

Welch, Kathleen E. *Electric Rhetoric: Classical Rhetoric, Oralism, and a New Literacy*. Cambridge, MA: MIT Press, 1999.

Zinberg, Israel. *A History of Jewish Literature: Italian Jewry in the Renaissance Era*. Translated by Bernard Martin. New York: Hebrew Union College, 1974.

Zonta, Mauro. *Hebrew Scholasticism in the Fifteenth Century: A History and Source*. Amsterdam: Springer, 2006.

4

"The Pretty Heiress from Our Old House"
Figuring the Yiddish-Hebrew Relationship in Rhetorical Works by Itzik Manger and Ya'akov Fichman

HANNAH S. PRESSMAN

Introduction: Yiddish in Space

In many ways, the Yiddish language is a perfect fit for the exciting new conceptualization of Jewish rhetorical studies presented in this volume. As outlined by Janice Fernheimer, a central concern for Jewish rhetoric is "making space" in two senses. Not only does the field prioritize providing space for emerging discourses within the contours of Jewish rhetorical practice, but it also seeks to make space for Jewish rhetoric among the broader disciplinary streams with which it is in dialogue: Jewish studies, rhetoric, composition, linguistics, philosophy, and critical theory. Accordingly, Fernheimer's remedy for "the uncertain *place* of Jewish rhetorics" is a sustained effort to make "space for connection, border crossing, and relationship building" (582, 585). In other words, the problem of situating the field of Jewish rhetorics—discerning where it belongs and with what it engages—is actually its own solution.

Situating Yiddish is also a productively problematic proposition. The language itself has always been characterized by contact with the non-Jewish languages of its host countries. In Max Weinreich's *History of the Yiddish Language*, his magnum opus in Yiddish sociolinguistics, Weinreich traces the evolution of Yiddish from its medieval origins in the Loter region of the Rhine Valley. When Jews settled in the area known as Ashkenaz, a "fusion language" emerged from Jewish interactions with neighboring Germans. What distinguished the Yiddish language, like the Jewish community in which it developed, was its "high degree of contact" combined with "a high degree of independence" (Weinreich, *History*, 177). Weinreich declares: "Apartness, but not segregation (in other words, distinctness but not separation)—the Ashkenazic reality must be sought between these two extreme points" (ibid., 177–78).

Perhaps the most compelling aspect of Weinreich's theory of Yiddish—and what links it to Fernheimer's proposal for mapping Jewish rhetorics—is its predominantly spatial orientation. The medieval cities of the Loter region consisted of *mokem* (the non-Jewish town) and *di Yidishe gas* (the Jewish street). Tellingly, the phrase *di Yidishe gas* also came to mean simply "among Jews," as if the circumscribed urban street space contained the whole of Jewish communal opinion.[1] Weinreich explains that "between the two parts of the city was a partition, but there was also constant communication," and he cites rabbinic testimony about the domestic proximity through which "servants and maids and also Gentile men constantly come into our houses" (ibid., 177; see also Harshav, 24–25). This nuanced portrait of twelfth- and thirteenth-century Jewish society leads to a nuanced view of the Yiddish language as well: firmly protective of certain religious and cultural boundaries, but also freely mixing with local people, languages, and customs. Furthermore, the influences were mutual, as non-Jewish residents also absorbed Jewish songs, idioms, and folklore (Weinreich, *History*, 182–83).

Widening our gaze from this telescopic view of medieval Ashkenaz to the spread of Yiddish across Central and Eastern Europe in subsequent centuries, we can properly understand Yiddish as a language that belonged to particular places—Warsaw, Vilna, Odessa. Pulsing with its original Hebrew, Aramaic, and Old Romance source material, modern Yiddish includes Germanic and Slavic elements as evidence of its geographic peregrinations. One recent survey describes Yiddish as "a borrowing, shifting, fusing, and 'plurisignifying' mix within its diasporic, multilingual settings." Its syncretic nature has affected the surrounding field of Yiddish studies as well: "Yiddish, always a border-crossing language, has continually pushed the boundaries of vigorous disciplinary exchange" (Rabinovitch, Goren, and Pressman, 2–3). Because of its provenance as a language that leaped from the Jewish street into non-Jewish areas and back again, Yiddish is uniquely situated to mark new discursive spaces, test-drive emerging methodologies, and connect previously disparate concepts.

It is in that spirit of linguistic, cultural, and disciplinary border crossing that I offer the following examination of Yiddish rhetorical practices. Perhaps "the uncertain *place* of Jewish rhetorics" will feel a little more *heimish* (homelike) as a result.[2]

Jewish Languages at War

Weinreich popularized the saying that "a shprakh iz a diyalekt mit an armey un flot" (a language is a dialect with an army and navy) ("YIVO," 13).[3] Indeed, Jewish discourse on the relationship between Yiddish and Hebrew runs the gamut from the harmonious to the militant. These two languages enjoyed a symbiotic coexistence for centuries, creating generations of Jewish writers whose Yiddish-Hebrew bilingualism (or multilingualism) enriched their cultural output (Niger; Feldman). However, when Jewish nationalism adopted the European romantic model of "one people, one language, one land" in the early twentieth century, Hebrew and Yiddish began to vie for the status of supreme language of the Jewish people (Halkin, 50). The resulting *riv haleshonot* (language quarrel) had aesthetic, political, and rhetorical implications and—in at least one documented case that gives new meaning to the phrase "a war of words"—involved a physical confrontation between advocates of the opposing tongues.

The battle was fought as an offshoot of a broader ideological conflict between Zionism, which maintained that Jewish sovereignty must be realized in Palestine, with a revived Hebrew language as its cultural tool; and diaspora nationalism, which held that Jewish national life could flourish around the world.[4] The translator and critic Hillel Halkin, who dates the language quarrel as lasting roughly from 1900 to 1940, wryly observes:

> Whatever their politics, the Jewish writers of Eastern Europe did all they could to avoid being torn apart by the bitterly contested divorce of Yiddish and Hebrew. Many refused to choose between them.... How does a writer reject a father-tongue or a mother-tongue?
>
> The most tragic thing about the language war was that it pitted one Jewish nationalism against another, the most Jewish Jews against the most Jewish Jews.... Nevertheless, the Jewish language war had to be fought. (54)

As Halkin here makes clear, despite its basis in larger questions about the collective Jewish future, the language quarrel was ultimately a personal matter affecting individual writers' affiliation with their *mame-loshn* (mother-tongue).[5] This historical episode and its lingering cultural aftermath thus offer a rich area to link with the critical concerns of Jewish rhetoric, a field that privileges the language-identity connection.

Defiant declarations, essays, and conference dispatches comprise the central discourse of the language quarrel. At the landmark Czernowitz language conference of 1908, for example, a cluster of Yiddish writers tried to pass a resolution that would have declared Yiddish the Jewish people's national language (Halkin, 50). These tensions played out vividly in 1914, when Haim Zhitlovsky (1865–1943), the "greatest theoretician" of Yiddishist ideology (Gottesman, xv), visited the Yishuv, the Jewish protosettlement in Palestine. The Russian-born Zhitlovsky promoted an Ashkenaz-centric brand of secular Jewish nationalism: as early as 1898, he was predicting the imminent failure of Zionism and proposing a diaspora Jewish identity nurtured by Yiddish culture.[6] Accounts of "the Zhitlovsky incident" in 1914 differ. At the very least, Zhitlovsky was shouted down by pro-Hebrew activists, and according to Yael Chaver, he was allegedly attacked by Gymnazyah Hertzliyah students while attempting to leave his hotel. One eyewitness even recalled that stones were thrown and shots fired. Chaver reads the debate in the Hebrew press immediately following the incident, as well as the episode's exclusion from later histories of the period, as symbolic of the extent to which Yishuv culture viewed Yiddish as a threat to Hebrew (18–19).

Regardless of what actually happened, this episode illustrates the passions elicited by the language quarrel, while also conjuring the spectacle of "a war of words" between pugilistic linguists. Indeed, the rhetoric of the period sometimes adopted the militaristic tone appropriate to a war. One anti-Yiddish group in the Yishuv called itself Gdud Meginey Hasafa (Brigade for the defenders of the [Hebrew] language). With the motto "Ivri, daber Ivrit!" (Hebrew person [Jew], speak Hebrew!), the brigade's members were known for tearing down signs written in "foreign" languages (Zuckermann, 48). Yishuv-era literary discourse also expressed antagonistic views. For example, commenting on a 1927 reception for visiting Yiddish writers, the Hebrew modernist poet Avraham Shlonsky called bilingualism a "catastrophe" comparable to tuberculosis and declared: "We want Israeli breathing to be *completely Hebrew*, with both lungs!" (quoted in Brenner, 367). By presenting the languages as dueling opponents in a *riv* or even a *milḥama* (war),[7] and by invoking tropes of attack and defense, victory and defeat, the cultural activists of the Yishuv period fed into the broader military discourse that dominated public discussion about the struggle for Jewish political autonomy.

Advocates on both sides continued publicly demonstrating their preferences even after the establishment of Israel in 1948, when Hebrew had "won" its fight to be the national language. Thus, the Jewish language quarrel of the early to mid-twentieth century offers productive opportunities to witness Jewish rhetoric in action—rhetoric that often seeks to effect an intervention in the audience's relationship to language itself. This essay examines two heretofore understudied core texts that functioned as rhetorical salvos in modern Jewish language debates; I have intentionally selected literary pieces rather than political speech acts. Composed in Yiddish by highly regarded Jewish writers, these works offer fascinating perspectives on the rhetoric surrounding Jewish language choice in the years immediately preceding and following the establishment of the state of Israel—a time when the very future of the Zionist enterprise seemed to hinge on having the ideal language and cultural apparatus to support the new Jewish polity in the physical space of Palestine.

The two texts, which I am presenting here in my original translations, were published during the same decade. Taken together, they effectively represent the dynamics of twentieth-century Jewish language discourse. I first offer an interpretation of Itzik Manger's 1942 poem "Yiddish." Subsequently, I analyze an excerpt from Ya'akov Fichman's 1949 essay "Tsvishen Hebreish un Yiddish (Di Oyfgabe fun *Di goldene keyt*)" (Between Hebrew and Yiddish [the task of *Di goldene keyt*]). Both Manger and Fichman were part of a generation of Jewish writers who moved from one landscape to another in the early twentieth century, and their texts reflect the profound impact of those border crossings. My goal is to showcase the use of Yiddish as a tool in Jewish rhetorical practice, although the Yiddish language is also a subject of that rhetoric. My essay concludes with thoughts about the future connections between Yiddish and Jewish rhetorics, two fields with border-crossing inclinations of their own.

Itzik Manger's Exilic Lament

As noted above, the first text I have selected to illuminate Jewish language discourse is the poem "Yiddish" by the popular Romanian-born writer Itzik Manger (1901–69). Manger was born Isidore Helfer in Czernowitz, Romania (site of the famous language conference mentioned above). His father, a tailor with bohemian tastes, created the marvelous Yiddish term *literatoyre*, which combines the Yiddish words for "literature" and "Torah." This idea of *literatoyre* influenced much of Manger's writing, which often took Jewish sacred texts and gave them a humanizing Yiddish twist (Roskies and Wolf, xv). He is perhaps most famous for his *Khumesh-lider* (Bible poems, 1935) and *Megile-lider* (Songs of the Megillah, 1936), which transposes the Book of Esther's Purim story to Jewish life in interwar Poland.[8] "Yiddish" appears in his 1942 collection *Volkens ibern dakh: lid un ballade* (Clouds over the roof [song and ballad]).

Manger presented himself as a romantic folk poet or wandering minstrel, and, ironically, he spent most of his adult life wandering from one landscape to another: from Warsaw to France and England during the Second World War, then to Montreal, New York, and eventually Israel, where he died in 1969. Manger described his ten years in England (1940–51) as the worst period in his life, a time when clouds (*volkens*) were constantly over his roof (*ibern dakh*). He had left behind him the vibrant clubs and Yiddish theaters of Warsaw and Paris, and the catastrophe befalling European Jewry was becoming more apparent with every passing year. Meanwhile, a new center of Jewish life was evolving in Palestine, where the revival of the Hebrew language was taking place. Stuck between Jewish homelands, Manger lived out the war years safe but miserable in cloudy England, adrift and unmoored from his people and his *mame-loshn*.

Thus Manger's Jewish rhetorical voice is precisely that of the exile—a stance, in Michael Bernard-Donals's words, of being "never quite at home in one's place of residence." In the Jewish scriptural tradition, the author of Psalm 137, sitting by the rivers of Babylon, exemplifies this speaking position that is "always fraught and never secure" (609). *Volkens ibern dakh* itself functions as a document of exile, as the dates and places accompanying certain poems form a map of Manger's gradual journey out of Europe: Warsaw 1938, Paris 1939, Marseille 1940, Algiers 1940, Liverpool 1940, and London 1941. Couched within Manger's exilic travel log, "Yiddish" functions as a song of lament in much the same vein as Psalm 137, whose composer sits "outside of his homeland and outside (and literally beside) himself in both anger and sorrow" (Bernard-Donals, 618). Facing a precarious future for the Jews of Europe, in the middle of a war that would eventually destroy almost half of the world's Yiddish speakers, Manger writes his poem as half a hymn of praise and half an elegy for his beloved Yiddish language.

"Yiddish"

1 Yiddish, a beautiful princess, just as beautiful as the holy tongue
2 Only younger. You have a sign every month
3 You get "this," which the old woman would want
4 And pays the United Israel Appeal[9] for it with gold.

5 I know that I'm a fool with a tassel,
6 But who isn't a fool, I beg your pardon,
7 When he loves the simple Daudet[10] like a song of King David
8 And hates Arele Barele[11] with the little golden cow?

9 Yiddish, our sunset, our swan song,
10 Sound and reverberation. A mournful bang bang.
11 Gold that the German Jew "Jud Süss"[12] underestimated,

12 Yiddish, the pretty heiress from our old house,
13 Your beauty is lonely, your loneliness large,
14 It's a wonder that your heart has not yet burst.[13]

First, we must note that Manger's song of lament is composed as a fourteen-line sonnet, a notable formal choice that reflects Manger's absorption of English literature during his unhappy decade in England. In fact, this poem is part of a section called *Sonneten far mayn bruder Notte* (Sonnets for my brother Notte), one of Manger's many literary tributes to his inspiring younger brother Notte (1903–42). Following the typical romantic tropes of the sonnet, Manger addresses his poem to a beautiful and distant lady. The object of his affections, the Laura to his Petrarch, is the Yiddish language.

More germane to my tracing of Jewish language discourse's volatile history, however, Manger's choice of the sonnet form should be understood as an intentional borrowing from a high Western literary tradition. This gesture affects my rhetorical evaluation of "Yiddish" because for decades leading up to this moment, Jewish nationalist discourse had figured Yiddish as low culture, a vulgar *zhargon* unable to express the highest aesthetic values (Miron). In contrast, modern Hebrew, with its basis in the biblical canon, was portrayed by Zionism as the elite Jewish language and therefore the proper medium for artistic endeavors. The aesthetic valuing of Hebrew and disparaging of Yiddish was among a cluster of dichotomous traits mapped onto these two languages (healthy/sick, beautiful/ugly, active/passive, new/old, male/female), stemming from the broader ideological worldview known as *shelilat hagolah* (negation of the diaspora). As Yael Zerubavel has shown, in order to symbolically link the national revival to the ancient land of Israel, Zionist collective memory created a "semiotic framework" that portrayed the period of exile—and Yiddish—as historical aberrations (*Recovered Roots*, 22–33). Manger's direct association of Yiddish with the sonnet, a form used by Petrarch and Shakespeare, stakes the claim that, contra Zionist rhetoric, Yiddish could and should participate in the most elite cultural activity.

"Yiddish" plays with and sharply undermines the Zionist, pro-Hebraic worldview in a number of other ways. Manger vividly presents the two languages as female generational rivals of contrasting ages and fertility. The poem opens by calling Yiddish "a beautiful princess, just as beautiful as the holy tongue / Only younger." Manger here slyly references Hebrew's exalted status as *loshn-koydesh*, the language of holy scripture, while simultaneously reminding the reader that Yiddish, though already a thousand years old, is still a much newer language than Hebrew. He revisits this theme in the final verses, calling Yiddish "the pretty heiress from our old house" in line 12. Although acknowledging that Yiddish contains a linguistic heritage from Hebrew,[14] this line reinforces Yiddish's youthful beauty and vitality versus the worn-out state of its biblical relative.

With this move, Manger has effectively reversed the central ideological association of these two languages in Jewish nationalist discourse. Hebrew, construed by Zionism as the language of the future, morphs into an old woman, pointedly indicated in line 3 by the Hebrew-sourced Yiddish word for "old woman," *di skeyne*. In contrast, Yiddish is no longer an ugly relic of the diaspora, but a vibrant young woman. The rebellious significance of this rhetorical gesture cannot be exaggerated. Exiled in cloudy England during the war, and aware of the Yishuv's growth, Manger nevertheless attempts to overturn the prevailing national narrative with a poem.

Intertwined tropes of fertility, money, and value deepen the texture of Manger's persuasive text. In the first stanza, he suggests that the young lady he is addressing is menstruating, getting "a sign every month"—or the even more modest euphemism, *das* ("this")—to signify her ability to bear children. Past her childbearing years, the old woman compensates for the loss by investing in the United Israel Appeal. Manger thus suggests that Hebrew, a barren language, is trying to recapture some of her youth through supporting Jewish settlement in Israel. This rhetoric of value, reinforced by references to gold in lines 8 and 11, suggests Manger's recognition of language's role as capital in the high-stakes game of modern Jewish nation building. Two figures in the poem are guilty of ignoring the treasures of Yiddish culture: the old woman representing Hebrew and the German-Jewish author of *Jud Süss*, Lion Feuchtwanger, who famously chose to write in German rather than Yiddish. By neglecting Yiddish, the gold that is right in front of them, they have doomed it to its lonely existence, on the periphery of cultural creation and on the verge of destruction. Manger's poem thus serves as a harsh indictment of both the Zionist enterprise and Jewish authors who have turned their backs on their mother tongue.

In the gendered economy of "Yiddish," women and money combine to represent the global Jewish realpolitik. By engaging with the economic tropes of money, donation, and inheritance, Manger suggests something very powerful about the values—emotional, political, and aesthetic—that attach to language. As a rhetorical act, his poem suggests the price paid by both the perpetrators and the victims of the Jewish language conflict. Occupying the "never secure" position of the exilic Jewish speaker, he ends his sonnet with an expression of immense loneliness and heartache that could as easily apply to himself as to the Yiddish language. However, within six years of this poem's publication, the state of Israel would be established, forever altering the equation of exile and homeland in the Jewish collective consciousness.

Ya'akov Fichman's Call for Unity

As a counterpoint, I turn now to a Yiddish text whose tone is quite distinct from Manger's plaintive sonnet: Ya'akov Fichman's 1949 essay, "Tsvishen Hebreish un Yiddish (Di Oyfgabe fun *Di goldene keyt*)" (Between Hebrew and Yiddish [the task of *Di goldene keyt*]). Fichman (1881–1958) was both a poet and a highly regarded Hebrew literary critic, perhaps best known as the editor of various collections of works by Haim Nahman Bialik, the national Hebrew poet. Born in Belz, Bessarabia (southern Russia), and educated in the traditional *ḥeder* system,[15] Fichman immigrated to Israel in 1912 but returned to Europe several times before immigrating permanently in 1925. He won the Bialik Prize for literature twice, and his career included editorial work for major and minor figures in Hebrew letters (such as Abraham Mapu, S. Y. Abramovitsh, Peretz Smolenskin) as well as contributions to pedagogical ventures during the Yishuv's formative period. Fichman felt a sense of duty to fill the lacunae in Hebrew criticism in the early twentieth century; in so doing, he helped create the sentimental education of his entire generation (Yoffe, 8–9).

Fichman is emblematic of the transitional generation of Hebrew poets who witnessed two monumental shifts in their lifetimes: first, the center of Jewish daily life and cultural activity switching from Yiddish to Hebrew; and second, within Hebrew poetry, the basic syllabic accent switching from Ashkenazi (penultimate stress) to Sephardi (ultimate stress).[16] Fichman's critical discourse is characterized by the poetic language that he deploys as well as by an openness to change. For example, although more conservative Hebrew critics balked at the influence of poetic modernism in the 1920s, Fichman took the position that true renewal of Jewish national culture would require some measure of innovation ("Yashan veḥadash," "Binyan"). The theme of anticipating the need for stylistic change appeared throughout Fichman's career as a literary critic and, indeed, fueled his impassioned pleas for Hebrew-Yiddish symbiosis in the essay in question here.

To begin with, we must examine the circumstances surrounding the provenance of "Between Hebrew and Yiddish." Given the thorny politics of the language quarrel described above, why would someone located squarely in the camp of Hebrew culture contribute to a Yiddish journal in 1949, the precise moment when a Jewish state had just been established with Hebrew as its official language? In truth, this move is not so surprising given the full context of Fichman's career, which, like that of many Jewish writers of his generation, was bilingual until the language quarrel forced his hand. B. Y. Michali stresses that, compared with his peers, Fichman neither completely separated from the *mame-loshn* nor imported his Yiddish works into Hebrew. Instead, he simply stopped writing in Yiddish while living in Palestine and returned to it when the occasion arose (77–79).

One of those rare occasions was the launching of *Di goldene keyt* in 1949 by Avrom Sutzkever, a Yiddish poet and Holocaust survivor who remained the journal's editor until he ended its production in 1995 (Novershtern). The journal's title is translated as "The Golden Chain" and refers to the continuity of Jewish tradition across generations.[17] The preeminent journal of secular high Yiddish literature and criticism in Israel, *Di goldene keyt* attracted the best artists of the time, including Marc Chagall. Positioning himself in the space "between" for his contribution to Sutzkever's inaugural issue, Fichman provides a moving meditation on Jewish bilingualism, which demonstrates two crucial points. First, at this late stage in his career, Fichman is still considering the impact of modernism on the Hebrew poetry of his time and of the future. Second, he is quite preoccupied by the connection between language and identity. My analysis probes this latter aspect of "Between Hebrew and Yiddish" in order to highlight the rhetorical tropes mobilized by a Hebrew critic with Yiddish sympathies. For historical, aesthetic, and rhetorical reasons, Fichman's language discourse in 1949 provides an intriguing counterpoint to the rhetoric of Itzik Manger's "Yiddish," published only seven years earlier.

At its heart, "Between Hebrew and Yiddish" is an earnest attempt to promote a kind of mutual fertilization (7) between estranged sister languages at a crucial turning point in the history of Jewish peoplehood. Replete with metaphors of soil and planting, the essay uses natural imagery in line with Fichman's critical discourse throughout his career.[18] Fichman begins the essay by attributing his own absence from Yiddish belle-lettres over the past three decades to the overwhelming dominance of Hebrew in the Yishuv: "Here we are soaking in a Hebrew atmosphere, and it consumes us like an elemental force: we can no longer breathe outside of it" (7). (This language echoes the poet Shlonsky's phrase from the 1920s, quoted above, that "we want Israeli breathing to be *completely Hebrew*.") Not exactly apologetic, Fichman is at least "ashamed" of the collective inability of his peers to produce in the othered Jewish language. He then offers a vision of bilingualism that promotes "the rooting of our great classics in both languages," claiming that a Hebrew author with "roots" in Yiddish would create inherently superior poetry, and vice versa (7). To prove his point, he cites Sholem Aleichem and Haim Bialik as examples of great Jewish writers who "organically" unified both languages.

Aware of the difficult ideological implications of promoting a Hebrew-Yiddish collaboration in the wake of the language quarrel, Fichman implores his readers not to think politically about the issue. Instead, he focuses on the aesthetic and sociocultural consequences of continuing the current state of estrangement. His culminating argument includes a dire warning to his readers as well as a vision of hope for what he calls the creative youth. These two paragraphs, excerpted from the essay's final section, serve to illustrate the powerful rhetoric of Fichman's approach:

> This is perhaps the last generation wherein Yiddish poets grew up from Yiddish-Hebrew soil. Moreover in its newer poets Yiddish has reached such maturity, such fullness in sound and color. I have no doubt that they all come more or less from

Hebrew tradition, even if they bear only its breath, its scent. The tragedy of Yiddish lies therefore not only in language assimilation, which these days does not bypass any land and against which it is so difficult to fight, but also in the fact that the Yiddish poet himself is becoming more adrift, having almost no Yiddish environment and becoming all the more severed from the Hebrew source as well.

The task of *Di goldene keyt* ought to be in the first place to combat the mutual estrangement between Hebrew and Yiddish writing, to once again create a kind of atmosphere that should not only tear out the truly unfounded antagonism between both literatures, but also make possible their mutual fertilization. Hebrew and Yiddish poets need to help one another, and above all they should *know* one another and mutually influence each other as well. Even today, when Hebrew as a spoken language possesses thousands of living sources—when here we have lived to hear Hebrew spoken from the sweet mouths of little Jewish children, we are still very much in need of an influx and influence from Yiddish—from its melodiousness and picturesque nature that were cultivated through the generations, and that yielded such an abundance of Hebrew work from our greatest poets ("Between Hebrew and Yiddish," 8).[19]

As at other points in his career, Fichman here demonstrates an acute awareness of his position as a critic witnessing major paradigm shifts in the evolution of Jewish culture in the twentieth century. His designation of the Yiddish poet as "adrift" hits remarkably close to Manger's position as an exile in England in the 1940s. Note also Fichman's passing observation that such poets have "almost no Yiddish environment": this is an oddly muted comment, whose indirect reference to the catastrophe of the Holocaust reflects a reluctance to enlist human tragedy to support an aesthetic polemic. However, Fichman does emphasize the extraordinary nature of the historical moment in which he finds himself in 1949, poignantly marking the significance of Hebrew words issuing "from the sweet mouths of little Jewish children."[20] His rhetorical approach here is largely sentimental: an invocation of "the tragedy of Yiddish," contrasted with a celebration of Hebrew's "living sources." These are the emotional extremes between which Fichman locates himself in order to convey the urgency of the Jewish language situation.

Fichman's proposed solution, which is in effect his programmatic platform for Sutzkever's new journal, is to "make possible [the] mutual fertilization" of the two languages. The way to ensure both languages' survival, he claims, is to encourage Hebrew and Yiddish poets to become better acquainted, to really "*know* one another." By employing the terms of intimacy and relationship, Fichman underlines the highly personal consequences of language choice: estrangement on an individual (human) level will result in destruction on a collective (cultural) scale. In no uncertain terms, he is here calling for the full ceasing of military operations between Hebrew and Yiddish. Cooperation, assistance, growth: this is the new reality that *Di goldene keyt* can help to achieve. Finally, this text also hinges on the appeal to continuity between generations, the very concept represented by the title of *Di goldene keyt*. Fichman establishes a chronological framework for his reader: from "our greatest poets" of the past three centuries ("infused" with the spirit of both languages), to "the last generation" of bilingual Jewish poets, to the "newer poets" of Yiddish with diminished Hebrew knowledge, and finally to the Israeli children now growing up only speaking Hebrew. This gloomy picture suggests that Jewish bilingualism may well become a relic of the past unless readers act now to support the coexistence of the two languages. In Fichman's perspective, there is no time like the present to make a crucial change that will propel Hebrew culture forward.

In "Between Hebrew and Yiddish," Fichman seizes the opportunity offered by Sutzkever to intervene in the tense language situation that still plagued Jewish culture in Israel's early years. Tapping into the natural imagery of soil, roots, and growth, Fichman cunningly applies the agricultural tropes of the Hebrew labor movement to his paean for intra-Jewish linguistic harmony. It bears emphasizing that Fichman is going sharply against the grain of the prevailing Zionist rhetoric not only by writing in Yiddish, but also by advocating that Yiddish poets who are "adrift" be brought back into the fold after decades of cultural exile.

On the Future of Yiddish or Jewish Rhetorical Studies

Published during the same decade, these two Yiddish texts nevertheless register as worlds apart. Manger's poem and Fichman's essay employ strikingly different rhetorical strategies for portraying the Yiddish-Hebrew relationship. Yet both writers are also mobilizing Yiddish to disrupt mid-century cultural norms in the wake of the Jewish language quarrel. Much like the writers' own geographic peregrinations, these works illustrate the predicament of modern Jewish culture—and peoplehood writ large—in the turbulent years surrounding Israel's establishment.

Granted, one could argue that hierarchical power relations are ultimately responsible for the contrasting rhetorics of these Yiddish texts. Fichman, safely ensconced in the Hebrew cultural center, can easily afford to extend an olive branch to Yiddish, while Manger, perched on the cultural periphery, necessarily resists the language that has taken over.[21] Yet both writers clearly are deeply concerned about future Jewish cultural growth, as evidenced in their overlapping use of fertility tropes. Moreover, both choose to launch their critiques of the cultural status quo, and the political and ideological forces that shaped it, via Yiddish, the internally othered Jewish language. Their texts wield Yiddish artfully and rhetorically in order to disrupt the prevailing cultural discourse.

The fascinating codas to the winding narratives of these writers' lives further complicate any attempt to categorize them as representing one side of the twentieth century's Jewish language quarrel. Manger immigrated to Israel in 1958 and lived there until his death in 1969. In a poem he wrote before moving, he declared: "For years I wallowed about in the world, / Now I'm going home to wallow there" (*The World According to Itzik*, 106). Manger found a new audience in Israel, reflected in the enormous popularity of long-running musical productions of his *Megile-lider* and the establishment of the Itzik Manger Prize for outstanding Yiddish writing in 1968. As for Fichman, in the 1950s, near the end of his life, he produced a collection of autobiographical fragments and other works in Yiddish (*Regnboygn*), an achievement about which he was "overjoyed" (quoted in Korn, 181). Perhaps participating in *Di goldene keyt* allowed him to break the geographical dichotomy that had structured his language choices up to that point.

Another coda must be provided for the evolving place of Yiddish in Israel, which is now being traced in the valuable work of scholars like Yael Chaver and Shachar Pinsker. Notably, three years after Fichman's essay was published, Hebrew University of Jerusalem had established a Department of Yiddish, a move that had been loudly protested by Gdud Meginey Hasafa in the 1920s. Further steps in recent decades have reflected a new institutional openness toward Jewish languages other than Hebrew. In 1985 the Center for the Study of Jewish Languages and Literatures was founded at the Hebrew University of Jerusalem, and in the 1990s the Israeli parliament established the National Authority for Yiddish Culture and the National Authority for Ladino Culture.[22] This official acceptance happened in parallel with renewed Israeli interest in connecting with "exilic Jewish roots," a trend that has grown since the 1970s and involves traveling to a family's country of origin, the revival of communal celebrations, and the secular study of Jewish texts (Zerubavel, "The 'Mythological Sabra,'" 137–38). In 2003 *Haaretz* hailed "the great Yiddish comeback" and described groups of young Israelis who gathered to explore their "Ashkenazi identity" (Shalom).

"Yiddish" and "Between Hebrew and Yiddish" are just two voices in the diverse chorus of twentieth-century Jewish language discourse, but they evoke the personal ramifications of sweeping political changes. It seems to me that such compelling explorations of voice and positionality are chief among the fruitful possibilities offered by considering Yiddish within the rubric of Jewish rhetorics. And herein might also lie the answer to Samuel Edelman's question: "What can the Jewish tradition of argument contribute to other traditions and the evolving global sense of rhetoric?" (121). Once so connected with particular locations and populations, the language of the Jewish street now exists largely in its "postvernacular" phase, taking on symbolic values beyond its original communicative function (Shandler, 4). In this era of "neo-Ashkenaz" (Hadda, 15) or "the new Ashkenaz" (Horn, 471), the relationship between language and identity is being radically redefined.

Today diverse Yiddish cultural practices are inspired by the same principles of fusion and evolution that were at play in medieval Ashkenaz, which Weinreich's work so deftly traced (*History*). This emerging discourse, now generated around the world by Jews and non-Jews, musicians and novelists, cooks and pop culture impresarios, demands a place in the disciplinary contours of Jewish cultural studies. Understanding the meanings of the newest generation of Yiddish self-inscriptions, as well as locating these aesthetic gestures in the rich history of Jewish language discourse, requires a sharp set of critical tools and comparative perspectives—which the field of Jewish rhetorics is uniquely positioned to provide. By bringing examples of Yiddish rhetoric into this volume, I hope that I have illustrated the rich potential for dialogue between *di Yidishe gas* and the Jewish rhetorical tradition.

NOTES

1. *Yidishe gas* also served as the title of a post-Holocaust collection of poetry by the pivotal Yiddish writer Avrom Sutzkever, whom I will discuss later in this essay.

2. One exciting recent example of a synthesis in these two fields is Jordan Finkin's *A Rhetorical Conversation*, which applies "conversational analysis" to show "Yiddish literature's receptivity to spoken-language trends" (45, 89).

3. Weinreich attributed the saying to a member of the audience at one of his lectures and called it a "wonderful formulation of the social fate of Yiddish" ("YIVO," 13). On Weinreich's centrality to the academic study of Yiddish in Europe and America, see Kalman Weiser, "Coming to America."

4. See Amos Kiewe's "Theodore Herzl's *The Jewish State*" for an in-depth analysis of the prophetic rhetoric through which Theodore Herzl argued for the necessity of a Jewish state. For an exploration of streams of Jewish nationalism that resisted the model of the sovereign nation-state, see Noam Pianko, *Zionism and the Roads Not Taken*.

5. The Hebrew writer David Shahar provides a humorous depiction of the language war through two characters in his Palace of Shattered Vessels series, which portrays the vibrant, multiethnic community in mandate-era Jerusalem (see, for example, *Summer in the Street of the Prophets* and *A Voyage to Ur of the Chaldees*).

6. I refer here to Zhitlovsky's article "Tsionizm oder sotsyalizm" (Zionism or Socialism), which was published in the Bundist (Jewish socialist) newspaper *Der yidisher arbiter* (The Jewish worker). Tony Michels suggests that in this essay Zhitlovsky may have been the first person to discuss *yidishe kultur* (Yiddish culture) as a concept (29).

7. The terms *riv haleshonot* (language quarrel) and *milḥemet hasafot* (language war) are often used interchangeably, and they also appear in reference to the clash over whether German or Hebrew would be the language of university instruction in Palestine in the early 1910s (Chaver, 17–18).

8. Jeremy Dauber offers insightful comments on the rhetorical and thematic techniques of Manger's masterpiece, whose approach to the Jewish traditional text borders on the postmodern. See also David Roskies, *A Bridge of Longing*, 230–65.

9. Keren Hayesod (The foundation fund), known in English as the United Israel Appeal, was established in London in 1920.

10. Alphonse Daudet, French writer (1840–97). Allusions to different literary traditions are typical of Manger's work; this reference also reminds the reader of Manger's recent sojourn in France.

11. Besides probably indicating the biblical Aaron, this may also be a reference to a Yiddish children's text or fairy tale of uncertain origin.

12. The German-Jewish writer Lion Feuchtwanger (1884–1958), who published a well-known German novel *Jud Süss* (The Jew Süss) in 1925. *Jud Süss* tells the story of Joseph Süss Oppenheimer, an eighteenth-century court Jew who was the financial advisor to a German duke. A notoriously antisemitic Nazi film version of the story was produced in 1940.

13. My thanks to Gennady Estraikh for his helpful consultations on my translation of this poem.

14. Hebrew and Aramaic words together form the stratum of Yiddish called *loshn-koydesh*, regarded by Weinreich as a phenomenon of "internal Jewish bilingualism" (*History of the Yiddish Language*, chap. 4). Regarding Hebrew's holy status, see Katz's philosophical study of how Jewish religious rhetoric has construed the Hebrew alphabet as "the ontological and ethical foundation of the universe" (134).

15. *Ḥeder*, literally meaning room, was the name for the traditional Jewish text-based educational system for boys. For a comprehensive anthology of works about the *ḥeder* in both literary and historical contexts, see Etkes and Assaf.

16. For extensive background on the poetic shift, see Segal.

17. It is also the title of a 1909 play by the great Yiddish writer Y. L. Peretz.

18. See, for example, Yoffe, 14–15; Fichman, *Regnboygn*, 26–29. See especially Fichman's use of the phrase *pe'at sadeh* (the corner or edge of the field), a phrase relating to harvest gleanings in Leviticus 19:9, which serves as the title of his 1945 poetry collection as well as a lyrical posthumous prose fragment.

19. My thanks to Rebecca Margolis for her helpful feedback as I prepared this translation.

20. The Israeli writer Amos Oz has expressed a similar sentiment about children's expressions marking modern Hebrew's ascendance: "But for me the revival of Hebrew occurred when the first boy said to the first girl 'I love you' in Hebrew. Or was it the girl who said it to the boy? This had not happened for seventeen centuries" (quoted in Guppy).

21. Here I intentionally use the concepts of center and periphery from Itamar Even-Zohar's influential polysystem theory, which presupposes a literary center, consisting of canonized culture that exerts control over the system, and a periphery, consisting of noncanonized repertoire that generates alternatives to the center.

22. My thanks to David Bunis for the helpful information he provided. It goes without saying that tracing the details of the evolving relationship between Hebrew and Yiddish in Israel is beyond the scope of this essay, but I hope to have conveyed one aspect of this fascinating history.

BIBLIOGRAPHY

Bernard-Donals, Michael. "'By the Rivers of Babylon': Deterritorialization and the Jewish Rhetorical Stance." *College English* 72, no. 6 (2010): 608–20.

Brenner, Naomi. "A Multilingual Modernist: Avraham Shlonsky between Hebrew and Yiddish." *Comparative Literature* 61, no. 4 (2009): 367–80.

Chaver, Yael. *What Must Be Forgotten: The Survival of Yiddish in Zionist Palestine*. Syracuse, NY: Syracuse University Press, 2004.

Dauber, Jeremy. "Manger and *Megile*: A Yiddish Folk Bard Takes on the Book of Esther." *Midstream*, February 2004, 27–31.

Edelman, Samuel M. "Ancient Traditions, Modern Needs." *Journal of Communication and Religion* 26, no. 2 (2003): 113–25.

Etkes, Immanuel, and David Assaf, eds. *Haḥeder: meḥkarim, te'udot, pirkei sifrut vezikhronot* (The *ḥeder*: studies, documents, literature and memoirs). Tel Aviv: Institute for the History of Polish Jewry and Israel-Poland Relations, Tel Aviv University, 2010.

Even-Zohar, Itamar. "Aspects of the Hebrew-Yiddish Polysystem: A Case of a Multilingual Polysystem." *Poetics Today* 11, no. 1 (1990): 121–30.

Feldman, Yael S. *Modernism and Cultural Transfer: Gabriel Preil and the Tradition of Jewish Literary Bilingualism*. Cincinnati, OH: Hebrew Union College Press, 1986.

Fernheimer, Janice W. "*Talmidae Rhetoricae*: Drashing up Models and Methods for Jewish Rhetorical Studies." *College English* 72, no. 6 (2010): 577–89.

Fichman, Ya'akov. "Binyan" (Building). *Hatekufah* 21 (1924): 343–49.

———. *Pe'at sadeh: Shirim*. Jerusalem: Schocken, 1945.

———. *Regnboygn: zikhroynes eseyen un lider*, edited by Ya'akov Batashansky and Y. L. Gruzman. Buenos Aires: Besaraber landslayt-farayn in Argentine, 1953.

———. "Tsvishen Hebreish un Yiddish (Di Oyfgabe fun *Di goldene keyt*)" (Between Hebrew and Yiddish [the task of *Di goldene keyt*]). *Di goldene keyt* 1 (1949): 7–9.

———. "Yashan veḥadash" (Old and new). *Hatekufah* 16 (1922): 504–6.

Finkin, Jordan D. *A Rhetorical Conversation: Jewish Discourse in Modern Yiddish Literature*. University Park: Pennsylvania State University Press, 2010.

Gottesmann, Itzik Nakhmen. *Defining the Yiddish Nation: The Jewish Folklorists of Poland*. Detroit, MI: Wayne State University Press, 2003.

Guppy, Shusha. "Amos Oz, the Art of Fiction no. 148." *Paris Review* 140 (1996). http://www.theparisreview.org/interviews/1366/the-art-of-fiction-no-148-amos-oz. Accessed 25 January 2014.

Hadda, Janet. "Imagining Yiddish: A Future for the Soul of Ashkenaz." *Pakn Treger* (spring 2003): 10–19.
Halkin, Hillel. "The Great Jewish Language War." *Commentary*, December 2002, 48–55.
Harshav, Benjamin. *The Meaning of Yiddish*. Stanford, CA: Stanford University Press, 1990.
Horn, Dara. "The Future of Yiddish—in English: Field Notes from the New Ashkenaz." *Jewish Quarterly Review* 96, no.4 (2006): 471–80.
Katz, Steven B. "Letter as Essence: The Rhetorical (Im)Pulse of the Hebrew Alefbet." *Journal of Communication and Religion* 26, no. 2 (2003): 126–62.
Kiewe, Amos. "Theodore Herzl's *The Jewish State*: Prophetic Rhetoric in the Service of Political Objectives." *Journal of Communications and Religion* 26, no. 2 (2003): 208–39.
Korn, Yitzhak. *Jews at the Crossroads*. East Brunswick, NJ: Cornwall, 1983.
Manger, Itzik. *Volkens ibern dakh: lid un ballade* (Clouds over the roof: song and ballad). London: Farlag Alayneniu, 1942.
———. *The World According to Itzik: Selected Poetry and Prose*. Translated by Leonard Wolf. New Haven, CT: Yale University Press, 2002.
Michali, B. Y. "Ḥativat-yiddish beshirato" (The Yiddish segment of his poetry). In *Arugot: kovetz lezikhro shel Ya 'akov Fichman* 2 (Flowerbeds: a Collection in memory of Ya 'akov Fichman), edited by Nurit Govrin, 2:77–88. Tel Aviv: Eked, 1976.
Michels, Tony. "Socialism with a Jewish Face: The Origins of the Yiddish-Speaking Communist Movement in the United States, 1907–1923." In *Yiddish and the Left*, edited by Gennady Estraikh and Mikhail Krutikov, 24–55. Oxford: Legenda, 2001.
Miron, Dan. *A Traveler Disguised: The Rise of Modern Yiddish Fiction in the Nineteenth Century*. Syracuse, NY: Syracuse University Press, 1996.
Niger, Shmuel. *Bilingualism in the History of Jewish Literature*. Translated by Joshua A. Fogel. Lanham, MD: University Press of America, 1990.
Novershtern, Avraham. "'Walk through Words as through a Minefield': Avraham Sutzkever z'l." *Yad Vashem Studies* 38, no. 1 (2010): 47–59.
Pianko, Noam. *Zionism and the Roads Not Taken: Rawidowicz, Kaplan, Kohn*. Bloomington: Indiana University Press, 2010.
Pinsker, Shachar. "Choosing Yiddish in Israel: Yung Yisroel between Home and Exile, the Center and the Margins." In *Choosing Yiddish: New Frontiers of Language and Culture*, edited by Lara Rabinovich, Shiri Goren, and Hannah S. Pressman, 277–94. Detroit, MI: Wayne State University Press, 2013.
Rabinovitch, Lara, Shiri Goren, and Hannah S. Pressman. Introduction to *Choosing Yiddish: New Frontiers of Language and Culture*, edited by Lara Rabinovitch, Shiri Goren, and Hannah S. Pressman, 1–10. Detroit, MI: Wayne State University Press, 2012.
Roskies, David G. *A Bridge of Longing: The Lost Art of Yiddish Storytelling*. Cambridge, MA: Harvard University Press, 1995.
Roskies, David G., and Leonard Wolf. Introduction to Itzik Manger, *The World According to Itzik: Selected Poetry and Prose*, xiii–xlvi. New Haven, CT: Yale University Press, 2002.
Segal, Miryam. *A New Sound in Hebrew Poetry: Poetics, Politics, Accent*. Bloomington: Indiana University Press, 2010.
Shahar, David. *Summer in the Street of the Prophets; and, A Voyage to Ur of the Chaldees*. Translated by Dalya Bilu. New York: Weidenfeld and Nicolson, 1988.
Shalom, Efrat. "The Great Yiddish Comeback." *Haaretz*, 19 May 2003.
Shandler, Jeffrey. *Adventures in Yiddishland: Postvernacular Language and Culture*. Berkeley: University of California Press, 2006.

Weinreich, Max. *History of the Yiddish Language*. Translated by Shlomo Noble. Chicago: University of Chicago Press, 1980.

———. "YIVO and the Problems of Our Time." *YIVO-Bleter* 25, no. 1 (1945): 3–18.

Weiser, Kalman. "Coming to America: Max Weinreich and the Emergence of YIVO's American Center." In *Choosing Yiddish: New Frontiers of Language and Culture*, edited by Lara Rabinovitch, Shiri Goren, and Hannah S. Pressman, 233–55. Detroit, MI: Wayne State University Press, 2012.

Yoffe, A. B. Introduction to *Ya'akov Fichman, Musag hashirah hamodernit: masot, dyokna'ot, reshimot* (Ya'akov Fichman, the concept of modern poetry: essays, portraits, notes), edited by A. B. Yoffe, 7–17. Tel Aviv: Agudat Hasofrim, 1982.

Zerubavel, Yael. "The 'Mythological Sabra' and Jewish Past: Trauma, Memory, and Contested Identities." *Israel Studies* 7, no. 2 (2002): 115–44.

———. *Recovered Roots: Collective Memory and the Making of Israeli National Tradition*. Chicago: University of Chicago Press, 1995.

Zuckermann, Ghil'ad. "Hybridity versus Revivability: Multiple Causation, Forms and Patterns." *Journal of Language Contact* 2 (2009): 40–67.

5

The Jewish Rhetoric of the Twentieth Century
Chaïm Perelman, *Double Fidélité*, and the Pre-Holocaust Roots of the New Rhetoric Project

DAVID A. FRANK

There are two anchors for the modern understanding of Chaïm Perelman's New Rhetoric Project (NRP).[1] First, Perelman's 1958 collaboration with Lucie Olbrechts-Tyteca, titled the *Traité de l'argumentation: La nouvelle rhetorique* (translated as *The New Rhetoric: A Treatise on Argumentation*), is viewed as one of the most significant systems of rhetoric developed in the twentieth century. James Crosswhite argues it is "the single most important event in contemporary rhetorical theory."[2] In his historical survey of rhetoric and philosophy for the *Oxford Encyclopedia of Rhetoric*, Sir Brian Vickers states that the NRP is "one of the most influential modern formulations of rhetorical theory"; it is the only system of twentieth-century rhetoric mentioned in the entry.[3] Wayne Booth, in his *Rhetoric of Rhetoric*, writes that a "major revolution occurred" with the publication of the *Traité* and that Perelman launched "an amazingly deep, rich, all-inclusive exploration of rhetorical resources, both from classical giants, especially Aristotle, Cicero, Quintilian, and from Renaissance anti-Cartesians on to 1969."[4] Compared to the twentieth-century rhetorics of I. A. Richards, Kenneth Burke, and others, Booth found Perelman's effort to be the "most complex effort to explore all the rhetorical resources for combating the 'absolutism,' 'Cartesian,' and 'views of truth.'"[5] Like Vickers, Booth believes that Perelman's new rhetoric may be the "most influential" of those he reviewed. Thomas Conley, in his *Rhetoric in the European Tradition*, observes that Perelman's body of work is a "landmark in the renaissance of rhetoric" in the twentieth century.[6]

The second anchor for the contemporary reception of the NRP is that it is Aristotelian, constituting a rescue, renewal, and renaissance of the classical tradition of rhetoric. Crosswhite draws a lineage from Aristotle and

Plato to Perelman;[7] Vickers writes that "the coherence of [Perelman's] new rhetoric to the tradition of the old" can be seen in his references to the anonymous author of *Rhetoric ad Herennium*, Aristotle, and Cicero ("Philosophy," 492); Booth joins Perelman with Aristotle and other classical giants; and Conley links Perelman to a broader twentieth-century movement of "New Ciceronianism," which included the rhetorically inflected works of Richard McKeon, Stephen Toulmin, and Jürgen Habermas.[8]

Perelman's work did help prompt a rhetorical turn in twentieth-century thought. However, although Perelman certainly appealed to the classical tradition, the NRP is founded on an essentially cosmopolitan Jewishness, expressed in a Talmudic sense of reason and argument. I have made this case in earlier works.[9] The Jewish voice I have identified in Perelman's NRP critiqued the foundational assumptions of Western and Enlightenment thought and challenged the first philosophies of Aristotle and Descartes. Perelman's critique of the first philosophy and the Enlightenment focused on the fact that both presented a constricted definition of reason, limiting it to deduction, the eternal, and the timeless.[10] Perelman offered Jewish thought as a countermodel to the classical tradition of rhetoric, doing so in the spirit of rapprochement with classical thought, not its effacement. This attempt at rapprochement was designed to distinguish between first and regressive philosophies; intended to recognize the coexistence of philosophical pairs, antimonies, and contraries that are often nested in opposition; and included a system of argument designed to encourage pluralism and reasoned argument.[11]

In a speech that Perelman delivered in 1980 when he received an honorary doctorate from Hebrew University of Jerusalem, he reflected on what he called his "intellectual itinerary."[12] This itinerary was designed to resist the Western tradition of restricting the rational to clear and distinct ideas, mathematical models, and the constrictiveness of Enlightenment definitions of values, knowledge, and truth. Hosted by a university that he saw as at the crossroad between cultures, Perelman told his audience that the NRP was a "theory of argumentation that draws from dialectical reason and logic from Greco-Roman antiquity, but also Talmudic methods of reasoning. It is to the study of this theory, and its extensions in all domains that I have dedicated, for more than twenty years, the majority of my work."[13] Perelman seemed to realize after the publication of the *Traité* and what Jean-Philippe Schreiber calls his *teshuvah*, or a more explicit return to Judaism, that his itinerary had been affected by Talmudic thought. Before the 1970s, Perelman rarely cited Jewish texts or sources of thoughts explicitly. Late in his life he returned to the Torah, Talmud, and the halachic texts to embellish the themes developed in the NRP.[14]

In these post-*Traité* embellishments, Perelman juxtaposed the Jewish sense of justice (*tzedek*) with its counterparts in Greco-Roman and Christian cultures,[15] called on two famous stories in the Talmud justifying pluralism and argumentation (about the dispute between the schools of Hillel and Shammai that God found to be equally reasonable and about the Oven of Akhnai, in which the rabbis defeated God's representative in an argumentative dispute), and pointed to Jewish patterns of reason and argumentation as countermodels to the Western tradition.[16] I have argued that the urgent need that Perelman felt existed for the NRP and his post-1958 commemoration of Jewish thought can be traced, in part, to the Holocaust and to his post-Holocaust desire to demonstrate the need for both a state with a Jewish majority (Israel) and for a Jewish presence in nation-states in which Jews are a minority.[17]

The NRP, I suggested earlier, is Perelman's and Olbrechts-Tyteca's response to the Holocaust. I now believe I have overstated the case. To this point in my study of Perelman's work, I have given too much emphasis to the NRP's status as a post-Holocaust rhetoric. I now believe that the NRP is primarily a response to Perelman's prewar experience as a Jew in Poland and Belgium, which he and Olbrechts-Tyteca then adapted to a post-Holocaust world. Perelman did not see the Holocaust as proof that antisemitism was an essential feature of European culture or as evidence that Jews could not live with gentiles, or that Israel was the only answer to the Jewish Question. Perelman's experience in prewar Poland and Belgium taught him to appreciate European cosmopolitan values and to fear the rise of antisemitism.

His views on antisemitism, the possibility of Jewish and gentile rapprochement, and the state of Israel as one of many options available to Jews were developed in response to the Enlightenment and the dilemmas confronting Western European Jews with the universalism of the French Revolution and emancipation. Indeed, the first line of *The New Rhetoric* declares that it should be seen as a "break" from the Enlightenment's constrictive definition of reason and, I suggest here, the Enlightenment's definition of Jewish identity. This break and Perelman's answer to the Jewish Question were captured in the phrase *double fidélité*, a notion that effectively reversed the "dual loyalty" slur. The doctrine of *double fidélité* held that Jews could be faithful both to the universal aspirations of the Enlightenment and to the values of Jewish civilization. Similarly, Perelman maintained that reason should not be restricted to the boundaries of deductive rationalism set forth by the logical positivists.

The Enlightenment, the French Revolution, and the emancipation of the Jews posed a paradox for Jewish thinkers. The universalism unleashed by the three movements threatened to render membership in ethnic groups obsolete. To receive the benefits of universal human rights, Jews were expected to give up their identification as Jews. In a 1933 essay titled "Enlightenment and the Jews," Hannah Arendt placed this paradox in its historical context: "The modern Jewish Question dates from the Enlightenment: it was the Enlightenment—that is, the non-Jewish world—that posed it. Its formulations and its answers have defined the behavior and assimilation of Jews."[18] The Enlightenment defined the Jewish world as tribal, clannish, and antithetical to universalism. Perelman's notion of *double fidélité* provided an elegant solution to the Enlightenment paradox. This solution and his new rhetoric addressed Perelman's status as a Jew in a post-Enlightenment Europe and the problem of reason.[19]

Chaïm Perelman and *Double Fidélité*

The philosophical vision that Perelman brought to the NRP was informed by his pre-Holocaust experience as a Jew in Poland and then Belgium. Perelman was born in Poland in 1912 and emigrated to Belgium with his family in 1925. Schreiber's historical account of Perelman's life is telling, providing the historical experience that led him to create the doctrine of *double fidélité*.[20] As Amos Elon documents in *The Pity of It All*, the Europe preceding the darkness of the Holocaust did host both antisemitism and a flourishing Jewish culture that complemented a European cosmopolitanism. Perelman's family was an illustration of the latter. His parents represented two major impulses in Eastern European Jewish thought: his father drew from the Jewish rationalist tradition (*maskilim*) and his mother from the Eastern European Jewish Hasidic traditions. Perelman's family enacted the somewhat uneasy synthesis of Jewish, European, Polish, and Zionist outlooks. The four children spoke Polish at home and were taught French by the family's nanny. A portrait of Theodor Herzl hung on a wall in the Perelman home.

Although supportive of the Zionist movement, Perelman's father emigrated east to Belgium rather than south to Palestine in 1925, suggesting support for the *Gegenwartsarbeit* (Focus on the defense and development of Jewish identity in the diaspora) rather than the *Palastinaarbeit* (Emphasis on the creation of a Jewish state in Palestine) expression of Zionism.[21]

Perelman reached the age of reason in a Europe seemingly open to Jews' aspiration to live at peace with gentiles. Indeed, as Elon notes, Hitler in the second half of the 1920s was not a dominant topic of conversation, and Jews were members of the Weimar Republic's cabinet.[22] The Belgium that the Perelmans moved to was relatively open to Jews, and that was particularly true in Antwerp, the city where the family first settled. A brilliant student, Perelman entered the Université Libre de Bruxelles at the age of sixteen. Marcel Barzin and Eugène Dupréel, two of his professors, recognized his talent and supported him with grants and teaching opportunities.

Perelman was awarded a scholarship in 1936 to attend the University of Warsaw. There he studied with the famous Tadeusz Kotarbiński, a founder of the Lvov-Warsaw school of logic. The members of this school focused on formal logic, the methods of science, and semantics, limiting the domain of reason to deductivism. They sought the liberation of reason, prevented in this way of defining it from making value judgments, effectively reducing claims made by fascists and antisemites to literal nonsense and meaninglessness.[23]

The definition of reason advanced by the Lvov-Warsaw school did not and could not prevent the outbreak of anti-Jewish riots at the University of Warsaw during the 1935–36 academic year. "Ghetto benches" designed to segregate Jewish students from non-Jewish ones were authorized by Polish authorities for the first time in December 1935. They remained in place during Perelman's one-year stay in Poland. Jewish students were attacked daily in Warsaw during his time at the university. The disease of antisemitism was becoming an epidemic in Poland.

Yet Perelman also witnessed opposition to antisemitism in Poland. Józef Piłsudski, the leader of Poland during this period, was known for his tolerance in dealing with Polish Jews and for opposing antisemitism. Kotarbinski, who would become a friend of Perelman, valiantly defended his Jewish students.[24] Resisting the temptation to essentialize Poland as antisemitic, in the face of massive evidence to the contrary, Perelman reminded the readers of his first postwar article, "La question juive" (The Jewish Question), that the kings of Poland had welcomed the Jews after their expulsion from Western Europe.

Perelman returned to Belgium in 1936, became a Belgian national, and served in the army. However, he also remained proud of his Jewish heritage and refused the pressures of assimilation.

Perelman's being both a loyal Belgian and a Jew required a tricky balancing act, one central to the doctrine of *double fidélité*. Without question, complete assimilation for Perelman and an embrace of the Enlightenment philosophy would have been safer and easier. However, he did not allow antisemitism to force him to assimilate, nor did he, after 1935, follow the Zionist trajectory advocated by Ze'ev Jabotinsky and others who believed that Jewish existence in Europe and outside of the Jewish state of Israel was impossible. Perelman sought to reconcile what appeared to be two opposing positions on the Jewish Question, as noted above: one that identified Palestine and a Jewish state as the answer to European Zionism (*Palastinaarbeit*), and a second that called for resistance to antisemitism to remain focused in the diaspora (*Gegenwartsarbeit*). Perelman and his wife, Fela, adopted the latter approach, turning down opportunities to flee Belgium. His definition of Zionism seemed to prioritize the Jewish people and their values rather than Israel as the source or terminal point of Judaism. His definition of Judaism turned on his understanding of antisemitism and assimilation.

For Perelman, antisemitism was a function of the natural opposition and antagonisms resulting from the formation of humans into social groups that had majority or minority status.[25] The conflict between Judaism and Christianity, defined as groups, is similar to the conflicts that erupt between nations, sports teams, and other social groups. The conflicts between majority and minority groups, Perelman maintained, could become intense and explained the nature of antisemitism. Because Jews had lived in Europe as a minority group, they had often been the object of the majority group's prejudice and scapegoating. Zionism, Perelman concluded, offered an answer to the problem of social groups' conflicts because it would offer Jews the status of a majority group. Perelman saw Palestine as a geographical site for Jewish refugees from European social groups' conflicts. He did not use the phrase *Eretz Israel* or suggest that the land had a metaphysical or theological meaning that was central to Jewish identity.

To Perelman, the question of Jewish assimilation was a priority. He refused the false choice presented to European Jews by the Enlightenment: either enjoy membership in the universal brotherhood of humankind or remain a member of a tribe. Having heard Herzl's call for a reborn Jewish nation, which appropriated Jabotinsky's rhetoric of pride in the Jewish culture and nation, Perelman celebrated Jewish history and identity in articles published in 1935, arguing that Jews could remain Jews and loyal citizens of Belgium.[26] This argument captured the spirit and intent of *double fidélité*.

Jews in France and Belgium sought to solve the dilemma of identity created by the Enlightenment and emancipation with the term "Israelite," a descriptor of Jewish identity that Perelman seemed to accept. Jewish thinkers sought to move beyond the word "Jew" as a marker of identity, bundled together as it was with a host of negative connotations. In contrast, the Israelite was a citizen of France, Belgium, or another nation-state who was, at the same time, a loyal and proud Jew. The Israelite yoked the universal values of the Enlightenment together with those of Jewish civilization, bringing into alignment European nationality and Jewish identity.[27] The rise of Hitler and other totalitarian leaders and the invasion of Belgium on 15 May 1940 cast grave doubt on the validity and viability of *Gegenwartsarbeit*, *double fidélité*, and the notion of the Israelite.

Double Fidélité and the Belgian Holocaust

The Nazi invasion of Belgium prompted many Belgians—including Fela Perelman and Noemi, Fela and Chaïm's daughter—to flee south into France. Chaïm Perelman was mobilized to serve in the Belgian army, which quickly surrendered. Those who fled eventually returned to Belgium, and Perelman returned to the professorship at Brussels University that he had abandoned in his flight. The German occupation of Belgium became increasingly brutal. The occupation authorities forced Jews who were on the staff and faculty at ULB to resign; Perelman submitted a letter dated 20 December 1940 acknowledging he was a Jew, and he was dismissed by the university.

An exchange between Fela and Chaïm Perelman about a passage in his *De la justice* makes it clear that the Perelmans saw the Nazi occupation as temporary, something that would eventually yield to the Resistance and the Allied forces. Noemi Perelman wrote: "While in the underground, during the darkest hours, he [Chaïm Perelman] was writing his book on justice. My mother always said she is responsible for one line in that book. Perelman had written, 'The Nazis are saying that...' and my mother said, 'You should say, "The Nazis *were* saying..."' because the book will not be published as long as the Nazis are saying.'"[28] Both anticipated a time beyond the Nazis.

The ULB served as an important center for the Resistance, justifying Chaïm Perelman's commitment to the institution. The Perelmans did far more than hold seminars and write books; they helped lead the Resistance.[29] They played a major role in the formation of an arm of the Resistance, the Comité de Defense des Juifs (CDJ), which worked in collaboration with the national resistance movement, the Front de l'Indépendance. The CDJ focused on the rescue of Belgian Jews, assisted by a host of non-Jewish Belgian citizens. There were, of course, a great number of Belgians who either actively supported the occupation or who did little to resist it, and we must keep in mind that Belgium during this period could be best described as a moral gray zone.[30] Among the non-Jewish Belgian citizens who joined the Resistance was the wife of a ULB professor, Lucie Olbrechts-Tyteca. She worked with Fela Perelman, who chaired a committee of women who saved Jewish children by placing them with Catholic families.[31] In collaboration with Belgian gentiles, the Perelmans helped save the lives of many Belgian Jews.

In spite of the relatively successful efforts of the Belgian Resistance, more than one-third of Belgian Jews perished at the hands of the Nazi occupiers.[32] The vast majority of the Belgian Jews who were murdered during the Holocaust were transported from the northern Belgian town of Malines to Auschwitz. When Belgium was liberated on 4 September 1944, Perelman and other members of the CDJ rushed to Malines from Brussels to save Jews who were incarcerated at the Malines transit camp. After the liberation, Chaïm and Fela Perelman dedicated themselves to finding homes for Jews who were defined as displaced people. The Perelmans assisted many Jews who sought refuge outside Europe, including in Palestine and South America.

Perelman contributed to the reconstruction of the Jewish community and Europe. In addition to helping displaced persons, he and his wife worked with Richard McKeon and UNESCO to think through what the postwar global community should be like, and he embarked with Lucie Olbrechts-Tyteca, whom he met during the Resistance, on a ten-year effort to expand the range of reason beyond the confines of analytical philosophy. It is reasonable to see the products of Perelman and Olbrechts-Tyteca's collaboration as a response to the Holocaust, but the evidence suggests that the new rhetoric project looked before the Holocaust to reclaim the best of European culture before the rise of Hitler and other European totalitarians. An anecdote recounted by Crosswhite captures this point quite well:

Helmut Schanze of the University of Aachen ... told a story [to me] about Perelman's insisting on being driven into Germany immediately after the war. While surveying one leveled city, Perelman reportedly said, "This is not Europe." If the violence and destruction that result from national and ethnic conflict are not the truth of Europe, then what is? Certainly not the modern contraction of reason that helped to produce it. *The New Rhetoric* is one way of saying, again, what Europe might be, what forms of reason might prevent its collapsing into violence again.[33]

To Perelman, the "truth" of Europe was not captured in a snapshot of a leveled German city. Rather, it was in the pluralistic, cosmopolitan, tolerant values he had witnessed and experienced before the war. Perelman believed that he could remain in Belgium and support Zionism and the state of Israel, that the Germany of the Third Reich was not Europe, and that Jews could flourish in the diaspora.

Without question, a number of contemporary rhetorical theories attempt to work through the Holocaust, and the NRP is one of them. Indeed, as noted above, the first article that Perelman wrote after the defeat of Nazi Germany was "La question juive." This article was followed by a cluster of short articles on such topics as democracy, truth, and first philosophies that sought to address the failure of reason to prevent the inhumanity of the recent war. Perelman and others had to admit that logical positivism did not provide the resources necessary to counter bad values and actors. He turned to rhetoric as an answer to the crisis of reason and, I believe, as a response to the Jewish Question. He and Olbrechts-Tyteca unfolded the identity and political doctrine of *double fidélité* into a philosophical foundation that could support a new rhetoric.

Double Fidélité in the New Rhetoric Project

Philosophies and rhetorics are crafted as responses to the problems human face. Christian Delacampagne argues that the crises of reason and the Jewish Question were intertwined after the Second World War: "Precisely because it constituted the ultimate scandal of modern reason, the Nazi genocide forces us to consider the Jewish question at this 'turning point' of history."[34] Reason had failed to prevent genocide, and Perelman joined other postwar thinkers in an autopsy of this failure.[35] With the NRP, he addressed the scandal of modern reason and answered the Jewish Question by announcing—in the first sentence of *The New Rhetoric*—that it constituted a "break" with the

Enlightenment definition of reason. This break explicitly broadened the domain of reason and implicitly opened up space for Jewish thought and existence. Writing in the aftermath of the Holocaust, Perelman and Olbrechts-Tyteca note two routes to fanaticism. The first route is radical skepticism about the rationality of values. Those who adopt this route accept the Enlightenment demand that truth must possess the conditions of timelessness, invariability, and permanence. Lacking these qualities, the skeptic can make no commitment to value propositions nor take principled action. In an address to his students, Perelman lamented the fact that the reigning prewar doctrines of scientism and analytical philosophy could not provide the value resources necessary to confront fascist ideologies.[36] The second route to fanaticism is through a commitment to an absolute truth, which is placed beyond the reach of discussion and argument. The Enlightenment assumptions about the nature of truth inform both the radical skepticism and totalitarianism that Perelman faced before and during the war.[37] The framework of *The New Rhetoric* confronts the contraction of reason by the Enlightenment by unfolding a nonformal expression of reason and establishing a realm of pluralism, enriched by epideictic discourse, dissociation, and argumentation, all nested within a system of regressive philosophy.[38] This framework uses the doctrine of *double fidélité* to allow those involved in the *vita activa* to enjoy the benefits of reason.[39] Perelman's rejection of positivism should be properly understood. In fact, he did not so much reject positivism as criticize how restrictive it is. Rhetoric allowed Perelman to see the limits of positivism and then to set forth a vision of reason within a realm of rhetoric, one that included but was not limited to positivism. Indeed, he made use of the terms of logic offered by positivism and analytical logic, embedding them in the world of experience and rhetoric and thus suggesting that the tools of logic we use are affected by our experience.

In face of the value monism enforced by the totalitarian movements Perelman experienced in the war, he developed a philosophy of irreducible pluralism,[40] similar to the philosophy of liberty and pluralism outlined by Isaiah Berlin.[41] Their philosophy of irreducible pluralism assumes that it is possible for humans to hold values that are in conflict with each other or even completely incompatible, and that humans might pursue different ends from each other. The idea that two parties in a conflict might both be right or wrong was a principle derived from the two Talmudic stories discussed by Perelman in his writings. In addition, this philosophy was lived out in Perelman's prewar

Poland and Belgium, although antisemitism lurked in waiting, in Perelman's view, eventually finding expression in social groups' conflicts and violence.

Irreducible pluralism by itself could not address the crisis of reason or the Jewish Question. Berlin did outline an elegant description and justification of pluralism, but he could not quite escape the criticism that his theory of pluralism ended up in relativism. Perelman embraced and developed a similar philosophy of pluralism, but he offered rhetoric and argumentation as vehicles for making those value judgments. Argument in the Talmudic tradition is prominent, given the assumption that the achievement of truth is a difficult if not impossible goal, one that must be approached with significant humility.[42] Perelman complemented the Western tradition of rhetoric with a Talmudic understanding of argument.

Perelman and Olbrechts-Tyteca's theory of the epideictic offered a grounding for argument in a pluralistic culture. The epideictic, in their new rhetoric, was quite different from that developed by Aristotle: a genre designed to celebrate and entertain, but not to provoke action. In their reconceptualization, Perelman and Olbrechts-Tyteca identified the epideictic as the category of rhetoric that drew on preexisting values and commitments to inspire the audience to do something.[43] I have noted the importance of their citation of Simone Weil's *The Need for Roots* to explain their view of a revised epideictic.[44] Perelman and Olbrechts-Tyteca observe that Weil "examined the means that the French in London might have used during World War II to rouse their countrymen in France" to oppose the German occupation with more energy and vigor (*The New Rhetoric*, 53). Weil called for the French government in London to express thoughts "already in the hearts of the people, or in the hearts of certain active elements in the nation."[45] Weil's major theme in *The Need for Roots* was the disease of "up-rootedness." The epideictic, in Perelman and Olbrechts-Tyteca's rendering, inoculated against this disease by featuring tradition and shared values. In quoting Weil, Perelman and Olbrechts-Tyteca highlighted preexisting value commitments made by the French to resist the German occupation, which were dormant and needed actualization with the discourse of Charles de Gaulle.

Conclusion

The evidence does support the claim that the NRP is one of the most important rhetorics of the twentieth century, which is the consensus of most historians of rhetoric. The same consensus holds that the NRP is an extension of Aristotle's rhetoric and constitutes a modern rescue of the classical tradition. I support the first consensus but question the second. Although the NRP does constitute a rescue of the classical tradition of rhetoric, it does so by addressing the severe foundational problems that result from that tradition's dependence on the philosophical assumptions of Perelman's understanding of Enlightenment thought (as it is understood by Perelman).[46] The NRP is a cosmopolitan Jewish rhetoric in classical garb. Without question, the NRP can be located, as can Jewish thought, within the classical tradition, and Perelman does cite Aristotle, drawing as necessary on the ancient Greek and Roman rhetoricians to develop a new rhetoric. Yet the philosophical position that Perelman develops both challenges the limitations of the classical rhetorical tradition and builds into his new rhetoric the strengths offered by Jewish thought.[47] The NRP is meant as an act of rapprochement, effectively representing Perelman's *double fidélité* to classical and Jewish thought. The Jewish thought he draws on is inflected by his experience as a Polish and then a Belgian Jew between 1912 and 1940, the Holocaust, and his postwar *teshuvah*, leading him back to Talmudic sources of reasoning.

In my ongoing efforts to write a history of the NRP, I made a categorical mistake in assuming it was a primarily a post-Holocaust project. Although the bulk of the new rhetoric was written in the decade after the Holocaust, the research I offer here suggests that Perelman did not view the Holocaust as proof that the Jewish experience in Europe was and should be over. His own experience, both in Poland and Belgium, suggested that it was possible to be both Belgian and Jewish (even in the face of antisemitism), and it called for a sociological pluralism that he imported into the philosophy of the NRP.

Perelman's identity, articulated in *Gegenwartsarbeit*, the symbol of the Israelite, and *double fidélité*, was translated into the philosophical aspirations of the NRP. The philosophy of the NRP is an attempt to address the crises of reason, answer the Jewish Question, and offer a system of communion. Reason, as it was practiced in the Talmud and in Perelman's Jewish culture, was expansive. As Susan Handelman has explained, the rabbis developed a system of reason that understood the syllogism but that went beyond classical reason in developing modes of logic and rationality.[48] As Perelman observed in his Hebrew University lecture, he saw a need to complement the classical system's version of logic with the grounded reason offered by the Talmud and his culture of origin.

I write in the centenary year of Perelman's birth, and as I write, Europe and the world are still responding to the shooting of three children and a rabbi at Ozar Hatorah Hebrew School in Toulouse, France, on 12 March 2012. The suspected gunman proclaims a version of radical Islam, leading some people to conclude that "Europe's Jewish communities have become the overseas front line of the Jewish state" and that Europe has yet to fully contain antisemitism.[49] Yet many hundreds of Parisians, including Muslims and Jews, marched in silence in the aftermath of the shootings to honor the dead, and the French Council of the Muslim faith condemned the violence.[50] These events suggest that the antisemitism Perelman faced remains a potent force; the resistance to this disease by Europeans of good will proves that his faith in *double fidélité* was not naïve or misplaced; and his vision of a human community ruled by rhetoric, not violence, remains prophetic.

NOTES

1. I fully appreciate the role played by Lucie Olbrechts-Tyteca in the construction of the NRP. Perelman and Olbrechts-Tyteca, both in collaboration and separately, developed the themes of the NRP over a forty-five-year period. As Michelle Bolduc and I demonstrate in "Lucie Olbrechts-Tyteca's New Rhetoric," which provides a more complete explanation of her motivations and contributions to the NRP, Perelman set the agenda and established the foundational philosophical framework for the NRP. Olbrechts-Tyteca made major contributions as well. My effort here is to clarify how Perelman's understanding of his Jewish identity and his efforts to navigate antisemitism before the Holocaust affected the development of the NRP.

2. James Crosswhite, *The Rhetoric of Reason*, 35.
3. Brian Vickers, "Philosophy," 491.
4. Wayne C. Booth, *The Rhetoric of Rhetoric*, 73.
5. Ibid.
6. Thomas M. Conley, *Rhetoric in the European Tradition*, 297.
7. Crosswhite, *The Rhetoric of Reason*, 312, 96.
8. Conley, *Rhetoric in the European Tradition*, 296–97.
9. David A. Frank, "Arguing with God, Talmudic Discourse, and the Jewish Countermodel," "Dialectical Rapprochement in the New Rhetoric," "The Jewish Counter-Model," and "The New Rhetoric, Judaism and Post-Enlightenment Thought."
10. See the exchange between Perelman and Rosen on Perelman's severe critique of the classical tradition: Stanley H. Rosen, "Thought and Action"; Chaïm Perelman, "Reply to Stanley H. Rosen."
11. See David A. Frank and Michelle K. Bolduc, "Chaïm Perelman's 'First Philosophies and Regressive Philosophy.'"
12. Chaïm Perelman, "My Intellectual Itinerary," n.p.
13. Ibid.
14. For the most explicit evidence of his return to Jewish sources, see Chaïm Perelman, "Juridicial Ontology and Sources of Law."

15. Chaïm Perelman, *The Idea of Justice and the Problem of Argument*.
16. Frank, "Arguing with God."
17. David Frank, "A Traumatic Reading of Twentieth-Century Rhetorical Theory," 3.
18. Hannah Arendt, *The Jewish Writings*, 3.
19. Amos Elon, *The Pity of It All*.
20. Jean-Philippe Schreiber, "Chaïm Perelman and Double Fidelity." I draw on this unpublished manuscript for the details on Perelman's family and biography.
21. On the distinction between the two expressions, see Hagit Lavsky, *Before Catastrophe*, 65.
22. Elon, *The Pity of It All*, 380.
23. Gunnar Skirbekk and Nils Gilje, *A History of Western Thought*, 428.
24. Anita Burdman Feferman and Solomon Feferman, *Alfred Tarski*, 42.
25. Chaïm Perelman, "La question juive."
26. Chaïm Perelman, untitled item in *Le tribune juif*, 51.
27. See Maurice Samuels, *Inventing the Israelite*.
28. Noemi Perelman, "Chaim Perelman," 11.
29. See Lucien Steinberg, *The Jews against Hitler*.
30. On the Holocaust and the gray zone, see Primo Levi, *The Drowned and the Saved*, chap. 2.
31. For more about this story, see Frank and Bolduc, "Lucie Olbrechts-Tyteca's New Rhetoric."
32. Dan Mikhman, *Belgium and the Holocaust*.
33. James Crosswhite, "Is There an Audience for this Argument?," 136.
34. Christian Delacampagne, *A History of Philosophy in the Twentieth Century*, 173.
35. Tony Judt, *Past Imperfect*.
36. Chaïm Perelman, "Le libre examen, hier et aujourd'hui." See also Chaïm Perelman and Lucie Olbrechts-Tyteca, *The New Rhetoric*, 62.
37. Michel Foucault called this the "Enlightenment Blackmail of Reason" ("What Is Enlightenment?," 41–42).
38. See Frank, "Dialectical Rapprochement in the New Rhetoric."
39. David A. Frank and Michelle Bolduc, "From *Vita Contemplativa* to *Vita Activa*."
40. Chaïm Perelman, "The Philosophy of Puralism."
41. Isaiah Berlin, *Four Essays on Liberty*.
42. David Kraemer, *The Mind of the Talmud*; Jacob Neusner, *Talmudic Thinking*.
43. Perelman and Olbrechts-Tyteca, *The New Rhetoric*, 52–53.
44. Frank, "The New Rhetoric." See also Simone Weil, *The Need for Roots*.
45. Weil, *The Need for Roots*, 185.
46. See Frank and Bolduc, "Chaïm Perelman's 'First Philosophies and Regressive Philosophy.'"
47. See the exchange between Perelman and Rosen cited above: Rosen, "Thought and Action"; Perelman, "Reply to Stanley H. Rosen."
48. Susan Handelman, *The Slayers of Moses* and *Fragments of Redemption*.
49. Claude Kandiyoti, "Lessons from the Toulouse Shooting."
50. Azra Haqqie, "Jews and Muslims March in Solidarity in France."

BIBLIOGRAPHY

Arendt, Hannah. *The Jewish Writings*. New York: Schocken, 2007.
Berlin, Isaiah. *Four Essays on Liberty*. New York: Oxford University Press, 1969.

Booth, Wayne C. *The Rhetoric of Rhetoric: The Quest for Effective Communication*. Oxford: Blackwell, 2004.

Conley, Thomas M. *Rhetoric in the European Tradition*. New York: Longman, 1990.

Crosswhite, James. "Is There an Audience for This Argument? Fallacies, Theories, and Relativisms." *Philosophy and Rhetoric* 28, no. 2 (1995): 134–45.

———. *The Rhetoric of Reason: Writing and the Attractions of Argument*. Madison: University of Wisconsin Press, 1996.

Delacampagne, Christian. *A History of Philosophy in the Twentieth Century*. Baltimore, MD: Johns Hopkins University Press, 1999.

Elon, Amos. *The Pity of It All: A History of the Jews in Germany, 1743–1933*. New York: Metropolitan, 2002.

Feferman, Anita Burdman, and Solomon Feferman. *Alfred Tarski: Life and Logic*. Cambridge: Cambridge University Press, 2004.

Foucault, Michel. "What Is Enlightenment?" In *The Foucault Reader*, edited and translated by Paul Rabinow, 32–50. New York: Pantheon, 1984.

Frank, David A. "Arguing with God, Talmudic Discourse, and the Jewish Countermodel: Implications for the Study of Argumentation." *Argumentation and Advocacy* 41 (fall 2004): 71–87.

———. "Dialectical Rapprochement in the New Rhetoric." *Argumentation and Advocacy* 33 (1998): 111–37.

———. "The Jewish Counter-Model: Talmudic Argumentation, the New Rhetoric Project, and the Classical Tradition of Rhetoric." *Journal of Communication and Religion* 26 (2003): 163–94.

———. "The New Rhetoric, Judaism and Post-Enlightenment Thought: The Cultural Origins of Perelmanian Philosophy." *Quarterly Journal of Speech* 83, no. 3 (1997): 311–31.

———. "A Traumatic Reading of Twentieth-Century Rhetorical Theory: The Belgian Holocaust, Malines, Perelman, and de Man." *Quarterly Journal of Speech* 93, no. 1 (2007): 308–43.

———. "From *Vita Contemplativa* to *Vita Activa*: Chaïm Perelman and Lucie Olbrechts-Tyteca's Rhetorical Turn." *Advances in the History of Rhetoric* 7 (2004): 65–86.

———. "Lucie Olbrechts-Tyteca's New Rhetoric." *Quarterly Journal of Speech* 96, no. 2 (2010): 141–63.

Frank, David A., and Michelle K. Bolduc. "Chaïm Perelman's 'First Philosophies and Regressive Philosophy.'" *Philosophy and Rhetoric* 36, no. 3 (2003): 177–207.

Handelman, Susan A. *Fragments of Redemption: Jewish Thought and Literary Theory in Benjamin, Scholem, and Levinas*. Bloomington: Indiana University Press, 1991.

———. *Slayers of Moses: The Emergence of Rabbinic Interpretation in Modern Literary Theory*. Albany: State University of New York Press, 1982.

Haqqie, Azra. "Jews and Muslims March in Solidarity in France." Timesunion.com, 31 March 2012. http://blog.timesunion.com/muslimwomen/jews-and-muslims-march-in-solidarity-in-france/3611/.

Judt, Tony. *Past Imperfect: French Intellectuals, 1944–1956*. Berkeley: University of California Press, 1992.

Kandiyoti, Claude. "Lessons from the Toulouse Shooting." *Haaretz* 30 March 2012.

Kraemer, David. *The Mind of the Talmud*. New York: Oxford University Press, 1990.

Lavsky, Hagit. *Before Catastrophe: The Distinctive Path of German Zionism*. Detroit, MI: Wayne State University Press, 1996.

Levi, Primo. *The Drowned and the Saved*. Translated by Raymond Rosenthal. New York: Summit, 1988.
Melzer, Emanuel. *No Way Out: The Politics of Polish Jewry, 1935–1939*. Cincinnati, OH: Hebrew Union College Press, 1997.
Mikhman, Dan. *Belgium and the Holocaust: Jews, Belgians, Germans*. Jerusalem: Yad Vashem, 1998.
Neusner, Jacob. *Talmudic Thinking: Language, Logic, Law*. Columbia: University of South Carolina Press, 1992.
Perelman, Chaïm. Untitled item. *Le tribune juif*, 31 July 1935, 51–52.
———. *De la justice*. Brussels: Universite Libre de Bruxelles, 1945.
———. *The Idea of Justice and the Problem of Argument*. Translated by John Petrie. London: Routledge and Kegan Paul, 1963.
———. "Juridicial Ontology and Sources of Law." *Northern Kentucky Law Review* 10 (1983): 387–98.
———. "La question juive." *Synthèses* (1945): 47–63.
———. "Le libre examen, hier et aujourd'hui." *Revue de l'Université de Bruxelles* (1949): 39–50.
———. "My Intellectual Itinerary." Speech delivered to the faculty of Hebrew University, Jerusalem, 1980.
———. *The New Rhetoric and the Humanities: Essays on Rhetoric and Its Applications*. Dordrecht, Holland: Reidel, 1979.
———. "The Philosophy of Pluralism." *Philosophie exchange* 2, no. 4 (1978): 49–56.
———. "Reply to Stanley H. Rosen." *Inquiry* 2 (1959): 85–88.
Perelman, Chaïm, and Lucie Olbrechts-Tyteca. *The New Rhetoric: A Treatise on Argumentation*. Translated by John Wilkinson and Purcell Weaver. Notre Dame, IN: University of Notre Dame Press, 1969.
Perelman, Noemi. "Chaïm Perelman: A Life Well Lived." In *The Promise of Reason: Studies in The New Rhetoric*, edited by John T. Gage and Chaïm Perelman, 8–17. Carbondale: Southern Illinois University Press, 2011.
Rosen, Stanley H. "Thought and Action." *Inquiry* 2 (1959): 65–84.
Samuels, Maurice. *Inventing the Israelite: Jewish Fiction in Nineteenth-Century France*. Stanford, CA: Stanford University Press, 2010.
Schreiber, Jean-Philippe. "Chaïm Perelman and Double Fidelity." Unpublished manuscript.
Skirbekk, Gunnar, and Nils Gilje. *A History of Western Thought: From Ancient Greece to the Twentieth Century*. London: Routledge, 2001.
Steinberg, Lucien. *The Jews against Hitler: Not as a Lamb*. Corrected ed. London: Gordon and Cremonesi, 1978.
Vickers, Brian. "Philosophy." In *Oxford Encyclopedia of Rhetoric*, edited by Thomas O. Sloane, 489–92. Oxford: Oxford University Press, 2001.
Weil, Simone. *The Need for Roots*. Translated by Arthur Wills. New York: Putnam's Sons, 1952.

Socrates as Rabbi
The Story of the Aleph and the Alpha in a Postinformation Age

STEVEN B. KATZ

The Aleph and the Alpha: A Midrash

In this tale by me, Schlomo ben Shmuel, Aleph and Alpha found themselves on an information highway in the same data stream. After greeting each other with a bow (for aleph is often silent now), Aleph asked: "So tell me, Alpha, why are you recognized as the Greek origin of the letter *a*, when in the history of the West the Hebrew Aleph came first?" Alpha replied: 'Because the Phoenicians brought Semitic letters, including you, to Greek shores.' Then Alelph said to Alpha: "In the history of language, the seafaring Phoenicians rather than Semitic cultures are given credit for the alphabet. Surely alphabets are not simply objects to be traded." 'No indeed,' Alpha responded, 'the alphabet was appropriated by the conquering Romans for Latin, and adopted as the writing system of Romance and other languages, while your language almost perished in Diaspora.' Aleph repeated, "But why Greek, when the Romans conquered the Jews as well?" Alpha replied: 'In the name of Daniel and Bright, Hebrew is not a true alphabet, but an *abjad*, a writing system without vowels, making your language ambiguous and obscure. The Greeks added letters for vowels, making meaning as well as pronunciation clearer.' "How obscure? Alpha, if it pleases you, the ambiguity presented no problem throughout the history of the Jewish people and in fact has been a holy source of interpretation, creativity, consolation, meditation, joy, revelation, and ethics." 'Forgive me for saying this, Aleph, but even your chosen people of the Book had to learn by tradition and the authority of rabbis. How much greater the difficulty for other peoples who are not Jewish to interpret your language!' "How obscure? The rabbinic period developed sets of hermeneutic principles to apply to the letters themselves and reveal hidden ethical meanings. Such hermeneutic principles might even be useful for people living in a postinformation age of virtual realities—social media, cybernetic bodies, digital objects."

Alpha interrupted: 'Subsequent cultures replaced the opaque letters of your G/d with the clear, transparent signs of science.' Taken aback by this information transfer, Aleph thought for a nanosecond, then asked: "Why clear?" Alpha replied: 'To see *through* the letters to the meaning outside them.' "To see *into* the letters and the possible meanings there! But why clear? Blessed be the name of Rabbi Munk, for many rabbis and mystics of my faith believe that the Hebrew letters are not transparent signs but opaque, physical substances—that the aleph-bet is the substance of the proto-alphabet God used as blueprint to speak the universe into being, and thus every material part of each letter is invested with moral meaning and needs to be interpreted!" Then Alpha responded: 'I mean no disrespect to your country of origin, race, religion, creed, or culture, but not all people accept your God, still less the creation stories of the Hebrew letters.' Aleph interjected: "Why clear? In reverence of Rabbi Dan, many religious Jews today believe that the *world* is the transparent language, and language the opaque fiery matter of the real world."

Before Alpha could reply Aleph added that there were several stories throughout Talmud as well as the Midrash, and later, Kabbalah, about the letters as living beings, and unlike inanimate objects, having their own ideas and agency: "Why clear? You see with your own eyes that I, the Aleph, the first letter in the aleph-bet, and also the Hebrew number 1, am quite alive." 'But how is that different from objects possessing agency, as in object-oriented philosophy (OOP)? Your God, blessed be his Name (just in case), did not begin the Torah with you.' Aleph countered: "How is it different? What you say is true, Alpha; the subject is much debated by Rabbi Jonah and Bar Kappara and Rabbi Judah in a midrash much like this one, known as the *Bereshith* (In the beginning) in *Midrash Rabbah*, the 'Great Midrash.'" 'I'm familiar with it and some of its expounders, although I question its fancifulness, ambiguity, and inconclusiveness as a philosophical work.' "How is it different? Ethics. In divine recompense I, Aleph, am used as the first letter of one of God's sacred names that like the holiest of all, the Tetragrammaton, יהוה, which non-Jews pronounce 'Jehovah' or 'Yahweh' but in Hebrew literally cannot be said, and whose meaning, like reality, remains partially hidden." Alpha quickly responded: 'For me and my followers, meaning must be as rational as ratios, mathematically clear as Apollo's sunlight, complete as omega.' "How is it different? Alpha, I too mean no disrespect to your country of origin, race, religion, creed, or sexual orientation, but the Hebrew letters that form the Western alphabet are originary and contain ethical meaning." 'Not chronologically. And I cannot believe that there is any meaning in the material shapes and forms of letters, whether Greek or Hebrew. Letters are just objects, containers of ideas, and conveyors of sound. The best alphabets are not opaque, but transparent, and step aside, allowing meaning to shine through.'

"Why transparent?" 'In a postinformation age, communication must be rapid and seamless.' "Why transparent? What about the sophistic or Ciceronian unity of form and content at the level of the letter?" 'My dear Aleph, in memory of Walter Benjamin, I must disagree with you: the "ritual aura" of things, be they objects or art (or, in our case, alphabets) derived from traditional notions of authoring or origin, no longer holds any meaning or power; the purpose of art is not mimesis, but technological reproduction of itself.' "This is well known and accepted among warring tribes of postmodernist literary and rhetorical scholars," observed Aleph. "The notion of self-signification within finite yet unbounded systems reminds me of Einstein—as well as Freud, Alpha—but also may have contributed to OOP, an ontology I confess I don't fully understand." 'That is the point, Aleph: we don't understand empirical objects; philosophers and rhetoricians have not given them their due.' "It appears to me that your letters, like nonliterate, digital objects, are all solipsistic surface, all self-referential data, neither essence nor attribute, just medium." 'On the contrary, Aleph, in OOP, Objects, whether they are alive nor not, are "actants" with agency.'

"Why transparent? Alpha, here I must invoke the venerable name of Kenneth Burke to assert that in the rhetoric you describe, the object that functions causally, almost mechanistically and without thought, free will, or even consciousness, yet regarded as an agent, is either mysticism or illusion." 'But, Aleph, for Latour's sake, OOP accounts for heretofore unnoted acts and relevant agents in social networks without needing to consider the drama of human motive; OOP therefore increases the range of rhetoric by refocusing the field on Objects, rather than only humans who have dominated discussion and debate for millennia.' "Alpha, in the universe you surmise (and for the sake of Baudrillard, may his memory be for a blessing), humans don't always engage in symbolic action but rather in sheer causal motion, whether physical or virtual." 'That is true, Aleph, but in your orthographic way of seeing the world, I note that the *O* in 'objects' is often capitalized, thereby giving them an essentiality in language that undermines the attempt to close the duality we are discussing. Bridging this duality is the greatest advance in Western philosophy." "Is it an advance? In trying to close the abyss, the founders of OOP must adhere to two philosophical assumptions concerning Objects, correct?" 'That is correct, Aleph. You are learning fast, despite your lack of vowels. Go on.' "First, for the prophets Graham Harman and Levi Bryant, Objects must be assumed to exist in and of themselves. Second, no Object can ever be known in its entirety, since our knowledge of the Object is limited by our own relations to it, and thus we must assume that a vast, perhaps infinite, number of relations remain unknown." 'Excellent, my ontological friend. Maybe we are related (as objects) after all.'

"Is it an advance? Harman says that we become aware of Objects only when we need or use them, or when they break down." 'You are correct in this as well. These conditions too are defined by our limited relations with the objects as objects in overlapping spheres—the realm of relations in which each object in its incomprehensibility exists in the realm of relations in which *we* exist as objects.' "Is it an advance? We 'know' from the experience of Western philosophy and science that only the most naïve empiricists, or logical positivists, would openly believe such a thing." 'I believe it is a new kind of empiricism, Aleph, thus: metaphysical awareness is enfolded into flat or two dimensional "objects"; in regarding all objects as actants, we prepare the ground of rhetorical theory for new technological or artificial life-forms.' "Is it an advance? Or an empiricism that is really another metaphysics?" 'Latour himself pointed out in *Factish Gods* that we *Have Never Been Modern*.' "Perhaps misreading Latour, I understand that all debates of assumptions and issues—metaphysical or objective, transcendental or methodological—are packed into objects like little 'black boxes' that we take as fact. For Latour, *Pandora's Hope* is perhaps that objects in social networks of facts are reopened so that we may understand their nature and call them into question—" 'Aleph!' Alpha interrupted, 'that's why Harman and others correctly if strangely call this metaphysical empiricism "speculative realism." A long time ago Herbert Simon said that we *do not* have to know what's inside "the black box" (whether economic rationality, decision science, the knowledge of the artificial, or human mind [or again, letters]), only that it is rational and will behave rationally in a rational system.'

"But, my dear Alpha, a rational system? Does this new of empiricism capture the experience of being human as well as object? If 'black boxes' by definition preclude the consideration of things like affect and values, humans themselves might be led to a fundamentally 'objective' conception not only of communication, but also of emotions and ethical behavior." 'In a postinformation age, emotions and values are "soft facts," Aleph, that—as Aristotle in his rational wisdom knew—are unwanted "owing to a defect in our hearers" and fall outside the communication equation (of which I as alpha am often a part).' "A rational system? What is missing can be summed up in a simple question: what are the ethics of the relations between humans, and objects? Perhaps this is where the Hebrew letters and hermeneutics, differentiated from but related to the Greek, might supplement or underwrite, if not unlock and replace, communication (non)ethics in a postinformation age. If I am not for myself, who am I?" 'Aleph, for me the question is: what is my nature, function, and relation?' "Let us continue our search on the network for answers to these questions, even though, as Baudrillard the prophet predicted, we will be dispersed beyond consciousness." 'Yes, let us search,' Alpha agreed. 'Let us seek out and find the great Greek rabbi, Socrates, who is purported to be in a nearby data stream, and ask his atoms, which according to Plato may float around the world for at least 9,000 years!' "Yes, let us seek Reb Socrates!"

A Postinformation Solipsistic Commentary on This Midrash

Multiplicities of Socrates

There are more versions of Socrates than you can shake a caduceus at. In the twentieth century alone, we have Socrates as (A) the true Platonist, the founder and standard-bearer of the bifurcation of the beautiful mind and the ugly body—thus an embodiment of the Western philosophical tradition (see Cornford); (B) the philosopher-critic of rhetoric and instigator of the search for truth through interactive questions and answers, now instantiated in instructional technology (see Weaver; Ulmer); (Γ) the half-historical, half-literary figure, cutting and comic, who is a true but playable mouthpiece for Plato, wondering (*sic*) through all but two of Plato's dialogues, the hapless main character with a philosophical purpose (see Boyarin, *Socrates*); (Δ) the granddaddy of dialectic, of literate linear logical thinking in dialogue form; (E) a marker of the line between orality and literacy (see Ong; Havelock) and a shill for an age on the verge of virtuality, the half-conscious harbinger of the cusp of literacy and electracy; (Z) a rebel for education, a trailblazer of truth, and a martyr for virtue unaware of First Amendment rights; (H) contra Plato's apology ("Socrates' Defense"), in which the city of Athens executes Socrates on the charge of "corrupting the youth," an ideologically astute and antidemocratic leader of a rearguard action for Plato's political elitist causes (see Stone); and (Θ) a surrogate or spokesperson for the binary opposed to *cogito* in Western philosophy, perhaps in "real" life a sophist himself—and thus for us a metaphysical straw man, a foundationalist without shoes (see Derrida).

In the end, Plato's Socrates is a highly complex individual or caricature, a literary device or character, who plays many roles in and out of history, literature, philosophy, and rhetoric, and is as malleable as he seems stubborn—he is steadfastly almost anything we want him to be. Most important for this chapter, he is the subject of Daniel Boyarin's book, coincidentally titled *Socrates and the Fat Rabbis*, in which Boyarin explores the common conceptions of Platonic and rabbinic dialogue by juxtaposing the Plato (or Socrates) of classical Greece, and the rabbis who wrote Midrash (discussed below) later on. Boyarin argues that both Plato and the rabbis productively combine, in dialogic form, the serious with the grotesque, and he refocuses our reading of Platonic dialogue and rabbinic midrashim by taking into account the interaction of these heretofore incompatible conventions and genres. Boyarin's book thus subverts, or at least problematizes, traditional ways of looking at Platonic and midrashic dialogue as separate from each other—as history or philosophy versus fiction—and of long-held tendencies to view tragedy and comedy as distinct genres.

Thanks to the polyvalence of texts, in which a simple conjunction (and) and a preposition (as) become almost as highly significant as two letters or words might in Hebrew hermeneutics, I can still write a chapter titled "Socrates as Rabbi" despite the similar title of Boyarin's book. Aside from titles, the difference between *Socrates and the Fat Rabbis* and "Socrates as Rabbi" is that Boyarin demonstrates how the dreaded and the ridiculous dialogically function in and out of their very different historical and intertextual contexts (also see Boyarin, *Intertextuality*). My midrash above suggests that I am looking at two contradictory but related orthographic and philosophical traditions for an ethical system on which existence as an alphabet in a postinformation age can be grounded. To examine these traditions, we must begin by briefly exploring how hermeneutic principles guide meaning and ethics in each of them. In turn, that requires us to discover how Greek topoi and rabbinic *baraitot* are similar and different, by looking at how each functions in texts as virtual realities.

Internal or Eternal Arguments: Hebrew Topoi, Greek Baraitot?

The Greek topoi for constructing arguments, as articulated by Aristotle in *On Rhetoric* and elsewhere are well known and do not need to be restated here. However, acting like Jewish topoi, the *Baraita* of the 32 Rules, also known as the *middot* (measures, rules), are specific hermeneutic principles derived from texts *outside* the Talmud[1] for analyzing, arguing, interpreting, and commenting on other texts (either Torah, the written law; or the later Mishna, the oral law redacted by Judah ha-Nasi). The development of the *baraita* of the 32 Rules was coterminous with the writing of the Babylonian and the Palestinian Talmuds (Mishna and its commentary, the *Gemara*, together constitute each Talmud) during two rabbinic periods in Jewish history (the Tannaim and the Amoraim) stretching from approximately 200 BCE to 400 CE. In this essay, following Herman Strack and Günter Stemberger's authoritative treatment of them, I also will be using the terms *baraita* (or plural, *baraitot*) and *middot* interchangeably to refer to these hermeneutic principles.

The *baraita* also are applied to Midrash like those addressed by Boyarin in *Socrates and the Fat Rabbis*: vast collections of rabbinic compositions of allegories and interpretations often loosely based on Torah, and presented in a genre of argumentative forms that include fantastic stories, homilies, sermons, and legends—of God, angels, biblical patriarchs and matriarchs, rabbis past and present (and even future) involved in the debates, and the living Hebrew letters. The *baraita* of the thirty-two rules are divided by Strack and Stemberger (16–30) into three groups: the rules of Rabbi Hillel, the rules of Rabbi Ishmael, and the rules of Rabbi Eliezer ben Yose ha-Gelili. I will merely summarize these groups here.

According to Strack and Stemberger, the *middot* of Hillel include *Qal va-homer* (the a fortiori "lesser to greater," or "lighter to heavier"); *Gezerah shavah* ("equal ordinance or statute," or argument by analogy); *Kelal u-ferat u-ferat u-kelal* ("the general and the particular, the particular and the general," by which general or particular are qualified); and *Ke-yose bô be-maqom aher*, somewhat similar to the previous item in another passage. What one notices here is the similarity between these *baraitot* and Greek forms of argument prevalent at the time. As Strack and Stemberger observe, these rules most resemble Hellenistic reasoning, though "the direct adoption from the Hellenistic world cannot be established, even if the correlation and terminology of the rules may go back to Hellenistic influence" (17; see also Katz, "Letter as Essence").

However, one also should notice the focus on the application of *baraita* to text. The other rules in this group, such as *Binyan av mi-shnê ketuvim* ("the expression for the same kind of derivation based on two biblical passages") are all about hermeneutics for interpreting writing, as opposed to topoi for inventing rhetorical (oral) arguments. But—as Strack and Stemberger point out and Boyarin (*Socrates and the Fat Rabbis*) seems to confirm—even this group of *middot* (for instance, *Dabar ha-lamed meʿinyanô* ["argument from the context"] which deals with the relation and meaning of passages in proximity) "frequently leads not to a natural exegesis of context, but to often far-fetched expositions based on the accidental proximity of two terms" (Strack and Stemberger, 20). However, orthodox Jews do not consider the placement of anything in Torah, even a tiny mark, coincidental (see Strack, 98; Katz, "Letter as Essence" and "The Alphabet as Ethics.") The rules of Ishmael (a rabbi who, in opposition to others, believed in "plain interpretation" [*peschat* instead of *drash*]), incorporate the rules of Hillel but primarily rely on the *Qal va-homer* and on argument by analogy (*Gezerah shavah*) (Strack and Stemberger, 21). The rules of Rabbi Eliezer include many principles for interpreting texts, including distant or divergent passages in the Bible (these rules are not in the same order as those in the other groups). The first *middot* of Rabbi Eliezer's rules includes "*Ribbui*," "'increase, inclusion,' where the Bible uses the words *af* and *gam* ('also,' or the accusative particle *et*)" in recounting, so that Samuel's servant in slaying a lion "(*gam et ha ʾari*)" kills four: "one each in addition for *gam*, *et*, and the *article*" (Strack and Stemberger, 23–24); and "*Mi-ut*," 'restriction, exclusion, reduction,' indicated by the works *akh* and *raq* ('only' and *min* ['from, out of'])." What is evident here with just these two rules is that relatively insignificant letters or words in a text, say the direct object marker את (*et*), which in Hebrew has no semantic meaning, or the single but powerful ו (vov), which is the conjunction "and" but in biblical Hebrew also can act as a *vov-hahipuch* (*vov*-consecutive)—which, when prefixed to a simple verb can change it from past (perfect, or completed action) into future (imperfect, incomplete action) tense, and vice versa. As Strack notes, "in the same manner a plural is made to yield an implication, or a superfluous [*vov*], or the duplication of a word" (98; see also Munk).

I do not have space to list all of the thirty-two *middot*, which are concerned with logical induction and deduction, as well as a fortiori reasoning in both directions (see Strack and Stemberger, 18–30). However, of particular interest to us are the latter of the *baraita* of the thirty-two rules, which focus on manipulating and interpreting the letters of the aleph-bet itself. Indeed, one of the primary differences between the Greek topoi and the *baraita* of the thirty-two rules is the inordinate attention to Hebrew text as a hermeneutics of reality, also noted by Susan Handelman (see also Boyarin, *Intertextuality*, xii). Following *Mashal* (meaning "parable, allegorical interpretation") in Strack and Stemberger's compendium we find "Neged" (Strack, 97), "equivalence," in which corresponding numbers are regarded as equivalent (the forty years that the post-Egyptian Hebrews spent in the desert, the forty days Moses was on Mt. Sinai, etc.); *Ma'al* (paronomasia), the relation of words based on similar sound—or, in the case of Hebrew, the same consonants; *Gematria*, the "calculation of the numerical value of Hebrew letters to discover hidden relations and meanings" (Strack and Stemberger 29), or "[s]ecret alphabets or substitution of letters for other letters" (Strack, 97); or *Athbash*, "the use of a secret alphabet in which the first letter of the Hebrew alphabet corresponds to the last, the second to the last but one, etc." (Strack and Stemberger, 29), or otherwise systematically changing the order of letters in a word or substituting other letters to arrive at other words; "*Notarikon*, [d]ivision of a word into two or more" (Strack and Stemberger, 29), or where each letter of a word can be read as standing for the first letter of another word (i.e., other words are signified and embodied by each letter of the word being interpreted). Note that *notarikon* is a Greek word. But the difference between Jewish topoi concerned with the meaning of the size, shape, crown, order, and the permutation of the *letters* of the aleph-bet and the Greek *baraitot* as presented in Plato's dialogue devoted to the subject is highly significant, and is discussed below.

The Socratic Drash: This Is Not Your Mother's Tongue
In Plato's "Cratylus," Socrates discusses the reality of the text—if and how the shapes and sounds and ordering of the letters of the Greek alphabet

might mirror reality. What is remarkable about this treatise is that Plato usually does not have Socrates analyze this elemental level of language, preferring instead to focus on meaning based on the classification and the logic of words in relation to ideal truths. But in "The Cratylus," Socrates rather flamboyantly takes up the mimetic question—with a few hermeneutic procedures—of whether the letters and sounds of the names of people and things have meaning. He is interested not only in whether language imitates nature, but also in whether the Greek letters themselves can mime essences.

Beginning with the idea that language doesn't originate from gods (who would know the right names of things [391e]) or legislators (who would all disagree), the discussion, primarily between Socrates and Hermogenes, concerns a subject that Cratylus has broached: what is the relation between *onoma* (name) and the form or essence of a thing (389e). On first blush, Socrates seems to agree with the notion that letters can adequately represent the essence of things, and he goes through a number of examples to demonstrate the claim. In his analysis of Greek words, Socrates appears to employ the Hellenistic *notarikon*, a process through which two or more words can be derived from one (in this case, a name). For instance, the Trojans in Homer called their young king "*Astyanax* (king of the city)" (392d): "a king (αναξ) and a holder (εκωρ) have nearly the same meaning as the Trojan king's name" (393b).

So, for example, Socrates engages and agrees with the following parsings: "Orestes (the man of the mountain) ... appears to be rightly called ... to express the brutality and fierceness and mountain wilderness of his hero's nature" (394e); and "Agamemnon (admirable for remaining) is one who is persevering in the accomplishment of his resolves" (395b–c). In the case of Tantalus, the unfortunate, with the stone suspended (ταλαντεια) over his head even after death, people might want "to call him ταλαντατος (most weighed down by misfortune)" (395e). Even Zeus comes under Socrates's hermeneutic scrutiny: "Zeus ... has an excellent meaning, though hard to understand because [it is] really like a sentence, which is divided into two parts, for some call him *Zena* (Ζηνα ['author of life']) and use one half, and others who use the other half call him *Dia* (Δια ['lord and king of all']); the two together signify the nature of the god, and the business of a name ... is to express the nature.... Wherefore we are right in calling him *Zena* and *Dia*" (396a).

In fact, many of the *middot* can probably be found in Plato's treatises, especially if one believes that they, like the topoi and grammar itself, constitute not only the way we speak but also the way we think. But the letters out of which the words are made will not be the subject of another treatise, nor will the hermeneutic principles that are applied to interpret the letters of words. Assuming principles opposite to those in the latter *baraita* of the thirty-two rules, Socrates points out that the names of other kings neither share letters while being alike nor share letters while not being alike: "The etymologist is not put out by the addition or transposition or subtraction of a letter or two, or indeed by the change of all the letters, *for this need not interfere with meaning*" (394b; emphasis added). In keeping with both serious and comic purposes of the *baraita*—for, as Boyarin (*Socrates*) might point out, the rabbis also used the *middot* for both, especially in Midrash—Socrates's purpose is to ridicule this most outrageous of all mimetic beliefs and any such Greek hermeneutic practices. Another major difference, then, between the topoi of the Greek letters and the *middot* of the Hebrew letters is the potency (or lack thereof) of the alphabet. In "The Cratylus," the letter becomes the final point of separation between names and meaning (a quadruple problem: nature is an imitation of Forms; rhetoric is an imitation of nature; writing is an imitation of rhetoric; and the letters are an imitation . . . of writing, not of Form or essence).

To illustrate, Socrates analyzes the suitability of the spelling out of the names of the letters. Socrates says that some letters (mostly vowels, which he lists, and consonants like β [beta]) "give no offense" (393e), and that the spelling of others does not matter: "Whether the syllables of a name are the same or not the same makes no difference . . . so long as the essence of the thing remains in possession of the name and appears in it" (393d). Even though he employs hermeneutic principles that resemble some *baraitot*, Socrates does not subscribe to the power of alphabets: the sharing of letter(s) in different names of people, places, or things does not mean they have anything in common (394c)—a major assumption in many of the *middot*. Furthermore, in "The Cratylus," letters, like words, have no ontological connection to ideas or essences. This distinction between Greek and Hebrew thought is critical (see Handelman; Boman). Even though Socrates in "The Cratylus" focuses on letters and sounds in relation to essences and things, Socrates "as rabbi" worships the supreme essences that lie beyond all letters, words, and things.

For the Platonic Socrates, letters as signs point only to the base materiality of both language and the physical world: "How real existence is to be studied or discovered is, I suspect, beyond you and me. But... the knowledge of things is not to be derived from names" (339b). For Boyarin (*Socrates*), the base, the grotesque, the ugly, and the ridiculous, mixed with the serious, the philosophical, and the dreaded, is not mere play, excess, or error on the part of Plato, but dramatic philosophy. So too with Midrash. We will now see that with the same or similar hermeneutical principles, Plato arrives at the opposite conclusion from that of the medieval kabbalists, even though Kabbalah was heavily influenced by neo-Platonism.

The (Re)Turn of the Mystics: Kabbalah

Begin combining letters, few, many, shift them and combine them until your heart is warm. Pay attention to the movement of the letters and to what you can produce by combining them. And when your heart is warm... you see that through the combination of letters you grasp things that you could not have known by yourself or with the aid of tradition.

Kabbalah of Abraham Abulafia, quoted in Umberto Eco, *Foucault's Pendulum*

The *baraita* of the thirty-two rules that the rabbis used in late antiquity to develop Talmud and Midrash—rules similar to those that Socrates ridicules in "The Cratylus"—also can be seen to have been used by the kabbalists to bring hermeneutics to full mystical flower in the Middle Ages. In particular, we will look at the use of *middot* in early parts of *The Zohar* (the book of splendor, or light). Although the improbable claim has been made that *The Zohar* was written by the Patriarch Abraham (Kaplan, *Sefer*), it is generally agreed that this mystical treatise was most likely written by Abraham Abulafia, who lived in thirteenth-century Spain. As we did with the *baraita* and "The Cratylus," in this section of my commentary we will focus on only a tiny sample from a very large body of work (like the *Midrash Rabbah*, *The Zohar* alone is an enormous multivolume work). Thus, I do not make claims to represent the use of *middot* even in these midrashim and kabbalah, but rather only to present a few little samples to see how the *baraita* as hermeneutic principles seem to work, and what their significance for us posthumans might be.

Many notable scholars have drawn connections between Midrash and Kabbalah (see, for example, Scholem; Dan; *The Zohar*, 379, where Harry Sperling and Maurice Simon point out that Midrash is obscured where it is most used). Several scholars have treated the Kabbalah as rhetoric or declared that that is what it is (see, for example, Handelman; Katz, "Epistemology"). Yet we must keep in mind Boyarin's entreaty not to draw too many connections between Midrash and Kabbalah (*Intertextuality*, xii). The Kabbalah of the thirteenth century was not only the product of another diaspora in which schools of kabbalists sprang up on Spanish, Mediterranean, Western soil. Rather, that soil was also highly rich in neo-Platonism, which, like plutonium, affected and irradiated Jewish mystical thought as much as it did Christian. In addition, at the time, kabbalism, particularly in relation to rabbinic culture of the Talmud, was (and still is in most circles) perceived as a radical, even heretical, break with rabbinical tradition—although others believe that kabbalism has equaled or even supplanted the more legalistic rabbinic tradition as the spiritual basis of Judaism in the twentieth century (Scholem). With these caveats, we now briefly turn to *The Zohar* and, once again, an account of *Bereshith*, "in the beginning," and God's use of the aleph-bet to create the universe. Indeed, the *middot* in "*Bereshith*" are appropriately so procreative and prolific that it is hard to even present them.

The opening passages of Genesis, in the prologue of *The Zohar* (2a-b), begin with a description of the application of various letters—syllables of sound that God used to designate the grades of creation, the number 600,000 (an example of both *baraita Neged* [corresponding significant number], and the *baraita* referring to an antecedent that is placed subsequently). This is followed by *Gematria*, a discussion of the letters of God's name (*Yod Hey Vov Hey*, the Tetragrammaton) and their translation into numbers. And this is followed by the relation of the numbers of verses and events that range well into the biblical future, "a biblical section [that] refers to a later period than the one that preceded it" (see Strack, 97–98; Strack and Stemberger, 30). In addition, *Debar shehu' shanui* (Repetition . . . to bring out a point), is used throughout (Strack, 96). And this is only the first paragraph!

Through a reversal of the order of the letters of God's name (*Notarikon*, or *Athbash* [a secret alphabet]), we are then given the famous story (it also appears in Talmud and Midrash) of the Hebrew letters each arguing before God why it should be first in creation. Each letter steps forward and states its case, using one or more of the *middot*—usually *Notarikon* but also others—to depict a moral or physical quality whose name commences with it, or to derive an important future verse or event based on it. And God replies to each letter, using the same or similar *middot* to adduce an opposing moral or physical reason, or an opposing future verse or event, why the letter should not begin the world. (See 2b–3b, where—based on "*Kal wa-homer sathum*" [Strack 96]—Aleph, in humility and before its turn, withdraws once God has granted the honor to *beth*.) Then the higher and lower worlds are created with the capitalized and lowercase forms of the letters, which could be any number of *middot*, depending on how a rabbi might want to interpret this passage of *The Zohar*. Thus begins a world made out of letters—a world quite different from the mimetic one of Socrates. As pointed out by Sperling and Simon (*The Zohar*, 379), sections 15a–22a and 29a–31a are particularly rich (and obscure) in *middot*. Here I merely point or wave to them as I go flying by. Albeit brief, the presentation of these two examples begins to show the ways the Greek and Hebrew topoi of the letters of their respective alphabets differ. We find that it is far less a matter of the difference in the hermeneutics themselves, or even in the letter shapes of two different languages, and more a matter of ontology—geometric forms versus the moral gestures of the letters, both of which can be interpreted using the *baraita*. Not only do we see incorporated in the Greek and the Hebrew alphabets both the comic and the serious, as Boyarin predicted (*Intertextuality*), but we also see that both of these rhetorics are mystical. Plato does not believe that the letters of the alphabet contain any truth at all; rather, he believes that truth exists in a nonmaterial realm outside of language and nature. Abraham (or Abulafia) not only believes the aleph-bet is true essence, but that the still-burning letters constitute the fundamental matter of a moral and physical universe (see Munk; Kaplan). *Kal wa-homer sathum*—in this orthographic materialism, as opposed to Socrates's dialogue, writing is not only a moral act but also a sacred one, and texts themselves are sacred (particularly the Bible, but also other writing, evidence of which I have discussed elsewhere [see, for example, Moskow and Katz; Katz and Rhodes]). This point is essential for the series of conclusions to this commentary on the midrash with which I began this chapter.

Conclusion: What's God "Got to Do, Got to Do with It?"

א. The questions that we rush to ponder as we go flying by are: Does this Jewish perspective of the aleph-bet, perhaps a distinguishing mark of its rhetoric, have an ethical role to play in a postinformation age? Why is the question of orthographic ontology important to us, who now live almost wholly in a digital and virtual world? Everything. In *The Sacrament of Language*, the contemporary secular philosopher Giorgio Agamben explores the nature of oath and blasphemy but quickly arrives at the nonreferential notion that in God's name(s), "essence and existence coincide": "To promote the name of God means to understand it as that experience of language in which it is impossible to separate name and being, words and things" (52). In just a few pages of this relatively short "archeology of the oath," Agamben moves from the writing of Catholicism and Kant to the writing of the rabbis. For Agamben, it is not in the history of myth, religion, or law that the power of the oath is discovered, but in the philological and philosophical context of language as The Name, on which these fundamental social institutions reside.

ב. But does the alphabet have to be about God? No. As postmodernists such as Derrida have argued, we are already written. This is not (just) metaphysical or mystical. We *are* written. This is especially true in our digital culture. We are now more rapidly becoming, and already exist as, media objects and letters, directed or drifting haplessly, colliding and reinvented via telepresence through networked streams of data, at home or on the job—another distinction that is disappearing (see Moses and Katz). This is not a superficial phenomenon or a passing fad, but a fundamental change in the human perception and experience of existence and consciousness, a leap into virtual being that will supplement or supplant evolution with a new theory of postevolution (see Hayles; Baudrillard; Ulmer). The opaque attributes of objects and letters both represent and embody epistemologies that lead not only to symbolic action in social reality but also to physical action in material reality. We have been manipulating the letters of the aleph-bet without fully realizing how social and physical realities are thereby altered as well (see, for example, Bennett; Latour, *Reassembling*; Morton). At the most elemental level, we are avatars, digital letters in virtual environments (see Ulmer).

ג. Are we merely imitations of reality, or do we constitute it? In my midrash, which is the story of the West, the Aleph—with its physical textuality and hermeneutic ambiguity—has no standing, while the Alpha—with its visual transparency and clarity of focus—has full ontological status. But the Alpha has no ethical basis other than its function as reference, which results in such communication values as accuracy, clarity, brevity, and maybe sincerity. The Aleph, on the other hand, is full of ethicity, since its values are internal and dependent on shapes, sizes, and orders of letters—which (like the Aleph's values) are ultimately rooted in a love and reverence for language. History is written by the alphabet that wins. Who gets to write history gets to be history. Clearly, our history belongs to the Alpha. But....

ז. Can the aleph-bet help us? Beginning with the Bible, it is well documented that the aleph-bet has been the focal point of Jewish life and has helped the Jewish people survive for millennia. But the rhetoric of the aleph-bet may provide an alternate ethical framework that offsets technological tendencies in a postinformation age, tendencies that (en)frame us, as Heidegger might say, in increasingly realized technological conceptions of the human body, conceptions of ourselves as digital, virtual, and post-posthuman. Unless we consider data themselves as a language sufficient to constitute us, to constitute flesh (the way Jean-Luc Nancy seems to want); unless we want to think of rhetoric as procedural code and phenomenology (Bogost, *Alien*) of being as only about objects (which Nancy doesn't), we may need *baraita*—either the rabbis' or someone else's, like Ulmer's—to help us interpret our new electrabet.

ח. How are the hermeneutical principles of the aleph-bet different from the philosophies of today? We currently hold a middle ground between Platonic and sophistic views of language in relation to reality and knowledge. We think names are just matters of political correctness, yet we grade papers and exams as if writing were the essence of thinking—or at least an accurate reflection (imitation) of it. (And the results of our interpretation have real, physical consequences in the students' lives.) Latour's brand of OOP (see, for example, *Reassembling*) is more closely aligned with social and epistemic rhetoric, whereas other strains of OOP move toward a metaphysical empiricism (see Bryant). A problem in OOP may not be a lack of morals, but, more precisely, the fact that the morals are packed away and hidden inside the black box of the object, which is then ideologically and ethically considered a transparent, *object*ive fact. In Judaism, especially mysticism, the letters are opaque and overflowing with moral wisdom and mystery; they are to be interpreted endlessly as a way of life. Literally: the black boxes are *tefillin*, containing the scrolled prayers of the *Shema* that declare the unity and covenant between the name of G/d (the unknowable Object) and Israel (in its handwritten but highly conventionalized in shape and font size [see Katz, "Alphabet"]); and the *V'havata*, the commandments to wear this aleph-bet on our foreheads and to display them on the doorposts of our house and on our gates in the box of the *mezuzah*.

א. Can *baraita* allow us to get inside the black boxes of our Greek-born letters? We may be able to apply *middot* to open Latour's *Pandora's Hope* and pull out the assumptions of the O/objects by hermeneutically reading them and turning them back into texts. *Baraita* as sets of hermeneutic principles need to go beyond mere mimesis or referential logic to provide a counter-literate system that parallels what Foucault called Principles of Reversal, which not only allow us to recover the hidden assumptions, arguments, and metaphysics embedded in objects as alphabets, but also help us recover a fuller conception of the human or cybernetic body and its relationship to objects as actants or agents in closer physical and moral relations, rather than as actants in partial, mechanical relations (see Katz and Rhodes). In this sense, *baraita* might ethically underwrite object-oriented philosophies and rhetorics in a postinformation age.

ב. Using *Notarikon* ourselves, does the second O in OOP not only replace humanistic ontologies, but also wholly displace (hide) sanity, sanctity, and the sacred? Does OOP need to displace the human ethics of hermeneutics to advance as a philosophy? If the answer to the last question is yes, that is a huge ethical problem. But OOP is also orthographic. If OOP is regarded as a hermeneutics of letters (those letters being etymological, historical, philosophical, and aesthetic objects), *baraita* may represent an alternative approach to the mystical ontology of the alphabet underlying both literacy and electracy. If we recognize the black boxes as letters—and, just as important, the letters as black boxes, full of superstitions and assumptions to be arrived at, revealed, and played with, using *baraita*—we also may recognize that those boxes are arks containing the silent prayers of letters. In the *Tanach* (Old Testament), even G/d, it seems, needs hermeneutics to think, argue, and act ethically (see Metzger and Katz).

NOTE

1. *Baraita* literally means "outside." The *baraita* are, precisely, outside the Mishna but contained in the *Tofseta* (Supplement) that antecedes the *Gemara* of the Palestinian Talmud, and they "document the concern for the precise and detailed definition of a text" (Strack and Stemberger, 16).

BIBLIOGRAPHY

Agamben, Giorgio. *The Sacrament of Language: An Archeology of the Oath*. Translated by Adam Kotsko. Stanford, CA: Stanford University Press, 2010.
Aristotle. *On Rhetoric: A Theory of Civic Discourse*. Translated by George Kennedy. 2nd ed. New York: Oxford University Press, 2007.

Baudrillard, Jean. *The Ecstasy of Communication*. Translated by Bernard Schütze and Caroline Schütze. Edited by Sylvère Lotringer. Brooklyn, NY: Semiotext(e), 1988.

Benjamin, Walter. *The Work of Art in the Age of Its Technological Reproducibility and Other Writings on Media*. Translated by Edmund Jephcott et al. Edited by Michael W. Jennings, Brigid Doherty and Thomas Y. Levin. Cambridge, MA: Belknap Press of Harvard University Press, 2008.

Bennett, Jane. *Vibrant Matter: A Political Ecology of Things*. Durham, NC: Duke University Press, 2010.

Bogost, Ian. *Alien Phenomenology, or What It's Like to Be a Thing*. Minneapolis: University of Minnesota Press, 2012.

Boman, Thorleif. *Hebrew Thought Compared with Greek*. New York: Norton, 1960.

Boyarin, Daniel. *Intertextuality and the Reading of Midrash*. Bloomington: Indiana University Press, 1990.

———. *Socrates and the Fat Rabbis*. Chicago: University of Chicago Press, 2009.

Bryant, Levi R. *The Democracy of Objects*. Ann Arbor, MI: Open Humanities Press, 2011.

Burke, Kenneth. *A Grammar of Motives*. Berkeley: University of California Press, 1969.

Cornford, Francis MacDonald. *Before and after Socrates*. Cambridge: Cambridge University Press, 1960.

Dan, Joseph. *Jewish Mysticism: Late Antiquity*. Vol. 1. Northvale, NJ: Aronson, 1998.

Derrida, Jacques. *Of Grammatology*. Translated by Gayatri Chakravorty Spivak. Baltimore, MD: Johns Hopkins University Press, 1974.

Eco, Umberto. *Foucault's Pendulum*. Translated by William Weaver. New York: Ballantine, 1990.

Foucault, Michel. "The Discourse on Language." In Michel Foucault, *The Archaeology of Knowledge and the Discourse on Language*, translated by A. M. Sheridan Smith, 215–37. New York: Pantheon, 1972.

Handelman, Susan A. *Slayers of Moses: The Emergence of Rabbinic Interpretation in Modern Literary Theory*. Albany: State University of New York Press, 1982.

Harman, Graham. *Towards Speculative Realism: Essays and Lectures*. Winchester, UK: Zero-Hunt, 2010.

Havelock, Eric A. *The Muse Learns to Write: Reflections on Orality and Literacy from Antiquity to the Present*. Binghamton, NY: Ballou, 1986.

Hayles, N. Katherine. *How We Became Posthuman: Virtual Bodies in Cybernetics, Literature, and Informatics*. Chicago: University of Chicago Press, 1999.

Heidegger, Martin. *The Question Concerning Technology and Other Essays*. Translated by William Lovitt. New York: Harper, 1977.

Kaplan, Aryeh. *Sefer Yetzirah: The Book of Creation*. San Francisco: Weiser, 1997.

Katz, Steven B. "The Alphabet as Ethics: A Rhetorical Basis for Moral Reality in Hebrew Letters." In *Rhetorical Democracy: Discursive Practices of Civic Engagement*, edited by Gerald Hauser and Amy Grimm, 195–204. Hillsdale, NJ: Lawrence Erlbaum Associates, 2004.

———. "The Epistemology of the Kabbalah: Toward a Jewish Philosophy of Rhetoric." *Rhetoric Society Quarterly* 25 (1995): 107–22.

———. "The Hebrew Bible as Another, Jewish Sophistic: A Genesis of Absence and Desire in Ancient Rhetoric." In *Ancient Non-Greek Rhetorics*, edited by Carol Lipson and Roberta Binkley, 125–50. Lafayette, IN: Parlor, 2009.

———. "Letter as Essence: The Rhetorical (Im)pulse of the Hebrew Alefbet." In "Jewish Rhetoric," edited by David A. Frank. Special issue, *Journal of Communication and Religion* 26, no. 2 (2003): 125–160.

Katz, Steven B., and Vicki W. Rhodes. "Beyond Ethical Frames of Technical Relations: Digital Being in the Workplace World." In *Digital Literacy for Technical Communication: 21st Century Theory and Practice*, edited by Rachel Spilka, 230–56. London: Routledge, 2010.

Latour, Bruno. *Pandora's Hope: Essays on the Reality of Science Studies*. Cambridge, MA: Harvard University Press, 1999.

———. *Reassembling the Social: An Introduction to Actor-Network-Theory*. Oxford: Oxford University Press, 2007.

Metzger, David, and Steven B. Katz. "The 'Place' of Rhetoric in Aggadic Midrash." Special issue, *College English* 72, no. 6 (2010): 638–53.

Morton, Timothy B. *Ecology without Nature: Rethinking Environmental Aesthetics*. Cambridge, MA: Harvard University Press, 2009.

Moses, Myra, and Steven B. Katz. "The Phantom Machine: The Invisible Ideology of Email (A Cultural Critique)." In *Critical Power Tools: Technical Communication and Cultural Studies*, edited by J. Blake Scott, Bernadette Longo, and Katherine V. Willis, 71–105. Albany: State University of New York Press, 2006.

Moskow, Michal Anne, and Steven B. Katz. "Composing Identity in Cyberspace: A 'Rhetorical Ethnography' of Writing on Jewish Discussion Lists in Germany and the United States." In *Judaic Perspectives on Composition*, edited by Andrea Greenbaum and Deborah H. Holdstein, 85–109. Creskill, NJ: Hampton, 2008.

Munk, Michael L. *The Wisdom in the Hebrew Alphabet: The Sacred Letters as a Guide to Jewish Deed and Thought*. New York: Mesorah, 1983.

Nancy, Jean-Luc. "Corpus." In Jean-Luc Nancy, *Corpus*, translated by Richard A. Rand, 1–121. New York: Fordham University Press, 2008.

Ong, Walter J. *Orality and Literacy: The Technologizing of the Word*. New York: Methuen, 1982.

Plato. "The Cratylus." Translated by Benjamin Jowett. In *Plato: The Collected Dialogues*, edited by Edith Hamilton and Huntington Cairns, 421–74. Princeton, NJ: Princeton University Press, 1961.

———. "Socrates' Defense (Apology)." Translated by Hugh Tredennick. In *Plato: The Collected Dialogues*, edited by Edith Hamilton and Huntington Cairns, 3–26. Princeton, NJ: Princeton University Press, 1961.

Scholem, Gershom. *Major Trends in Jewish Mysticism*. New York: Schocken, 1974.

Simon, Herbert. *The Sciences of the Artificial*. 2nd ed. Cambridge, MA: MIT Press, 1982.

Stone, I. F. *The Trial of Socrates*. New York: Anchor, 1989.

Strack, Herman L. *Introduction to the Talmud and Midrash*. New York: Atheneum, 1976.

Strack, Herman L., and Günter Stemberger. *Introduction to the Talmud and Midrash*. Translated by Markus Bockmuehl. Minneapolis, MN: Fortress, 1996.

Ulmer, Gregory L. *Avatar Emergency*. Anderson, IN: Parlor, 2012.

Weaver, Richard M. *Language Is Sermonic*. Edited by Richard L. Johannesen, Ralph T. Eubanks, and Rennard Strickland. Baton Rouge: Louisiana State University Press, 1985.

The Zohar. Translated by Harry Sperling and Maurice Simon. Vol 1. New York: Soncino, 1984.

7

Maimonides's Contribution to a Theory of Self-Persuasion

DAVID METZGER

The Case for Internal Rhetoric

As Jean Niencamp has pointed out in her provocative study, *Internal Rhetorics*, we have learned to think of persuasion as something that we do to others or that others do to us. By means of language, someone prompts another person to adopt a particular course of action or a particular opinion, whether for good or ill. The conventional rhetorical story is scripted as follows: there is a rhetor who speaks or writes, and there is an audience who listens or reads. There is also a text: a particular use of language that negotiates the potential conflicts between the rhetor's desires and the audience's inclinations.

Introducing the possibility of some such thing as self-persuasion does not dismiss the hermeneutical promise of this common-sensical understanding of rhetoric, nor does it question rhetorical research's focus on the civic dimensions of language use (persuasion, communication, and teaching). However, an examination of self-persuasion may put us in a position to develop further the predictive and descriptive powers of our rhetorical models by focusing our attention on the active role that an audience or a listener may play in being persuaded. Indeed, the concept of self-persuasion may even have implications for the study of rhetoric, inasmuch as it challenges us to make more explicit the often-unexpressed interdependence of rhetoric, ethics, and psychology.

For the time being, let us define "internal rhetoric" as the means by which individuals discourse with themselves: the ways that we persuade, communicate, and teach ourselves. Niencamp's work has already provided us with a historical survey of internal rhetorics that conform to this definition. After discussing the Greeks (principally Homer, Isocrates, and Plato), she moves on to Bacon, Shaftesbury, and Smith. She ends her survey with the modern period, where she finds contributions to a theory of internal rhetoric in the work of Kenneth Burke, Chaïm Perelman, Lucie Olbrechts-Tyteca, and George Herbert Mead, among others.

One of the strengths of Niencamp's historical narrative is that it allows her to develop a theory of self-persuasion in conversation with people whose work has already been identified with the development of rhetorical thinking in the Western European tradition. Her historical narrative thereby addresses the concern that the conceptualization of internal rhetoric may reflect only the concerns of a limited and highly specialized group of scholars. Niencamp's thematization of internal rhetoric also invites us to consider others whose work might be understood to contribute to this ongoing discussion. She does so by asking us also to consider three common themes that emerge from her historical survey: the association of intellection with speech; the development of a self comprised of multiple intellectual or perceptual agencies (most clearly identified with the field called faculty psychology; and the identification or use of internal rhetoric to describe the discursive (persuasive, pedagogical, and communicative) dimensions of moral agents as well as the construction of moral agency.

From just this snapshot of internal rhetoric, it may be possible to suggest that Maimonides (Rabbi Moshe ben Maimon, or the Rambam) may be a participant in an ongoing conversation on the subject of internal rhetoric. Over the course of this essay, we will see Niencamp's thematization of internal rhetoric surface in the Rambam's writing. We will also see how the sharp demarcation between internal and external rhetorics becomes more and more problematic as we chart how the rhetorical dimensions of his ethics and the ethical dimensions of his rhetoric unfold.

Born in Cordoba, Spain, Maimonides (1135–1204) spent most of his life in Egypt, where he was a leader of the Jewish community as well as one of the physicians appointed to the court of Saladin's son, al-Afdal.[1] The product of both a traditional Jewish education and the neoclassical revival in Arabic secular education, Maimonides has understandably become known for the reconciliation or negotiation of Jewish tradition with classical philosophy and thought that is evinced in his *Moreh Nevukhim* (Guide for the perplexed), as well as his multivolume *Mishneh Torah*, a monumental reconstruction of halacha (Jewish law).

Even before moving to Egypt in 1165, Maimonides's study of classical philosophy was evinced in a short treatise on logic, based—some scholars suspect—on Al-Farabi's commentaries and paraphrases of Plato and Aristotle. It is also important to mention this short compendium on logic because it provides us with a sense of how rhetoric figured in the Rambam's secular Arabic education—an understanding of rhetoric that, as we will see, is compatible with our working definition of "internal rhetoric." As is well-attested in medieval Arabic philosophical literature, rhetoric was understood to be part of the Aristotelian *Organon*: rhetoric was one of the divisions of knowledge arranged under the heading of "logic."[2] The medieval expansion of the *Organon* to include rhetoric (and poetics) is itself a subject worthy of consideration. Here, however, we will consider how Maimonides—in a short passage from chapter 14 of his "Treatise on the Art of Logic"—makes a move that is essential for the theorization of an internal rhetoric. In this passage, he associates intellection with speech:

> According to the technical usage of the ancient learned men of past communities, "logic" is an equivocal term having three meanings. The first is the power peculiar to and by which he intellectually apprehends the intelligibles, masters the arts, and distinguishes between the base and the noble. The learned call this meaning the rational [*natiq*, speaking] power. The second meaning is the intelligible itself which man has intellectually apprehended. They call this meaning "internal reason" [*al-nutq al-dakhil*, inner speech]. The third meaning is the expression in language of the notions impressed upon the soul. They call this meaning "external reason" [*al-nutq al-kharij*]. ("Treatise on the Art of Logic," 158)

Without the association of intellection and speech, our discussion of internal rhetoric would be simply an assertion of the constructed nature of thought. Rhetoric, in these terms, would be better understood as the rhetoricality of all human activities, including thought, where, in the words of John Bender and David Wellberry, rhetoricality "manifests the groundless, infinitely ramifying characteristics of discourse in the modern world . . . allowing for no explanatory metadiscourse that is not already itself rhetorical" (quoted in Niencamp, 3). But this is not what the Rambam asserts in the passage above. Rather, we find the elaboration of intellection and speech in terms of three specific activities: the ability to learn and use an art or technique to produce an object, the recognition or registration of something as an object of thought (an intelligible), and the ability to communicate what is recognized as an object of thought. In addition, we find a division between internal speech and external speech, with external speech bridging the gap between what the soul experiences and what it expresses. In the next section of our discussion, we will see how the concept of an internal rhetoric, for the Rambam, also involves the association of rhetoric and morality, understood here as the ability to discern what is base and what is noble.

Maimonides's Rhetoric and the Possibility of Self-Persuasion

In the fifth chapter of his magisterial *Introduction to the Code of Maimonides*, Isidore Twersky provides us with a brief but insightful treatment of Maimonides's rhetoric.[3] As we would expect from the title of this chapter ("Language and Style"), Twersky provides a short but carefully considered treatment of Maimonides's theory of language, after which he identifies certain stylistic choices, norms, and ideals of the Rambam. Unexpectedly, one finds that style increasingly acquires a certain moral and evidentiary weight as Twersky's discussion develops:

> Brevity for Maimonides is not only a sign of wisdom but also a sign of divine origin. A salient feature of the Mishnah which he extols, and which contributed to its authoritativeness, is its terseness. Beyond these formal-structural reasons, brevity is also a pedagogic device: it leads to clarity and precision. Brevity, like oral transmission, eliminates or minimizes confusion; a pointed and unencumbered statement is a rather safe antidote to erroneous and undisciplined interpretation. Any superfluity should be avoided; self-evident or widespread items should not be repeated; excessive speech is wasteful, if not sinful. (*Introduction*, 337)

Twersky then develops this insight regarding brevity's moral depth into a general program for further examination of Maimonides's rhetoric, as well as a short catalogue of the kinds of discursive or textual data that Maimonides's texts—in this case, his *Mishneh Torah*—make available for rhetorical study:

> The use of rhetorical strategies—in general, the relation of *brevitas* to *amplificatio*—needs to be scrutinized. We must seek special reasons, and in fact we are readily able to identify certain categories—emphasis, polemical needs, particularly confrontation with entrenched authority or rejection of an erroneous, even heretical view, reflective-persuasive communication, ethical-philosophical flourishes, innovations, anticipatory avoidance of misunderstandings—which account for the spasmodic intrusion of lengthiness and sometimes repetitiousness in the otherwise uniformly crisp and concise construction. (*Introduction*, 339)

Twersky's "rhetorical strategies" clearly share a concern with "external rhetorics"—the rhetoric of the one communicating, persuading, or teaching the many or some other one. But there is an important exception to this rule: "reflective-persuasive communication." Although Twersky does not delineate the relationships among reflection, persuasion, and communication, he does identify something like our area of concern.[4] Granted, it is not clear if the phrase "reflective-persuasive communication" means that reflection can be understood as a form of persuasion; "reflective-persuasion" might, in this instance, refer to language use that persuades us to reflect, without also meaning that reflection is a self-persuasive act. The problem here is not whether we think in language or not. After all, faculty psychologies often create an internal rhetorical scene in which reason, passion, and imagination "duke it out" or have a dialogue without making such an assumption.[5] The problem involved in identifying an internal rhetoric is to determine to what extent the metaphors we use for thinking (for example, "thinking is an internal dialogue") are themselves the tools that enable us to reflect, to think about thinking. Perhaps reflection is not persuasion. Nonetheless, to what extent does our ability to think and to learn depend on our speaking about reflection as a type of self-persuasion?

This question—which I identify as an area of concern for internal rhetoric—is particularly important where Maimonides's ethics is concerned, since the Rambam is not merely concerned with providing a typology of ethical subjects and the particular goods that these ethical subjects choose to pursue. He is also interested in helping individuals make better choices, which may also include helping these individuals understand that they have, in fact, chosen to pursue the good according to their capacity for understanding it.[6] This is not to say that everyone fully actualizes her or his capacity for understanding the good.[7] Rather, the very promise that individuals can change their behavior, produce new behaviors, or more fully actualize their ethical capacities by way of their behaviors involves the development of a model or metaphor that helps individuals see the choices that are available to them. The power of this model or metaphor might then be measured in terms of its internally persuasive power: how it helps individuals seek, accept, understand, and heed advice from others and how it helps individuals test the advice that they give themselves.

Self-Persuasion and Self-Deception: The Negative Dimensions of Internal Rhetoric

Within the conceptual framework of internal rhetoric, my intent is to examine Maimonides's use of medicine as a metaphor for a moral therapeutic in

"Hilḥot Deot" (The laws of character traits). "Hilḥot Deot" appears in the first book (*Sefer HaMadah* [The book of knowledge]) of Maimonides's *Mishneh Torah*, a monumental reconstruction or reorganization of halacha.[8] As we will see, medical metaphors appear in Maimonides's *Shemoneh Prakim* and his *Moreh Nevukhim* (Guide for the perplexed). But in "Hilḥot Deot," this metaphor cannot be understood simply as a way of engaging the obligatory force of reason, as we see—for example—in Aristotle. We may indeed find that the Rambam believes that metaphor is one of the tools by which a rhetor may engage reason and its dictates, but we cannot forget that reason itself may be a tool used by a covenantal community to explore its obligations to the deity. That is, reason may be both a tool and a trap where the construction of divine or moral sciences is concerned. This is not to deny that there is a "rationalist" thrust in Maimonides's work.[9] Rather, the trap of reason is our failure to understand that there are limits to what human beings can know.

One of Maimonides's more explicit identifications of self-persuasion is couched in just such a cautionary tale, in chapter 32 of *Moreh Nevukhim*:

> If you admit the doubt, and do not persuade yourself to believe that there is a proof for things which cannot be demonstrated, or to try at once to reject and positively to deny an assertion the opposite of which has never been proved, or positively to deny an assertion the opposite of which has never been proved, or attempt to perceive things which are beyond your perception, then you have attained the highest degree of human perfection, then you are like "R. Akiva, who 'in peace entered [the study of these theological problems], and came out in peace.' If on the other hand, you attempt to exceed the limits of your intellectual power, or at once to reject things as impossible which have never been proved to be impossible, or which are in fact possible, though their possibility be very remote, then you will be like Elisha Acher; you will not only fail to become perfect, but you will become exceedingly imperfect. Ideas founded on mere imagination will prevail over you, you will incline toward defects, and toward base and degraded habits, on account of the confusion which troubles the mind, and of the dimness of its light, just as weakness of sight causes invalids to see many kinds of unreal images, especially when they have looked for a long time at dazzling or at very minute objects." (*Moreh Nevukhim*, trans. Friedlander, chapter 32, 42–43)

Again, we note that the concept of self-persuasion is not wholly alien to the Rambam's thinking.[10] Deceiving oneself is the beginning of an extended series of intellectual actions that ends with imaginings overcoming the subject's intellect. Here, self-persuasion seems to be limited to those instances when we have been thinking incorrectly. Knowing the limitations of human apprehension limits the negative effects of self-deception or self-persuasion. If we are thinking correctly—understanding the limits of what can be or has been demonstrated as well as what human beings can know through demonstration—then we have not persuaded or deceived ourselves so much as we have developed a chart of external reality that is as accurate as is humanly possible. We might well ask why someone would choose to deceive himself or herself into thinking that a proposition has been demonstrated when, in fact, it has not been. Maimonides identifies a common source for our engagement with truth and error: the desire to apprehend. Error occurs when, prompted by the desire to know, we jump over the fence of what humans can know. The result is not only that we imagine what is not the case to be true, but also that we begin to desire what is not the case.

This is reminiscent of Aristotle's treatment of rhetoric, in which the enthymeme (a shortened form of the syllogism) is used to convey the truth value of a particular deduction even when the audience is unable to understand the demonstration leading to that conclusion. But there is an important difference between Maimonides and Aristotle. Aristotle is limiting himself to the field of external communication. His (external) rhetor is attempting to communicate a demonstrable truth to an audience that is incapable of following the demonstration of that truth. Ideally, Aristotle's rhetor is someone who understands the demonstration and who is capable of communicating its truth in a semilogical form. In the passage above from *Moreh Nevukhim*, Maimonides's internal rhetor is trying to understand something that is beyond the human capacity for knowledge or demonstration. And she or he can do so only by means of an act of self-deception. Since the rhetor's or thinker's inaccurate chart of the world exists only in the rhetor's own mind, Maimonides might be said to limit himself to the field of internal rhetoric in this instance. In fact, he distinguishes between Rabbi Akiva and Elisha Acher in terms of the dominance of one of two intellectual faculties. Whereas Akiva's chart of the world and his understanding of G/d are associated with the rational faculty, the imaginative faculty dominates the movement of Elisha Acher's thoughts beyond what can be apprehended. Both Maimonides and Aristotle accept that the goal of human knowledge making is that the truth value of a statement should exist both inside and outside an individual's thinking. However, Aristotle concerns himself with the problem of how to get the truth inside. At least in this instance, Maimonides is concerned instead with how to get some degree of the falsity out.

But before jumping to the conclusion that Maimonides provides us with the internal counterpart to Aristotle's external rhetoric, we must consider another important difference between these two thinkers. In his discussion of rhetoric in *On Rhetoric*, Aristotle limits himself to those instances in which it is impossible for a given individual or audience to understand something that is possible for others to know (1357a). For Aristotle, rhetoric bridges the gaps between varying intellectual powers. In the discussion of self-persuasion noted above, Maimonides limits himself to those instances in which an individual has attempted to move beyond the limits of human knowledge, treating what is impossible for anyone to know as if it were something that she or he could possibly know. Maimonides associates self-persuasion with the act of deceiving oneself. For him, an internal rhetoric would bridge differences of opinions by identifying them as either differences associated with our varied intellectual abilities or differences associated with our varied acceptance or recognition of the intellectual limitations that all human beings share. In other words, for Maimonides self-persuasion and internal rhetoric are not interchangeable terms because an internal rhetoric would promise to assist those whose self-persuasion has led them astray and made them morally sick.

Self-Persuasion and the Medical Metaphor in "Hilḥot Deot"

Having agreed that the conceptual category "self-persuasion" might be applied to Maimonides's work without fear of committing an act of scholarly violence, how are we to study this so-called self-persuasion? My approach will be to examine a metaphor that Maimonides may have introduced into his work as a tool for moral reflection: just as there are physical illnesses, so there are moral or spiritual illnesses. We will take note of how this metaphor is identified with actions whose qualities might be identified more or less reliably for an individual self (a self privy to its own reflections). And we will consider the explanatory limitations of this metaphor inasmuch as metaphor is treated here as a tool for reflection and not as reflection itself.[11] This approach to the study of metaphor is elaborated by Werner Jaeger in his essay "Aristotle's Use of Medicine as Model of Method in His Ethics." Following Aristotle, Jaeger treats metaphor as a way of making apparent (*phanera*) to the eye of analysis what is hidden (*aphane*) from the senses or the deliberations we base principally on the evidence of the senses (57). However, if

Jaeger's reading of Aristotle is correct, it would appear that Maimonides is less concerned with identifying the epistemological features of ethics as a body of knowledge (like medicine) than he is with introducing this metaphor as a self-persuasive or reflective tool that enables an individual to gauge and correct her behavior herself or for an individual to seek and accept the advice that others might offer with regard to his behavior.[12]

With these suppositions in mind, let us now turn to the metaphor of medicine introduced in chapter 2 of "Hilḥot Deot":

> To those who are physically sick, the bitter tastes sweet and the sweet bitter. Some of the sick even desire and crave that which is not fit to eat, such as earth and charcoal, and hate healthful foods, such as bread and meat—all depending on how serious the sickness is. Similarly, those who are morally ill desire and love bad traits, hate the good path, and are [too] lazy to follow it. Depending on how sick they are, they find it exceedingly burdensome. Isaiah [5:20] speaks of such people in a like manner: "Woe to those who call the bad good, and the good bad, who take darkness to be light and light to be darkness, who take bitter to be sweet and sweet to be bitter." Concerning them [Proverbs 2:13] states: "Those who leave the upright paths to walk in the ways of darkness." (Maimonides, *Mishneh Torah*, vol. 2, Halacha 2.1, 30–32)

The Rambam's discussion of physical illness is developed in two stages: illnesses of the body can confuse our perceptions (the bitter tastes sweet, and the sweet bitter); and illnesses of the body can lead us to desire what is not properly food (dirt, for example). Not surprisingly, we see a similar development in his discussion of spiritual illness, even though the order of the exposition is reversed. Whereas his discussion of physical illness begins with misperception followed by desire, his discussion of spiritual illness begins with desire ("those who ... desire and love bad traits"), followed by misperception ("Woe to those who call the bad good"). It is important to note this reversal, since it may underscore an important difference between physical and spiritual illnesses. In Maimonides's discussion of physical illnesses, it seems as if misperception leads to improper desire; in other words, "that which is not fit to eat" tastes good to the sick person, so the sick person desires to eat it. This relationship between misperception and desire may also be true of spiritual illnesses, but that remains to be seen.

In our discussion of a passage from chapter 32 of *Moreh Nevukhim*, we saw that the desire to apprehend what human beings are incapable of knowing prompted certain individuals into self-persuasion (or misperception). Do we see a similar construction in Maimonides's discussion of the morally ill? If so, then the notion of an internal rhetoric (with all its promise to correct individual misperceptions) could very well be confused with what activities that some would more comfortably understand to be ethics.

Concerning the morally ill, we are told that if they are spiritually sick, finding the good will be difficult. It is true that Maimonides introduces the phrases "the good path" (*haderech hatovah*) and "lazy to follow it" (*umitalatslim lalechet bah*) at this point in his discussion of spiritual illness. And we are told that the spiritually ill desire and love bad traits. For this reason, the spiritually ill are not motivated to follow the good way (the ways of the good); indeed, they are discouraged from following the good way because they find doing so to be onerous (heavy). The metaphor seems to be quite transparent: physical illness is related to spiritual illness; that which is not properly food is related to bad traits; good food is related to the good way. But it is not clear whether the relationship between misperception and desire with regard to physical illness is the same, or merely similar to, the relationship between desire and misperception where spiritual illness is concerned.

The difficulty here is not simply a matter of identifying the source of good and bad traits. In "Hilḥot Deot" the Rambam provides us with that information. There are traits that are possessed from birth and traits that are not possessed from birth. Of those possessed from birth, there are those that are acquired as actualities and those acquired as potentialities. Of those that are not possessed from birth, there are those one has learned from others and those one has learned on one's own. Of those one has learned on one's own, there are those that come from one's own thoughts and those that one has heard would be proper for one (but not just anyone) to have.

The difficulty illustrated here may be that it is imperative for the morally ill to make a distinction between desire and misperception when that distinction is supported only in those instances where one is seeking a cure for oneself or for another. The mean, from the standpoint of an internal rhetoric, is a diagnostic tool available to ourselves and to those whom we have enlisted to help us. If we extend our discussions of the cures for moral illness outside of the domain of a moral therapeutic, then we understandably run into certain difficulties or misperceptions regarding the exceptions to the rules of the mean that Maimonides identifies himself. Lawrence Kaplan makes a similar point with regard to the *Shemoneh Prakim*:

> But if "the commandments of the Torah are, in fact" *not* "the specification of the ideal behavior in accordance with the mean," what then, is their function in EC 4 [*Shemoneh Prakim*, chapter 4]? In order to answer this question, we must look at the title of the chapter: "On Medical Treatment for the Diseases of the Soul." That is, though EC 4 begins by defining both the good actions and the virtues in terms of the mean, the bulk of the chapter is concerned with the justified deviations from the mean as a mode of "medical treatment for the diseases of the soul. And it is in this connection that Maimonides very carefully and skilfully [*sic*]" introduces his explanation of why "the Law forbids what it forbids and commands what it commands." But it should be emphasized . . . that these deviations from the mean are always in service of attaining the mean, which never loses the function allotted to it at the chapter's beginning as the defining criterion for both the good actions and the virtues. (8)

In other words, the very difficulty or need that one might have in determining whether desire or misperceptions cause moral illnesses, this may itself be a symptom or sign that one is morally ill.

Support for this reading appears in *Moreh Nevukhim*, where the Rambam also uses the metaphor of eating to develop his discussion of the limits of human knowledge. We must note that the following discussion of the metaphor of eating appears in the same chapter of *Moreh Nevukhim* where the idea of self-persuasion or self-deception appears:

> How marvelous is this parable, inasmuch as it likens knowledge to eating, a meaning about which we have spoken. It also mentions the most delicious of foods, namely, honey. Now, according to its nature, honey, if eaten to excess, upsets the stomach and causes vomiting. Accordingly Scripture says, as it were, that in spite of its sublimity, greatness, and what it has of perfection, the nature of apprehension in question—if not made to stop at its proper limit and not conducted with circumspection—may be perverted into a defect, just as the eating of honey may. For whereas the individual eating in moderation is nourished and takes pleasure in it, it all goes if there is too much of it. . . . This means that you should let your intellect move about only within the domain of things that man is able to grasp. For in regard to matters that it is not in the nature of man to grasp, it is, as we have made clear, very harmful to occupy oneself with them. (Maimonides, *Moreh Nevukhim*, trans Pines, vol. 1, chapter 32, 69–70)

In "Hilhot Deot" the emphasis is placed on those who desire what is inappropriate because, even though it is bitter, it tastes sweet to them; these individuals will pursue the good because, once they have been accustomed to it, the good will be pleasurable to them. In *Moreh Nevukhim*, the emphasis is placed on those who pursue the good (eat the honey) beyond what it is possible for human subjects to acquire (eat). The spiritual problem, as *Moreh Nevukhim* frames it, is not that individuals have misapprehended the good (honey is, after all, good), but that—prompted by their desire for the good—certain individuals have sought to apprehend (and they believe they have apprehended) what it is impossible for human beings to know. In other words, the desire for the good is the trigger for spiritual illness—hence the differing and perhaps even counterintuitive roles of misperception (as cause of desire in physical illnesses) and desire (as cause of misperception in spiritual illnesses) that we noted in *Mishneh Torah* above. Although the physically ill desire what they misperceive to be good in *Mishneh Torah*, the spiritually ill misperceive the good because of their desire for it in *Moreh Nevukhim*.

The Mean as a Treatment for the Morally Ill

We are now in a position to understand something about Maimonides's notion of the treatment for both physical and spiritual illnesses. Our question is: if the distinction between physical and spiritual illnesses is as sharp as has been suggested above, how can we account for the fact that Maimonides looks to the mean and to the *mitzvot* as therapeutic tools?

We have already noted the identification of the mean with the treatment for both physical and spiritual illnesses in a passage from *Shemoneh Prakim*: "So, just as when the equilibrium of the physical health is disturbed and we note which way it is tending in order to force it to go in exactly the opposite direction until it shall return to its proper condition, and just as when the proper adjustment is reached we cease this operation and have recourse to that which will maintain the proper balance, in exactly the same way must we adjust the moral equilibrium" (Twersky, *A Maimonides Reader*, 369). The key to understanding the mean as a treatment for spiritual illness is also provided in "Hilḥot Deot": "Since the Creator is called [*nikrat*] by these terms and they make up the middle path which we are obligated to follow, this path is called 'the path of God' [*Derech HaShem*]" (Maimonides, *Shemoneh Prakim*, vol. 1, Halachah 1.7, 30). This is not to say that whatever characteristics we identify as the middle points of character are, in fact, accurate characterizations of the deity. Rather, the prophets associated these characteristics with the deity in order to persuade individuals that these middle points of character are actualizations of the good to which a human being might aspire. Using the language of *Moreh Nevukhim*, we might say that the prophets identify the development of positive character traits with the desire to know the attributes of the deity. If the boundaries of human comprehension are not overrun by the imagination, this desire to have knowledge of the deity also serves as a guide for distinguishing between misperception and perception. Using the language of the *Mishneh Torah*, the Rambam asks how a person might accustom himself or herself (*yargil adam atzmo*) to these character traits. The task of acquiring these traits would, I believe, fall under the heading of internal rhetoric because this task is one way to correct a moral ill both at the level of misperception and at the level of desire. At the level of misperception, we accustom ourselves to these traits by performing actions that "conform to the standards of the middle road temperaments" (*vishalesh bamaasim sheoseh al-pi hadeot haemtsaiyot* [*Mishneh Torah*, vol. 2, Halacha 1.7, 28]). And the test for success with regard to moral matters seems to be a matter in which the authority of the self would be privileged: "He should do this constantly, until these acts are easy for him and do not present any difficulty" (*ad sheyihyu maasehem kalim alav, ve lo yiheye vahem torach alav* [ibid., 1.7, 30]). Others may also have an opinion with regard to the actions that we perform, but it would be difficult—if not impossible—for others to gauge the ease with which these actions are performed. Inasmuch as the one who misperceives is also the one who administers the test of success, is it possible that a person might misperceive (persuade herself or himself) that an action is easy, presenting no difficulties? This is certainly a possibility if it is also possible for us or for the person so affected to identify a desire responsible for such a misperception. But if the desire is to do good or to know the good through one's own actions, our feelings with regard to the ease with which we perform actions must also meet a standard that is not wholly within the province of an individual self (namely, the mean or the middle road). The mean is both the aim and the content of prophetic speech (the middle path is the path of God). The mean also functions as a purposeful limit to what we might want to say about our obligations to the deity and what we may wish to know or say about the deity. The mean—associated with the Law, as seen above—gets in the way of our desire to know more than we can, which could easily prompt our imaginings rather than our reason without enacting the Law's noble purpose. The Rambam does lay out the varied landscape for an internal rhetoric, following Niencamp's definition, given in fuller form above: the association of intellection with speech; the development of a self comprised of multiple intellectual or perceptual agencies; and the identification or use of internal rhetoric to describe the discursive dimensions of moral agents as well as the construction of moral agency. But Maimonides does so without pushing for an internal rhetoric at the expense of an external one. After all, when the prophets assigned certain traits to the deity, they did so in order to encourage us to perform actions that would foster the development of these traits. And those who have identified the presence of bad traits in themselves are told to seek outside help: "What is the remedy for the morally ill? They should go to the wise, for they are the healers of souls. They will heal them by teaching them traits, until they return them to the good path" (*Mishneh Torah*, vol. 2, Halachah 2. 1, 32). Yet our attention to external rhetoric should not cause us to omit all consideration of internal rhetoric. For example, we find the following with regard to anger: "Anger is also an exceptionally bad quality. It is fitting and proper that one move away from it and adopt the opposite extreme. He should school himself [*vilamed atsmo*] not to become angry even when it is fitting to be angry" (ibid., vol. 2, part 3, 38). In fact, we have been commanded to do so: "They [the early sages] have directed that one distance himself from anger and accustom himself [*atsmo*] not to feel any reaction, even to things which provoke anger" (ibid., vol. 2, part 3, 40). This prohibition against anger has been the subject of much discussion, since it is one of the exceptions to the rule of the mean (the middle road is good) that Maimonides notes. One might rather glibly suggest that, since both the *mitzvot* and the mean are tools used to effect moral development, a person should use each only to the point at which it produces some good. But the issue is much more complex, even if one does not immediately recoil from the suggestion that one might or should ignore a commandment when it is no longer useful. One would need to identify the party, the person, the intellectual faculty, or the authority capable of making such a determination. In fact, the arguments regarding whether Maimonides had a use for Aristotle's notion of *phronesis* might be contextualized in this regard. For Aristotle, *phronesis* is the ability to discern the middle point in all of its varied, particular, and highly contextualized forms, and the mean is a philosophical tool for describing and predicting our exercise of that ability. For Maimonides, the mean is a tool we can use to test our understanding of the relationship between the external and internal dimensions of human experience (the relationship between external actions and moral traits), and—as such—it represents one of the basic building blocks for an internal rhetoric: it is a test for the quality of our misperceptions. We can see this distinction between Aristotle and Maimonides in the latter's discussion of anger, which departs considerably from Aristotle's. Students of rhetoric will recall Aristotle's discussion of anger in book II of *On Rhetoric* (1378b). There, anger is treated as one of the emotional appeals. If one wishes to convince an audience to accept a particular course of action, it is possible to do so by associating the proposed course of action with the audience's future relief from anger. Anger is understood to be a negative emotion, an emotion that causes pain in those who experience it. The positive emotion associated with anger is revenge, positive in the sense that it produces pleasure. According to Aristotle, those experiencing anger may accept a proposed course of action if they perceive that action as revenge (which the angry experience as pleasure). I would associate Aristotle's treatment of anger with external rhetoric, since he restricts his discussion to the use of anger as a way of effecting change in others. Maimonides's treatment of anger is also concerned with affecting the behavior of others:

> If one should wish to arouse fear in his children and household—or within the community, if he is a communal leader—and wishes to be angry at them to motivate them to return to the proper path [*lemutav*], he should present an angry front to them to punish them, but he should be inwardly calm. He should be like one who acts out the part of an angry man in his wrath, but is not himself angry. (*Mishneh Torah*, vol. 2, Halachah 2.3, 38–41)

Notice that Maimonides does not suggest the audience will identify itself with the authority figure and be angry too; the goal is not to persuade the audience by providing it with the pleasure of revenge. Indeed, the audience is motivated to return to the good by suffering the displeasure of the authority figure. We might say that the authority figure's anger puts a face on some wrong that the community has committed, a wrong that might otherwise be disguised—by rationalization, misperception, or desire—as something else. In short, the authority figure's anger allows the audience to recognize its wrong(s) as such, especially if the audience does not assume it has special knowledge of the authority figure's internal state. External rhetoric assumes here a therapeutic dimension that, for the most part, is assumed to be the province of the internal rhetor, inasmuch as the audience's obligatory response involves its choice of an affective response. And internal rhetoric must, if Maimonides can be said to anticipate that a community or an individual might choose to be angry with the rhetor rather than fearful or shamed by the rhetor's angry display. We can catch a glimpse of the dynamic relationship between internal and external rhetorics presented here if we accept the prohibition against anger discussed in "Hilḥot Deot" (*Mishneh Torah*, vol. 2, Halachah 3.3, 38). If a member of the external rhetor's audience is angered by the rhetor's speech, then that individual should accustom herself or himself to feeling no reaction at all, even when experiencing conditions under which anger would appear to be warranted. In addition, we discover that our anger at the rhetor may not be justified because we cannot rely on the "reality of the rhetor's anger as warrant for our own." We see a similar relationship between internal and external rhetorics even when we might expect that the Rambam's concern is wholly with the ethics of external rhetoric—such as in the statement that "a person is forbidden to act [*lehanhig atsmo*, to accustom himself] in a smooth-tongued and luring manner" (ibid., vol. 2, Halachah 2.6, 46)—where we find in the Hebrew text a reference to the self (*atsmo*). Maimonides's goal, here following a well-known dictum from the Babylonian Talmud, is that one should not be one thing in one's mouth, and another in one's heart. The quality of an action, even verbal action, is determined by the internalization of external judgment and the externalization of an internal quality. This leads Maimonides—in what remains of the second chapter of *Hilkhot Deot*—to consider "silence" as a potential area of concern for rhetoricians ("silence is a safeguard [fence] for wisdom" [*Mishneh Torah*, vol. 2, Halachah 2.4, 42]) as well as to consider how what we might categorize as feelings could be understood as actions for which we might be held responsible: "One should neither be constantly laughing and a jester, nor sad and depressed, but happy" (ibid.). Is it merely a coincidence that, as rhetoricians have begun to consider the possibility of an internal rhetoric, they have also begun to examine silence and "feeling" as areas of academic study?

Maimonides's contribution to these current discussions may be to caution us against treating these subjects wholly from the standpoint of an external rhetoric (for example, studies of how our silence might affect others are warranted in addition to studies of how we might silence ourselves). In addition, although the discussion in this essay of internal and external rhetorics has not resolved the tensions between philosophy and religion (the mean and/or the *mitzvot*), I hope that I have opened up the conceptual possibility that Maimonides's contribution to current discussions of the relationship of ethics and rhetoric may very well be his attention to how the dynamic relationship of external and internal rhetorics marks a shift in our responsibilities and obligations to each other and God. For students of Jewish philosophy, the idea of internal rhetoric may be particularly helpful in directing our attention away from the question, "Does the law have no intrinsic value or obligatory force?" (a Jewish corollary to the conundrum of holiness examined in Plato's *Euthyphro*), and toward the question, "How do individuals experience the obligatory force of the law?"[13] For students of rhetoric, Maimonides provides us with another case study in the development of internal rhetoric—an example of how the Aristotelian corpus had to be revised to meet the conceptual requirements of an internal rhetoric. The notion of internal rhetorics is not unique to Jewish thought, as Niencamp's survey clearly demonstrates, but the history of Jewish discourse resonates with the study of internal rhetorics. In fact, the notion of some such thing as an internal rhetoric persists among various Jewish rhetorical projects—for example, from the elaboration of *kavvanah* (intention) in halachic discourse to the propadeutic morality of *musar* literature. Indeed, further development of the history of Jewish rhetorics may demonstrate that internal rhetoric is more than a leitmotif in the philosophy of rhetoric. It is a category of knowledge making that moves somewhere between rhetoric and ethics in other rhetorical traditions, an episteme with its own set of questions and concerns to which the internal rhetor is compelled to respond.

NOTES

1. These details and other biographical information can be found in Sherwin Nuland, *Maimonides*.

2. For an extensive and highly nuanced discussion of rhetoric in medieval Arabic thought, see Deborah Black, *Logic and Aristotle's Rhetoric and Poetics in Medieval Arabic Philosophy*.

3. Ralph Lerner's *Maimonides' Empire of Light* provides another important addition to the study of Maimonides's rhetoric by focusing on the politics of public instruction as well as the persuasive strategies deployed in the Rambam's letters. A sampling of the Rambam's extensive corpus of letters can be found in Twersky's *Maimonides Reader* and in Maimonides's *Epistles of Maimonides*.

4. We may even find that Twersky's phrase, "reflective-persuasive communication," is more descriptive than external or internal rhetorics, challenging us not only to question the extent to which we rely on what George Lakoff and Mark Johnson have called the "conceptual metaphor of containment" to frame our "rhetorical understandings" (28, 31). In this essay, I will use the terms "internal rhetoric" and "self-persuasion" more or less interchangeably.

5. The concern of this essay is not Maimonides's psychology per se. (For a brief overview of Maimonides's faculty-based psychology, see Isaac Husik, *A History of Jewish Medieval Philosophy*, 281–82.) Regarding the relationship of faculty psychologies and "internal rhetoric," see Niencamp, *Internal Rhetorics*, 43–77.

6. This summary of Maimonides's general approach may place unwarranted emphasis on the idea of choice. It may be more proper to say that conditions of the soul cause individuals to perform certain actions, as we see in the discussion of "illnesses of the soul": "The ancients maintained that the soul, like the body, is subject to good health and illness. The soul's healthful state is due to its condition, and that of its faculties, by which it constantly does what is right, and performs what is proper, while the illness of the soul is occasioned by its condition, and that of its faculties, which results in its constantly doing wrong, and performing actions that are improper" (Twersky, *A Maimonides Reader*, 366). I cite here a selection provided by Twersky from Joseph Gorfinkle's English translation of Shmuel ibn Tibbon's Hebrew translation of Maimonides's Arabic text. Although Maimonides's discussion of the soul's health in "Hilhot Deot" may focus more on the conditions that prompt certain behaviors than the behaviors themselves, it is fair to say that he is concerned with both: "Just as the wise man is recognized [*nicar*] through his wisdom [*bechochmato*] and his temperaments [*uvdeotav*] and in these, he stands apart from the rest of the people, so, too, he should be [*yiheye*, will be] recognized [*nicar*] through his actions [*bemaasav*]" (Maimonides, *Mishneh Torah*, vol. 5, section 1, page 82).

7. Despite my Aristotelean mode of expression, similar generalizations are made by others who have explored Maimonides's use of this medical metaphor (in particular, see Alexander Broadie, "Medical Categories in Maimonidean Ethics"). I have skirted the difficult issue of the relation and/or differences between intellectual and moral virtues here, for fear of muddying the waters even further.

8. Broadie ("Medical Categories") and David Eisenman ("Maimonides' Philosophic Medicine") provide helpful discussions of the aptness of the medical metaphor in Maimonides's thought.

9. In fact, I am assuming here a "rationalist predisposition" on the Rambam's part, a predisposition carefully delineated in Twerksy's "Some Non-Halakic Aspects of the Mishneh Torah," which identifies several examples of Maimonides's interpellation of *chokmah* (literally, wisdom—the appeal and power of reflection) into traditional halachic formulations.

10. Shlomo Pines translates this passage differently. Instead of "if you do not persuade yourself," Pines has "if you do not deceive yourself" (68–69). The Arabic is *wala'tahdac nafsika* (you should not lie to yourself). Both Pines and Friedlander, however, agree that the action described here is reflexive, if not reflective. I thank my colleague Larry Kutler for his assistance with the Arabic text.

11. Here, reflection is not the same thing as self-persuasion. Since the Rambam has limited self-persuasion to intellectual activities that lead to error, we must treat self-persuasion as a species of reflection. But reflection includes those intellectual activities that assist the self-persuaded to restore their intellectual capacities and save themselves from the assault of the imagination.

12. Future examinations of this metaphor will need to take into account Maimonides's treatment of the subject and of discursive properties of metaphor, such as we find in *Moreh Nevukhim*.

13. This is a slightly different formulation than we find in Kaplan's "An Introduction to Maimonides' 'Eight Chapters,'" but Kaplan may point us in the right direction when he writes: "The key categories of EC [*Shemoneh Perakim*] enable us to unify these important concerns and to resolve the many enigmas set forth above are the two pairs of opposites: virtue and vice, and obedience and disobedience" (6).

BIBLIOGRAPHY

Aristotle. *On Rhetoric: A Theory of Civic Discourse*. Translated by George Kennedy. Oxford: Oxford University Press, 2006.

Black, Deborah L. *Logic and Aristotle's Rhetoric and Poetics in Medieval Arabic Philosophy*. Leiden: Brill, 1990.

Broadie, Alexander. "Medical Categories in Maimonidean Ethics." In *Moses Maimonides: Physician, Scientist, and Philosopher*, edited by Fred Rosner and Samuel S. Kottek, 119–26. Northvale, NJ: Aronson, 1993.

Eisenman, David J. "Maimonides' Philosophic Medicine." In *Moses Maimonides: Physician, Scientist, and Philosopher*, edited by Fred Rosner and Samuel S. Kottek, 145–50. Northvale, NJ: Aronson, 1993.

Husik, Isaac. *A History of Jewish Medieval Philosophy*. New York: Macmillan, 1916?

Jaeger, Werner. "Aristotle's Use of Medicine as Model of Method in his Ethics," *Journal of Hellenic Studies* 77 (1957): 54–61.

Kaplan, Lawrence. "An Introduction to Maimonides' 'Eight Chapter.'" *Edah Journal* 2, no. 2 (2013): 2–23.

Lakoff, George, and Mark Johnson. *Metaphors We Live By*. Chicago: University of Chicago Press, 2003.

Lerner, Ralph. *Maimonides' Empire of Light*. Chicago: University of Chicago Press, 2000.

Maimonides. *Epistles of Maimonides: Crisis and Leadership*. Translated by Abraham Halkin. Philadelphia: Jewish Publication Society, 2009.

———. *Mishneh Torah: A New Translation with Commentaries* [in Hebrew and English]. 28 vols. Translated by Eliyahu Touger. New York: Moznaim, 1986–2007.

———. *Moreh Nevukhim* [The guide for the perplexed]. Translated by Michael Friedlander. New York: Dover, 1956.

———. *Moreh Nevukhim* [The guide for the perplexed]. Translated by Shlomo Pines. 2 vols. Chicago: University of Chicago Press, 1974.

———. "Treatise on the Art of Logic." In *Ethical Writings of Maimonides*, edited by Raymond Weiss and translated by Charles Butterworth, 155–64. New York: Dover, 1983.

Niencamp, Jean. *Internal Rhetorics: Toward a History and Theory of Self-Persuasion*. Carbondale: Southern Illinois University Press, 2001.

Nuland, Sherwin. *Maimonides*. New York: Schocken, 2005.

Twersky, Isadore. *Introduction to the Code of Maimonides*. New Haven, CT: Yale University Press, 1982.

———. "Some Non-Halakic Aspects of the Mishneh Torah." In *Jewish Medieval and Renaissance Studies*, edited by Alexander Altman, 95–118. Cambridge, MA: Harvard University Press, 1967.

Twersky, Isadore, ed. *A Maimonides Reader*. Springfield, NJ: Behrman, 1972.

8

Rabbi Moses ben Nachman, Sophist?

PATRICIA BIZZELL

How is it possible to consider the great medieval rabbi and exegete, Rabbi Moses ben Nachman (1194–1270; Nachmanides, or Ramban) to be a sophist? Such an identification is not only anachronistic, but it also seems to be a contradiction in terms. Scholars agree that the ancient Greek sophists were profoundly skeptical about the possibility of humans acquiring knowledge of absolute Truth. As Susan Jarratt puts it, "rejecting traditional religion as an explanation for natural phenomena, [the sophists] evinced a special interest in human perceptions as the only source of knowledge in all fields" (xviii; for another rehearsal of this characterization by a contemporary Jewish scholar, see Boyarin, 89–93). In contrast, Ramban affirmed the existence of a source of absolute Truth and of communication that humans have received from this source, namely the holy Torah. Although Ramban knew the Greco-Arab philosophical traditions well, he was steeped in traditional rabbinic Judaism and also attracted to Kabbalah, mystical Jewish knowledge of the divine that he learned from Provençal sources and expanded on in his own work (see Septimus, 12–13). He believed that Truth could be known by both rational and nonrational means.

My intention here is not to make a historical argument about Ramban's knowledge of the ancient Greek sophists (if any) or their influence on him (if any). Rather, my project is simply to describe the strange harmonics created when someone like me comes to Jewish studies with habits of mind ingrained by years of studying the history of rhetoric in the West. Certainly it seems odd to cast a great medieval rabbi as a proponent of a philosophical method associated with the Greek pre-Socratics, whose ur-text is the *Dissoi Logoi*, which appeared around 400 BCE. Its author is not known, though he (or possibly she) was probably a student of Protagoras, who is generally credited with developing the method this text instantiates. The text explores opposing arguments on several topics, such as whether wisdom and moral excellence can be taught, and pits abstract terms such as seemly and shameful against each other. The sophistic movement that grew out of this method excelled in verbal display that entertained patrons and attracted students, but it also taught serious intellectual exploration and the concept that when absolute Truth is unavailable, a consideration of all plausible truths gets humans as close to correct answers as possible (see Bizzell and Herzberg, 47–48).

Reading Ramban, I seem to observe a sort of "*dissoi-logoi*-like" thinking as he sifts through a wide range of sources to untangle interpretive cruxes. In the first part of this essay, I will provide some examples of this sort of thinking in Ramban's biblical exegesis. In the second part, I will show how, when reading critical commentary on Ramban from his own time to the present, I seem to encounter characterizations that echo scholarly opinion about the sophists. I will sample these characterizations and let the reader decide whether my sense of similarity is correct. I will conclude with some comments on the implications of this kind of project for rhetorical study and, perhaps, for contemporary argument pedagogy.

[1]

I have labeled the *dissoi-logoi*-like thinking I detect in Ramban a "both/and approach." Ramban's characteristic both/and approach can be seen in his most characteristic work, his biblical exegesis. A series of sophistic moves may be seen, for example, in his interpretation of Exodus 20:8, "remember the Sabbath day, to keep it holy." This text provides an ideal location for the both/and approach, since the commandment it expresses is phrased two different ways: in Deuteronomy 5:12 it reads "observe the Sabbath day." The rabbis of the Talmud also take a both/and approach to this passage (and indeed, a multifaceted approach is characteristic of Talmudic argument in general, although I argue that it is developed to an unusually sophisticated degree by Ramban; I will have more to say about this in my conclusion). The rabbis insist that both verbs, "remember" and "observe," are necessary, as both were expressed by the divine voice "with one utterance" (quoted in Ramban, 306). Ramban reviews the Talmud's explanation for needing both verbs: to remember involves a positive commandment—that is, to do whatever is required to enact the commandment; whereas to observe involves a negative commandment—that is, to not do anything that violates or impedes enacting the commandment. Normally, women are exempt from positive commandments, but because it was desired that they be obligated to honor the sabbath, a negative commandment—which normally does require obedience from women—had to be included.

"But I wonder!" says Ramban about this Talmudic explanation (308). If God intended both verbs, why were not both written on the two sets of tablets? Ramban answers his own question by speculating that "remember" was the verb on the tablets, but "observe" was also pronounced by the divine voice and Moses reported that fact orally. Notice that Ramban does not set aside the Talmudic explanation; instead, he supplements it. However, he quickly turns to a type of explanation that interests him more, from Kabbalah. Thus, he says that "remembrance" is a "daytime" activity and "observance is at night" (309). Both verbs are needed because the sabbath begins in the evening and continues through the following day.

In this connection, Ramban mentions the words with which the sabbath is officially welcomed in the Friday night prayer service: "Come, O Bride" (ibid.). He mentions also the wine blessing uttered during the day on Saturday (the Jewish sabbath): for "the sanctification of the Great One" (ibid.). He further associates remembering with "the attribute of love" and observing with "the attribute of justice" (ibid.). What is going on here? I do not know, but I speculate that he is alluding cryptically to the union of two divine attributes (*sefirot*, in kabbalistic terms) that takes place on the sabbath, according to Kabbalah. The two verbs allude to two divine attributes that are coded male and female. Ramban believed that Kabbalah should be studied only face to face with a wise teacher, so he does not spell out his meaning clearly (see Idel). But however the *sefirot* line up, I think it is safe to say that this section enacts the greatest, most mystical both/and in his interpretation of this verse (I draw in this paragraph on Sendor).

Ramban is not done yet, however. He has another set of contraries to reconcile—namely, the controversy between the two major commentators and legal authorities from the beginning of the Common Era, Rabbis Shammai and Hillel, about the proper practice of remembering. Shammai thinks people should be mindful of the sabbath every day of the week, to the extent that if they happen to acquire anything especially good, such as a tasty food or a new garment, they should save it for enjoying on the sabbath. Hillel, in contrast, thinks that people should trust in God to provide enjoyments for the sabbath when the time comes, so they do not need to set things aside throughout the week. Ramban notes that the rabbinic tradition sides with Hillel, at least in the matter of whether food delicacies and other items need to be set aside. But he argues that the view of Shammai has been preserved in the Jewish names for the days of the week:

> Other nations count the days of the week in such a manner that each is independent of the other. Thus they call each day by a separate name or by a name of the ministers [in heaven, such as Sunday, which means "sun's day," Monday which means "moon's day," etc.], or by any other names which they call them. But Israel counts all days with reference to the Sabbath: "one day after the Sabbath," "two days after the Sabbath." . . . And I say further that this is the intent of Shammai the Elder's interpretation. (313; bracketed interpolation by Chavel)

As far as I can determine from the notes of the translator, Charles Chavel, Ramban makes an original connection here between Shammai's view and the Hebrew terms for the days. For example, Sunday is called *Yom Rishon* (first day [after the sabbath]).

To give one more example of both/and thinking from Ramban's exegesis, I turn now to a more difficult text, his commentary on Leviticus 16:8, a verse in which Aaron, the high priest, is commanded to bring two he-goats before the Lord as sin offerings, "and he [Aaron] shall place lots upon the two goats, one marked for the Lord and the other marked for Azazel" (Jewish Publication Society, 244). The one designated for the Lord is then slaughtered, but the one for Azazel is sent alive into the wilderness. The use of a goat for a sin offering is not unusual in ancient Jewish ritual practice, but the offering to Azazel is shocking. If you know nothing else about the Jewish religion, you surely know that its cornerstone is worship of no other god than the Lord. A huge problem, then, emerges when the Jews appear to be commanded here to make an offering to some other entity, seemingly put on a par with the Lord since both get the same offering (a goat). Ramban is going to steer a tortuous path between two readings of this problematic text. As he often does, he starts with the most prominent earlier medieval exegetical authority (still preeminent today), Rashi (known by this acronym made from his Hebrew name and title, Rabbi Solomon ben Isaac). Rashi's reading concurs with prior rabbinic authorities in attempting to explain away Azazel, not as the name of some sort of divinity but rather as merely a description of the sort of wilderness into which the Azazel goat is sent. In Hebrew, *az* means hard or strong, and doubling it (*azaz*) intensifies this meaning; *el* can mean to. Thus in this reading, Azazel merely suggests that the goat is sent to a very hard place, or (in Chavel's translation of Ramban's citation of Rashi) "a flinty precipitous peak" (Ramban, 217).

Without saying aye or nay to this reading, Ramban now turns to the interpretation of another important earlier medieval commentator, Rabbi Abraham Ibn Ezra, who grasps the goat by the horns, as it were, and intimates that Azazel is actually the name of a lesser sort of divinity, a demon to whom the Jews did indeed once offer sacrifices. Ibn Ezra implies that the two goats are brought before God's altar, but only one is slaughtered while the other is sent away, in order to dramatize the fact that the Jews no longer make offerings to the lesser deity—the logic being that if the Azazel goat were intended as a sacrifice, it would be ritually slaughtered like the goat for the Lord. But no, it is simply sent into the wilderness alive. Ramban spends some time on Ibn Ezra's reading, engaging in a sort of etymological investigation and wordplay also associated with the Greek sophists. He unpacks a series of associations and puns revolving around the Hebrew word *saʿir*, which can mean both goat and hairy (goats are hairy), including Jacob's brother Esau (known as a hairy man) and a type of demon known as a satyr (half man, half goat). Ramban implies that Ibn Ezra sees the goat as a typical animal to sacrifice for a sin offering because the head goat demon, named Sammael rather than Azazel in the rabbinic literature, is actually given power by God over the Jews on the Day of Atonement, to destroy them if they do not repent effectively. They do repent effectively, however, when they demonstrate that they no longer sacrifice to goat demons (see 217–18).

Ramban then proceeds to his own interpretation, which modifies that of Ibn Ezra. Yes, the Jews used to worship divinities other than the Lord, but these were not demons—instead, they were angels. Once the Jews gained knowledge of the Lord from Torah, they realized that they were not to worship the angels as gods. But God inserted into the atonement ritual this moment of the Azazel goat so that the power of at least one angel could still be acknowledged—namely, the angel "of the sphere of Mars," who rules over wilderness, "wars, quarrels, wounds, plagues, division and destruction" (220); as well as, among the nations, Rome, associated in rabbinic tradition with Esau (and certainly the most warlike nation known to the rabbis of the Talmud); among the animals, goats; and, among the demons, satyrs. This angel, terrifying as he may be, is still the Lord's servant like all the other lower divinities, and the Lord simply wishes to acknowledge him by ordering some of the Lord's other servants, humans, to set aside a portion for him. We are certainly not sacrificing to him because, and here Ramban concurs with Ibn Ezra, we do not slaughter the goat for him in the prescribed ritual manner. But it is wise for us to obey the command to acknowledge him on a day of atonement when we are particularly vulnerable to being given into his power as punishment for our sins, if we do not repent effectively (see 220–21). (The rabbinic tradition tends to see the advent of all the ills over which this angel has power as coming on people as punishment for their sins.)

So far, I have explained how Ramban saves Ibn Ezra's reading, making it somewhat less diametrically opposed to that of Rashi—who wanted Azazel to be merely a place name. But what about that reading of Rashi's? For Ramban's solution to be both/and, Rashi's reading has to be folded back in somehow. Ramban finds a way. His argument is that, although, as Ibn Ezra contends, sending the goat into the wilderness does acknowledge the power of a divinity other than the Lord, this power is not, as Ibn Ezra suggests, a demon named Azazel. It is an angel, as Ramban has just explained. But Azazel is not the name of this angel. Rather, says Ramban, Azazel is a place name, after all, but he does not parse its meaning as Rashi does. Rather, he notes that *aiz* is another Hebrew word for goat, and *azal* can mean "going." So Azazel as a place name does not mean a flinty peak but rather, simply, "the place where the goat goes" (222, note 92)—or, "the place of going to the goat" (remember, the goat is associated with the angel who is supposedly acknowledged by this action). Quite the complicated both/and here!

Contemporary readers will have noticed that throughout this analysis, Ramban appears to acknowledge the existence both of demons and satyrs and of higher angelic powers who are still under the Lord's control. David Novak confirms (79–80) that Ramban believes such entities exist, and that he believes they can be studied and to some degree manipulated by astrology and necromancy. For instance, Ramban's commentary on Exodus 20:3 avers that in the commandment to worship no other gods, the Lord acknowledges not just that humans think there are other gods, but that there are in fact other nonhuman powers that humans might worship; what humans have to understand is that these entities are not in fact divinities and should not be worshiped (see Ramban, 295). Why would someone as highly rational as Ramban give credence to the existence of demons and angels? In part the answer lies in the fact that there is much testimony to their existence in the rabbinic sources, which Ramban by no means felt empowered to set aside (we might imagine that in this he evinces an attitude similar to that of the ultrarational Samuel Johnson, the eighteenth-century British philosopher who averred that he believed in ghosts because there was so much testimony to their existence). But Ramban can make a stronger case than this, as he concludes this exegesis:

> I cannot explain more, for I would have to close the mouths of those who claim to be wise in the study of nature, following after that Greek [philosopher Aristotle] who denied everything except that which could be perceived by him [through the physical senses], and he, and his wicked disciples, were so proud as to suspect that whatever he could not conceive of through his reasoning was not true! (222; bracketed interpolations by Chavel)

For Ramban, acute ratiocinator that he is, it still seems the height of both foolishness and arrogance to imagine that the human senses and human reason are adequate to encompass everything that is. Certainly they are not adequate to understand the *Ayn Sof* (no end), the limitless, omnipotent, omniscient Lord. To come closer to that understanding (which, nevertheless, still will elude him, as he realizes), Ramban needs Kabbalah. Perhaps for this reason, Novak suggests that "in some ways Nahmanides was more rationalist than Maimonides" (the third great medieval rabbi, Moses ben Maimon or Rambam, and noted as a "rationalist"; see Davidson) because Ramban admits that reason has limits and restricts its operations to a sphere in which "he could more easily demonstrate the truth of reason's claims" (Novak, 4–5), while also admitting where reason cannot resolve our difficulties. Indeed, Novak argues that Ramban's view of what is possible in arguments about nature is consistent with that propounded by Thomas Kuhn, the contemporary historian of science whose account of the rhetorical nature of scientific revolutions has done so much to foster postmodern thinking (Novak, 56). Novak argues that today we would call Ramban's views in this matter an attack on "scientism" (78).

[2]

These examples of Ramban's exegetical arguments can help us understand why Bernard Septimus claims that "the selective fusing and shaping of divergent traditions is a major theme in [Ramban's] thought" (34). Similarly, Menachem Lorberbaum states: "Nachmanides stands at a cultural crossroads: he helped transmit Ashkenazic (Franco-German) *halakhah* [Jewish law] to Spain, integrating the methods and concerns of the Tosafists [heirs of Rashi] into the classic Andalusian tradition [including Ibn Ezra], and went on to forge new approaches to the analysis of Talmudic material" (94). Michelle Levine explains the origins of this habit of mind in Ramban's eclectic education, which, in the words of Ephraim Kanarfogel, "integrated an unusually wide array of disciplines, methodologies, and concerns" (quoted in Levine, 6):

> Born and bred in Gerona, Catalonia, which was part of Christian Spain in his time, Nachmanides is exposed to more than one exegetical school of thought. From his teachers, who were students of the Tosafists, he is trained in Talmudic and midrashic literature [commentary on the Talmud] and educated in the Northern French exegetical tradition. Nachmanides also absorbs the methodology of Andalusian *peshat* exegesis, which seeks to establish the meaning of the biblical text by focusing on its language, context, literary style and genre, and historical milieu. He imbibes further the exegetical methods of the Provençal school. Moreover, his writings reveal the significant influences of kabbalistic, philosophical, and scientific teachings, which he learns from Spanish and Provençal sources. (Levine, 5–6)

This sort of education would have suited Ramban well to be a sophist. The pre-Socratics were well known for their itinerancy, as they traveled around Greece making their living by teaching philosophy and speech. Furthermore, "from their experiences of different cultures" in different cities, as Jarratt explains, "they believed and taught that notions of 'truth' had to be adjusted to fit the ways of a particular audience in a certain time and with a certain set of beliefs and laws" (xv). Given the fortuitous location of his upbringing, Ramban did not have to travel to experience diverse cultures and intellectual approaches, as the scholars noted above have observed, and we have seen him lay them side by side and negotiate among them in his biblical commentary.

For their emphasis on "concepts of *kairos* (timeliness) and *to prepon* (fitness)" derived from their comparison of cultures, the sophists have often been accused of using rhetoric for stylistic display, self-aggrandizement, and, at worst, "the amoral manipulation of an audience" (Jarratt, xv, xvi). Distrust of Ramban's rhetorical dexterity and eclectic habits of mind have caused some to level similar charges against him, accusing him of "diplomatic insincerity," as both Isadore Twersky (9) and Septimus (15) note. Among the many social roles he filled was that of the polished courtier, circulating amid powerful adherents of an antithetical religion (Christianity) much as his intellectual forebears had done in the Moslem courts of Andalusia (Septimus 25). The kind of rhetorical suavity required of someone in such a precarious political position might strike some contemporary scholars in more secure locations as ethically questionable. Indeed, some feel that Ramban was "insincere" when he defended Rambam from attacks by the Tosafists and also the "Montpellier anti-rationalists," who condemned his extreme rationalism, even though Ramban did not accord as much supreme power to reason as Rambam wanted to do (see Septimus, 14). Ramban was being "diplomatic" because he wanted to quiet the intense controversy over Rambam's work that was ripping the Jewish world apart. Others say that Ramban was "insincere" when, during the 1263 Barcelona Disputation, he stated that a Jew need not believe in all the Aggadot, a quasi-heretical position. He was being "diplomatic" in order to fend off some Aggadot that his Christian interlocutors claimed attested to a Jewish belief that the Messiah had already come (see Bizzell).

Septimus attempts to rescue Ramban from these charges. He argues that Ramban was genuinely able to appreciate what was good both in Rambam's thought and in that of his opponents (Septimus, 15), and that Ramban did not really misrepresent his own position on Aggadot—which he did not take "at face value"—so much as represent it selectively for argumentative advantage in an extremely difficult situation (16–17, note 21). It seems to me that an even stronger defense of Ramban can be constructed if we view him as a sort of sophist. He is not so much a hypocrite or waffler as he is a man who cannot help but see multiple sides of any question. He sees them, and he explores them. We see this both/and pattern in his thinking over and over again.

According to Septimus, in dealing with Aggadot, Ramban makes strategic use of Kabbalah. He neither rejects Aggadot as superstitions, like Ibn Ezra does, nor accepts them unquestionably, like Rashi does; rather, Septimus implies, Ramban uses Kabbalah to provide mystical meanings for Aggadot that would otherwise have to be discarded as patently irrational (Rambam tries to save some of the same Aggadot by devising rational explanations for them, primarily as hedges against idolatry; see Septimus, 19). Yet—a point reiterated by Moshe Idel—Ramban was not entirely hostile to Rambam, and he employs nonkabbalistic allegory as a legitimate method of exegesis as well. For Ramban, Kabbalah is only one (if the most esoteric and best) way of knowing. Idel contrasts this view with that of the Zohar kabbalists who aggressively reject all secular philosophy, and Rambam, who tends to reject mysticism (Idel, 69–70). Yet Idel says that Ramban was "ambiguous" about the value of philosophy (69). I respectfully disagree. I think Ramban clearly valued philosophy highly; it's just that he valued other ways of thinking too. "Ambiguous" implies that Ramban was unsure of how he valued philosophy and Kabbalah, respectively, and I think what we have here is not ambiguity, but intellectual ambidexterity.

A crux in the controversy over Rambam's work derived from Kabbalah's radical notion that human actions can somehow support or nourish God. Rambam, of course, rejected this idea utterly, regarding it as irrational in the extreme to imagine that the unknowable Master of the Universe could need anything from humans or be diminished by their failure to provide him support. Ramban steered a middle course between Rambam and a more radical kabbalistic position (which would evolve in even greater strength in the later work of the Zohar). Ramban pointed out that God, who is everywhere, is of course present within God's creation; it is the life and health of this creation, with God within it, that is sustained by human action (especially by the performance of *mitzvot*—that is, acts in obedience to Jewish law). God is also elsewhere; God is the great *Ayn Sof* who exists before and beyond creation and whose existence is quite unaffected by human action. In other words, God both is, and is not, affected by human action. A both/and solution (see Novak, 13).

Perhaps because he takes this kind of position, Ramban certainly advocates performing *mitzvot* and exercising spiritual discipline and physical self-restraint—these are the kinds of actions that support God and lead to close union (*devekut*) with God. But these actions are to be performed in the course of one's daily life on earth. Ramban imagines a sort of both/and existence—keeping up the worldly pursuits necessary to raising a family and contributing to one's community while striving at the same time to reach a higher and higher spiritual level. As Bezalel Safran points out, this view contrasts sharply with that of Rabbi Azriel, Ramban's fellow Gerona kabbalist, who sees one's life in this world as utterly antithetical to union with God, and as something to be shed as soon as possible in an ecstatic mystical experience that ravishes the soul even as it terminates the earthly existence that is a barrier to that union.

A profound and fundamental example of both/and thinking in Ramban has to do with another element in the controversy over the work of Rambam. As Genesis states, a central tenet of the Judaic worldview is that God made the world. Jewish thinkers generally adhered to the view that the Genesis account meant creation ex nihilo, from nothing. It had to mean this to affirm God's complete control over the world, or so they thought: if God created the world, God could then manipulate it as God sees fit, to bend natural laws so that just rewards and punishments are meted out, for example. Rambam was inclined to adhere, in contrast, to the Aristotelian view that the world had always existed, although he insisted that this did not abrogate God's complete control. Combined with Rambam's tendency to minimize the number of actual miracles, explaining away as many as possible in terms of natural causes, his position led some to think that he denied divine providence altogether. Ramban's solution to the ex nihilo/always existing debate is to imagine, as David Berger explains, that "creation is a process of emanation from the divine Nothing, not the sudden appearance of matter from ordinary nothingness" (112). This emanation did appear at a particular moment, but it did not evolve out of what Berger calls "ordinary nothingness." Thus it seems that the Genesis and the Aristotelian accounts can be harmonized. Here is another example of both/and thinking, which may be condemned as sophistical manipulation or appreciated as subtle accommodation.

[3]

In this essay I have attempted only what Daniel Boyarin calls a "typological parallelism" between ancient Greek sophistic rhetoric and the argumentative strategies of Rabbi Moses ben Nachman (133). In *Socrates and the Fat Rabbis*, Boyarin tries to do more than this, to excavate "a cultural relationship ... between Plato and the Babylonian Talmud" (ibid.). The textual problem that gives rise to Boyarin's study is the abrupt mixture in the Talmud of jests and scatological material with the most profound religious and philosophical questions. How did such a seemingly inappropriate mixture come to be? Boyarin believes that he detects the same mixture in the work of Plato, especially that which responds to the Sophists, such as the *Gorgias*. It is "seriocomic" (4), even "Menippean satire" (26), and Boyarin argues that this sort of Greek writing influenced the framers of the Talmud:

> The ways that I imagine such cultural exchange, namely between Christian or "pagan" Greek-writing intellectuals and Babylonian Jewish intellectuals, are drawn from the models and methods of folkloristic research. Diffusion among cultures of

motifs, stories, sayings, proverbs, legends, is, of course, a very well-known phenomenon.... I certainly do not imagine Babylonian Rabbis *reading* Platonic dialogues—there just isn't evidence for that for the seventh century [CE], even though a century or two later they certainly were—but rather that literary modes and religious ideas reached them via the modes of diffusion of the kinds of literature that we design as folklore. (135–36)

It would be risky to accept Boyarin's claim for cultural diffusion, given the controversy over his work that he himself notes (133), and in which I am not equipped to join. I would not want to build a case on his breezy assumption that rabbis of a later period, approaching Ramban's own, *were* reading Platonic dialogues, such as the *Gorgias* or the *Protagoras*, and so may have encountered sophistic thinking there, even if filtered through Plato's disapproval. But I do not think that Boyarin's interpretive argument rests on his convincing us of such diffusion, and I am hoping that mine does not either. I risk following Boyarin at least to the extent of suggesting that we can perhaps understand complicated texts better by reading them in light of each other: Plato's dialogues and the Babylonian Talmud, or works of the sophists and Ramban. Boyarin might even agree with me; he finds classical parallels even as far back as Kohellet (Ecclesiastes), which reminds him of the *Dissoi Logoi* (see 10).

My own interest, however, lies primarily not in forging links between classical Greek and medieval Jewish thinkers, but rather in understanding in yet another manner how rationality can be used as a means of persuasion in religious argument—and in argument more generally. In my essay on the 1263 Barcelona disputation, I suggest that Ramban's attempts there to present rational arguments were not motivated by the hope that rational arguments could induce agreement between himself and his Christian interlocutors. Indeed, he knew full well that his monastic opponents and the Catholic king who sponsored the disputation had determined ahead of time that the Jewish position would be judged inferior. As I mentioned earlier, such rhetorical situations required great rhetorical suavity of the courtier-rabbi, who may have aimed with his close ratiocination to persuade his audience not that he was correct about the religious matters under dispute, but rather that he was, if capable of ratiocination, a human being, and thus deserving of at least basic human rights.

Sergey Dolgopolski's work suggests that Ramban may have developed his ability to argue in situations where agreement was, a priori, not possible from his experiences in Talmudic study. Dolgopolski sees in Talmudic argument a method that treats "disagreement as an end rather than as a means" (ix), in contrast with Western philosophy's goal of reaching agreement. Starting with Plato, this goal has been deemed possible because all humans by virtue of being human are supposed to have implanted in their souls memories of the ideal forms of the world they inhabited before birth. The work of philosophy, in this view, is to clear away misunderstandings and obscurities created by the necessity of people's representing these universal ideas to themselves in particular human languages. Although this task is to be accomplished primarily by invoking the universal rules of logic, Dolgopolski attributes to Aristotle the recovery of a subordinate, but still important, role for rhetoric to play, in using language(s) to persuade humans to abandon their errors and reach agreement on the Truth—that is, the ideas that match the eternal forms (see 251–53).

According to Dolgopolski, because Western philosophy believes agreement can be attained, it works toward that goal in the future and pushes errors—that is, disagreements—into the past, to be forgotten. The conception of time here is linear. In contrast, disagreement can be described as an end in itself for the student of Talmud, because the student knows that disagreement has been attained in the past and preserved in the pages of the Talmud. This is a holy text that it is his or her task to understand, not to edit. In effect, Talmudic disagreements are timeless—we are not going anywhere with them, we are not trying to make them disappear, unlike in classical Western philosophy, which feels free to set aside any traditional learning that contradicts its current positions (see Dolgopolski, 24). Rather, we are charged with understanding them.

What does argument look like if your goal in pursuing it is not to eliminate all incorrect positions and establish the correct one unequivocally? What if your goal, rather, is to understand all the positions presented? Dolgopolski describes the Talmudic method this way: "The rabbis insisted that recalling always involved *teaching* the tradition, rather than merely *repeating* it. The dynamic between recalling, teaching, and repeating is more rhetorical than it is logical" (43). In approaching the Talmud, the goal of the learner or teacher (in Hebrew, learning and teaching come from the same root) is to discover the text's invention—that is, the new point it makes about the issue at hand. Discovering this point cannot be merely a matter of testing the text's logic—that is, testing it against some preestablished and presumably universal standards. Rather, one must employ refutation. If you agree with the text's new point, you are not done. You must try to excavate the position against which the text is asserting its insight, the position it comes to correct or refute—there must be one, or else the text is useless and would never have been promulgated. If instead you find any difficulty in accepting the new point you uncover, you should pursue your objections as far as you can, but mainly to understand the new point better, rather than to demolish it. Thus "refutation does not therefore serve a destructive purpose, but instead is a way to refine a speculation further and to make the invention found in the [textual] oration even more persuasive" (82).

This method stands in strong contrast to typical academic agonism, in which the goal is to drive the opponent from the field. In contrast, this method sits comfortably within the timelessness of Talmud study, in which there is no hurry to get to the one main point that will guide future action. We are not concerned about the future. Rather, we are concerned about contemplating the text in front of us and understanding it deeply. One could almost explain the difference with the image of two types of conversation, one in which your interlocutor hardly waits for you to finish speaking before interrupting you with objections (Western), and another in which your interlocutor listens patiently and asks only a few questions to make sure you have quite said everything you want to say, before venturing his or her own opinion (Talmudic).

Adopting this method does not throw us into a world of utter relativism. As I noted at the outset of this essay, Ramban is not like a Sophist in that he believes in a source of absolute Truth to which humans have access. Dolgopolski says: "As opposed to a Sophist, who was professionally disinterested in any truth, a Talmudic sage has the same desire for truth as a philosopher would have" (24). The difference between the Talmudist and the philosopher is that for the Talmudist, tradition with all its disagreements cannot be set aside—or, as Dolgopolski puts it, "retaining the correct connections demands keeping the mistaken connections in view" (100). The difference between the Talmudist and the sophist is that connections or argumentative positions are not proliferated simply for the sake of showing that one is clever enough to do it. Rather, the idea is that from the plethora of positions, new insights emerge.

This is another way of describing what I have called in this essay a both/and approach. As I have shown, for example, Ramban does not agree with either Rashi or Ibn Ezra about how to understand the goat sent to Azazel. However, in fully exploring their ideas, he finds a way to retain both rabbis' ideas in a sort of discourse cloud that also encompasses his own invention. In refuting them, he does not erase them but rather incorporates them into his chain of reasoning that leads to the interpretation he prefers. Dolgopolski characterizes this approach as "hermeneutical charity" (272–73). It suggests an interesting alternative model to the way academic argument is usually taught today—that is, almost entirely in terms of winning and losing.

BIBLIOGRAPHY

Berger, David. "Miracles and the Natural Order in Naḥmanides." In *Rabbi Moses Naḥmanides (Ramban): Explorations in His Religious and Literary Virtuosity*, edited by Isadore Twersky, 107–28. Cambridge, MA: Harvard University Press, 1983.

Bizzell, Patricia. "Rationality as Rhetorical Strategy at the Barcelona Disputation, 1263: A Cautionary Tale." *College Composition and Communication* 58, no. 1 (2006): 12–29.

Bizzell, Patricia, and Bruce Herzberg. "Dissoi Logoi." In *The Rhetorical Tradition: Readings from Classical Times to the Present*, edited by Patricia Bizzell and Bruce Herzberg, 47–55. 2nd ed. Boston: Bedford Books of St. Martin's Press, 2001.

Boyarin, Daniel. *Socrates and the Fat Rabbis*. Chicago: University of Chicago Press, 2009.

Davidson, Herbert A. *Maimonides the Rationalist*. Portland, OR: Littman Library of Jewish Civilization, 2011.

Dolgopolski, Sergey. *What Is Talmud? The Art of Disagreement*. New York: Fordham University Press, 2009.

Idel, Moshe. "'We Have No Kabbalistic Tradition on This.'" In *Rabbi Moses Naḥmanides (Ramban): Explorations in His Religious and Literary Virtuosity*, edited by Isadore Twersky, 51–74. Cambridge, MA: Harvard University Press, 1983.

Jarratt, Susan C. *Rereading the Sophists: Classical Rhetoric Refigured*. Carbondale: Southern Illinois University Press, 1991.

Jewish Publication Society. *JPS Hebrew-English Tanakh*. 2nd ed. Philadelphia: Jewish Publication Society, 1999.

Levine, Michelle J. *Naḥmanides on Genesis: The Art of Biblical Portraiture*. Providence, RI: Society for Biblical Literature, 2009.

Lorberbaum, Menachem. *Politics and the Limits of Law: Secularizing the Political in Medieval Jewish Thought*. Stanford, CA: Stanford University Press, 2001.

Novak, David. *The Theology of Nahmanides Systematically Presented*. Atlanta, GA: Scholars, 1992.

Ramban (Nachmanides). *Commentary on the Torah*. Vol.2: *Exodus*. Translated and annotated by Rabbi Dr. Charles B. Chavel. New York: Shilo, 1974.

Safran, Bezalel. "Rabbi Azriel and Naḥmanides: Two Views of the Fall of Man." In *Rabbi Moses Naḥmanides (Ramban): Explorations in His Religious and Literary Virtuosity*, edited by Isadore Twersky, 75–106. Cambridge, MA: Harvard University Press, 1983.

Sendor, Rabbi Meir. "The *Zohar*." Lecture at Hebrew College, Newton Centre, MA, 31 January 2006.

Septimus, Bernard. "'Open Rebuke and Concealed Love': Naḥmanides and the Andalusian Tradition." In *Rabbi Moses Naḥmanides (Ramban): Explorations in His Religious and Literary Virtuosity*, edited by Isadore Twersky, 11–34. Cambridge, MA: Harvard University Press, 1983.

Twersky, Isadore. Introduction to *Rabbi Moses Naḥmanides (Ramban): Explorations in His Religious and Literary Virtuosity*, edited by Isadore Twersky, 5–11. Cambridge, MA: Harvard University Press, 1983.

Is Midrash Comics?
A Fish Story about Graphic Narrative, Visual Rhetoric, and Rabbinic Hermeneutics

SUSAN HANDELMAN

Jonah entered the mouth of the whale like a man entering a great synagogue, and stood. The eyes of the fish were like shuttered windows [אפמריות] which shone, and he could see all that was in the sea and the underworld. R. Meir said: there was a pearl which hung from within the belly of the fish that lit up all that was in the seas and in the Underworld, and of this it says, "Light is sown for the Righteous."

Midrash, Pirke d' R. Eliezer, chap. 10

Several years ago, while attending a Rhetoric Society of America conference in Minneapolis, I wandered into a local Barnes and Noble looking for examples of graphic novels to use in a new seminar I was preparing on graphic narrative. As I stood looking at the many works from Batman to Will Eisner to Daniel Clowes to Japanese manga, I became aware that standing next to me were two boys about seventeen years old, with mohawk haircuts, tattoos, and pierced noses, looking as intently at those shelves as I was. Nothing like that had ever happened when I was looking at books on literary and cultural theory! As Art Spiegelman, the author of the Pulitzer Prize–winning graphic Holocaust narrative *Maus*, told the *Comics Journal* in 1995, "It seems to me that comics have already shifted from being an icon of illiteracy to becoming one of the last bastions of literacy. If comics have any problem now, it's that people don't even have the patience to decode comics at this point.... I don't know if we're the vanguard of another culture or if we're the last blacksmiths" (61).

It was Spiegelman's *Maus*, completed in 1991, that made comics and graphic narratives acceptable in the eyes of the adult reading public and academic critics. Theorists and practitioners of the medium often insist on using the word "comics" as a singular noun that requires a singular verb.¹ So the title of this essay, "Is Midrash Comics?," is neither ungrammatical nor meant to be simply provocative. It is a way of asking central questions about the rhetorical relationship between text and image in this form of rabbinic interpretation. Although much has been written on the textuality of midrash, there has been little relating it to contemporary theories of visual rhetoric or graphic narrative. Visualization, of course, was one of the venerable techniques of persuasion in the art of public speaking in Greek and Roman rhetorical theory. Rabbinics scholars such as Marc Bregman, Elliot Wolfson, and Daniel Boyarin began to look at questions of visuality in rabbinic texts some years ago.² I would like to carry the discussion further by using contemporary theories of comics and graphic narrative to examine an exemplary midrashic text, and then consider the implications for a renewed sense of Jewish rhetoric.

I have chosen a particularly extravagant midrash from the collection *Pirke d' R. Eliezer*, commenting on the book of Jonah. As a biblical text, the story of Jonah itself contains comic and satiric elements, fantastical caricatures, and imaginative breadth. But I think my chosen example will serve us well as we ask larger questions about midrash and visual rhetoric. This midrash imagines and visualizes what occurs when Jonah enters the huge fish's mouth, converses with it, and saves the fish from being eaten by no less a creature than the Leviathan. Jonah then acts as a type of superhero, rescuing both the fish and himself through the visual display of his circumcised penis as his weapon. As a reward, the fish agrees to Jonah's request to take him on an undersea voyage and shows him everything in the seas. It's a kind of Jewish *Moby Dick*.³ The following is the translation of chapters 9 and 10 of *Pirque de-Rabbi Eliezer and the Pseudepigrapha* by Rachel Adelman from her superb *The Return of the Repressed*.⁴ Chapter 9, just before the one in which our text appears, provides the larger context for our story. It interprets Genesis 1:20–23 and the emergence of various swarms of creatures above the earth and in the seas, including the sea monsters (*ha-taninim ha-gedolim*) on the fifth day of creation. This is the link our chapter 10 will use to connect Jonah's fish to the Leviathan, a creature that has many associations in Jewish tradition with both primordial creation and end-of-time messianic eras that our midrash will further engage.⁵

> On the fifth day, [God] caused the Leviathan, the Elusive Serpent, to crawl from the waters. Its dwelling is in the lowest waters and, between its two fins, rests the foundation hinge [הבריח התיכון] of the universe. All the great sea monsters

[התנינים הגדולים] in the oceans are food for the Leviathan. The Holy One, blessed be He, plays with him daily. He opens his mouth and the sea monster, whose designated day has come to be eaten, (tries to) escape and flee, but enters the Leviathan's mouth. The Holy One, blessed be He, plays with it, as it says: "(this is) the Leviathan that You formed to sport with" (Ps. 104:26). (Adelman, 244; bracketed interpolations and parentheses by Adelman)

Chapter 10 says:

The fifth day ... R. Tarfon said: the fish had been appointed to swallow Jonah since the Six Days of Creation, as it says: "And God appointed a huge fish to swallow Jonah" (Jonah 2:1). Jonah entered the mouth of the whale like a man entering a great synagogue, and stood. The eyes of the fish were like shuttered windows [אפמיות] which shone, and he could see all that was in the sea and the underworld. R. Meir said: there was a pearl which hung from within the belly of the fish that lit up all that was in the seas and in Underworld, and of this it says, "Light is sown for the Righteous" (Ps. 97:11). The fish said to Jonah, "Don't you know that my day has come to be swallowed by the jaws [lit. mouth] of the Leviathan?" Jonah said, "Take me to him and I shall save you, as well as myself, from his jaws." He [the fish] took him [Jonah] to him [the Leviathan]. He [Jonah] said to the Leviathan, "It was for you that I descended to see your abode [in the sea], and I will descend again, in the future, to place a rope through your tongue, and haul you up to sacrifice you for the great feast of the Righteous in the Days to Come." As it says: "Can you draw out the tongue by a rope?" (Job 40:25;). And, not only that, but look at this seal of our forefather Abraham. Look to the covenant [*brit*—mark of circumcision]' and flee!" And the Leviathan saw the seal of Abraham our forefather and fled from the presence of Jonah a distance of two days. (Adelman, 240–41; bracketed interpolations by Adelman)

Jonah then said to the fish, "Well, I saved you from the jaws of the Leviathan, so now show me everything in the seas and the depths." It showed him the paths along the bottom of the Sea of Reeds [*yam suf*], Israelites had walked upon, as it says: "... the weeds [*suf*] entwined around my head" (Jonah 2:6). It showed him the Great River [*nahar*] of Oceanus, as it says: "... the floods [*nahar*] engulfed me" (v. 4). It showed him the place where the breakers of the sea and its waves emerge from, as it says: "... all Your breakers and billows swept over me" (v. 4). It showed him Gehenna, as it says: "From the belly of Sheol I cried out" (v. 3). And it showed him the nethermost underworld of Sheol, as it says: "You brought my life up from the pit, O Lord my God" (v. 7). It showed him the foundation pillars of the earth, as it says: "I sank to the base of the mountains" (v. 7). From this verse, one learns that Jerusalem stands upon seven mountains. There, it showed him the Foundation Stone, set in the depths, and he saw, there, the sons of Korah standing and praying, and he knew he was below the Temple of God. (Adelman, 249–50; bracketed interpolations by Adelman)

The fish then said to Jonah, "Behold, you are now standing below the Temple of God. Pray and you will be answered." Jonah said to the fish, "Stand on your tail, for I would like to pray." He began to pray: "Master of all the Worlds, Whom we call 'He-who-casts-down and He-who-raises-up,' I have gone down, now raise me up! You Who are called 'He-who-causes death, and He-who-grants-life,' I have reached death, now raise me up, bring me back to life!" But he was not answered until he uttered the following words: "Whatever I vowed I shall fulfill" (Jonah 2:10)—to slaughter the Leviathan before You on the day of Israel's salvation. "And I, with a voice of gratitude, will sacrifice to You" (ibid.). As soon as he said this, the Holy One, blessed be He, indicated to the fish to vomit Jonah up onto dry ground as it says: "And God told the fish to vomit Jonah up onto dry ground" (v. 12). (Adelman, 254–55)

The text is endlessly rich and complex, and I can touch on only a few aspects of it here. I recommend Adelman's book for an excellent summary of the background, textual history, and literary and psychological readings of this passage. A further caveat: I am not trying to make grand claims about the entire genre of Midrash, an ancient rabbinic exegetical activity spanning over a thousand years; nor do I want to engage in any of the complex historical and philological questions about the editing and background of midrashic texts, or the intentionality of the authors. I'm writing this as an "essay" in the word's original sense (from the French *j'essaie*, I try)—as a tentative, personal, exploratory attempt to look at things from a new angle and see what insights that might yield. To use a visual metaphor, the scholarly methods we use are like various pairs of glasses we put on that reveal different views, none of which is panoramic or all-encompassing (what the rhetorical theorist Kenneth Burke might call a terministic screen).

The Hebrew root of the word midrash—*drsh*—means to search out, seek, inquire, or demand. Midrash visualizes, scripts, plays with, and caricatures the biblical text whose meaning it probes. It dissolves the linearity of the text, making us read back and forth simultaneously, on multiple levels; it disrupts regular chronology and topography; and it thus grapples imaginatively with the traumas of Jewish history and engages in ethical debate. One also often senses in so many midrashim that the authors are slyly winking at us. Or, as one of my favorite contemporary Jewish thinkers, Rabbi Yéhouda Léon Askénazi, once put it: "A Rabbi who does not laugh, is not a serious Rabbi" (quoted in Aviner, 15). In sophisticated comics—graphic novels and narratives—there is a similar uneasy and challenging relationship between text and image: one has to read back and forth, filling in the gaps between panels, and there are complex nonlinear juxtapositions of time and space.

As Hillary Chute—one of the best contemporary literary theorists of comics—writes, it is a genre dealing with fiction, narrative, and historicity:

> Comics might be defined as a hybrid word-and-image form in which two narrative tracks, one verbal and one visual, register temporality spatially. Comics moves forward in time through the space of the page, through its progressive counterpoint of presence and absence: packed panels (also called frames) alternating with gutters (empty space). Highly textured in its narrative scaffolding, comics doesn't blend the visual and the verbal—or use one simply to illustrate the other—but is rather prone to present the two nonsynchronously; a reader of comics not only fills in the gaps between panels but also works with the often disjunctive back-and-forth of *reading* and *looking* for meaning. (452)

Graphic narratives at their best, Chute continues, also involve an "affective, urgent visualizing of historical circumstance" and ethical engagement (457). As researchers in visual studies and graphic narrative always stress, we read images and we imagine texts; reading and seeing are complex activities, engaged in a profound interrelationship. I do not have room here to examine the complexity of this relationship, but it's useful to stop for a moment to enumerate what W. J. T. Mitchell—to my mind, one the best scholars writing in the field of visual studies today—calls the "four fundamental concepts of image science": the pictorial turn, the image-picture distinction, the meta-picture, and the biopicture (14). The pictorial turn does not signify just the rise of purely visual media like video, cinema and television. Mitchell explains:

> Media are always mixtures of sensory and semiotic elements, and all the so-called visual media are *mixed* or hybrid formations, combining sound and sight, text and image. Even vision in itself is not purely optical, requiring for its operations of coordination of optical and tactile impressions. Second, the idea of a "turn" toward the pictorial is not confined to modernity, or to contemporary visual culture. It is a *trope* or figure of thought that reappears numerous times in the history of culture, usually at moments when some new technology of reproduction, or some set of images associated with new social, political, or aesthetic movements has arrived on the scene. (15)

Mitchell's image-picture distinction is fundamental for the analysis I want to present of the midrash on Jonah. Image and picture are not the same, as Mitchell notes:

> "You can hang a picture, but you can't hang an image." The picture is a material object, a thing you can burn or break. An image is what appears in a picture, and

what survives its destruction—in memory, in narrative, and in copies and traces in other media. The golden calf may be smashed and melted down, but it lives on as an image in stories and innumerable depictions.... The picture, then, is the image as it appears in a material support or specific place. This includes the mental picture, which (as Hans Belting has noted) appears in the body, in memory or imagination.... [An image] is thus the perception of a relationship of likeness or resemblance or analogous form—what C. S. Pierce defined as the "iconic sign," a sign whose intrinsic sensuous qualities remind us of some other object. (16–18)

Mitchell has influenced the way I think about visual rhetoric, but he lacks scholarly familiarity with Jewish tradition, Hebrew, and rabbinic hermeneutics. One of the principles I have absorbed from Askénazi (whose work I have discussed at length elsewhere, in trying to define what Jewish rhetoric)[6] is the need to return to Hebrew to understand the meaning of Jewish ideas and texts. In other words, the language one uses is inseparable from the conceptuality that the language and its grammar entail. That is an important (and rhetorical) caveat for discussing Jewish rhetoric. Using English words such as "image," "picture," "vision," "representation," and "imagination" involves a conceptuality that differs from that entailed in the many Hebrew words used for images and seeing, such as *hazon, demut, mabat, tzelem, re'iyah pesel, tavnit, temunah, tzurah, histaklut,* and *dimayon* in biblical, rabbinic, and kabbalistic literature. To understand the profound and pervasive notions of seeing and visual rhetoric in Jewish texts, one would need to first thoroughly survey the numerous Hebrew words denoting seeing or images, then note where they appear and try to decipher meanings from those contexts.

In an essay on hearing and seeing, Askénazi discusses the dialectic between these two faculties in Jewish tradition. The biblical revelation at Sinai, he notes, is described as "witnessed"—both seen and heard—by the Jewish people. There is an especially interesting and cryptic line in Exodus 20:15: "[And] all the *people saw the voices* and the lightning and the sound of the horn." It is indeed true, Askénazi notes, that Jewish tradition is careful about vision because using it can risk idolatry, so one needs to first listen or hear in the sense of being taught to comprehend. As Askénazi puts it, "hearing is first and only those who have heard in truth will be able to see" ("Écoute et vision," 2:549; my translation).

But there is a deeper, subtler dialectic between the two faculties. As Askénazi observes, the Mishna (Jewish oral law that is part of the Talmud but was put in writing around the second century CE, after the destruction of the second Temple and end of the prophecy) uses a conventional phrase to mean "come and study": *Ta Sh'ma*—literally, come and hear. In contrast, the Zohar (one the foundational documents of Jewish mysticism, whose contents were collected, edited, and written down in the fourteenth century), uses the phrase *Ta Hazeh*—literally, come and see. Why these two different formulas? asks Askénazi. He answers that there was an initial time of revelation, during which the witnesses had seen and heard. Revelation later was hidden, so in the Talmudic period the imperative becomes: Come and understand by study what you have seen. Afterward, the kabbalistic teaching is: Come and see what you have understood by studying. In other words, if one is not initiated into hearing, into the rabbinic tradition of understanding what was first revealed and now hidden, then there is a risk of idolatry. So the Talmud says: "Come and understand, Israel, what you saw." And if you have understood, then the tradition of the Zohar intervenes: What you understood, come to see ("Écoute et vision," 2:550).

The Fish Story

With these preliminary theoretical reflections in mind, let's now look further at our midrash on Jonah. In the Bible, Jonah is the prophet who flees the mission to which God has called him: to go east to the city of Nineveh and proclaim its impending destruction due to its wickedness. (Nineveh was one of the oldest and largest cities of ancient Mesopotamia.) Instead, Jonah escapes in the opposite direction, to the coastal city of Jaffa, in the Land of Israel. There he finds a ship going even further west, to Tarshish. He pays his fare, gets settled on board, and falls asleep. No grand rhetoric here, in the classic tradition of Israel's ancient prophets Amos, Isaiah, and Hosea. Instead, silence and unconsciousness. God then sends a great storm, placing the ship in mortal danger; the pious non-Jewish sailors investigate and discover the storm is due to Jonah's presence and flight. Jonah responds by asking them to throw him overboard. The sea stops raging, and God sends the fish to swallow Jonah. Here is the biblical passage from Jonah 2:1–11 that our midrash interprets:

> And the Lord appointed a great fish to swallow up Jonah. And Jonah was in the belly of the fish three days and three nights. Then Jonah prayed to the Lord his God from the belly of the fish. And said, I cried to the Lord out of my distress, and he heard me; from the belly of Sheol I cried, and you heard my voice. For you cast me into the

deep, in the heart of the seas; and the floods surrounded me; all your billows and your waves passed over me. Then I said, I am cast out from your sight; yet I will gaze again on your holy temple. The waters surrounded me, even to the soul; the depth closed around me, the weeds were wrapped around my head. I went down to the bottoms of the mountains; the earth with her bars closed on me for ever; yet have you brought up my life from the pit, O Lord my God. When my soul fainted inside me I remembered the Lord; and my prayer came to you, to your holy temple. Those who pay regard to lying vanities forsake their loyalty. But I will sacrifice to you with the voice of thanksgiving; I will pay that which I have vowed. Salvation belongs to the Lord. And the Lord spoke to the fish, and it vomited out Jonah upon the dry land. (Adelman's translation)

Jonah's prayer is an eloquent piece of rhetoric, a poetic psalm interpolated into the prose narrative, whose nuances and tropes our midrash will play on, literalize, and concretize, as we will soon see. It is a commonplace of literary commentary on this biblical text to also note an ironic and satiric core.[7] The prophet is a clumsy antihero, doing the opposite of what he's supposed to; then he gets swallowed by a fish and is forced finally to pray from its belly. In the Jewish cycle of holidays, Jonah is the biblical book read on Yom Kippur, the holiest and most solemn day of the Jewish calendar, in which Jews are called to return to God and are cleansed of their sins. Yet in the book of Jonah, it's the non-Jewish sailors and residents of Nineveh who become the paradigms of pious repentance, not the reluctant Jewish prophet or any other Jewish figure. Even when Jonah accepts his mission, he does so with little enthusiasm. When Nineveh's inhabitants do repent and the city is saved, Jonah is angry and wishes for death at the end of the book.

The image of the large fish that swallows Jonah and Jonah's ardent, stylized prayers from the fish's belly seem especially exaggerated and grotesque—very much like a "comic." Indeed, the image of Jonah and the fish has been cloned endless times: it is particularly beloved by cartoonists, graphic artists, and advertisers. Perhaps there is a kind of meta-picture here as well, to use Mitchell's term. A meta-picture, he writes, is one in which the "image of another picture appears, a kind of 'nesting' of one image inside another, as when Velázquez paints himself in the act of painting Las Meninas" (18). As Mitchell also indicates, any picture can be a meta-picture if it becomes a device to reflect on its nature as a picture. I suggest that our biblical text here is using an outlandish image of a man praying inside a huge fish as a way to comment on its own narrative and themes, and to signal to the reader the impossibility of any literal meaning. The midrash on Jonah then carries that gesture further, with an ironic rhetorical self-consciousness: it images the nature of its imaging and brings another huge fish to swallow Jonah's fish. Then, on a third level, we have the final triumph in the days of the Messiah, with the picture of the righteous eating the Leviathan itself.

Let me try to explain further. One of the main themes of the book of Jonah is *teshuvah* (literally, return, but often awkwardly translated as repentance), which involves a reflexive and rigorous looking back on one's life and deeds, a rewriting and reimagining of one's life story, as it were. In other words, this cartoonish man-in-the-fish image embedded in the biblical narrative is a kind of meta-pictorial device used to embody that double consciousness of *teshuvah*—of the need to look at ourselves looking at ourselves. We are inevitably reluctant to truly see ourselves. We naturally evade our less attractive sides, trying to escape that difficult work; we find endless reasons to rationalize our behavior and see ourselves as more righteous than others. So to see rightly, we have to see differently; we have to have our vision distorted. We need to be shocked out of our normal ways of doing and being.

But in the Jewish notion of *teshuvah*, there is also much hope and flexibility: time is reversible. As the Talmud famously says, "great is teshuva, for it transforms intentional sins into merits" (*Yoma*, 86b). In other words, the past is not irrevocably over; the past itself can be changed; time is not linear. There is no Greek sense of fate and tragic destiny, or Christian sense of original sin, or Marxist dogma of irreversible deterministic history. As Askénazi puts it, Jewish history is "a drama but not a tragedy" ("Le couple," 209). Indeed, the Leviathan—representing the seemingly overwhelming forces of chaos, death, and destruction—is also portrayed as God's plaything in our text.

Now let me try to relate this back to midrash and visuality. In visuality, there is a certain kind of simultaneity; one sees all at once, as it were. Humans process images 60,000 times faster than they do texts. "Time," someone once said, "is God's way of not having everything happening at once."[8] Physicists indeed speak about the way in which the universe is both in time and outside of time. Outside of time, everything happens at once. That is very hard for humans to understand, since we are temporal creatures. But the midrash pushes the limits of our understanding. It not only reads the text in nonlinear ways, but it also transforms Jonah into a superhero battling the primordial sea monster of Creation and Apocalypse. That is, it rhetorically makes us see all at once: past, present, and future simultaneously, with a kind of God's-eye vision of creation, covenant, struggle, and redemption. It does this not through sermonic preaching or philosophical argument, but through its pedagogical and rhetorical combination of text and image. And like comics, it does so in an accessible and popular way.

All these techniques challenge us to see anew, defamiliarize the text (to use the term of Russian Formalist critic Viktor Shlovksky), upset our conventional ways of reading and understanding. And, as Askénazi once put it in another context, they keep the discussion from being "too serious to be serious" (*Parachat Béréchit*, 28). To cite another brilliant humorist, Mark Twain, "humor must not professedly teach and it must not professedly preach, but it must do both if it would live forever" (202). I would suggest that a specifically Jewish religious rhetoric must somehow ultimately situate its audience in relation to this larger redemptive vision, as part of the divine comedy. (Even in secularized Jewish rhetoric, one often finds these theological elements transformed, and also often in an ironic or satiric way. In *Maus*, for instance, the horrific experience of the Holocaust is intertwined with ironic and comic scenes of the narrator Artie's interactions with his father.) This seeing brings what is outside or at the end of time into time; that is, it both gives us a glimpse of that redeemed world and performatively moves the world further toward the messianic goal. So it is also the source of the laughter of Rabbi Akiva, in the famous Talmudic story (*Makkot*, 24b), as he views the ruins of the Temple destroyed by the Romans in his generation. Asked by his colleagues why he laughs instead of weeping at this sight as they are, he answers that now he has witnessed how the prophecies of destruction have come true, so surely the prophecies of the rebuilding and redemption will also eventually come true.

This entire sensibility, I think, is also at the heart of the spiritual seeing in the midrash on Jonah, with its disruption of linear chronology and geography, its mixture of past, present, and future, and its intense graphic images. In sum, Jonah in the fish is not a naïve image or simply part of folklore. Of course, I am using "image" here in the sense of Mitchell's definition: "a highly abstract and rather minimal entity that can be invoked with a single word. It is enough to name an image to bring it to mind" (18). In fact, the text of Jonah does not specifically use any Hebrew word for whale but rather refers to a huge fish (*dag gadol*). We tend to envision a whale, due to the conventional translations and associations: whales are probably the largest fish that could swallow a person whole, though of course whales are actually mammals and not fish.

Moreover, this has not been a strictly verbal dual; Jonah also intimidates the Leviathan by showing him the mark of his circumcision in another strong display of visual rhetoric, as it were. In biblical and rabbinic literature, the mark of circumcision is often called the *brit milah* (circumcision of the covenant), or *ot brit* (sign of the covenant) since the act of circumcising signifies the entry of the male Jewish baby into covenant of Abraham and the Jewish people. So part of Jonah's secret weapon is a word-thing, a graphic sign of God's unbreakable embodied relationship with the Jewish people and God's saving power. There may even be a parodic reference here to a famous line in the Yom Kippur liturgy, when the book of Jonah is read in the afternoon service: "*La brit habet ve al tefen la yetzer* [לַבְּרִית הַבֵּט וְאַל תֵּפֶן לַיֵּצֶר], look to the *brit* and don't incline to your desire]."[9] I cannot help but also sense a seriocomic tone here, a double consciousness in the juxtaposition of these solemn words from the liturgy with Jonah's use of them to scare off the huge monster.

It's the ironic or satiric literal sense of Jonah in the fish's belly as a comic, a kind of intentionally distorted cartoon image, that our midrash in chapter 10 from *Pirke d' Rabbi Eliezer* builds on so well. In both the biblical and the midrashic texts, Jonah has been taken into an alternative reality, an upside-down world. And along with him, we are swallowed into the depths of the text, the psyche, history, and the world of images that lies under the surface of words. At these levels of reality, there is a different kind of vision. The reader has to follow the back-and-forth interpretation of the verses from Jonah's biblical prayer, where the metaphors are now literalized, pictorialized, and made into a topography and map of his voyage. The "weeds [*suf*] entwined around my head" (*Pirke d' Rabbi Eliezer*, 2:6) metamorphose, as in a surrealist painting, into the paths along the bottom of the Sea of Reeds [*yam suf*], on which the Israelites had walked as they left Egypt. "I sank to the base of the mountains" (2:7), which becomes the foundation stone of the Temple. This reimaging of the metaphors parallels Chute's description of how "comics spatially juxtapose (and overlay) past and present and future moments on the page" (453): the midrashic interpreter has taken the verses of Jonah's biblical prayer and pictorialized and divided them into visual sequential frames of his journey with the fish, where past, present and future are overlaid.

In an essay on *Maus*, Chute analyzes Spiegelman's masterwork and notes how he uses his comics panels as "windows" to open up and order the traumatic nonlinear account of his father's Holocaust testimony, the memories of which his father wants to forget, and critical personal papers which he has destroyed. Chute notes:

> In the introduction to his 1977 collection *Breakdown*, . . . Spiegelman attaches the concept of narrative to the spatializing, "materializing" work of comics:
>
> MY dictionary defines COMIC STRIP as 'a narrative series of cartoons . . . .' A NARRATIVE is defined as 'a story.' Most definitions of STORY leave me cold. . . . Except for the one that says 'a complete horizontal division of the building . . . [From Medieval Latin HISTORIA . . . a row of windows with pictures on them].'" (quoted in Chute, "The Shadow of a Past Time," 209; bracketed interpolations by Spiegelman)

Something similar, I suggest, is happening in our midrashic narrative, which presents us with a "row of windows," a visual sequencing of Jonah's underwater journey, and also deals with trauma and survival—serious and comic at once, so consonant with Jewish life and history.

Fish Eyes

What else can we understand about those eyes or windows of the fish that enable Jonah to see an alternate world? The text does not use the regular Hebrew word for eye, *ayin*; the word used instead, *afmioth* (אפמיות) is somewhat obscure. Based on her philological research, Adelman notes differences in manuscript versions of our midrashic text. The word *afmioth* has been translated as "skylight," "windows of glass," "flaps," and "shutters." Regardless of the precise spelling or translation, this is a special visual apparatus that allows Jonah to see anew—to see into the dark depths of himself and the world and have a visionary glimpse of history and redemption. The midrash specifically focuses us on the eyes of the fish, although they are not even mentioned in the biblical text, which directs us more to the fish's belly.

What would it be like to see as a fish? This is also both a serious and comic question. There is something actually quite extraordinary about fish vision. Fish navigate in the depths with little light; their eyes never close and are much larger in proportion to their bodies than human eyes are. Fish eyes have fixed irises and round lenses, and most have no eyelids. Placed on both sides of the head, a fish's eyes give it 180-degree vision. We have some everyday sense of this from the ultrawide camera lens called a fisheye lens, which uses strong visual distortion to create a hemispherical panoramic image. The small fisheye lenses in the peepholes of doors also give us a wide-angle spherical view. The point here, of course, is not biology or the science of optics, but the rhetorical effects and associations of the image of the fish eye in our midrashic narrative. The fish eyes are the windows through which a Jonah, closed in on himself, can open up, see anew, see truly. Not a biological seeing but a psychological, spiritual, and historical reenvisioning of himself and the world; a *teshuvah*, or return, repentance, renewal. These fish eyes also make the reader see with a different kind of vision.

In sum, I am proposing that the fish eye itself is the image in the text that marks this alternative seeing, vision through distortion, and is also an embodiment or an icon of what it designates. Perhaps one might say that the genre of Midrash itself is a kind of fish eye, a way of looking with and through the text, without which the text is an empty shell. Could I push that simile further and apply it to rhetoric itself? To ways in which rhetoric is also an attempt to make an audience see differently, or to rhetoric's use of tropes and turns and various techniques of persuasion? If so, it is no wonder that many times in its history of conflict with philosophy, from Plato onward, rhetoric has been denigrated as a kind of deceptive fish story, unconcerned with pure truth. Similarly, comics has had a long history of being denigrated as a crass, superficial form of art. And comics especially works through fish-eye vision, a kind of wide-angle distortion.

To help explain that technique, I turn to Scott McCloud's classic *Understanding Comics*, one of the earliest and best attempts to theorize the formalist aesthetics of comics. McCloud is also a cartoonist, and the book is written as a graphic narrative in comics form. By "de-emphasizing the appearance of the physical world in favor of the idea of form," McCloud argues, "the cartoon places itself in the world of concepts" (41). He is referring to the ways in which comics caricatures, abstracts, and engages in "amplification through simplification." In cartooning, he continues, when an image is abstracted, "we are not so much eliminating details, as we are focusing on specific details. By stripping down an image to its 'essential meaning,' an artist can amplify that meaning in a way that realistic art can't" (30). So there is a special intensity to the image, and, as he notes, "simplifying characters and images towards the purpose can be an effective tool for storytelling in any medium. Cartooning is not just a way of drawing, it's a way of seeing" (31).

Why do the simple abstracted lines in cartoons or Midrash so attract and engage us? To take the common example of emoticons, why do we so easily read the sign :-), which are just a few set of dots and a lines, as a face? (The examples are mine, not his). McCloud observes that when we "look at a photo or realistic drawing of a face," we see it "as the face of *another*. But when you enter the world of the *cartoon*—you see *yourself*.... The cartoon is a *vacuum* into which our *identity* and *awareness* are *pulled*—an *empty shell* that we inhabit which *enables* us to travel in another *realm*. We don't just *observe* the cartoon, we *become* it! That's why I decided to *draw* myself in such a simple *style*. Would you have *listened* to me if I looked like *this??*" (36). In this quote, I've taken just the words from the balloons over the images in the panels his book. Here's the way it's actually appears:

In analyzing McCloud's two drawings of his face in the above panel, the one in "cartoon" style, and the other in "representational" style, Ora Elper commented to me that "those windows/eyes through which Jonah was enabled to see everything he saw—they are the round, blank glasses of your comics author. The fish—like that self-effacing teacher image—lends Jonah his eyes/perspective (as a fish) and through them Jonah is 'enlightened'—as the midrash says, מאירות ליונה [gave light to], enlightened Jonah."[10] If we look back at the cartoon figure McCloud draws of himself, his face has large, round, eyeglass frames but no eyes. Elper has made a stunning connection between those transparent, round, clear, and empty lenses of McCloud's and the *afmioth*, those window eyes of Jonah's fish through which he sees in our Midrash.

The leap from reading the words I cited from McCloud's book to looking at the actual reproduction of those same words as they are drawn and integrated with images, panels, and gutters (the empty spaces between the panels) in the graphic narrative also feels somewhat like the leap from reading the biblical text of Jonah to the midrashic version of *Pirke d'R. Eliezer*. When McCloud writes that "the cartoon is a *vacuum* into which our *identity* and *awareness* are *pulled*—an *empty shell* that we inhabit which *enables* us to travel in another *realm*. We don't just *observe* the cartoon, we *become* it," I think he is also giving us a tool to explain what happens when we read or look at that fish image in the biblical text. It, too, is a kind of "vacuum" that pulls us in and enables us, like Jonah, to travel to another realm. This is precisely what the midrash picks up and then exaggerates or amplifies—lending new eyes to both the reader and Jonah. In other words, the cartoon image is analogous to the physical belly of the fish—"an *empty shell*" for Jonah to inhabit that enables him to travel into other psychic and historic realms, where his vision merges with the fish's and he can see into the depths. Our midrash even likens it to a synagogue: "'And God appointed a huge fish to swallow Jonah' (Jonah 2:1)]. He entered its mouth like a man entering a great synagogue, and stood."

Fish belly as synagogue? I sense the simile too is both serious and tongue-in-cheek. Both are open spaces that close around what or who enters them and then become platforms for transformation. In both places, prayer from the straits opens up the supplicant. The fish story genre of Midrash similarly opens up the biblical text. In other words, for the Jew, the Torah narrative is a kind of large, dark belly into which one is swallowed, which one lives with and through as one is tossed about in the stormy waters of Jewish history and life. How does one survive and maneuver in those narrow straits and turbulent depths? What does one seek? What is the goal of Midrash or Jewish religious rhetoric itself, if not also a spiritual transformation, a way of seeing or living the text and journeying with it through the long, agonizing process of history, enduring and building despite chaos and death—with one's eyes not failing, but still looking, still longing for that ultimate messianic completion of Creation? And so also being able, like Rabbi Akiva, to still laugh in spite of it all? Or, as Jonah puts in his prayer in the biblical text: "For you cast me into the deep, in the heart of the seas; and the floods surrounded me; all your billows and your waves passed over me. Then I said, I am cast out from your sight; yet I will gaze again on your holy temple" (2:5)—the holy temple in Jerusalem, that center toward which Jews have prayed through all their exiles and suffering, believing in a future of rebuilding and redemption.

The rabbis famously say that "God's salvation comes in the blink of an eye" (*Pesikta Zutra, Lekah Tov*, Esther, chap. 4). That eye movement takes only a fraction of a second. Of this, our midrash as comics has given us a smiling wink. In one of the most exceptional uses of the metaphor of the eye, from one of the minor tractates of the Babylonian Talmud, it is written:

> Abba Issi ben Yochanan said in the name of Samuel ha Katan: "This world is like a person's eyeball. The white of the eye is the ocean surrounding the world; the iris is the inhabited world; the pupil of the eye is Jerusalem; and the face [the reflection of the observer] in the pupil is the Holy Temple. May it be rebuilt speedily in our days." (*Derekh Eretz Zuta*, 9)

NOTES

1. Academic definitions of "comics" are as much debated as the term "visual rhetoric." I use these terms rather loosely and interchangeably in this essay. There are many definitions and arguments about what constitutes each field. The literature is vast, and many academic areas intersect in visual rhetoric, including rhetoric, art history, linguistics, semiotics, cultural studies, and technical communication. The broadest definition of "visual rhetoric" would be the study of how images affect audiences and societies. For a good introduction to and overview of various debates in the field of comics, see Hillary Chute, "Comics As Literature?," whose publication in *PMLA*, the most prestigious journal of literary studies, was a sign that the field had very much arrived.

2. My *Slayers of Moses* dealt with midrashic hermeneutics and literary theory before the rise of the field visual rhetoric in the 1990's. Daniel Boyarin's "'The Eye in the Torah'" first discussed the question of visuality. Elliot Wolfson's *Through a Speculum That Shines* is a study of visualization particularly in medieval Jewish mysticism. *Vision and Imagination in Medieval Jewish Mysticism*, appeared in 1994. See also Marc Bregman, "Aqedah: Midrash as Visualization." For recent work from a different angle, see, for example, Maya Katz, *The Visual Culture of Chabad*.

3. I thank Marc Bregman for bringing this wonderful text to my attention many years ago in our discussions of the creative hermeneutics of Midrash. He playfully called it the "Yellow Submarine."

4. For a close parallel version of the text from *Pirque de-R. Eliezer* in another midrashic collection, see *Tanhuma*, on Lev. 5.

5. The Leviathan is mentioned six times in the Hebrew Bible. Job 41:1–34 describes it in detail, and some of those verses are used in our midrash on Jonah. The Babylonian Talmud also emphasizes the creature's eyes and associates it with primeval creation and the End of

Days (*Bava Batra 74b-75a*). There are many parallels between Jonah and Job, for which there is no room for discussion here.

6. See Handelman, "The Philosopher, the Rabbi, and the Rhetorician."

7. For a comprehensive and excellent critical scholarly overview of this passage and the book of Jonah, see Uri Simon, *The JPS Bible Commentary: Jonah*.

8. The physicist Gerald Shroeder quoted this sentence to me in a conversation. When I asked him for the source, he wrote in an e-mail message of 20 December 2012: "Written on the wall of the Men's room in the Pecan Street café, Austin Texas."

9. This phrase is part of the well-know *piyut* (liturgical song) "Ki Hinneh K'homer," sung by the assembled congregation several times on Yom Kippur in the various requests for forgiveness. An alternative reading would be to see the words addressed to a human person, to "look to the *brit*, the sign of circumcision, and don't turn to your desires," or addressed to God to look to the sign of the *brit*, the circumcision that sealed God's covenant with Abraham and his descendants for all time.

10. Ora Wiskind Elper, e-mail message to the author, 24 July 2012.

BIBLIOGRAPHY

Adelman, Rachel. *The Return of the Repressed: Pirqe de-Rabbi Eliezer and the Pseudepigrapha*. Supplements to the *Journal for the Study of Judaism* 140. Leiden: Brill, 2009.

Askénazi, Yéhouda Léon [Manitou]. "Écoute et vision." In Yéhouda Léon Askénazi, *La Parole et l'écrit: Penser la tradition juive aujourd'hui*, 2:549–54. Paris: Albin Michel, 2005.

———. "Le couple, créateur de l'histoire." In Yéhouda Léon Askénazi, *La Parole et l'écrit: Penser la tradition juive aujourd'hui*, 1:206–26. Paris: Albin Michel, 1999.

———. *Parachat Béréchit*." Jerusalem: Foundation Manitou, 1993.

Aviner, Shlomo. *Pirurum me-Shulkhan Gavoah: Me-Torato Shel ha-Rav Yéhouda Léon Askénazi Manitou*. Jerusalem: Beit El, 1991.

Boyarin, Daniel. "'The Eye in the Torah': Ocular Desire in Midrashic Hermeneutics." *Critical Inquiry* 16 (spring 1990): 534–43.

Bregman, Marc "Aqedah: Midrash as Visualization." *Journal of Textual Reasoning* 2, no. 1 (2003). http://jtr.lib.virginia.edu/volume2/number1/bregman.html. Accessed 26 January 2014.

Chute, Hillary. "Comics as Literature? Reading Graphic Narrative." *PMLA* 123, no. 2 (2008): 452–65.

———. "'The Shadow of a Past Time': History and Graphic Representation in Maus." *Twentieth-Century Literature* 52, no. 2 (2006): 199–230.

Handelman, Susan A. "The Philosopher, the Rabbi, and the Rhetorician." *College English* 72, no. 6 (2010): 590–607.

———. *Slayers of Moses: The Emergence of Rabbinic Interpretation in Modern Literary Theory*. Albany: State University of New York Press, 1982.

Katz, Maya Balakirsky. *The Visual Culture of Chabad*. Cambridge: Cambridge University Press, 2010.

McCloud, Scott. *Understanding Comics: The Invisible Art*. New York: Harper Collins, 1993.

Mitchell, W. J. T. "Visual Literacy or Literary Visualcy?" In *Visual Literacy*, edited by James Elkins, 11–30. New York: Routledge, 2008.

Simon, Uri. *The JPS Bible Commentary: Jonah*. Translated by Lenn Schramm. Philadelphia: Jewish Publication Society, 1999.

Spiegelman, Art. Untitled interview by Gary Groth. *Comics Journal* 181 (1995): 52–114.
Twain, Mark. "Humorists." In *Mark Twain in Eruption: Hitherto Unpublished Pages about Men and Events*, edited by Bernard DeVoto, 200–3. New York: Capricorn, 1968.
Wolfson, Elliot. *Through a Speculum That Shines: Vision and Imagination in Medieval Jewish Mysticism*. Princeton, NJ: Princeton University Press, 1994.

10

S. Yizhar's *Khirbet Khizeh* and the Rhetoric of Conflict

SHAI GINSBURG

September 2, 1949. The last military operation of the 1948 War—the First Arab-Israeli War, the Israeli War of Liberation and Independence, the Palestinian *Nakba* or Catastrophe—was concluded merely six months earlier. The ceasefire agreement between Israel and Syria, the final of four such agreements between the newly established Jewish state and its neighboring states that officially brought the war to a close, was signed less than two months earlier. A notice in the daily newspapers ʿ*Al ha-Mishmar* and *Davar* announces the publication of S. Yizhar's new novella *Sipur ḥirbet ḥizʿa* (The story of Ḥirbet Ḥizʿa, translated into English as *Khirbet Khizeh*).[1] The laconic language of the ad is suggestive: "The cry of conscience of a Hebrew warrior as he clashes with the cruel face of our war."

Yizhar's novella relates a harrowing tale indeed. Spanning a day from sunrise to sunset, it chronicles a military operation to expel the Palestinian villagers of Khirbet Khizeh and transport them across the cease-fire lines. The Israeli troops who carry out the operation appear, by and large, to have no qualms about it; even the narrator—the only one of the perpetrators to articulate his compunctions—offers only a feeble protest. The expelled offer no resistance, so the operation proceeds unhindered to its prescribed end. Though the novella is fictitious—there was no Palestinian village by that name—Yizhar has insisted on the veracity of the events that it recounts, and his readers likewise conceived of it as a true account.[2] The novella was—and still is—considered a moral deliberation on Israelis' conduct during the 1948 War in general and on Israel's treatment of the Palestinian civilian population during that war in particular.[3]

Khirbet Khizeh was immediately recognized as a literary achievement, and it also enjoyed commercial success. In less than two years, it received dozens of reviews and sold more than 4,000 copies, a considerable number given the size of the Hebrew readership at the time.[4] As Anita Shapira notes, it "is one of the few fictions on the history of the War of Independence that has been incorporated into the scholastic canon of Hebrew literature. Since 1964 it has been a regular part of the high school literature syllabus and is even a selected work in the final secondary school *bagrut* matriculation exam."[5] As such, its cultural presence is conspicuous. Indeed, it became a staple not only of 1948 Hebrew fiction, of Hebrew war fiction in general, and of Hebrew fiction about the Israeli-Palestinian conflict but also of the Israeli Hebrew literary canon as a whole.

To be sure, Yizhar's concluding paragraph left an indelible impression on its readers and proved to be one of the most memorable passages of modern Hebrew prose fiction:

> The valley was calm. Somebody started already talking about supper. Far away on the dirt track, close to what appeared to be its end, a distant, darkening, swaying car, in the manner of heavy cars laden with fruit or produce or something, was gradually being swallowed up. Both painful humiliation and rage of helplessness would turn into a kind of casual shameful irritation. Everything was suddenly so open. So big, so very big. We all had become small and insignificant. Soon a time would arise in the world when it would be good to return from work, to return exhausted, to meet someone, or walk alone, to say nothing and walk.... All around silence was falling, and very soon it would close upon the last circle. And when silence had closed in on everything and no one disturbed the stillness, and the latter would sigh noiselessly for what was beyond silence—then God would come forth and go down to the valley to roam and see whether it was according to the cry of it. (*Khirbet Khizeh*, 89–90 112–13)

These final words bring to a climax Yizhar's deontological deliberation in *Khirbet Khizeh*. Yet these words also betray the fact that such a deliberation is inextricably bound to rhetorical considerations. I shall suggest, in fact, that this deliberation allows Yizhar to probe Hebrew rhetoric vis-à-vis the *raison de la guerre* of the newly established Jewish polity—indeed, vis-à-vis the very *raison d'état* of the latter. It leads him to ask, more precisely, whether the new state is indeed the vessel of traditional Jewish rhetoric as it claims to be or whether it marks a "breaking of the vessel" and a break away from this rhetoric.[6]

Yizhar's *Khirbet Khizeh* culminates with a great cry that alludes to the story of Sodom and Gomorrah (an allusion that Yizhar's Hebrew readers would not have failed to recognize). Both those who applauded the novella and those who found fault with it saw such biblical allusions—of which the great cry is but the apex—as evincing Yizhar's endeavor not only to cast the present story of war and atrocity as a biblical drama but, more than that, to lay claim to the mantle of the biblical prophet; where the two groups differed was whether he did so in good faith or not. Binyamin Yitzḥtak Michali for instance contends that "Yizhar's stories validate the continuity of the Jewish moral understanding.... [T]he ancient Jewish *ethos* was awoken and commenced to flow in the vessels of young Hebrew fiction."[7] Rhetorical continuity was thus read as continuity of ethos and morality. In what follows I shall reason, however, that Yizhar's is a story of crisis and break rather than one of continuity, a crisis that Yizhar's rhetoric both unfolds and enfolds.

The biblical rhetoric with which Yizhar brings his narrative to its end is often measured against and contrasted with the rhetoric of the operational order, which Yizhar "quotes" at length near the beginning of his novella. Indeed, Yizhar sets the order as the starting point of his narrative:

> One could ... mention straightaway that which had been the purpose of that entire day from the start, that "operational order" number such and such, on such and such day of the month, in the margin of which, in the final section that was simply entitled "miscellaneous," it was said, in a line and a half, that although "the mission must be executed decisively and precisely," nevertheless, "no violent outbursts or disordered conduct"—it said—"would be permitted," which only indicated straightaway that there was a reason for this, and that anything was possible (and yet, that everything is also planned and foreseen). And that you couldn't assess correctly this straightforward conclusion before returning to the opening and also scan the noteworthy clause that immediately warned of the mounting danger of "infiltrators," and "terrorist cells," and (in a wonderful turn of phrase) "operatives dispatched on hostile missions"; and also the subsequent and even more noteworthy clause, which was explicitly saying that, "the inhabitants of the area extending from point X (see attached map) to point Y (the same map) should be assembled—loaded onto transports, and conveyed across our lines; blow up the stone houses and burn the clay huts; detain the youths and the suspects, and clear the area of 'hostile forces,'" and so on and so forth—so that it was now obvious how many good and honest hopes were being invested in those who set out when they were burdened by all this "burn-blow-up-detain-load-convey," so that they would burn and blow up and detain and load and convey with such decorum and with a restraint born of true culture, and this would be a sign where the wind blows, of decent upbringing, and, perhaps, even of the Jewish soul, that great one. (*Khirbet Khizeh*, 7–9)

Khirbet Khizeh as a whole appears like a close reading of the rhetoric of this operational order. Such a reading reveals that what appears as straightforward is anything but that; it reveals that the operational order and its language serve to obfuscate the true nature of what is being ordered. Thus, the order's affirmation that no violence would be permitted notwithstanding spells out the violence to be unleashed: assemble, load, convey, detain, and blow. Simultaneously, however, the order enfolds as much as it unfolds: its topographical and functionalist vocabularies alongside its passive grammatical constructions allows it to charge the operation without naming its designated location, agents, and victims.

More than a mere prescription of a particular military action, the operational order marks a crisis of language in general and of Hebrew rhetoric in particular, a crisis brought about by the *raison de la guerre*. More specifically, the rhetoric of the order works to produce a breach between language and human action in the world. No more can language be trusted to correspond to action and the world (problematic and uncertain as such correspondence may be). On the contrary, language communicates to mystify both—the traditional accusation against rhetoric since at least Plato's dialogues—so that their true significance, ontological as well as deontological, is no longer manifest.[8] The operational order, that is, embodies bad rhetoric: an empty, morally suspect parlance. Herein lies the source of the moral crisis Yizhar explores, for military rhetoric, inasmuch as it produces a crisis of language, undercuts the demand to assess human conduct and assign it a moral value.

Yizhar's novella can be read as an endeavor to recover what the operational order elides. It is an endeavor to identify "the area extending from point X (see attached map) to point Y (the same map)" as the Palestinian village of Khirbet Khizeh; to identify its victims as the women, children, elderly people, and invalids who live in the village (as the narrator makes clear, no able-bodied man who could be considered an enemy combatant is left in the village); and to identify its agents as the Israeli-Jewish narrator and his comrades. Ultimately, this recovery turns into a process of moral exploration that reaches its climax in the concluding passages of the novella, with the allusion to the biblical story of Sodom and Gomorrah.[9]

Yizhar's turn to biblical rhetoric, then, is designed to mend the break effected by military rhetoric. His biblical allusion, however, is anything but innovative or extraordinary. Such allusions were, and continue to be, a key figure of Hebrew literature in general, and of modern Hebrew literature in particular.[10] Still, the heated public debate prompted by the novella suggests that more is at stake here than a mere literary figure, mere "rhetorical intertextuality."[11] Indeed, Yizhar's allusion to the Bible has to be read for its political and legal dimensions as these were manifested, first and foremost, by the Declaration of the Establishment of the State of Israel, delivered on 14 May 1948. The first sentence of the declaration reads: "In Eretz-Israel arose the Jewish people, where its spiritual, religious and political identity was shaped, where it attained state sovereignty, where it created cultural values of national and universal significance and gave to the world the eternal Book of Books."[12] The sentence, which opens by tracing the origins of the Jewish people to the territory it designates as "Eretz-Israel," concludes with a reference to the Hebrew Bible. The sentence binds together national identity, political sovereignty, and culture; it further establishes their interchangeability as the foundation of the polity to be proclaimed and the claim of that polity to the said territory. Such interchangeability serves to ground the particular claim for Jewish sovereignty in universal values as embodied in and by the Book. In fact, the particular and the universal become inextricably intertwined; the exclusive claim for territory and for sovereignty as a Jewish territory and Jewish sovereignty—rather than the territory of its inhabitants and their sovereignty—is hinged on the all-inclusive appeal of the Hebrew Bible. In between Eretz-Israel and the Book of Books, no room is left for the non-Jewish Palestinian present or for the Jewish diasporic past. The two, so it appears, would challenge the claims at the heart of the declaration. For the non-Jewish presence, rooted as it were in territory, may suggest that other national entities have a rightful claim over Eretz-Israel and the diasporic Jewish past, in its vast cultural production, may suggest that Jewish identity is not necessarily bound to that territory.[13]

It is within the nexus of the claim for exclusive territorial rights and exclusive sovereignty through the appeal to the Hebrew Bible that one has to read Yizhar's biblical allusion. One should note that within the rhetoric of the Declaration of the Establishment of the State of Israel, the reference to the Hebrew Bible serves as a fetish: even as the declaration hails the Hebrew Bible as "the eternal Book of Books," its language and argumentation conspicuously lack specific references to the biblical texts—a surprising fact, given the prevalence of such allusions, as just noted, in Hebrew belles-lettres.[14] Its formulation remains within the general, though vague, references to the "vision of the Prophets of Israel" as the foundation of "the principles of liberty, justice and peace" of the new state and to the "Rock of Israel" in the concluding paragraph as what secures the declaration.[15] The claim for continuity—of rhetorical continuity taken as political and legal continuity—is more a fetish than a reality. Yizhar's extended allusion to the story of Sodom and Gomorrah—his explicit appeal to the biblical God in an endeavor to gauge the events of *Khirbet Khizeh* vis-à-vis the principles of liberty, justice, and peace—thus appear to test not only the biblical fetishism of the Declaration of the Establishment of the State of Israel, but also the very *raison d'état* used to proclaim the state.

Yizhar embeds in his concluding passage the language of two biblical verses in particular: "And the Lord said, Because the cry of Sodom and Gomorrah is great, and because their sin is very grievous; I will go down now, and see whether they have done altogether according to the cry of it, which is come unto me; and if not, I will know" (Genesis 18:20–21). The two verses announce a legal drama whose participants are—in addition to the people of Sodom and Gomorrah—God's emissaries as investigating magistrates, the Patriarch Abraham as a defense attorney, and God as a presiding judge and executioner. Within this legal drama, the transgressions of the two cities are corroborated, their verdict pronounced, and their punishment deliberated and ultimately meted out. The legal drama centers on the exchange between Abraham and God in which Abraham argues on behalf of the accused in an endeavor to reduce their punishment. Inasmuch as that exchange highlights the linkage between language, persuasion, and moral principles, it is rhetorical in the classical sense and marks, in effect, a scene of rhetoric.

From its very beginning, however, the story of Sodom and Gomorrah is intertwined with the divine promise to Abraham. The two cities are first mentioned when Lot, Abraham's nephew, parts ways with Abraham because "the land was not able to bear them, that they might dwell together.... And Lot lifted up his eyes, and beheld all the plain of Jordan, that it *was* well watered every where, before the Lord destroyed Sodom and Gomorrah, *even* as the garden of the Lord.... But the men of Sodom were wicked and sinners before the Lord exceedingly" (Genesis 13:7–13). God follows Lot's departure with a promise: "Lift up now thine eyes, and look from the place where thou art northward, and southward, and eastward, and westward: For all the land which thou seest, to thee will I give it, and to thy seed for ever" (Genesis 13:14–15). It is no surprise, then, that the trial of Sodom and Gomorrah in Genesis 18 immediately follows God's pronouncement that Sarah would soon give birth to a son and a reiteration of the promise: "Shall

I hide from Abraham that thing which I do; Seeing that Abraham shall surely become a great and mighty nation, and all the nations of the earth shall be blessed in him? For I know him, that he will command his children and his household after him, and they shall keep the way of the Lord, to do justice and judgment; that the Lord may bring upon Abraham that which he hath spoken of him" (Genesis 18: 17–19). Divine retribution and divine reward are coupled, as two sides of one coin.

Khirbet Khizeh should consequently be read from the double biblical perspective of covenant and trial. In fact, the novella overlays the narrative projected by the military order with the one projected by the biblical narrative, deploying each to probe the other. Consider, for instance, the first appearance of Khirbet Khizeh:

> Moishe, the company commander, gathered us together, and briefed us about the situation, the lay of the land, and the objective. From which it transpired that the few houses on the lower slope of another hill were some Khirbet Khizeh or other, and all the surrounding groves and fields belonged to that village, whose abundant water, good soil, and choice crops had gained reputation almost equal to that of its inhabitants, who were, they said, a band of ruffians, who gave succor to the enemy, and were ready for any mischief should the opportunity only arise; or, for example, should they happen to encounter any Jews you could be sure they would wipe them out, in a raging fury—such was their nature, and such were their ways. (Yizhar, *Khirbet Khizeh*, 10–11).

Khirbet Khizeh appears, then, in the image of the plain of Jordan before the Lord rained brimstone and fire on it, an image of Eden peopled with sinners, as a modern telling of the biblical story. Still, in Yizhar's novella, the gaze that observes, assigns guilt, and announces retribution is not God's, but Moishe's. Indeed, the novella points at the exchange of the divine promise of retribution and inheritance for a human promise, of divine destruction for human destruction. In transposing the biblical language and making it human, Yizhar follows a common practice in modern Hebrew literature. Yet such a transposition is also in defiance of biblical language, a human transgression and violation of the divine realm. To be more precise, whereas the biblical text distinguishes between observation, retribution, and inheritance—God places the territory, whether promised or doomed, in human view, but the actual moment of endowment or destruction is delayed until a future time, often undefined and unspecified—modern military rhetoric—a language divorced from the presence of the divine—conflates human observation, retribution, and inheritance in the present time.[16] In this conflation, the novella locates the offense it brings to divine trial in its final passage. In this context, that passage should be noted as an endeavor to reintroduce God—in fiction, it should be underscored—into the rhetoric of the state and its military, to retheologize it, if you will, as a measure against human violence.

Such an endeavor, however, is far from having a decisive effect. The said transgression turns not only the modern drama staged by the operational order (on behalf of the Declaration of the Establishment of the State of Israel) into a grotesque play of gratuitous violence and inequity, but the biblical drama of divine trial as well. As the Israeli troops enter the village, they find not the menacing and murderous men of Sodom and Gomorrah (Genesis 19:4–11) or, for that matter, of the fabled Khirbet Khizeh, but a very different crowd:

> For who were we dealing with after all, but for some women with babies in their arms (bleary-eyed driveling Arab babies wrapped in rags and good-luck charms) and a few other women clasping their hands and mumbling as they walked? There were also a few old men walking silently and solemnly as though towards Judgment Day and other middle-aged men, too, who felt they weren't old enough yet to be safe from the impending wrath . . . and a blind man led by a child, perhaps his grandson. (*Khirbet Khizeh*, 60–61, 72–73)

The sight of these human figures puts into relief the crisis of rhetoric, both modern and biblical. These figures render the deployment of tropes such as "infiltrators," "terrorist cells" and "operatives dispatched on hostile missions"—a deployment that serves to ground the ultimate objective of the operational order, the transport of the villagers "across our lines"—as a mere ploy. Simultaneously, however, these figures also render the biblical rhetoric of retribution and inheritance dubious. For they make it clear that the biblical narrative fails to identify culprits and innocents correctly. The villagers—cast as the contemporary embodiment of the people of Sodom and Gomorrah—are revealed to be faultless, whereas the troops—cast in Abraham's image—are revealed to be cold-hearted miscreants. Be that as it may, however, the villagers cannot escape their destruction as entailed in their assigned role as villains, nor can the troops be deprived of their bequest as entailed in their roles as the righteous. Their merits or demerits notwithstanding, the actors in this all-too-human drama cannot diverge from the course laid out by divine speech, as articulated in the biblical text. In so rearticulating the biblical story of Sodom and Gomorrah as its predestination, that is, the story of Khirbet Khizeh implicates biblical rhetoric in its inequity.

The sight of the human figures of Khirbet Khizeh prompts the narrator (who remains unnamed throughout the novella) to assume the role of Abraham and argue on behalf of the condemned. He indeed articulates to himself what he sees: "Something struck me like lightning. All at once everything seemed to mean something different, more correct: exile. This was exile. This was what exile was like. This was what exile looked like" (Yizhar, *Khirbet Khizeh*, 84). As critics have not failed to note, herein lies the moral crux of the narrative of *Khirbet Khizeh*. The anaphora underscores the metaphoric exchange between Palestinians and Jews, between past and present, as the narrator presents his contemporaneous Palestinians as the embodiment of historical Jews. It has not been noted, however, that this metaphorical exchange announces, in effect, a crisis of rhetoric. Following the biblical matrix of Yizhar's novella, the reader surely expects that when the moment arises, the narrator would echo Abraham's question, as he was contending with God over the fate of Sodom and Gomorrah: "Wilt thou also destroy the righteous with the wicked?" (Genesis 18:23). Yizhar's narrator, however, is unable to follow suit:

> I bumped into Moishe.
> "What are you looking at me like that for?" said Moishe.
> "This is a filthy war," I said to him in a somewhat choked voice.
> "Please," said Moishe. "So what do you want?"
> And there was something I really did want. And I had something to say. I just didn't know how to say anything that would be practical wisdom rather than merely excitement. He should be shaken. He had to understand, quickly and immediately, the seriousness of the situation.
> Instead of which Moishe told me, pushing his cap back away from his forehead, like someone exhausted from too much worries, like a man talking to his friend, scrabbling in his pockets after cigarettes and matches, and trying to clothe in words something that had just occurred to him, he answered me:
> "Just you listen to what I'm saying." Moishe's eyes sought mine as he spoke. "Immigrants of ours will come to this Khirbet what's-its-name, you hear me, and they'll take this land and work it and it'll be beautiful here!"
> Of course. Absolutely. Why hadn't I realized it from the outset! Khirbet Khizeh is ours. Questions of housing, and problems of absorption. And hooray, we'd house and absorb—and how: We'd open a grocery store, establish a school, maybe even a synagogue. There would be political parties here. They'd debate lots of things. They'd plow fields, and sow, and reap, and do great things. Long Live Hebrew Khizeh! Who

would ever imagine that once there had been some Khirbet Khizeh that we expelled and inherited. We came, we shot, we burned, we blew up, we thrust and we shoved and we banished. (*Khirbet Khizeh*, 107–8)

The narrator fails to turn his private language into a public one. His failure is a rhetorical failure, inasmuch as rhetoric marks a public performance of language; inasmuch as it marks a public delivery of an argument clearly and persuasively; and, indeed, inasmuch as rhetoric is classically discussed in the context of political, legal, or moral deliberation and as Quintilian, for instance, would have it, a public demonstration of the virtue of the orator.[17] The moral failure that Yizhar's novella explores is, therefore, one and the same with the breakdown of the scene of rhetoric.

The breakdown of the scene of rhetoric that the novella presents is especially striking for several reasons. First, the narrator has just—as we have seen—articulated the moral argument in a classical form. Second, the novella reveals the bad faith of the Declaration of the Establishment of the State of Israel in its call on the Arab inhabitants—central to its international ratification as stipulated out by the UN Resolution 181 on the Future Government of Palestine of 20 November 1947, popularly known as the Partition Resolution—to peaceably play a role in the development of the State. Third, and most important, the novella undercuts Yizhar's own rhetoric, inasmuch as that rhetoric hinges on one key trope: that of the Garden of Eden or, more precisely, of the expulsion from the garden. Yizhar's deployment of the trope builds on the biblical trope that lies at the heart of the story of Sodom and Gomorrah. Indeed, the Plain of Jordan is explicitly compared to Eden. For these reasons the story as a whole should be seen as an allegory of the narrative of bliss, sin, and fall from grace that is spatially articulated as the expulsion from the Garden of Eden. That narrative is central to Yizhar's fiction in general, but in *Khirbet Khizeh* its rhetorical implications are the most explicit.[18] The implications are not merely that Yizhar portrays Khirbet Khizeh as just a reincarnation of Eden, nor that he so renders the expulsion of its citizens as a reenactment of the expulsion from Eden, nor that he casts the Israeli troops in the role of the "flaming sword which turned every way" (Genesis 3:24), the personification of divine wrath and, even more strikingly, the emissaries of the principle of evil that brings about sin and expulsion in the first place. Rather, the point is that in deploying the trope of the expulsion from the garden, Yizhar sets against each other a state of bliss and a state of fall that uneasily correspond to Palestine before the creation of the State of Israel and to the State of Israel. In other words, he directs our attention to the *raison de la guerre*, to the very *raison d'état* of the newly established state—under whose aegis the expulsion of Khirbet Khizeh's residents is carried out—as producing a fall in the theological sense of the word.

The trope of the garden allows Yizhar to articulate a devastating critique of Zionist rhetoric in general. *Khirbet Khizeh* as a whole could be read as an inquest into two of the key maxims of Zionist rhetoric, maxims that were deployed and circulated to justify the Zionist endeavor first in Palestine and then in the State of Israel, at the very moment the two are about to be realized: "a Land without People for a People without Land" and "to Make the Desert Bloom."[19] The two maxims together chart a two-step reversal of the course of Jewish history of exile and wandering (as conceived, it should be added, by Zionist theoreticians), a reversal that seeks to undo expulsion and inhabit anew the deserted garden. Yet, as the novella makes clear, the Garden is neither empty nor desolate. Rather, it is emptied and desolated so it can be claimed, possessed, settled, and nurtured anew, turned into a blooming garden anew. The garden thus becomes more than a rhetorical trope: it is revealed as a means of destruction, designed to conceal the great violence, even brutality, that produced it. It is designed to conceal, in other words, the presence of Palestinians, their fate, and Israeli responsibility for that fate.

I am back at the concluding passage of *Khirbet Khizeh* with which I opened my discussion of Yizhar's novella. When all traces of its recent inhabitants disappear from view, the garden—as a place of blissful (though, in Yizhar's version, earthly) existence—is reinstated. It is at this point that the novella turns most explicitly to biblical rhetoric and embeds that rhetoric into its language as it brings its moral deliberation to a climax. In that turn we see a last effort to shatter the trope of the garden and, with it, both the *raison de la guerre* and *raison d'état* in which the trope is irrevocably implicated. Yizhar's language, however, even as it openly echoes the biblical text, is anything but true to its spirit. The scene at the end of the novella is, in fact, a far cry from the scene to which Yizhar alludes. The difference is rhetorical: as I have suggested, the biblical narrative of trial and moral deliberation sets a scene of rhetoric, but Yizhar's conclusion sets an eschatological scene of a final judgment without rhetoric. It is a scene beyond human life, history, and language altogether, "when silence had closed in on everything and no one disturbed the stillness, and the latter would sigh noiselessly for what was beyond silence (*Khirbet Khizeh*, 90, 113)." All that remains is the non-human cry of the land itself.

Yizhar's abrogation of rhetoric is unsettling. It foreshadows the public reticence of the author, who was elected to the Israeli parliament in February 1949 and who throughout his eighteen years as an MP never broached the subject of Israel's treatment of the Palestinians in public (that is, not in fiction). His concluding outcry notwithstanding, then, the abrogation of rhetoric seems to allow him to adjourn the trial of Khirbet Khizeh for the present. In between the constitutive ur-scene of expulsion and the eschatological scene of divine judgment, the novella spans—even if perfunctorily—a present time of human existence, blissfully ignorant of the great violence that brought it about and of the condemnation that awaits it when it is no longer. The demand for justice is to be heard again only at the end of time, when there will no longer be any human being to hear it and assume moral responsibility for it. God is summoned, then, as a *deus ex machina* to save the narrative from its moral aporia, from the simultaneous demand to assume moral responsibility and unwillingness to do so within human history. God remains beyond rhetoric, as the sole addressee of the cry, the sole anchor of the claim to morality.

NOTES

1. Although I quote the English translation, I have modified it in numerous places to make it closer to the Hebrew original. The novella was published together with the short story "*Ha-Shavuy*" (The POW), which had initially been published the previous November in the monthly magazine *Molad*. The story was later translated as "The Prisoner."

2. See, for instance, Yizhar's "*Be-Terem Aharish*" and "*Lo Ukhal le-Haharish Aheret*" (the previously unpublished introduction to *Khirbet Khizeh*); Uri S. Cohen, "'Al Hitnatsluto ha-Ma'ashima shel S. Yizhar."

3. See, for instance, Todd Hasak-Lowy, *Here and Now*, 101–42; David Kenaani, "Ba-Shayara uve-Tsida"; Shalom Kraemer, *Hilufey Mishmarot be-Sifrutenu*, 266–74; Adia Mendelson-Maoz, *Ha-Sifrut ke-Ma'abada Musarit*, 93–110; Dan Miron, *Mul ha-Ah ha-Shotek*, 317–25; Yochai Oppenheimer, *Me-'Ever la-Gader*, 166–95.

4. For the sake of comparison, Moshe Shamir's 1947 novel *He Walked in the Fields*, the best seller of the time, was published in a first edition of 3,000 copies. A second, paperback, edition sold 20,000 copies between 1948 and 1956. See Gershon Shaked, *Ha-Siporet ha-'Ivrit 1880–1980*, 3:283.

5. Anita Shapira, "Hirbet Hizah," 2. For a summary of the critical reception of the novella, see Haim Nagid, "Mavo."

6. Whereas no critic has failed to note Yizhar's distinctive language, the uniqueness of the language of *Khirbet Khizeh* within Yizhar's *oeuvre* has received little attention. For general con-

siderations of Yizhar's language, see, for instance, Dan Miron, introduction; G. Shaked, *Ha-Siporet ha-ʿIvrit*, 4:189–229.

7. Binyamin Yitzḥak Michali, "Ha-Etos she-Hikhziv: ʿAl 'ha-Shavui' ve-'Ḥirbet Ḥizʿa' le-S. Yizhar," 237. In this essay, Michali revisits his earlier assessment of Yizhar's war fiction.

8. See, for instance, Plato's "Gorgias."

9. See also my discussion of this passage in *Rhetoric and Nation*, 217–29.

10. See, for instance, Ruth Kartun-Blum, *Profane Scriptures*; Malka Shaked, *La-Netsaḥ Anagnekh*; David Jacobson, *Does David Still Play before You?*

11. Malka Shaked employs the term "rhetorical intertextuality" to define contemporary literary allusions to the Bible (*La-Netsaḥ Anagnekh*, 19).

12. I have diverged from the official English translation because it fails to reflect the grammar—and, hence, the meaning—of the Hebrew text. For the official English translation, see Walter Laqueur and Barry Rubin, *The Israeli-Arab Reader*, 81–83 (the quote is from 81).

13. For a historical account of the declaration and the formulation of its text, see Zeev Sharef, *Three Days*. For recent discussions of its different drafts, rhetoric, and status within Israeli law, see Orit Kamir, "'La-Megila,' Yesh Shtey Panim"; Yoram Shachar, "Ha-Tyotot ha-Mukdamot shel Hakhrazat ha-ʿAtsmaʾut"; Yizhar Tal, "Hakhrazat ha-ʿAtsmaʾut—ʿIyun Histori Parshani."

14. For a discussion of the book as a fetish in the postcolonial context, see my "Signs and Wonders."

15. The phrase "Rock of Israel" appears only twice in the Bible (Samuel 2 23:3 and Isaiah 30:29); it is significant that the writers of the declaration preferred it to more common expressions. As Shachar notes in "Ha-Tyotot ha-Mukdamot shel Hakhrazat ha-ʿAtsmaʾut," however, one should probably read the expression not so much as a biblical allusion as a reference to the "divine Providence" that appears in the last sentence of the US Declaration of Independence and, moreover, as a specific allusion to the concluding paragraph of the last blessing of the Morning *Shema* Prayer, known as the Blessing of Redemption. Shachar documents how the explicit allusions to the biblical text that anchored the claim to territory and sovereignty of the first draft of the Israeli declaration were elided in subsequent drafts.

16. The conflation of observation, retribution, and inheritance is embodied in the character of Moishe, the company commander. The biblical Moses is shown the Promised Land but is prohibited from entering it, in yet another conflation of pledge and retribution: "And the Lord said unto him, This *is* the land which I sware unto Abraham, unto Isaac, and unto Jacob, saying, I will give it unto thy seed: I have caused thee to see *it* with thine eyes, but thou shalt not go over thither" (Deuteronomy 34:4; emphasis added). In contrast, Moishe, his namesake, does not merely both show and observe the land, but he also proceeds to lead his men into and take over the territory, thus violating the biblical interdiction.

17. Quintilian, *The Orator's Education*, vol. 1, 2.14–17. See also Heinrich Lausberg, *Handbook of Literary Rhetoric*, 17–23.

18. See, for instance, Uri Shoham, "Ha-ʿArava ha-Ptuḥa, ha-Pardes ha-Sagur veha-Kfar ha-ʿArvi."

19. Diana Muir traces the maxim "a land without a people for a people without a land" to nineteenth-century Christian writers ("A Land without a People for a People without a Land"). Based on the paucity of references to the maxim in English in the first half of the twentieth century, Muir concludes that it was not central to Zionist rhetoric. She curiously fails, however, to examine its presence in other languages; it should be noted that at least until the Second World War, English was not one of the main Zionist languages, and German, Polish,

Yiddish, and Hebrew were more central to the circulation of Zionist terms and notions. Muir thus dates the first Zionist use of the term to Israel Zangwil in 1901 and fails to note earlier references to Palestine before the creation of the State of Israel as an empty territory in the Jewish press in other languages. For a critique of the two maxims, see Edward W. Said, *The Question of Palestine*, chap. 1.

BIBLIOGRAPHY

Cohen, Uri S. "'Al Hitnatsluto ha-Ma'ashima shel S. Yizhar,'" *Haaretz* 19 September 2009.
Ginsburg, Shai P. *Rhetoric and Nation: The Formation of Hebrew National Culture, 1880–1990.* Syracuse, NY: Syracuse University Press, 2014.
———. "Signs and Wonders: Fetishism and Hybridity in Homi Bhabha's *The Location of Culture.*" *New Centennial Review* 9, no. 3 (2009): 229–50.
Hasak-Lowy, Todd. *Here and Now: History, Nationalism, and Realism in Modern Hebrew Fiction.* Syracuse, NY: Syracuse University Press, 2008.
Jacobson, David. *Does David Still Play before You? Israeli Poetry and the Bible.* Detroit, MI: Wayne State University Press, 1997.
Kamir, Orit. "'La-Megila,' Yesh Shtey Panim: Sipuran ha-Muzar shel 'Hakhrazat ha-Medina ha-Tsiyonit' ve-'Hakhrazat ha-Medina ha-Demokratit.'" *Iyunei Mishpat* 23 (1999): 473–538.
Kartun-Blum, Ruth. *Profane Scriptures: Reflections on the Dialogue with the Bible in Modern Hebrew Poetry.* Cincinnati, OH: Hebrew Union College Press, 1999.
Kenaani, David. "Ba-Shayara uve-Tsida." *Orlogin* 5 (1952): 45–65.
Kraemer, Shalom. *Ḥilufey Mishmarot be-Sifrutenu: Ma'amarim u-Masot.* Tel Aviv: Hebrew Writers Association by Dvir, 1959.
Laqueur, Walter, and Barry Rubin. *The Israeli-Arab Reader.* 6th ed. New York: Penguin, 2001.
Lausberg, Heinrich. *Handbook of Literary Rhetoric: A Foundation for Literary Study.* Leiden: Brill, 1998.
Mendelson-Maoz, Adia. *Ha-Sifrut ke-Ma'abada Musarit: Kri'a be-Mivḥar Yetsirot ba-Proza shel ha-Me'a ha-'Esrim.* Ramat Gan, Israel: Bar-Ilan University Press, 2009.
Michali, Binyamin Yitzḥak. "Ha-Etos she-Hikhziv: 'Al 'ha-Shavui' ve-'Ḥirbet Ḥiz'a' le-S. Yizhar." *Moznayim* 35 (1972): 235–51.
Miron, Dan. Introduction to S. Yizhar, *Midnight Convoy*, ix–lv. London: Toby, 2007.
———. *Mul ha-Aḥ ha-Shotek: 'Iyunim be-Shirat Milḥemet ha-'Atsma'ut.* Jerusalem: Keter, 1992.
Muir, Diana. "A Land without a People for a People without a Land." *Middle East Quarterly* (spring 2008): 55–62.
Nagid, Haim. "*Mavo: Hitpatḥut ha-Bikoret 'al Sipurey S. Yizhar.*" In *S. Yizhar: Mivḥar Ma'amrey Bikoret 'al Yetsirato*, edited by Haim Nagid, 16–24. Tel Aviv: Am Oved, 1972.
Oppenhaimer, Yochai. *Me-'Ever la-Gader: Yitsug ha-'Aravim ba-Siporet ha-'Ivrit veha-Yisre'elit (1906–2005).* Tel Aviv: Am Oved, 2008.
Plato. "Gorgias." In *The Collected Dialogues of Plato.* Edited by Edith Hamilton and Huntington Cairns and translated by W. D. Woodhead, 229–307. Princeton, NJ: Princeton University Press, 1961.
Quintilian. *The Orator's Education.* Edited and translated by Donald A. Russell. 5 vols. Cambridge, MA: Harvard University Press, 2002.
Said, Edward W. *The Question of Palestine.* New York: Vintage, 1979.

Shachar, Yoram. "Ha-Tyotot ha-Mukdamot shel Hakhrazat ha-ʿAtsmaʾut." *ʿIyunei Mishpat* 26 (2002): 523–600.

Shaked, Gershon. *Ha-Siporet ha-ʿIvrit 1880–1980*. 5 vols. Tel Aviv: Hakibbutz Hameuchad, 1977–98.

Shaked, Malka. *La-Netsaḥ Anagnekh: Ha-Mikra ba-Shira ha-ʿIvrit ha-Ḥadasha*. Tel Aviv: Yediʿot Aḥaronot, 2005.

Shapira, Anita. "Ḥirbet Ḥizah: Between Remembrance and Forgetting." *Jewish Social Studies*, ns 7, no.1 (2000): 1–62.

Sharef, Zeev. *Three Days*. London: W. H. Allen, 1962.

Shoham, Uri. "Ha-ʿArava ha-Ptuḥa, ha-Pardes ha-Sagur veha-Kfar ha-ʿArvi." *Siman Kriʾa* 3–4 (1974): 336–46.

Tal, Yizhar. "Hakhrazat ha-ʿAtsmaʾut—ʿIyun Histori Parshani." *Mishpat u-Mimshal* 6 (2006): 551–90.

Yizhar, S. "*Be-Terem Aḥarish*." *Yediʿot Aḥaronot*, 24 February 1978.

———. *Khirbet Khizeh*. Translated by Nicholas de Lange and Yaacob Dwek. Jerusalem: Ibis, 2008.

———. "*Lo Ukhal le-Haḥarish Aḥeret*." *Haaretz*, 19 September 2009.

———. "The Prisoner." Translated by V. C. Rycus. In *Israeli Stories: A Selection of the Best Contemporary Hebrew Writing*, edited by Joel Blocker, 57–72. New York: Schocken, 1962.

———. *Sipur Ḥirbet Ḥizʿa*. Merḥhavya, Israel: Sifiriat Poʿalim, 1949.

Esther's Book
A Rhetoric of Writing for Jewish Feminists

SUSAN ZAESKE

In *Rootprints: Memory and Life Writing*, rhetorical and literary theorist Hélène Cixous reproduces a photograph of her younger brother, Pierre, and herself on Purim, she dressed as Esther and he as Ahasuerus. In the accompanying text, she writes that in childhood, "All the time I lived my life with the life of a small boy. I lived with the possibilities: I had a female possibility (that was me) and the masculine possibility with all its episodes.... I went through the stages of development of a little boy. It was fortunate." Linking her experiencing of female and male gender development with her writing practice, Cixous explains, "The brother is very strongly in me. He appears little in my texts, but he is certainly a constituent of my masculine universes." As she continues narrating her early life, Cixous dwells on her changing sense of self. She recalls her arrival in France in 1955 as a turning point in her identity for it was then that she "felt the true torments of exile." Growing up in Oran, French Algeria, she had known that she and her family were German Czechoslovak Hungarian Jews who also were "other Arabs." What she learned at lycée in Paris was that "my unacceptable truth in this world was my being a woman. Right away, it was war. I felt the explosion, the odour of misogyny. Up until then, living in a world of women, I had not felt it, I was a Jewess, I was Jew." Cixous resisted these antisemitic and antiwoman assaults on her sense of self by enlisting the power of writing: "From 1955 on, I adopted an imaginary nationality which is literary nationality." Drawing strength from the position of exiled other, which she deemed the "Jewoman," Cixous devoted her life's work to producing literary/rhetorical theory and practice that insists on the fluidity of the subject to empower writing to be a radically transgressive act.[1]

Cixous is far from the only Jewish woman who has connected her early sense of identity to memories of performing the role of Queen Esther. Jewish feminist and queer theorist Eve Kosofsky Sedgwick writes, "I have a snapshot of myself at about five, barefoot in the pretty 'Queen Esther' dress my grandmother made (white satin, gold spangles), making a careful eyes-down toe-pointed curtsey at (presumably) my father." As a child, Sedgwick welcomed parental attention won by wearing a pretty dress and gold spangles, but as an adult she cringed at the traditional Purim tableau captured by her father's camera. "Even today," she laments, "Jewish little girls are educated in gender roles—fondness for being looked at, fearlessness in defense of 'their people,' nonsolidarity with their sex—through masquerading as Queen Esther at Purim." Nevertheless, Sedgwick embraces the story of Esther as a tool to analyze how Proust and Racine dramatize Jewish self-identification or "coming out." Sedgwick confides that she finds the story singularly powerful because Esther's individual act that risks losing the love of her master "has the power to save not only her own space in life but her people."[2]

The photographic memories of Cixous and Sedgwick are only two instances of the multitude of Purim remembrances held in the minds of generations of Jewish women. They and other Jewish feminist writers have discovered in the Book of Esther a certain self-consciousness about writing, a surprising destabilization of the patriarchal written word hidden in plain sight in the Old Testament. While exposing dominant males as lacking control of the technology of writing, Megillat Esther honors a woman who saves the Jews and records in writing the history of her actions to avert a pogrom, a history for future generations to read and thus remember. Yet, rather than join the foolish Ahasuerus and his advisors by insisting that a text can be fixed forever, the Megillat Esther embraces impermanence and invites appropriation. It leaves questions unanswered, the narrative open to more reversals, and its characters available for identification and appropriation by readers. At the same time as it destabilizes patriarchal writing and rejects the notion of textual stability, for many Jewish feminists it reinscribes the figure of the seemingly mindless beautiful woman who uses her feminine wiles, competes against other women, and attempts to gain power in a male-dominated world. While Esther does progress beyond a brainless beauty queen, for many Jewish feminists she becomes an equally problematic self-sacrificing Jewish woman, always putting the needs of the Jews before her own. This tension in the narrative between demonstrating that a woman can succeed by seizing the transformative potential of writing and containing feminist agency has made a good number of Jewish feminists uncomfortable with the biblical story, and some of them have rejected Esther entirely. Yet, remarkably often, this tension has also provoked Jewish feminists to write with, against, and beyond the Book of Esther. Indeed, as Mieke Bal puns, the Purim story has generated "lots of writing."[3]

This essay begins by attending to the text of the Jewish Bible story to reveal the rhetorical theory of writing hidden in the Book of Esther. (To best understand this analysis, it is helpful to read or reread the biblical story.[4]) It then turns to examples of Jewish feminists appropriating Megillat Esther to inform their own rhetorical theories of writing and to use the story as a source of invention for feminist arguments. In this way, the essay demonstrates not only that the Book of Esther offers Jewish feminists a theory of the nature and necessity of writing but also that the ancient narrative has provoked Jewish women to embrace the power of writing to formulate new feminist endings to the Old Testament tale.

A Rhetorical Theory of Writing Hidden in Plain Sight

The Book of Esther is self-conscious. It opens by perseverating about its authenticity attempting to staunch the flow of this self-radiated anxiety calling attention to itself by citing a suspicious overabundance of dates, place names, and rituals. As it draws to a close, the text explicitly refers to its own conception, saying, "And the commandment of Esther confirmed these matters of Purim; and it was written in the book" (Esther 9:32). With this verse, the Book of Esther narrates itself into existence and gives itself a history, and an author. The verse implies that before Esther "confirmed"—bore witness to—the "matters of Purim," there was no historical record of the Jews escaping annihilation at the hands of Haman due to the bravery of Esther and Mordecai. There was no Purim story. Having given testimony to the events she witnessed, the verse reports, Esther explicitly commanded that her spoken words be set in writing in the form of a book, a book that bears her name. This, of course, is the very book being read by the reader, who is reading the verse that rehearses the memory of how the book became a book. And the story of how the book became a book is also the story of how

Esther went from silence, to speaking, to writing so that Jews may read and remember.[5]

This self-consciousness about the creative acts that brought the text into being is reinforced throughout the Book of Esther with remarkable attention to the rhetorical act of writing.[6] In the first chapter, the king's advisor urges: "Let it be written among the laws of the Persians and the Medes, that it be not altered, that Vashti come no more before king Ahasuerus" (Esther 1:19). In the second chapter, using Esther as a conduit, Mordecai reports men plotting against the king, who are ultimately hanged, and "it was written in the book of chronicles before the king" (Esther 2:22). The third fateful chapter emphasizes the role of writing in publicizing and legitimizing Haman's plot to massacre the Jews: "Then were the king's scribes called in the first month, on the thirteenth day thereof, and there was written, according to all that Haman commanded, unto the king's satraps, and to the governors that were over every province, and to the princes of every people; to every province according to the writing thereof, and to every people after their language; in the name of king Ahasuerus was it written, and it was sealed with the king's ring" (Esther 3:12). Although depicted as permanently fixed by the force of the king's signet ring, this text—this command made artifact through the use of the technology of writing—ultimately is impermanent. The force of the king's seal is unable to imbue the text with the power to fend off writing over, papering over, masking by new texts. And it is the petition of Esther that effects the papering over of the text: "If it please the king, and if I have found favour in his sight, and the thing seem right before the king, and I be pleasing in his eyes, let it be written to reverse the letters devised by Haman the son of Hammedatha the Agagite, which he wrote to destroy the Jews that are in all the king's provinces" (Esther 8:5). Ahasuerus replies to Queen Esther and Mordecai the Jew, saying: "Write ye also concerning the Jews, as it liketh you, in the king's name, and seal it with the king's ring; for the writing which is written in the king's name, and sealed with the king's ring, may no man reverse" (Esther 8:8). The king, who is as mistaken about his ability to control words as he is about his ability to control women, gives Esther authority to write in his name. And she does write; she writes the book which thereafter bears *her* name.

In the course of attending to writing, the text assumes a voice of its own, constantly commenting on what is happening to itself while the characters develop and the narrative churns along. Indeed, the text can be understood as a character within itself that experiences reversals of fortune akin to those dealt to Vashti and Haman. Vashti is the queen of all of Persia, but at the king's whim, she is deposed and never heard from again. Haman is the powerful vice chancellor, and just as he is poised to defeat his archenemy, he is hung on a gallows of his own making. Likewise, the lives of texts in the Book of Esther undergo jarring reversals. They are written—often dramatically commanded into being and legitimized through the brandishing of the royal seal—then published in multiple languages, then circulated throughout the empire "by posts on horseback, riding on swift steeds" (Esther 8:10). Yet, despite their celebrated nativity, the texts' commands are frequently reversed by rashly formulated, inane new edicts. In one case, a decree forbids a woman—Queen Vashti—to come to the king, only to be followed soon thereafter by another ordering all virgins in the empire to the king. This reversal of fate in the texts pertaining to the status of women in the empire foreshadows the reversal of fate in the texts pertaining to the status of the Jews exiled in Persia, which is the very heart of the Purim story. One decree orders the massacre of all the Jews, then another is issued to write over the first, authorizing the Jews to murder their enemies.

There is no portrayal of rewriting, only writing over—creating a new text to cover over the old rather than altering an existing text. Texts, like the characters in the Book of Esther, are always impermanent, unstable, unfixed, susceptible to change, the original being masked by the new text. Repeatedly, the biblical narrative depicts the suppression of an existing text through the pressing of a new text over the old. This ability to mask over undesirable existing texts creates the potential, indeed, the imperative, for more writing. As a character in the play, Text is revealed as both powerful and vulnerable, sharing with humans an aspiration for immortality, yet aware of the reality of its vulnerability to being forgotten. Text can be manipulated by those who possess the agency to interpret, formulate ideas, command, and call into action the technology of writing. In this accretion of texts, this palimpsest, the text of the Book of Esther gestures toward the abiding form of the Jewish rhetorical tradition—midrash.[7] In the megillah as in the midrash, new contexts, new interpretations, new authors lead to the composition of new texts. Rather than replacing the preexisting text, the new texts are piled one atop the other, creating a layered, ever-changing, living text that resists fixity or containment.

The Book of Esther reflects the midrashic tradition not only by emphasizing the power of writing but also by reinforcing the necessity of reading texts. It does so through the negative example of King Ahasuerus, who never reads or writes but always calls upon his chamberlains to read to him and to write for him. He is seemingly illiterate, unable to master or manage the technology of the written word, and consequently unable to formulate a cogent thought. Unable to read or write, he lacks control not only of his ideas but also of his own history, for it is Esther, not Ahasuerus, who writes the chronicle of the days of his reign "from India even unto Ethiopia" (Esther 1:1). Nowhere is the crucial role of reading made clearer than in the scene in which during the middle of the night the insomniac king calls for the book of records to be read to him. Through this reading of the written record, memory of Mordecai's good deed (his warning of a plot against the king) is restored, the king promotes Mordecai, and the stage is set for averting the massacre of the Jews. In this way, the Book of Esther reminds its readers that unless writing is read, it is a dead letter. Books must be read and reread and at different times in multiple frames of mind. Reading what has been written, moreover, is essential for remembering. The scene in which the king is read the "book of records of the chronicles" where Mordecai's good deeds are recorded, foreshadows the denouement of the story—Esther ordering the writing of a book that bears her name that chronicles the history of a woman saving the Jews from a pogram and commanding that the victory be celebrated every year so the events will be remembered.

Yet the author of Megillat Esther, whoever he, she, or they may have been, clearly understood that texts are impermanent, for that reality is dramatized throughout the narrative.[8] The character of the king represents those who insist that once a text comes into being it is permanent, unchanging. By rendering the king ridiculous, the author of the megillah conveys a foundational tenet of the rhetorical theory embedded in the story—texts are impermanent. Moreover, the Book of Esther demonstrates that there is rhetorical power in the reality of textual impermanence. The author embeds the tale with multiple literary-rhetorical hooks designed to firmly snag the reader's or listener's imagination, inviting prolonged personal engagement with the text, and ultimately new tellings or appropriations. A major appropriative hook in the megillah is the construction of characters who are at once vivid and well-defined yet who change over the course of the narrative, often coming to possess elements of their apparent enemies. A sufficient number of traits are fixed to render the character recognizable to the reader and to foster identification, yet at the same time identities are enough in flux to invite reinterpretation and reinhabitation. Reinhabited characters can take the narrative in new directions, especially given that narrative reversal occurs throughout the megillah. These reversals serve as another type of hook, inviting readers to engage their imaginations to invent new narrative directions and even new plots.

Other invitations to appropriation of the Book of Esther abound. One is the narrative's lack of resolution. Put simply, many questions are left unanswered. What happened to Vashti? Why did the king choose Esther? Did Esther and Vashti ever meet? Where is God in this biblical story? Yet another appropriative hook is the preponderance of vivid scenes of action—sumptuous banquets, exquisite beauty treatments, and life-threatening verbal confrontations. These scenes grab the visual imagination, calling for reenvisioning the settings, the characters, and the actions themselves. These strong scenic aspects, combined with the farcical plot and carnivalesque mood, make the megillah well suited for appropriation in visually intense forms such as paintings, graphic novels, plays, and films. (Unsurprisingly, scenes from the Esther story appear on the canvases of many great painters.[9])

Not only do appropriative hooks in the Book of Esther beckon Jewish feminist writers, but also the dramatization of enduring gender politics calls their attention. The Book of Esther depicts rhetorical dynamics of Jews living in a foreign court and also of women coping in a society intensely hostile to their gender. Unlike all other books of the Bible, notes Michael V. Fox, the Book of Esther is the only one with "a conscious and sustained interest in sexual politics."[10] The scroll raises issues such as how to survive in a context of male dominance, whether women can truly gain power by brandishing their sexuality, how women should relate to one another, and how to balance the needs of the community with one's personal needs and desires. In this way, the Book of Esther not only offers a theory of the nature and necessity of writing but also functions as a sourcebook of rhetorical invention, providing Jewish feminists with a compendium of issues and a set of characters and narrative possibilities to put into play to discover new answers to enduring questions.

Lots of Writing: Jewish Feminists Tell New Tales

Jewish American feminists inevitably remember their experiences of Purim. Joining Cixous and Sedgwick in writing about visual memories, Mary Gendler began her influential 1973 article "The Restoration of Vashti" by recalling, "When I was a child, Purim was one of my favorite Jewish holidays. I loved to dress up as Queen Esther in a long, flowing gown, put a sparkling crown on my head, and feel brave and loyal at the thought that I might risk my life to save my people." Writing about her experiences as a child and what she was observing in the mid-1970s, Gendler recalled that no one dressed up like Vashti because she disappears after the story's first chapter. As an adult, Gendler came to grasp the "deep significance" of playing the various characters in the Purim narrative. "When we, as children—or adults—dress up as someone, we are, in a sense, identifying with them," she writes. "The characters, in this way, serve as a kind of role model for us." Although as a girl she had dressed up as Esther, as a woman she came to find the Jewish queen in many respects objectionable. "In most ways she sounds like an ideal woman—beautiful, pious, obedient, courageous. And it is just this which I find objectionable. Esther is certainly the prototype—and perhaps even a stereotype—of the ideal Jewish woman—an ideal which I find restrictive and repressive." Gendler maintained that the message of the Esther story comes through loud and clear: "Women who are bold, direct, aggressive and disobedient are not acceptable; the praiseworthy women are those who are unassuming, quietly persistent, and who gain their power through the love they inspire in men. These women live almost vicariously, subordinating their needs and desires to those of others." Concludes Gendler: "We have only to look at the stereotyped Jewish Mother to attest to the still-pervasive influence of the Esther-behavior-model."[11] Gendler proposes, that "Vashti be reinstated on the throne along with her sister Esther, together to rule and guide the psyches and actions of women."[12]

After restoring Vashti to the attention of Jewish feminists, Gendler left to others the task of more fully reconstructing the previously maligned character. Breathing life into the character of Vashti, Norma Rosen invents an extended ending to the Book of Esther to demonstrate how Jewish feminists can fulfill her imperative to write new stories about biblical women. In her 1996 article "Midrash, Bible, and Women's Voices," Rosen wrote, "I have never met a woman who liked the Megillah of Esther. Too many aspects of the story make us squirm."[13] Among the aspects of the Esther story that made Rosen squirm is Esther's use of her sexual power, not her brains, to save the Jews. Rosen's new ending addresses this concern and also provides a model of her Jewish feminist rhetorical theory of writing. She argues that feminists must draw upon the midrashic tradition to use the power of writing "to give a voice to women in the Bible who have had nearly none." The reason it is imperative for feminists "to write some midrash yourself," she explains, is that stories from the Hebrew Bible "are the cultural heritage of western civilization. Women of the Bible, particularly their familial and societal relationships . . . hold powerful places in our imagination." Commentaries on the Bible, moreover, "particularly those expressing attitudes toward women, become the basis of tradition, carrying legal force."[14]

At the core of her rhetorical theory is a confidence that among Jews, texts are not only read but also interpreted and questioned. "Jewish tradition has always been more than text; it has also been the experience of the text. Not only what occurred or was said, but how it is interpreted—commentary," she maintains. That Jews can be trusted to read and engage texts creates the necessary condition for Jews to write. In Rosen's rhetorical theory of reading and writing, grounded in Jewish rhetorical practice and the midrashic tradition, texts matter, stories matter, for they are cultural productions that engage the imagination in ways that create memories, traditions, and attitudes. These, in turn, are filled with possibilities and limits, which influence behaviors, customs, and laws.[15]

Because texts matter, writing is imperative. The writing of fiction, in particular, is crucial according to Rosen's rhetorical theory of writing. Fiction, she maintains, "is a call to the imagination of a people to repair the work of reality." Novels, she explains, must be "a reflexive source of something like a wholeness still hidden from us, clues buried somewhere in the creative imagination."[16] In Rosen's rhetorical theory, fiction is the preferred form because of the potential that characters and narrative possess to explore the human condition dialectically rather than didactically. "Fiction writers rely on ambiguity; they put their ideas forward behind the protection of characters' masks," she explains. "Fiction writers find this congenial, not because they are afraid to speak the truth, but because they find truth to be slippery—or to put it more elegantly, truth is in the dialectic itself, in the interplay of ideas; ideas moreover that in life never express themselves purely but are always modified, sometimes grotesquely, sometimes nobly, by human behavior."[17]

Employing fiction to "witness-through-the-imagination" is a hallmark of Rosen's rhetorical theory of writing, not only in the feminist dimension of her theory and practice, but also as an American Jew committed to preserving memory of the Holocaust. Having written a Holocaust novel, *Touching*

Evil (1969), Rosen experienced what she calls the double bind of being an American Jewish writer alive during but physically separated from what was happening in Europe in the 1940s. She felt that the Holocaust was both impossible to write about yet impossible to avoid writing about. "European writers had come forth as witnesses and had, even when their writing had been most surreal, given something that felt like documentary," explains Rosen. "Witness-through-the-imagination could be the only role for the American writer: documenter of the responses of those who had (merely) 'heard the terrible news.'"[18] In this sense, Rosen's theory of writing echoes the Book of Esther, which is an instance of witness-through-the-imagination, for it is a work of fiction that purports to document historical events. The imaginary tale foregrounds the act of Esther witnessing a near massacre of the Jews and celebrates her for writing, for being a documenter so the news could reach future generations.

According to Rosen's rhetorical theory of writing, fiction offers the writer not only the powerful vehicle of character to sustain the life of ideas but also narrative, which when written well imbues texts with future lives. "A narrative once set in motion is no longer entirely in the control of its author. It takes on its own life; its integrity demands that narrative lines be followed to the end," she explains. Rosen likens the potential of narrative to the actions of the golem, purportedly created in the sixteenth century by Rabbi Judah of Prague to protect the Jews: "It was created for one purpose, but its own energies drove it to rampage wherever it could."[19] Bible stories such as the Book of Esther, explains Rosen, cry out for readers, who, her theory holds, are actively engaged in experiencing the text to ask questions left unanswered by the narratives canonized in the Tanakh and to imagine new characterizations, contexts, and narrative turns, especially endings. She implores feminists to rewrite Bible stories from the point of view of female characters in those stories as if they had knowledge of contemporary Jewish women.

Rosen provides an example of the kind of writing she implores Jewish feminists to undertake in "After Esther," a new ending to the biblical tale. Her narrative intersects with the canonized text at the point at which Haman has been put to death, the Jews have been raised up, and Esther is left to live out her life with King Ahasuerus. His penchant for drunken revelries persists, causing an unhappy Esther to dream of escape. One night Ahasuerus throws "a lavish, wine-soaked saturnalia for powerful neighboring potentates," during which the men engage in a bragging match and Ahasuerus boasts that his queen can be compared to the finest woman on earth. "Prove it!" yell the soused potentates. At that very moment, Esther is having one of her escape dreams, this one set in another place and time (implicitly, the contemporary United States). In her dream, Esther "steps onto a brilliantly lit stage wearing red spike heels and a white bathing suit with a no-string bra and a G-string bikini bottom." Dream Esther wins the beauty contest and, just as the biblical Esther submitted herself to the Persian King in order to save the Jews, dream Esther tolerates being felt up by the man who puts the crown on her head. But when she sees him fondling the runner-up, who struggles to retain her composure, dream Esther is incensed. She rips off her shoe and plunges its spiked heel through the hand of the offending man. Using the motif of a dream, Rosen effects a feminist awakening in the character of Esther. In helping another woman, dream Esther takes a step toward helping herself.[20]

Rosen reinforces her narrative argument that Jewish women must work together for survival rather than compete for male sexual favors by uniting Esther and Vashti. Dream Esther says to dream Vashti, "I always thought you were brave." Dream Vashti reveals that she deliberately allowed herself to be usurped to make room for Esther to be chosen queen. "How did it happen that the King chose me?" dream Esther asks. Dream Vashti replies, "Indeed, the Persians scorn Jewish women. Beauty spoiled by suffering, they say. I was the one who accustomed the king to such beauty. In Esther he recognized Vashti and looked for me in your arms!" Astonished at Vashti's insinuations that she is a Jew, dream Esther asks, "Then you, Vashti—are you . . . ?" Dream Vashti interrupts, "Let it be enough to say that I created the taste in Ahasuerus for the sad-eyed look of suffering Jewish beauty."[21] By imagining a new narrative in which these female characters meet, Rosen alleviates the enduring tension between Vashti and Esther, uniting them not only as women attempting to survive in a sexist society but also as Jews attempting to survive in exile. Rather than competing, they work as a team in the sexual arena, with dream Vashti serving as a mentor to dream Esther rather than Esther turning to Mordecai, as in the biblical narrative.

The resolution of tensions between Vashti and Esther is followed by refutation of the treatment of women by the Jewish community. Rosen exposes Mordecai as a self-promoting man who sold his niece into sexual bondage in the hopes of becoming a Jewish hero. In a dream, Mordecai commands Esther and Vashti to stop mourning their "tiny" fates. "If it's clearly for the good of the people, can't a Jewish girl be sacrificed without such hullabaloo? Didn't Abraham agree to sacrifice Isaac?" he implores. "The boy lay there, trussed, until an angel freed him. My girl wiggled free of her bonds and saved the Jewish people! Should I be blamed for that? These quibbles eat away at heroism." In Rosen's hands, Mordecai is not a Jewish hero, but a narcissist who disrespects women. She also refutes the notion that Esther "wiggled free of her bonds," by having dream Esther exclaim, "Storytellers say it never happened, that I never had sex with the King. That God in His mercy intervened." This is not the truth, she testifies. Then dream Esther utters the lament of the Jewish Woman: "But if widespread tragedy is averted, isn't it too petty, too ungrateful, to ask, 'And now what about my personal happiness? That's how it is with us. We move from cataclysm to cataclysm."[22] Through this dialogue, Rosen argues that the Megillah of Esther does disservice to contemporary women by praising Esther for her obsequiousness and for being "self-sacrificing in the most self-demeaning way in the service of the Jewish people."[23]

Rosen ends her story with a plea for women to take charge of their sexuality, to exercise sexual agency, and to unite with other women to fight male sexual domination. After hearing that the king has demanded that Esther appear naked before his guests, Vashti sneaks into the palace through secret passageways. She finds Esther in her chamber collapsed in terror. "Did you think, because you were Queen, that you could escape the fate of women? It may even be that you were put here for this purpose—to take your stand against our destroyers!" Rosen thus replaces the famous verse imploring Esther to save the Jews with a new one that implores her to save women. Yet Rosen's work nevertheless argues against those women who believe they can gain power through the assertion of their sexuality, stressing that, ultimately, males hold power in the sexual arena. "If I refuse," Esther says to Vashti, "I will be destroyed like you!" On the third night, the eunuchs come to Esther's chamber to lead her to the hall where the king is carousing with his guests. Esther removes her rich garments one by one until she is naked, barefoot, and crownless. Then she spies on the hip of a guard a jeweled dagger. She snatches it and plunges it into her chest: "Soon her own blood clothes her naked body in a royal garment of red, and under this covering the eunuchs carry beautiful Esther into the King's presence."[24]

With this dramatic ending, Rosen's midrash teaches that women must work together to resist male sexual domination but also that a defiant woman must ultimately be ready to take her own life—to die an empowered death. Rosen uses the power of fiction writing, reinhabiting the characters of Esther and Vashti to address the Old Testament narrative's unfeminist competition between women by dramatizing how they can protect one another rather than compete to gain male favor. By appending a dystopian conclusion, Rosen reverses the biblical ending from one of Esther surviving a threatened massacre to become a Jewish heroine, to Esther embracing death to become a feminist hero. In reversing the fate of Esther, Rosen calls upon the Jewish community to reverse its uncaring treatment of Jewish women. She concludes her new Esther story with a warning: "And so it came to pass. Again and again. For Queen Esther was dead. No one had thought it necessary to protect the protectress, or to grant the Jewish woman whom we call Queen her freedom."[25]

Like Rosen, in her play "Esther and Vashti" (2004), Carolyn Gage appropriates what she calls "the patriarchal text"—the biblical Book of Esther—to imagine means for women to unite to resist sexual colonization by men. Gage portrays Esther, a radical Jewish lesbian living in exile, and Vashti, a privileged Persian woman, as lovers. Vashti complies with family expectations and marries the king of Persia, leaving Esther burning with betrayal. Living in the palace, Queen Vashti fosters strong relationships among women, especially those in the harem,[26] and Gage further defines Vashti by emphasizing her ability to write. (In the play, the act of writing connects Vashti and Esther across the very different cultural, class, race, and religious spaces they and women like them inhabit.) Despite her ability to write and obvious intelligence, in the precarious patriarchal environment of the palace, even Vashti, a woman of privilege, the queen, is at risk. For one day the king orders Vashti to dance at a banquet for his officers, a venue where already a harem woman has been raped. Taking advantage of holes in the biblical narrative (what happened to Vashti after she was deposed?), Gage writes a new narrative in which Esther engineers Vashti's escape from the palace, and the two women go underground, hiding in the homes of Jewish women. When Esther is rounded up with virgins from throughout the empire and taken to the king, Vashti insists on going to the palace with Esther and dying with her, for she knows that Esther would kill herself rather than submit to sex with a man.[27]

The play's depiction of female solidarity in the face of male sexual domination reaches its height when Esther is about to be raped by a vicious army officer, Darius. Tiamat, a harem girl who had been gang-raped at an earlier banquet, dances into the room, positioning herself between Esther, who is pinned on the floor, and Darius, who is standing with his robe open. Suddenly, Tiamet grabs Esther's knife from the floor, swinging it upward and slicing off Darius's penis, then stabbing him in the back. At that moment the harem women led by Vashti rush into the chamber and advance on the men with their swords. The men's retreat is blocked by the Jewish women. When, during the battle, Haman's wife Zeresh, who is always working against other women, attempts to strangle Esther, Vashti stabs Zeresh, saving her lover and scoring a victory for the women united by killing a symbol of women competing against one another.[28]

Yet another new Purim story has been written by the young Jewish feminist Hallel Abramowitz-Silverman. At the age of seventeen, in 2013, Hallel published an article in the *Jerusalem Post*, describing her childhood memories of Purim. They differ significantly from those of previous generations of Jewish feminists, who hold in their mind's eye photographs of themselves twirling around dressed as Queen Esther. Abramowitz-Silverman wrote, "Shortly before my fifth birthday, listening to the megila, I heard Vashti say 'no' when the king summoned her. I perked up immediately and said excitedly 'Like Rosa Parks!' Later in the megila, I nervously awaited the king's response to Esther's uninvited visit."[29] Beginning in childhood, Abramowitz-Silverman understood the Purim story as being about "two courageous young women." Rather than struggling with a portrayal of Vashti as a diseased, donkey-eared enemy of the Jews, she found in this character, an example of a woman defiantly dedicated to a cause, comparable to the civil rights leader Rosa Parks. And in Esther she found a hero who displayed courage in the face of danger.

What is striking about Abramowitz-Silverman's article is not only how she writes about both of Megillat Esther's main female characters as heroes but also how she has used those characters to write her own life. A week before writing the article, she had been detained by Israeli police for wearing a tallit and singing at the Kotel along with other members of Women of the Wall, an international group of women who insist on their right to pray, chant, and wear prayer shawls at the Western Wall. Since 1989, members of Women of the Wall have been fighting to practice rituals at the Wall that Orthodox law reserves for men.[30] Conceptualizing the subversive actions she would take in the coming days in relation to Megillat Esther, Hallel pledged,

"I need to say 'no' like Vashti, and, like Esther, approach authority uninvited—in this case not Persian royalty but the Israeli police, the civil authorities who enforce the extremist desire to control my prayer." Having made that promise to herself, Hallel reported to her community by writing in her *Jerusalem Post* article: "On Tuesday this week I followed Esther's lead and showed up unannounced at the Kishle Police Station inside Jaffa Gate and requested an exemption for Purim." Abramowitz-Silverman's petition succeeded, which led her to write another pledge: "Now, on to Purim at the Kotel, I will follow Vashti's lead and refuse pompous demands, in this case that women keep quiet." Emboldened by Esther and Vashti, using Purim as a rhetorical vehicle for Jewish feminist protest, Abramowitz-Silverman exhorted: "I'm calling on the women of Jerusalem, young and old, secular and religious, to join me in costume celebrating the courage of Esther and Vashti, and of Women of the Wall. For those of you outside Israel, it would be a wonderful act of solidarity to wear a tallit over your costume when you, wherever you are, from the US to Persia—freely recite and hear the megila."[31] On Purim 2013, approximately eighty Women of the Wall activists participated in a reading of the Scroll of Esther at the Kotel. There were no incidents nor arrests.[32]

Conclusion: A Changed Purim Picture

By rereading and rewriting the Book of Esther over the past forty years, Jewish feminists have changed the picture of Purim. Yellowing snapshots of little girls posing as a pretty, self-sacrificing Jewish queen are now joined by news photos of a young woman inspired by the determination of Vashti and the bravery of Esther to raise her voice on Purim at the Kotel despite threats of arrest. This makeover has been accomplished by Jewish feminist writers who have been provoked to write over and against Megillat Esther because of its unsavory characterization of Jewish female heroism and dismissal of its only identifiable feminist character. Yet while rejecting the biblical story on those grounds, Jewish feminists have also embraced and extended the rhetorical theory of writing embedded in the Book of Esther. They have seized upon the scroll's lesson of textual vulnerability as an imperative to read and write in transformative ways. Taking hold of the many appropriative hooks in the story, they have created out of ancient characters new role models that refute sexist assumptions and portray feminist ideals.

In addition to offering a rhetorical theory of writing, the Book of Esther has served as a source of invention because it dramatizes issues women face when living under patriarchy. Foremost among those issues, in the original story as well in its feminist appropriations, is the problem of how women can resist male sexual domination. Attempts to rewrite the ending of the narrative to allow Esther to retain her sexual dignity tend toward dystopia, portraying suicide as the only available alternative to submitting to unwanted sex. These retellings have been countered by utopian endings that envision women uniting to resist male sexual violence, seizing the theme of Jewish revenge and forging it into a feminist ethic of self-defense. A major theme in Jewish feminist appropriations of the megillah is female solidarity, wrought by portraying Esther and Vashti as collaborators, co-religionists, and lovers. Whether inhabiting dystopian or utopian landscapes, these new versions of the story's central characters explore the enduring issues of Jewish women's relationship to one another, to their community, and to their god. They contemplate the question raised in the biblical book of how much the individual should sacrifice the self for the community, warning the Jewish community to employ an ethic of care toward its own women. In these ways, Jewish feminist writing has breathed new lives into the Book of Esther.

NOTES

1. Hélène Cixous, *Rootprints*, 202, 204. Timothy Beal draws connections between the biography of Cixous and the narrative of Esther and draws upon Cixous' critical methodology to read the Book of Esther (*The Book of Hiding*, esp. 87–88).

2. Eve Kosofsky Sedgwick, *Epistemology of the Closet*, 75–83.

3. Mieke Bal, "Lots of Writing," 77–102. "Lots" is a pun in relation to the *Book of Esther*, which establishes the holiday of Purim. Purim is named after the lots—"pur" in Persian—cast by Haman to decide the date for the proposed annihilation of the Jews.

4. This analysis is based on the version of Esther found in the Hebrew-to-English translation of the Tanakh (Jewish Bible) printed by the Jewish Publication Service, 1917. It is available online at www.jewishvirtuallibrary.org/jsource/Bible/Esthertoc.html.

5. Others who have commented on self-reflexivity in the Book of Esther include Bal, "Lots of Writing," 81–82, and Shirly Bahar, "Coming Out as Queen," 170.

6. Indeed, the Book of Esther pays such abundant attention to writing that Bal deems Esther's banquet a feast of writing. "For me, the Esther scroll is a celebration of writing, and, as the climax of the story, so is Esther's banquet.... Writing is also the medium that produced 'Esther'" ("Lots of Writing," 80). Danna Nolan Fewell also emphasizes that "writing is a major preoccupation within the story world of Esther—writing in response to certain situations and

writing in response to yet other writing. No single text is sufficient. There will always be yet another attempt to offer the final word" (*Reading Between Texts*, 11).

7. Beal also calls the Book of Esther a palimpsest (*Book of Hiding*, 29).

8. The Book of Esther was most likely written by an unknown author or authors during the third century, sometime after Alexander's conquest of Persia in 330 BCE. Despite the centrality of female characters and the humorous portrayal of male authority, most scholars simply assume that the Book of Esther was written by a man. Yet even those few who have considered female authorship conclude that at least parts of it were written by a man or from a male perspective. See Michael V. Fox, *Character and Ideology in the Book of Esther* and Kristin De Troyer, "Oriental Beauty Parlor, 47–70.

9. Scenes from the Book of Esther have been painted by, for example, Tintoretto, Rubens, Rembrandt, and Dali.

10. Fox, *Character and Ideology*, 209–10.

11. Mary Gendler, "Restoration of Vashti," 241—47. In a similar vein, Aviva Cantor Zuckoff declared in a 1972 article published in the feminist journal *off our backs*: "Megillat Esther has a definite patriarchal bias and could in no way be construed as a feminist or pro-feminist document" ("The Real Story of Esther," 2:6).

12. Ibid., 247. Alicia Ostriker also rejects Esther in favor of Vashti in her 1994 book *The Nakedness of the Fathers*, deeming Esther "the sexy Jewess" who succeeded in winning the "Miss Persia contest" while Vashti was "demoted for discipline problems." Ostriker writes that upon first reading the story while an undergraduate at Brandeis in the 1950s, "I preferred proud Vashti" to "Esther, the spoilt beauty queen who saved the Jews only because Mordecai twisted her arm (219)."

13. Norma Rosen, "Midrash, Bible, and Women's Voices," 440.

14. Ibid., 422–25.

15. Norma Rosen, *Accidents of Influence*, 17, 47.

16. Ibid., 47.

17. Ibid., 4.

18. Ibid., 10.

19. Rosen, "Midrash," 423–24.

20. Ibid., 441–42.

21. Ibid., 442–43.

22. Ibid., 443, 444.

23. Ibid., 441.

24. Ibid., 445.

25. Ibid., 445.

26. Carolyn Gage, *Esther and Vashti*, 26, 29.

27. Ibid., 49, 58.

28. Ibid., 78.

29. Hallel Abramowitz-Silverman, "The Great Kotel Schlep."

30. Allyn Fisher-Ilan, "Women of the Wall Blocked from Western Wall by Ultra-Orthodox Protesters." Women of the Wall have been harassed, arrested, and beaten in what is both a feminist struggle and a long struggle between Israel's secular majority and its ultra-Orthodox minority over lifestyle in the Jewish state.

31. Abramowitz-Silverman, "The Great Kotel Schlep."

32. Adam Soclof, "Women of the Wall Megillah Reading Undisturbed."

BIBLIOGRAPHY

Bahar, Shirly. "Coming Out as Queen: Jewish Identity, Queer Theory, and the Book of Esther." *Studies in Gender and Sexuality*, 13, no.3 (2012): 167–78.
Bal, Mieke. "Lots of Writing," *Semeia*, no. 54 (1991): 77–102.
Beal, Timothy K. *The Book of Hiding: Gender, Ethnicity, Annihilation, and Esther*. London: Routledge, 1997.
Cixous, Hélène. *Rootprints: Memory and Life Writing*. London: Routledge, 1997.
De Troyer, Kristin. "An Oriental Beauty Parlor: An Analysis of Esther 2.8–18 in the Hebrew, Septuagint and the Second Greek Text." In *A Feminist Companion to Esther, Judith and Susanna*, edited by Athalya Brenner, 47–70. Sheffield, UK: Sheffield Academic Press, 1995.
Fewell, Danna Nolan, ed. *Reading between Texts: Intertextuality and the Hebrew Bible*. Louisville, KY: Westminster, 1992.
Fisher-Ilan, Allyn. "Women of the Wall Blocked from Western Wall by Ultra-Orthodox Protesters," Reuters. www.huffingtonpost.com/2013/07/08/women-of-the-wall-ultra-orthodox-_n_3560599.html?utm_hp_ref=religion. Posted July 8, 2013, accessed July 9, 2013.
Fox, Michael V. *Character and Ideology in the Book of Esther*. Columbia: University of South Carolina Press, 1991.
Fuchs, Esther. "Status and Role of Female Heroines in the Biblical Narrative," *Mankind Quarterly* 23, no. 2 (Winter 1982): 149–60.
Gage, Carolyn. *Esther and Vashti: A Play in Two Acts*. Published by the author, 2004.
Gendler, Mary. "The Restoration of Vashti." In *The Jewish Woman: New Perspectives*, edited by Elizabeth Koltun, 241–47. New York: Schocken, 1976.
Horowitz, Elliott. *Reckless Rites: Purim and the Legacy of Jewish Violence*. Princeton, NJ: Princeton University Press, 2006.
Kogen, Lisa. "Women Speak: V Is for Vashti." *Women's League for Conservative Judaism Virtual Journal* (Winter 2012/2013). www.wlcj.org/articlenav.php?id=614. Accessed September 17, 2013.
Metzger, David, and Peter Schulman, eds. *Chasing Esther: Jewish Expressions of Cultural Difference*. Santa Monica, CA: Kol Katan Press, 2005.
Ostriker, Alicia. *The Nakedness of the Fathers: Biblical Visions and Revisions*. New Brunswick, NJ: Rutgers University Press, 1994.
Rosen, Norma. *Accidents of Influence: Writing as a Woman and a Jew in America*. Albany: State University of New York Press, 1992.
———. "Midrash, Bible, and Women's Voices." *Judaism* (Fall 1996): 423–45.
Sedgwick, Eve Kosofsky. *Epistemology of the Closet*. Berkeley: University of California Press, 1990.
Soclof, Adam. "Women of the Wall Megillah Reading Undisturbed by Israeli Police." *JTA*. www.jta.org/2013/02/25/life-religion/women-of-the-wall-megillah-reading-undisturbed-by-israeli-police. Posted February 25, 2013, accessed September 21, 2013.
Waldman, J. T. *Megillat Esther*. New York: Jewish Publication Society, 2005.
Women's League for Conservative Judaism. "Vashti's Banquet: A New Women's Celebration. www.wlcj.org/articlenav.php?id=63. Accessed September 17, 2013.
Zuckoff, Aviva Cantor. "The Real Story of Esther." *off our backs: a women's newsjournal*, February 28, 1972, 2:6.

12

"Shema Yisrael"
Listening in Judaism and What It Has to Teach Us

JOY ARBOR

Although the subject of listening is enjoying a spate of scholarship in rhetorical studies (see, for example, Ratcliffe; Glenn and Ratcliffe; Tompkins; Hyde), the traditional devaluation of listening as passive and naturalized and, hence, its undertheorization still limits our rhetorical theories as well as the US educational system. Students, for example, spend a great deal of their time listening to their teachers from kindergarten through college, but listening skills are rarely taught or even discussed (Barker and Watson, 7), though lectures remain the dominant teaching mode, while students listen and take notes. Perhaps listening receives so little attention because it is conflated with hearing, which, for most people, is innate, a physiological process that requires no intention. Listening may also be devalued because it is too closely associated with obedience.[1] For example, when parents complain that a child is not listening, they often mean that the child is not responding in the desired way—that is, obeying. Obviously, if listening is akin to blindly obeying, then there is little to theorize about. However, those of us in rhetorical studies know that audience members cannot be counted on to "obey" a rhetor's speech or writing just because they have listened to it. In rhetorical studies, the traditional focus on speaking—and, by extension, writing—may explain the relative lack of interest in listening. Yet the importance of analyzing one's audience (a word that comes from the Latin *audire*, to hear or listen, which reminds us that listening is necessary to the rhetorical act) and adapting one's rhetoric to that audience makes the dearth of theorizing about the nature of listening in the rhetorical act seem a curious omission. In Judaism, on the other hand, listening is conceptualized as active and intentional, requiring conscious focus, the development of skills, and the listener's willingness to risk—because listening is so difficult. Moreover, this conception of listening is fundamental, referred to in the most important Jewish prayers and tracts to such an extent that Sheldon Lewis asserts that "the commandment to 'hear' is central to Jewish tradition" (275), and Barbara Breitman, a Jewish spiritual director, asserts that "hearing is the quintessentially sacred act for Jews" (73).[2]

In order to help us resee the possibilities and value of a more complex and nuanced concept of listening in rhetorical studies, I focus in this chapter on three themes or concepts of listening found in Judaism: listening as an active, intentional process, which requires openness and vulnerability on the part of the listener; listening as a gift to the speaker; and listening as the foundation of ethics. I analyze texts in the Hebrew Bible (the Tanakh); *Pirke Avot* (often called "Ethics of the Fathers"), a tract of the Talmud that addresses ethics; and other Talmudic passages, as well as drawing from traditional and contemporary commentators of Judaism.[3] After exploring each concept, I turn my attention back to rhetorical studies and investigate what insights these alternative concepts of listening might give us. I conclude with a discussion of what a transformed concept of listening might mean for pedagogy. But first we need a foundation for our analysis, so I will begin by examining the Shema, Judaism's most important and recognizable prayer that begins with the exhortation to hear or listen.

The Shema

No discussion of Judaism, and certainly not one of listening in Judaism, would be complete without reference to the Shema, a central prayer considered to be the Jewish "confession of faith" (Berlin "Shema," 673) or "credo" (Skolnik, "Shema"). It is recited twice daily by observant Jews and is often the last words of pious Jews condemned to death. Derived originally from Deuteronomy 6:4, the Shema prayer is "*Shema Yisrael: Adonai elohenu Adonai eḥad*," most often translated as "Hear O Israel: The Lord is God, the Lord is One." Though many consider the Shema to be a testament to monotheism, others assert that this is an anachronistic reading, arguing instead that the Shema affirms that Adonai is the sole Lord of Israel (Berlin, Brettler, and Fishbane, headnote, 380). But whether what follows the directive to listen or hear affirms monotheism, or the relationship between the Israelites and God, the directive to listen "is a summons by Moses to Israel, 'Hear O Israel'; so the worshiper summons himself to pay heed to what follows, to 'lend an ear' to a significant message that requires his attention" (Lamm, 13). Although saying "listen" may seem like an ordinary way of getting people's attention, many commentators find the exhortation *"shema"* significant, explaining that it does not mean simply hearing with the ears. Instead it "implies understanding as well as apperception.... [T]rue hearing is cognitive as well as sensory" (ibid., 15). Rabbi Saadia ben Joseph, a great Talmudist of the tenth century, stated that the word *shema* had two meanings, both of which were "correct and necessary": one is to know or understand, and the other is to accept or commit (quoted in ibid., 15–16). Jews must understand the words of the Shema as well as commit to following them. Obviously, both the cognitive act of understanding what one hears and the more emotional act of acceptance or commitment require significant and active work on the part of the listener. Moreover, the practices surrounding the traditional liturgical pronouncement of the Shema mirror how this listening is rooted more in engaging in the active work of understanding than in passive hearing: "Jewish law requires special concentration on the meaning of the words of at least the first two verses (and many Jews cover or close their eyes to achieve such concentration)" (Skolnik, "Shema"). Further, the Shema is one of the few parts of the liturgy that may be read in other languages: "The Sages permit the Shema to be read 'in any language that you understand' (*shomei'a*, literally, "hear"), not only in the original Hebrew.... The Halakha [Jewish law] ultimately decided in favor of the Sages, and so the preferable translation of *shema* is not 'hear' but 'understand'" (Lamm 15). Listening as demanded in the Shema is not a passive act. Moreover, the Shema comes from the moment in Deuteronomy when Moses is giving God's law to the Israelites. The Israelites had to participate in God's speech act (by way of Moses) by choosing to be silent in order to listen. Lewis claims that "the Midrash [homiletic stories told by the sages in order to explain passages in the Torah] imagines an unusual quiet that enveloped the world at the time of revelation. Rabbi Abbahu seems to suggest that silence was the prerequisite to receiving Torah. Without that unusual degree of attention shared by all, the moment of revelation might have been missed" (144). Providing this encompassing silence so that God's law could be heard echoes the kabbalistic notion of initial creation: infinite God had to contract or withdraw Himself in order to make space for the world He wanted to create. The listener must first engage in action to make it possible for any speech, even God's word, to be heard. Considering the effort involved in moving one's self out of the way to make room for another and his or her words and stories not only highlights the deliberate activity of listening, but it also suggests a conception of listening that requires openness, provides a gift to the speaker, and lays the foundation for ethics.

Listening as an Act Requiring Attentiveness and Openness

The Shema entreats the people of Israel to listen, which implies that they have the choice not to. If people can choose to listen, they must do so actively, with intention. Beyond the exceptional text of the Shema, other texts in Judaism affirm a conception of listening as a deliberate act requiring attentiveness and openness. In Isaiah 55.3 we see again the choice and action of listening: "Incline your ears and go to Me; listen and your souls will live" (quoted in Freeman, 257). In this passage from Isaiah, we see the intention to try to listen harder in "incline your ears."

This active, intentional listening requires attentiveness and openness. *Pirke Avot* 6.6 lists forty-eight virtues, often called the forty-eight Ways of Wisdom. The second of these virtues is *Shmiat HaOzen*, literally "listening of the ear," which is most often translated as "listening attentively," showing again listening's vital importance in Judaism. Susan Freeman, a teacher of Judaism, affirms that "being compassionate and understanding, being open-minded and unbiased ... are key in the mastery" of *Shmiat HaOzen* (256). In Freeman's explanation of the connotations of this virtue, we begin to see a more complex, more challenging notion of listening, one that begins to explain why people must be exhorted again and again to listen: this attentive listening requires that we open ourselves, pay attention to others, and be compassionate and understanding. It can be incredibly difficult for a listener to get his or her preconceptions and beliefs out of the way to embody these qualities. Furthermore, these qualities, considered feminine in Western thought, leave one vulnerable.

Listening proves to be vital in *havruta*, a traditional Jewish way of working and debating with a study partner in order to understand a biblical or Talmudic passage and its relevance.[4] In Orit Kent's case study of *havruta* learning, she identifies "listening and articulating" as one of three pairs of core practices that study partners engage in. Listening and articulating serve as the foundation for developing ideas as well as the *havruta* relationship; each partner needs to be heard, as well as the text (Kent, 223). Listening carefully and attentively to one's study partner is crucial since one's ideas build on the other's in this interdependent learning and meaning-making experience; without careful and attentive listening, one shortchanges one's own learning as well as that of one's partner. Listening to understand one's partner requires important inner and outer work: "To understand the other, one needs to practice both outer and inner silence—creating an outer space for the other to articulate and also silencing the many internal voices that arise in one's own head so that s/he can truly pay attention to what the other is trying to say" (Kent, 230). When a listener struggles to understand, the listener must also be silent, not only refraining from speaking but also actively silencing one's internal voices, whether chatter or responses to the speaker, in order to really focus on the other and his or her statements. In short, one must consciously make space inside one's self for another's words and ideas. Although Kent's focus is *havruta*, I would argue that the attentive listener in Judaism must always perform the vital work of quieting one's internal voices to make space for the speaker's words, inner work that can be difficult and includes denying the self on behalf of another for a time.

This temporary quieting of the self in order to make space for another's words is a sign of humility. The vital importance of humility in listening is shown in the Talmud, when the school of Shammai and the school of Hillel were in dispute over a particular interpretation, each asserting that the law was on their side. Then a "voice from heaven" announced that both were "the words of the living God" but sided with Hillel. The Talmud explains that God, or the voice from heaven, decided in favor of the school of Hillel "because they were kindly and modest [and] they taught their own rulings as well as those of the School of Shammai, and even more, they taught the rulings of the School of Shammai before their own. This should teach you that one who humbles oneself is exalted by the Holy One and one who exalts oneself is humbled by the Holy One" (quoted in Chanin, Colflesh, Epstein, and Schoenfeld, 6). This ruling is groundbreaking on several levels. In this instance, God found important not the distinctions between the two arguments, but the ways in which the arguments were presented; the process was more important than the product. In order for the school of Hillel to quote from Shammai, Hillel must have listened attentively to Shammai's argument. Moreover, by reflecting Shammai's argument faithfully, Hillel showed respect for Shammai and Shammai's argument, and indicated that—though they had their own views and defended them—Hillel was not necessarily in possession of the whole truth. In short, Hillel showed humility. Rabbi Benjamin Hecht argues that "by quoting Beit Shammai first, Beit Hillel understood their full place within Torah. Another's opinion must be heard, recognized and respected—not just as [an] act of tolerance—for this very process of hearing, recognizing and respecting powerfully changes the actual nature of one's opinion and one's Torah" (quoted in ibid., 9). It is important to present others' views as fully worthy even though different, rather than ignoring other potential viewpoints or presenting them as straw men able to be easily refuted. To listen to and include these opposing views changes not only one's opinions but also the subject at hand. Hecht even goes so far as to say that the listening, open-mindedness, and respect (*anava*) Hillel demonstrates to Shammai is divine ("within Torah") (ibid.). Mitch Chanin, Mira Colflesh, Saundra Sterling Epstein, and Rabbi Rachel Schoenfeld state that this humility (*anava*) is a key Jewish value. The fact that opening ourselves to attentive listening means we run the risk of changing our views and our sense of the subject at hand may explain why so many of us are resistant to listening. Yet this humility, vulnerability, and openness are required to fulfill the commandment Jews are reminded of twice daily, in the Shema.

The idea that listening requires openness is not new in rhetorical studies. Krista Ratcliffe's "rhetorical listening,"[5] which seeks to facilitate cross-cultural communication that can prove difficult, "signifies a stance of openness that a person may choose to assume" (17). But, to me at least, assuming a stance of openness does not suggest the same kind of authentic receptivity that Judaism's attentive and humble listening requires. A stance of openness is still a position, while letting go of positions and moving one's self out of the way to receive the speaker's words, as the school of Hillel did, may be what is required to listen. This humility that getting one's self out of the way requires also makes the listener vulnerable. The work of moving one's beloved ideas away in order to listen to others whose stories or ideas are threatening to one's identifications (Ratcliffe's focus in *Rhetorical Listening*) or self is real emotional and spiritual work. Ratcliffe rarely addresses the difficulty and emotional work of her rhetorical listening, a critique I have made in another context (Arbor, 224–25). Because Ratcliffe rarely discusses emotion, it is difficult to assess whether emotional responsiveness is part of her rhetorical listening, though the difficulty and emotional work of listening are clearly part of listening in Judaism.

Beyond seeing Ratcliffe's rhetorical listening differently, this attentive listening reminds me that rhetors and scholars of rhetoric do the audience a disservice by considering the audience as a constraint or seeing listeners as those who must be cajoled and convinced or seduced. The work of the listener as conceptualized in Judaism reminds me that the audience is not capricious at all, but must be very invested in the rhetorical act—engaging in significant inner work—to be affected by the rhetor's words. Because listening takes a great deal of emotional and spiritual work, we should not wonder when people listen poorly or not at all, especially to rhetoric that asks them to change their ideas or actions.

Listening as a Gift

In Judaism, open, attentive, and understanding listening can expand the listener's knowledge and wisdom, as in the Shema, but listening also gives something to the speaker. This builds on the openness and vulnerability of the listener explored in the last section; the listener's inner work of moving out of the way to make way for the speaker is an act of generosity. In the study of *havruta* discussed earlier, Kent explains: "When one *havruta* partner tries to understand the other's ideas, the partner moves the other from an object of attention to a subject in his or her own right.... Listening to understand goes a long way to helping *havruta* members feel respected" (230–32). Here, the listener helps the speaker feel that he or she is respected and that his or her ideas are worth listening to. Beyond helping the speaker feel worthy of being listened to, in Judaism there is a connection between listening and its ability to overcome another person's resistance to speech. For example, Isaiah 50:4 states: "The Eternal God has taught me how to speak, even to those tired of speech. Morning by morning God awakens me, awakens my ear: teaching me to listen" (quoted in Chanin, Colflesh, Epstein, and Schoenfeld, 21). Even the great prophet Isaiah must learn to listen to God; listening is not innate or naturalized but must be learned every day, even by someone who is already good at listening. Here God has taught Isaiah how to speak "even to those tired of speech"—that is, people who do not want to, or cannot, listen. If God is teaching Isaiah how to listen, is it God that Isaiah is learning how to listen to? Or is he learning to listen to those he is trying to speak to—those who don't want to listen? Chanin and coauthors, who focus on Jewish approaches to interfaith dialogue, argue that

Isaiah is learning to listen to those he is trying to talk with: "Listening to people ... allows us to find out what words will be meaningful to them. Without listening, we can only recite a predetermined speech—we cannot talk with them, but only to them.... It is only by listening to someone that we can find out which ideas and feelings would be most useful to speak about" (Chanin, Colflesh, Epstein, and Schoenfeld, 21–22).

Here we have something familiar to us in rhetoric: analyzing the audience in order to lay the groundwork for persuasion. In rhetorical studies, listening may be undertheorized in general, but the importance of analyzing the audience is not; listening becomes one way to figure out what is useful to say in order to persuade. But there is another possibility here. If one listens to those who are "tired of speech," they will become more open to being spoken with. Listening to those "tired of speech" heals them in some way. Chanin and coauthors claim:

> Only when people feel heard are they truly able to hear the message that we might bring them. Many people today, as well as in Isaiah's time, are "tired of speech."... [P]eople often find themselves tired of speech when they are experiencing cynicism, anger, or despair. Words have not helped them to find clarity, peace, or hope, and they no longer want to listen.... At all of these time[s], people are likely to be resistant to hearing others. When another person listens to them carefully and shows that they care about and understand their concerns and feelings, the possibility for communication opens up. (Chanin, Colflesh, Epstein, and Schoenfeld, 22)

Those who are most closed down and resistant to listening to others may need to be listened to in an attentive and caring way. In this way, Isaiah's listening here becomes more than just a calculated bid to increase his own persuasiveness; Judaism's open, attentive, and emotionally responsive listening becomes a gift that has the power to heal. An argument between Moses and Aaron in *Parshah Shemini*, a specific weekly portion of the Tanakh, further demonstrates that listening can be a gift that heals the speaker. Aaron and Moses had a disagreement about the law. Moses got very upset and launched into a diatribe. According to Rabbi Eliyahu Hoffmann, the commentary of Rashi—a medieval rabbi who authored comprehensive commentaries on the Tanakh and Talmud and whose work is considered to be the "father" of all subsequent commentaries—indicates that Moses's diatribe went on for a long time. Then Aaron spoke concisely about his argument, and Moses immediately agreed that Aaron was correct and quieted down. Hoffmann asks: "What was in Aaron's short speech that calmed [Moses] down? . . . Aaron allowed Moshe [Moses] to express his anger. Instead of jumping in and indignantly proving that he was right (as he indeed was), he heard his brother out, and gave him the opportunity to say whatever he had to say. Once Moshe [Moses] had been heard, he was willing to listen. . . . The lesson implied is simply: If you want to be heard, learn to listen to what others have to say." This is an important rhetorical lesson: if you want someone to listen to you, you must listen to them.

But here, again, I argue that we have more than that; we have the cure of listening. In this case, Moses was angry, and his anger clouded his judgment. But once he had his say and was heard, he was ready to listen to Aaron's argument. If listening can be curative, then listening to an angry person, even if that person is in the wrong, can be a new kind of listening done for the rhetorical effect of calming the person down, in a way becoming another kind of rhetorical listening.[6] Judaism's concept of the gift and cure of listening can present those of us in rhetorical studies with a potentially powerful strategy to test out with those who may be resistant to listening. Furthermore, knowing that listening can sometimes be a gift to the speaker presents us with a new way of thinking about the purpose of the rhetorical act and the relationship between rhetor and listener. Rather than assuming that the listener is disempowered and that the speaker is empowered, we should realize that the gift of listening empowers the listener and makes his or her reactions extremely important for the rhetorical effect of giving and healing. In rhetorical studies, few scholars appear to discuss this aspect of listening. I argued that the gift of listening as conceptualized by the conflict resolution group called the Compassionate Listening Project offered rhetorical studies a new view of listening (Arbor, 226–28), and Michael Hyde's theory of the life-giving gift of acknowledgment sees listening as integral. Hyde argues that acknowledgment "functions to transform space and time, to *create* openings wherein people can dwell, deliberate, and know together what is right, good, just, and truthful" (7). If acknowledgment is fundamentally about others' honoring us by making a dwelling place in their lives for us to feel at home, then listening must be part of it. "Listening," Hyde asserts, "helps set the stage for the goodness of acknowledgment; it is a capacity for welcoming and . . . thus aids salvation" (152). The idea that listening and acknowledgment can aid in "salvation" may seem a bit extreme, until one considers Hyde's book's opening question: "What would be like if no one *acknowledged* your existence?" (1). Acknowledgment and being listened to may be everyday occurrences for us, but rather than overlook them, we should see their ubiquity as proof of their importance. Hyde's project asks us to consider how rhetorical competence is vital for the creation of dwelling places (ethos) where people can have their say. All I would add to his project is that this rhetorical competence depends on being able to give the gift of listening.

Listening as an Ethical Act

Because listening in Judaism calls for the cultivation of openness and other receptive qualities, it is tempting to see this listening as blind submission or obedience to a speaker's words. But in fact, listening in Judaism is often correlated with discernment and wisdom, the opposite of blind obedience. For example, in I Kings 3:5, God asks Solomon to choose the gift God will give him. Solomon asks God for a *lev shomea*—literally, a listening heart, though the phrase is more often translated as an "understanding heart." The Jewish Publication Society's translation of the same verse states: "Give Thy servant therefore an understanding heart to judge Thy people, that I may discern between good and evil; for who is able to judge this Thy great people?" Here Solomon asks for a heart that listens; only such a heart will give him the discernment to make ethical judgments about the people of Israel. God's subsequent praise and fulfillment of this request, coupled with Solomon's reputation as the wisest king in the Tanakh, suggest correlations between listening, wisdom, and ethical decision making. Not only does listening aid in making ethical decisions, but—according to Jewish law—the listener is ethically responsible for providing an audience for what is said, at least when it comes to damaging or evil speech, which is speech that damages another person's reputation. Communication scholar Erika Falk asserts: "Jewish rhetoric sees the listener playing an important role in the communication process. Judges have a responsibility not to *listen* to false testimony. Similarly it is prohibited for one to listen to casual lies" (19, emphasis in the original). Here the listener is prohibited from listening to false speech, with dire consequences predicted for the speaker and listener. *Pirke Avot* 2.1 discusses *lashon hara*, damaging speech that is true: "Evil speech . . . kills three people: the speaker, the listener, and the subject" (quoted in Chanin, Colflesh, Epstein, and Schoenfeld, 14). Here the listener is responsible for providing an audience for evil or damaging speech. Because listeners share the ethical responsibility for damaging speech, they should practice discernment in what they listen to and be responsive, ready to object to lying, false testimony, and *lashon hara* should they arise. Refusing to listen can be an ethical act, as in cases of lying or *lashon hara*, and listening too can be an ethical act. In fact, Judaism argues that listening is the foundation of ethics. In order to explore the connections between listening and ethics, Rabbi Jeffrey Summit helps us see the connection between listening and love by examining the relationship between the Shema and the V'ahavta,[7] the prayer that immediately follows it:

> Listening is a prerequisite for love, which is why, I think, the Shema is followed by the words, "and you shall love/V'ahavta." First listen, then you build the connections that enable you to love. While the text ... goes on to talk about loving God, the rabbis [whose commentary helped to shape Judaism in the diaspora] were much more interested in how you loved other people. Now, the rabbis weren't naïve. They recognized that you can't command emotion and you certainly can't love every person you meet. So they translated love into action: be exquisitely sensitive to the other human beings around you, their physical needs, their feelings, the quality of their lives. Be so connected to the people around you that you try to see the world through their eyes, where their happiness becomes your happiness, where you can't sleep well, if you do nothing, while others go to bed hungry. (quoted in Chanin, Colflesh, Epstein, and Schoenfeld, 20)

Here listening to God is tied to love, not just of God but of other people as well. If—as the great sage Hillel said—the Torah could be summed up as "love your neighbor as yourself" (quoted in Chanin, Colflesh, Epstein, and Schoenfeld, 20), then listening is an active and concrete first step toward loving one's neighbor, making listening an ethical and religious imperative. Furthermore, Elliot Rose Kukla asserts that the act of studying the Talmud (a text that is dialogic, with many different commentaries on a single page) teaches that listening is foundational to ethics: "[an] ethical encounter... begins with listening." Listening as an ethically responsible act encourages us to rethink power and responsibility in the rhetorical act. Although rhetorical studies sometimes seems to imagine a listener (or audience member) who is helpless and from whom nothing can be expected—or listeners who are easily swayed as long as we can get their attention—we may be denying the full humanity of other people when we ignore the fact that they must choose to make a space for us and our words. If listeners must choose to open themselves in order to make room for another's words, then rhetoric's traditional focus on the agency, intention, and eloquence of the rhetor misses an important aspect of the rhetorical act. Debra Hawhee argues that "invention-in-the-middle" is not created solely by the rhetor but springs from *kairos*, the propitious moment (17–18). Just as there cannot be *kairos* without a rhetor open to finding and harnessing the right moment, so there can be no *kairos* without an open and receptive listener. Furthermore, we must accept that refusing to listen may be an ethical act, as discussed above. (If most people felt that they were responsible for what they listened to, it is interesting to imagine what would happen to reality television, gossip magazines, and the like.)

Moreover, restoring listening to its proper and ethical importance may help resolve one of rhetoric's oldest ethical problems: the charge that rhetoric is immoral because it does not seek or lead to the truth. Socrates argues against rhetoric because it can make the worse argument appear to be the better one and favors dialogue as better leading to the truth (Plato, *Gorgias*); Judaism may be in sympathy with his second argument. But if we compare Plato's Socrates to the school of Hillel, as discussed earlier, we can see that Socrates did not listen in an open-minded and humble way to his interlocutors in *Gorgias* but used questioning as a way to undercut the arguments of his opponents. Socrates did not listen in the full Jewish sense, letting the truth of others potentially change him and his sense of the subject at hand. (Of course, the argument for dialogue over rhetoric is complicated by the fact that Socrates does eventually resort to monologic rhetoric.) Perhaps the way to an ethical rhetoric is not through the ultimate goal of rhetoric but through its communication ethics, its willingness to listen. The example of Hillel and Shammai suggests that our ethical standard lies not in claims to truth but in listening, understanding, and engaging with another's ideas and respectfully representing others' view even before our own. The belief that listening is the basis of ethics is not completely new to rhetorical studies. Hyde explains: "Listening is a moral act that, according to Levinas, defines 'the first ethical gesture,' for this is how we, in our being-for others, open ourselves to all that others have to say about who and how they are and what they need in order to be saved from the pain and suffering of Being" (152). A rhetoric that includes Judaism's conception of listening, with its emphasis on attentiveness, open-mindedness, humility, and responsibility, could transform rhetoric from an ethically suspect or morally neutral *techne* to an ethical art form as interested in ethical encounters as it is with truth. An emphasis on the activity and humanity of the listener alters our conception of rhetoric and our awareness of the audience. Instead of focusing on manipulation and social engineering, we concentrate on the foundation for potential dialogue and ethical relations between people, with the potential to transform both speaker and listener. In this way, rhetoric can be an ethical art that invites all people to have "a say in what is to become of them," as Hyde puts it in his theory of acknowledgment (57).

Clearly, more research is needed on listening, especially theories and strategies to help listeners become more open, so that we can learn to be better rhetors and listeners. But studying listening in Judaism in conjunction with recent scholarship in rhetorical studies makes it clear to me that most of our existing and exciting scholarship on listening is programmatic rather than descriptive—that is, it offers us specific methods that can be applied only if the listener learns about those methods, understands their reasoning, and is motivated to apply them. We still need to study listening more, so we can more fully understand the rhetorical act. Although some recent scholarship has been groundbreaking, it should not be seen as the basis for all explorations of listening as a rhetorical art.

Conclusion

In Judaism, listening is active, requiring attentiveness and openness; responsible; and ethical. Listening can even be a gift from the listener to the speaker. I have argued that the possibilities of this listening and the work of the listener should be investigated more in rhetorical studies. But these transformed ideas of listening can also make an impact in the subjects we choose to study and on the relations we have with students.

Most obviously, we can make listening a subject in our courses. We can problematize listening with our students, asking them to investigate the kinds of listening they engage in. Since most primary and secondary education requires students to listen, they have a great deal of experience to draw on. This listening may not require the kind of emotional responsiveness suggested by listening in Judaism, but it calls for a high degree of attentiveness. We can ask students to be more mindful of their strategies, if any, for doing the internal work necessary to quiet their internal chatter and make room for an educator's words. We can also teach listening in our rhetoric courses and teach advanced listening courses alongside advanced writing and rhetoric or speech courses.

When teaching rhetoric, we can use listening in Judaism to inform how we approach the audience, making sure to emphasize that the audience is made of people who have to work to listen and make space for us in their lives. Though the concept of audience has a great deal of power because rhetors shape written or spoken rhetoric for listeners to gain the desired effect, I believe the tone of this transaction suggests an instrumentalist relationship that may not attend to or respect the full humanity of the listeners, who are generously making space for the rhetor and his or her words in their lives. Encouraging a more respectful and ethical relationship with one's listeners will, I hope, encourage students to stop making comparisons between rhetoric and manipulative social engineering.

More specifically, when we ask students to investigate sources or interview people, we are implicitly asking them to engage in an encounter in which one can act ethically or unethically. Many textbooks seem to discuss ethics in reading and writing solely as matters of plagiarism, but the importance and character of listening in Judaism helps us see that the way we engage a source has ethical ramifications. It matters for the researcher as well as for the researcher's conception of the subject matter whether he or she tries to understand a source fully—in an open-minded way, letting it change him or her—or just dips into it as a way of arguing for or against a predetermined answer. Believing in the truth of one's argument is no reason to not listen: we remember that in the debate between the school of Hillel and the school of Shammai, God did not ultimately care about which argument was right. What God rewarded in the debate between Hillel and Shammai was being able to represent the other's arguments with humility and respect. We can use the example of Hillel and Shammai to model ethical engagement with others: listen, reflect back what the speaker says, and then represent those words faithfully and ethically.

Beyond our teaching of listening, Judaism's conception of the attentive listener can encourage us to consider how much, and what kind of, listening we ask our students to do and how we think of them as the audience of our rhetoric. Individuals have different abilities to listen attentively; refusals to listen may be due to laziness, the lack of motivation to engage in the internal work needed to listen, or even an ethical choice. In any case, we should be wary of assuming that just because we have said something, students understand it. Moreover, we need to listen to our students and their difficulties and their troubles; only then can we know what to say, what to offer them. We have to be willing to be changed and have their ideas change our sense of our subject. We show that we respect our students when we give them the gift of listening.

Judaism suggests that listening is foundational to ethics. If we want to live a good life, an ethical life, we must begin by listening. We have the humility to realize we do not know everything, we are not complete in ourselves, and so we listen: to ourselves, other people, our teachers, our students, and God. We have a piece of truth, a shard, and so we listen—which is hard work, holy work—for more.

NOTES

I would like to thank Michael Bernard-Donals and Janice W. Fernheimer for their help with this chapter. From the very beginning, they challenged and inspired me to undertake this project, giving me the gift of their confidence in me. At a key moment in the revision, their comments on this chapter spurred me to take my ideas to the next level. I would also like to thank Rabbi Amy Eilberg, who directed me to key texts in listening and Jewish perspectives on interfaith dialogue. I also thank an anonymous reviewer of the manuscript.

1. I suspect that the connection between listening and obeying also comes from the common understanding that the word for listen in Koine Greek is the same as the word for obey. My limited investigation indicates that the Koine Greek of the Christian Bible uses many words for listen and obey. For example, Jesus is quoted as saying the Shema, the profession of faith in Judaism analyzed at length in this chapter, to his disciples in the Christian New Testament (Mark 12:29–30). The Shema is most often translated into English as: "Hear O Israel: The Lord is God, the Lord is One." My studies indicate that the word actually used in the Christian New Testament for Shema was *akouo*, meaning to hear or understand. But there are other Koine Greek words that may prove to be more contentious, such as *peitho*, which is often translated as obey but means not blind obedience but action that comes from having been persuaded. Nonetheless, whether or not it is true that the word for listen is the same as that for obey, the claim may have power. Certainly misinterpretations and mistranslations may have occurred when the Hebrew of the Hebrew Bible (Tanakh) was translated into Koine Greek and then from the Greek into Latin.

2. The Hebrew word for listen is *shema*, which means hear or listen. But *shema* is not equivalent to the physiological process of hearing; instead, it includes meanings much more similar to listening. Although scholars and commentators use both "hear" and "listen" when discussing listening in Judaism, as Lewis and Breitman do in the quotes I have used here, I will continue to use "listening" to denote the intentional act.

3. Because of the limits of space, I do not explore listening in Kabbalah, the mystical aspect of Judaism. Since my focus is rhetoric, I also do not include a study of listening to wordless sound, such as music or the blast of the shofar.

4. *Havruta* is most people's image of traditional Jewish pedagogy, but historians of *havruta* argue that although learning in groups or even pairs is traditional in Judaism, even discussed in the Talmud itself, having *havruta* be the dominant model for learning in yeshivas (schools of traditional Jewish learning) is a recent development. Until around the time of the First World War—according to the contemporary Israeli historian Shaul Stampfer, as cited by Rachael Schultz—*havruta* was only one possible means of study, and it was particularly associated with helping weaker students. Stampfer speculates that during the wartime period, when yeshivas opened their doors not just to the intellectual elite as before but to all Jewish men, these weaker students needed to learn in *havruta* to understand the difficult texts that, before, only the elite were studying. So *havruta* became the dominant form of study in this effort to democratize Jewish study.

5. I refer to Krista Ratcliffe's rhetorical listening as such because Paula Tompkins conceptualized a rhetorical listening that is quite different. Although space does not permit me to discuss Tompkins's work here, I want to acknowledge it by distinguishing between the versions of rhetorical listening.

6. Although I greatly admire the work of both Ratcliffe and Tompkins, it has always confused me that they both named their programs "rhetorical listening." To me, just as a rhetorical question is a question posed not to elicit an answer but for rhetorical effect, the term "rhetorical listening" should mean listening that is engaged in not necessarily to learn something but for its effect on the speaker.

7. The V'ahavta (Deut. 5.5–9) is usually considered part of the Shema prayer and is recited twice daily, though saying only the part in the text and in note 1 above is enough to affirm one's Judaism. The Jewish Publication Society's version of the V'ahavta is as follows: "You shall love the LORD your God with all your heart and with all your soul and with all your might. Take to heart these instructions with which I charge you this day. Impress them upon your children. Recite them when you stay at home and when you are away, when lie down and when you get up. Bind them as a sign on your hand and let them serve as a symbol on your forehead, inscribe them on the doorposts of your house and on your gates." This prayer is the source for the injunctions to Jews to recite the Shema in the morning and the evening, wear tefillin (phylacteries), and put mezuzot (small boxes with the complete Shema and other biblical verses in them) at the entrances to one's home.

BIBLIOGRAPHY

Arbor, Joy. "With Our Ears to the Ground: Compassionate Listening in Israel/Palestine." In *Silence and Listening as Rhetorical Arts*, edited by Cheryl Glenn and Krista Ratcliffe, 217–30. Carbondale: Southern Illinois University Press, 2011.

Barker, Larry, and Kittie Watson. *Listen Up: How to Improve Relationships, Reduce Stress and Be More Productive by Using the Power of Listening*. New York: St. Martin's, 2000.

Berlin, Adele, Marc Zvi Brettler, and Michael Fishbane, eds. *Jewish Study Bible*. New York: Oxford University Press, 2004.

Berlin, Adele. "Shema." In *The Oxford Dictionary of the Jewish Religion*, edited by Adele Berlin and Maxine Grossman, 673–74. 2nd ed. New York: Oxford University Press, 2011.

Breitman, Barbara Eve. "Holy Listening: Cultivating a Hearing Heart." In *Jewish Spiritual Direction: An Innovative Guide from Traditional and Contemporary Sources*, edited by

Rabbi Howard Avruhm Addison and Barbara Eve Breitman, 73–94. Woodstock, VT: Jewish Lights, 2006.

Chanin, Mitch, Mira Colflesh, Saundra Sterling Epstein, and Rabbi Rachel Schoenfeld. "Dialogue in the Jewish Tradition." Jewish Dialogue Group. 2006. Www.jewishdialogue.org/resources/jewish-texts. Accessed 25 January 2013.

Falk, Erika. "Jewish Laws of Speech: Toward Multicultural Rhetoric." *Howard Journal of Communications* 10, no. 1 (1999): 15–28.

Freeman, Susan. "Shmiat Haozen: Attentiveness/Being a Good Listener. In *Teaching Jewish Virtues: Sacred Sources and Arts Activities*, by Susan Freeman, 255–68. Denver, CO: A.R.E., 1999.

Friedmann, Jonathan L. "The Suitability of Sound: Seven Functions of Sacred Music." *Journal for the Renewal of Religion and Theology* 5 (2009). www.renewtheology.org/paperJFriedmann0809.htm. Accessed 31 August 2013.

Glenn, Cheryl, and Krista Ratcliffe. *Silence and Listening as Rhetorical Arts*. Carbondale: Southern Illinois University Press, 2011.

Hawhee, Debra. "Kairotic Encounters." In *Perspectives on Rhetorical Invention*, edited by Janet M. Atwill and Janice M. Lauer, 16–35. Knoxville: University of Tennessee Press, 2002.

Hoffmann, Eliyahu. "Parshas Shemini." Torah.org. 2007. www.torah.org/learning/olas-shabbos/5762/shemini.html. Accessed 25 January 2013.

Hyde, Michael J. *The Life-Giving Gift of Acknowledgment*. West Lafayette, IN: Purdue University Press, 2006.

Jewish Publication Society. *The Jewish Bible: Tanakh, the Holy Scriptures*. Philadelphia: Jewish Publication Society, 1985.

Kent, Orit. "A Theory of *Havruta* Learning." *Journal of Jewish Education* 76, no. 3 (2010): 215–45.

Kukla, Elliot Rose. "The Twisted Wick: Talmud Study as Spiritual Practice for Post-Modern Jews." *Zeek.net*. 7 July 2006. www.zeek.net/707talmud/. Accessed 25 January 2013.

Lamm, Norman. *The Shema: Spirituality and Law in Judaism*. Philadelphia: Jewish Publication Society, 2000.

Lewis, Sheldon. *Torah of Reconciliation*. Jerusalem: Gefen, 2012.

Plato. *Gorgias*. Translated by James H. Nichols. Ithaca, NY: Cornell University Press, 1998.

Ratcliffe, Krista. *Rhetorical Listening: Identification, Gender, Whiteness*. Carbondale: Southern Illinois University Press, 2005.

Schultz, Rachael Geifman. "Havruta: Learning in Pairs." My Jewish Learning.com www.myjewishlearning.com/practices/Ritual/Torah_Study/How_to_Study_Torah/Havruta_Learning_in_Pairs_.shtml. Accessed 25 January 2013.

Skolnik, Fred. "Shema." In *The New Encyclopedia of Judaism*, edited by Geoffrey Wigoder, 532. New York: Macmillan, 1989.

Tompkins, Paula. "Rhetorical Listening and Moral Sensitivity." *International Journal of Listening* 23 (2009): 60–79.

13

Simulated *Shiur*?
Post-It Notes of an ArtScroll Amateur

JONATHAN BOYARIN

The Babylonian Talmud is the classic text of rabbinic Jewish culture and has been the core curriculum of traditional Jewish yeshivas for centuries. As popularly understood today, it is a commentary on and also incorporates the Mishna, the first monument of written rabbinic Judaism after the closing of the biblical canon. The Mishna is concise, telegraphic, and declarative in style, reflecting its original oral transmission. The text of the Babylonian Talmud was established by the sixth century, although its transmission remained largely oral for centuries after that. It is customarily printed with the classic medieval commentaries of Rashi and the Tosafists on flanking margins. Along with, and in a sense even more than Scripture, it is the core of the early modern Jewish curriculum.

This chapter discusses the phenomenon formally called the *Schottenstein Edition of Talmud Bavli*, subtitled *The Gemara: The Classic Vilna Edition, with an Annotated, Interpretive Elucidation, as an Aid to Talmud Study*. Everyone knows the work as "ArtScroll," the "ArtScroll Talmud," or the "ArtScroll Gemara" (Schottenschein, *Talmud Bavli*). ArtScroll is a well-recognized brand name in the Anglophone Orthodox Jewish world. It began as a printer of wedding invitations and is now the producer and purveyor of bilingual editions of the standard prayer book as well as the Pentateuch, crowding out older editions, as richly documented in the communications scholar Jeremy Stolow's *Orthodox by Design*.

The language of the Babylonian Talmud and its standard commentaries is the Hebrew-Aramaic mix known as *loshn-koydesh* (the holy tongue). The language of oral study or the reception of those texts has been the vernacular—Yiddish, Ladino, and the like, and now, quite commonly, English. ArtScroll's English "elucidation" seeks to replicate and make available to nonadepts in the original language of the texts the embodied mode of learning that is typical of traditional yeshivas but is far less common today. Here I seek to point out some of the commonplaces of that mode of learning and ArtScroll's techniques for conveying them in a written text. The challenge faced by the ArtScroll editors becomes clearer when we stress that the Talmud, even though written down, is understood as oral Torah. In deference to Scripture, the Talmud was not supposed to be written down, although it eventually was. It exists now primarily in (vast) written form, yet it is ideally studied through vocalization and argument, whether solo, tête-à-tête, in a small group, or in a vast room with a single lecturer. Indeed, an old-fashioned yeshiva is a noisy place, where no signs saying "Shh!" are to be found. ArtScroll uses contemporary typesetting technology to facilitate, even for a solitary learner, something like those traditional learning practices. The typesetting has three distinct rhetorical functions: to demarcate the authority of founding texts, both scriptural and rabbinic; to mark the presence of the virtual teacher of the lesson that the reader pays attention to by reading; and, through footnotes, to provide a glimpse into the vast history of post-Talmudic interpretation. At the same time, the last words of the edition's subtitle—"as an Aid to Talmud Study"—seem to reveal the editors' anxiety lest their edition be seen as an adequate substitute for the real experience of learning in a classic yeshiva setting.

Indeed, the question of what shifts, what persists, what is lost, and what is gained when ArtScroll becomes the primary source for Talmud study must be addressed both from outside (meaning both the vantage point of the English page, as it were, and also the vantage point of the ethnography or sociology of reading) and inside (grounded in the original text, with the eye of the trained philologist or philologically trained critic or, for that matter, the traditionally trained Talmud scholar). From my perspective as an aspiring Talmud scholar, ArtScroll provides a fundamental form of access I would not otherwise have; from my perspective as an ethnographer, the ArtScroll Talmud is another move in the language dance by which foundational Jewish texts are repeatedly (and not only sequentially, but also simultaneously) reoralized and retextualized (see Boyarin).

For the past several years, I have perused several pages of the ArtScroll Talmud daily, but whether by the standards of the yeshiva or those of the academy, I am not a professional Talmudist. My bits of background as a Talmud student up to the age of forty-five did not make me adept enough to study on my own either the Talmud, in its original *loshn-koydesh*, or the key marginal commentaries that for centuries have accompanied Talmud study. The various experiences I had had of study one-on-one with a teacher, one-on-one with a more learned peer, or in small classes had been both enriching and frustrating. Studying with others, I tended to be frustrated by questions of pace: sometimes my teachers went too slowly, since I wasn't concerned to understand everything fully before moving on, a fundamental feature of classic yeshiva study in which students may spend days on a single folio; and sometimes they went too fast, as when a friend decided that we should study together a mathematical analysis of the Jewish calendar by the early modern scholar known as the Tiferes Yisroel. I haven't a clue now as to what that text says, though I know I read every word.

At some point I learned about the new, bilingual Talmud edition that ArtScroll was then in the process of publishing, and I decided I wanted to study Talmud on my own. Where to begin? I decided I wanted to study about a holiday. I knew that the tractate *Pesachim*, on the holiday of Passover, was immense, so I sat down to learn *Shevuos* instead, which I supposed would be about the holiday of Shevuos, or Pentecost, the second of three annual pilgrimage festivals in the Jewish ritual calendar. I did not buy the book at that time. Rather I went, most Sabbath mornings, to Rabbi Dovid Feinstein's Misevtha Tifereth Jerusalem on East Broadway in the Lower East Side of New York City, where the ArtScroll Talmud is kept in a semiseparate library room off to the side of the large *beis medresh*, the common study hall. I did figure out pretty quickly that *Shevuos* was about oaths,[1] not a pilgrimage festival. I got through perhaps ten *blatt*, or folios (both words mean the same thing in plain English—leaves—and indicate both sides of a page). Eventually I conceived the project of—but what word to use here?—studying, learning, or reading the entire Babylonian Talmud at least once in my lifetime. The choice of verb to describe what I do with—or, perhaps better, within—the volumes of the ArtScroll Talmud is consequential. "Studying" is perhaps the most neutral of these three, suggesting an engagement that could take place in either an academic or a traditional religious setting. "Reading" seems almost casual, and when I do in fact use it to describe my time with ArtScroll, I do so almost as a form of self-disparagement, to make it clear that I don't confuse my relatively superficial study with "learning."

This last term (a direct calque of the Yiddish *lernen*) indicates the plenary and manifold rhetoric—embodied, social, oral, and written—that constitutes the process of Talmud work as it has developed over the past millennium and more. Solitary study is hardly nonnormative, but the classic *lieu d'étude* for the Babylonian Talmud is the yeshiva (literally, the sitting place). There masters and disciples or pairs of study partners struggle to realize and make their own the tradition of debate and interpretation, using body language, facial expression, intonation, patterns of deference and interruption, and eyes—which fly back and forth from each other's countenances to the page, around the page, to the commentators at the back of the volume, and which occasionally close in concentration, exasperation, or exhaustion. "Learning" is embodied even when solitary, but the ArtScroll elucidation is designed, *inter alia*, to elicit as much of this repertoire of active engagement as possible without assuming that the person who holds the work necessarily has access to the original texts around which learning traditionally takes place. The notion of learning has powerful affective value in traditionalist Jewish culture (for example, "My grandfather spent all his spare time learning" and "Women should be taught to learn, too"). But it also points toward a richly embodied rhetoric of shared, active, voluble, and even agonistic study. ArtScroll aims, at least in large measure, to make that rhetorical practice accessible to those who for various reasons—such as money, time, geography, and lack of early training—do not have regular access to learning in the traditional yeshiva world.

Traditionally, editions of the Talmud start with *Berachot*, the first tractate in the order *zera'im* (seeds), dealing with the laws of agriculture. But I started instead with the tractate *Bava Kamma*—the name really just means "first segment"—which deals with major aspects of rabbinic civil law. That is where I started, several years ago, at first just trying to do "a chunk" (such as up to "two dots," the full colon that indicates the end of a passage in an otherwise unpunctuated text, or until the beginning of the next page of text in the original *loshn-koydesh* layout) every day and then, gradually and inconsistently, reconceiving this as my personal *daf yomi* project, with the goal of daily getting through a leaf, front and back. I was aware of the worldwide *daf yomi* program, inaugurated in Poland in the 1920s, in which thousands of Jews commit to at least a quick study of one folio of the Babylonian Talmud each day, a schedule that allows completion of the entire Talmud in the course of about eight years. But I have never attempted to catch up with that schedule.[2] I am, to make it clear, studying on my own, without partner or class. This kind of study does not create the kind of group identity that one might find in a traditional yeshiva setting, where pairs of partners may spend hours on end together, six days a week, for years, or where a group of students may follow a revered master for hours each week, likewise for years. I don't have to listen to other people's questions about the text, which sometimes might offer me illuminations and sometimes might seem to provide nothing but irrelevant distractions. If I don't understand something, I can look over the text itself, the explication, and the footnotes—about which more below—but there's no one I can speak to if I want to express my puzzlement or, on very rare occasions, share what I think is an insight.

I do worry sometimes about the superficiality of my passage through each volume, but I comfort myself that I am, at the very minimum, engaging at least as actively as an ordinary attendee (not a director) of a real *daf yomi shiur*, which typically lasts forty minutes to an hour stolen from an ordinary workday. Similarly, when I come to the end of a tractate, I'm ambivalent about marking the event with a *siyum*, a ritual of completion, since those are precisely the moments when the pace of my progress through the Talmud becomes public, and I do not want to deceive anyone with the claim that, having come to the end, I have "learned" that tractate.[3] More to the point, perhaps, I don't want to leave myself open to the charge that as an ArtScroll Talmudist, I have no idea what real "learning" entails. Indeed, sometimes it seems that the mark of true "learning" is not to make progress by moving further through the printed text, but rather to elaborate problems within the text and explore ever further the near-infinite depth of possible interpretation.

Solitary study has its attractions for me, especially early in the morning. For years I'd wondered what the experience of reading by candlelight would be like. Finally I decided to try it, opening my ArtScroll before dawn with no electric light switched on. I recommend two good candles, or preferably three, and you may have to move them around the page a bit to get the best illumination. It is true, however, that the small pool of light helps one concentrate on the text. So does the traditional practice of chanting the text to myself, to which I usually resort on those rare occasions when I'm trying to make out the sense of the text by looking only at "the classic Vilna edition" rather than reading the original text phrase by phrase, integrated with its translation and "elucidation" in English. I hardly ever mark the volumes of my ArtScroll Gemara. When I do, it is only to correct the very rare typographical errors I find (the copyediting and proofreading are astonishingly careful). The one time I can recall entering a query directly on the text (I do know that this is not an uncommon practice, and that a printed Talmud volume is not conventionally treated as quite as sacred an item as a Torah scroll), I stuck a post-it note on the margin nearby that said: "first time I wrote directly in my ArtScroll gm." Otherwise I got through the three "gates"—*Bavas Kamma, Metsiya,* and *Basra*—without writing anything, and it wasn't until I opened the first volume of *Sanhedrin*, dealing with the laws of courts and evidentiary procedure, that I began sticking small yellow post-its next to points that, for whatever reason, struck me as worthy of particular note. "For whatever reason" indeed—for quite some time I wrote nothing on the post-its, and when I look at those passages now, I am often unable to remember what significance I saw there then. If nothing else, these post-its are some kind of downpayment on the promise that ArtScroll— and, indeed, the traditional printed Talmud edition on which it is based— reminds me to make at the end of every chapter of every tractate: *hadran alach* (we shall return to you), "What is the place for sacrifices?" (or whatever the title of the given chapter is). If there is something I have noted in that chapter that I might easily find again, that I may need or want to recall at some point in the future, then I can make the promise to visit the chapter again in somewhat better faith. I have in the past years also begun to use the ArtScroll Talmud in my university teaching, as it has the advantage of permitting group study both by those who have some Hebrew (at least know the Hebrew alphabet) and by those who have none. I can attest that this generally works well, at least in small doses. In both undergraduate and graduate seminars, I have students take turns reading out loud, so they get to practice the intonation that produces Talmudic syntax, and I always explain that the only rule is "You have to interrupt."

ArtScroll and the *Tsuras Hadaf*

The ArtScroll Talmud is remarkable not least for what might aptly be termed its visual rhetoric. As promised by the subtitle's reference to "the classic Vilna edition," the ArtScroll includes the *tsuras hadaf* (image of the page) for each page—each side of each leaf—of what we may loosely call here the "traditional" modern original-language Talmud. The *tsuras hadaf* is reproduced, in fact, as many times as necessary, with the corresponding English that inevitably "elucidates" only a fragment of the original page's Talmud text on the facing (right or left) page, as the case may be. Accordingly, in addition to the traditional pagination (such as 21a and 47b), each ArtScroll English page bears a superscript numeral indicating where it stands in the order of the several English pages pertaining to that same "original" page: such as $21a^2$ and $47b^4$.

These points are worth reiterating: ArtScroll always presents diptychs; every English page is accompanied, on its right or left, by an "original" page; every "original" page is explicated by anywhere from three to six English pages. In every respect other than level of piety, I may be close to the ideal ArtScroll reader, susceptible as I am to the sentimental attractions of the "Vilna edition" and to ArtScroll's retention of the Ashkenazi *sof* (for example, *Bechoros*). The repetition of the "original" page thus serves a sentimentalizing, grounding, or authorizing ideological role. However, anecdotal reports and my own casual observations in a neighborhood yeshiva suggest that more advanced students use the ArtScroll as an aid to help them through difficult passages, a quick guide to secondary commentaries or obscure terminology. Accordingly, while having the English available may tend to transform of the "Vilna edition" into pure textual icon, various degrees of interchange and dialogue between the facing pages of the diptych are more likely.

Aware of this reification of the *tsuras hadaf*, and with some retention of the knowledge that my original goal was eventually not to need the English, but to reach a point of fluency where I might only rely on an older (and larger) monoscript[4] edition, I try at times to make myself look over onto the original page for a few lines at least. At one point in my reading I was doing more and more of that, as is shown by the fact that my post-its tended for a while to be placed next to the "Hebrew" page, and sometimes to be written in Yiddish. But at certain points—especially when the flow of the Talmudic argument is relatively straightforward, when I'm in a hurry to complete my *blatt du jour*, or when the topic itself seems especially remote—I catch myself with my eyes scanning only the phrases of the *loshn-koydesh* original, but on the English page itself, thus skipping over the literal translation and elucidation that make up the vast bulk of the text appearing on that English page. All of this suggests the potential interest of a more intimate ethnography of solitary reading, perhaps even with a video camera recording the way the eye travels across the page (in this case, pages) presented to it. I suspect that, with this text at least but with nearly every reader, the results would show an almost inevitably selective—and perhaps it would even be safe to say a strategically selective—choice of the words presented to it. Thus, for example, one could also study all of the original commentary of Tosafos, whose remarkably wordy text is reproduced in the original. This is, I suspect, unlikely but would obviously require ethnographic study of the integration of ArtScroll into more traditional yeshiva settings, a process that, as I understand by hearsay, has been at least somewhat controversial. This is understandable, since the entire ArtScroll Talmud project presents a dilemma that has appeared previously in the history of Talmud scholarship—to wit, making the text more open to nonadepts weakens the chain of oral and personalized tradition guiding its reception. Thus, Talya Fishman notes that Rashi's monumental eleventh-century commentary "made it possible for literate Jews (including those who lacked access to a master) to make sense of the Talmudic text's truncated and epigrammatic formulations. . . . Rashi's Talmud commentary contributed, wittingly or unwittingly, to the attenuation of discipleship and the weakening of its many collateral assumptions" (132). Similarly, Elchanan Reiner remarks of the first printed edition of the entire Babylonian Talmud, the Bamberg edition of the early sixteenth century, that it created "a learning community without borders that didn't need even a house of study. [This] gradually liberated the text from the control of the traditional elite. . . . It became an open text."

What, then, is the "open text" of the ArtScroll elucidation? It is worthwhile to describe the layout of the English pages in some detail. Taken together, this layout scheme might be described as a rhetoric of print. This notion is fully consistent with the idea of Talmud as an interplay of oral and written Torah, and of Talmud study as an ongoing, centuries-long process of textualization, reoralization, and retextualization. The various typefaces on the English ArtScroll page produce a rich range of visual-comprehension distinctions and encourage active, mobile reading as opposed to straightforward, linear, sequential reading. At least the following eight typefaces are used:

1. Large bold capital letters for the page heading.
2. Bold Hebrew, with vowels, for the phrase-by-phrase transcription of the facing Talmudic text.
3. Bold English, upper and lower case, to indicate the "literal" translation of each original phrase, though careful study would demonstrate that the bounds between such supposedly "literal" translation and

interpretation is often hard to determine. In other words, the choice to assign some parts of a sentence to bold letters and some to non-bold letters (see the next item in this list) often appears arbitrary on closer inspection, thus illustrating the truism that there is no such thing as a "literal translation."

4. Nonbold English, upper and lower, for all of the extra words needed to make sense of the telegraphic "literal" translation; this I take to be ArtScroll's "elucidation," which I gloss, roughly, as "what a teacher would have to say in a live class for this text to make any sense to you." Although this also has the effect of constructing a readable, normative English sentence around the skeleton of the "literal" translation, the nonbold English also incorporates glosses and clarifications drawn from Rashi's commentary and from surrounding Talmudic passages. Here, as at so many points throughout the ArtScroll elucidation, the editors both guide and control the reading. This nonbold English text, along with the ample footnotes, reflects the ArtScroll editors' strict fidelity toward the authority of the medieval commentators known as Rishonim (the first ones).

5. Smaller bold capital letters for quotes from Mishna or Baraita, statements attributed to the rabbis of the Mishna and hence authoritative, but for various reasons not included in the text of the Mishna itself.

6. Nonbold italic for transliterated Hebrew words or phrases, and for citations to Hebrew commentaries.

7. Nonbold Hebrew, in footnotes for references to particular passages in commentaries.

8. Smaller bold capital letters, in italic, for scriptural quotations.

In addition to the phrase-by-phrase reproduction, "translation," and "elucidation" of the original language on each English page, there are footnotes at the bottom. Sometimes the "top" material will take up most of the page (see, for example *Bechoros* 25b[4]), and there will be relatively few footnotes. Occasionally the footnotes overwhelm the elucidation (for example, *Bechoros* 8b[7]). As a general rule, the footnotes rely in the first instance on, and summarize, the commentary of the twelfth-century northern French scholar known as Rashi, though they will not hesitate to note apparent difficulties or inconsistencies in Rashi, especially (though perhaps not quite exclusively) where later authoritative commentators have already taken issue with him.

The footnotes also make occasional reference to the more wordy commentary of Tosafos, but they certainly make no attempt at a comprehensive summary of Tosafos. Accordingly, as Tosafos is frequently so verbose as to represent the majority of the words on a page of the Vilna edition (see, for example, Bechoros 41b), it is often the case that most of the words on the facing page of the "original" edition are not really reflected in the English— neither in the elucidation nor the footnotes. The curious effect is that the pages of the "original" that have the most words printed on them are generally the ones I get through fastest. In contrast, in formal and organized yeshiva study the analyses of the Tosafists, often notoriously difficult, are given a great deal of close attention.

Extensive footnotes both further the in-text "elucidation" of the Talmudic argument and elaborate on related issues covered by the legion of later commentators. The ArtScroll editors[5] take extreme care to attribute the substance of their footnotes to traditional sources, most commonly to Rashi or to Rashi plus others, but they by no means always do this. I open, haphazardly, to *Bechoros* 38b[3] and find citations to both classic and less well-known commentaries, Rishonim (the earlier ones) as well as Acharonim (the later ones). Certain footnote text is set off by brackets, sometimes (apparently) to indicate further complications that may be illuminating but less central to the understanding of the text (see, for example, footnote 32 on the same page) and sometimes (clearly) to set off footnotes that are in ArtScroll's "own" voice—that is, not attributed to earlier authoritative sources. For a reader like me, the footnotes thus become a remarkable compendium of sources to which I might otherwise never have had access, including non-Talmudic rabbinic works, lesser-known medieval commentators, and a host of later commentators. Nonetheless, if the ArtScroll Talmud synthesizes and brings back into circulation selected points from major commentaries, it also "loses" them, since the editors have chosen not to reproduce even in the original language the commentaries appended to the end of each tractate of the Vilna edition.

Certain additional features of the ArtScroll Talmud are also worthy of note.

1. The innovative punctuation "- ? -" occasionally appears at the end of a paragraph of elucidation. As far as I know, this is an invention of the ArtScroll editors and has never been used elsewhere. This feature puzzled,

and indeed disturbed, my non-Talmudist graduate student Shenandoah Nieuwsma so much that she wrote a brilliant seminar paper about it, tentatively concluding that it is rhetorically superfluous. To me the feature is not puzzling at all, probably because I have some experience with the live give-and-take of oralized Talmud study. The punctuation does not indicate that ArtScroll is at a loss, but that the reader should realize a counterpoint has just been made and needs to be acknowledged. One possible gloss of "- ? -" in English is: "What are 'you' [in which case 'you' means the position taken by the text immediately preceding the paragraph of elucidation that concludes with '- ? -'] going to say about the point made in the paragraph that ends with '- ? -'" (or, more simply, "This whole paragraph constitutes a question."). The "- ? -", in other words, indicates that a move has just been made in the back-and-forth of the Gemara's discourse. It may also be understood as a prompt for oral reading, similar to the way that the medieval commentator Rashi often comments that a certain statement in the Gemara is made *bitmiya*—that is, "in surprise" or "skeptically." ArtScroll's "- ? -" and Rashi's *bitmiya*, that is, imperfectly stand in for the shrugs, eyebrow motions, vocal indications, and hand gestures that do so much to drive live debate.

2. As a student of Jewish sociolinguistics and of internal bi- and trilingualism, I am impressed by the consistent accuracy of copyediting in this very complex text, and also by the precision of the elucidation's English prose style. This is remarkable not only because of the tendency of the source language to interfere with the target in a text where virtually every sentence is both bilingual and bi-alphabetic (Hebrew and Latin), but also because in live and social Talmud study, terms from the source text quite commonly appear in the oral, target discourse of explanation, analysis, and dispute. In particular, although I was most eager to find interference from a presumptive native Yiddish, or indeed idiosyncratic English of any kind, I found it very rarely, to wit (these are, in my reading, almost exclusive and not merely selective examples, at least in the tractates cited):

   a. "When a consecrated animal produces a young," BT *Menachos* 80a[1], note 6. This sounds like a Yiddishism, though I cannot identify it.

b. Possible interference: "Rav Huna stated that the firstborn were replaced by the Kohanim already at Mount Sinai." *Zevachim* 115b², note 14. Here the term "already" seems a calque of the Yiddish *shoyn*, which in a context like this would mean something like "as early as."

c. A rare actual calque: "Those Amorites did not return after those wars [but were killed out]." *Avodah Zarah* 53b¹, note 7. The Yiddish term that almost certainly underlies the English "killed out" here is *oysgeharget*.

d. "A *bechor* that the circle of its eye is round like that of a man" (*Bechoros* 40a⁵, elucidation). Again a calque from the Yiddish form "*a w vos di x fun zayn y iz*."

3. The Ashkenazi-traditionalist orientation of the entire ArtScroll project (in the Talmud as elsewhere) is clearly signaled by the "s" transliteration of *sof* rather than its merger with *tof*, even extending to transliterations such as *Encyclopedia Talmudis*.⁶

4. Since the phrase-by-phrase reproduction of the "original" language on the English page is vocalized, ArtScroll indicates not only text but pronunciation. At certain points, at any rate, the ArtScroll editors seem to indicate a loyalty to traditional Ashkenazi pronunciations even where these are arguably not grammatically correct in the *loshn-koydesh*. These traditionalist transcriptions further add to the effect of listening to a *shiur* given by an old-fashioned teacher, properly grounded in the study world of the Eastern European yeshiva.⁷

5. The status throughout the ArtScroll Talmud of the question of the perfection of the Talmudic text (is it nonredundant and complete, or does it need philological attention?) is ripe for investigation, as both of these attitudes certainly appear. Accordingly, ArtScroll frequently attends to textual changes suggested by earlier religious authorities (*Bach* and *Shitah Mekubetzes*) that are likely to strike contemporary readers as constituting simultaneously emendations and interpretations. This seeming confusion about what, in the philology of written texts, is strictly separated out for methodological purposes is another indication that the Talmud is still an oralo-literate—that is, still open—text. However, ArtScroll draws on some of the techniques characteristic of academic philology, such as when its editors note interpolations of

marginal comments that seem to have been mistakenly integrated into the text by some copyist. At the same time, the footnotes will occasionally take the trouble to help explain why apparent redundancies in the Gemara are in fact necessary (see, for example, *Menachos* 23b[1], note 7). Even from a traditionalist perspective, which the ArtScroll editors would likely accept as an apt description of their own, the work of emendation and the effort to "elucidate" a text seen as perfect are not mutually contradictory, since the Talmud is fundamentally understood as a written record of a text whose basic character remains oral Torah. This in turn points once again to the persistent imbrication of the written and the oral that shapes the embodied and contingent nature of study and authority in the Talmud.

Toward a Provisional Conclusion

I understand and experience the ArtScroll Talmud as providing me with a simulated *shiur*, something like the experience of live group study, with the nonbold "elucidation" serving *in loco rabonis*—that is, as the master who directs the group session. And it may not be too much to insist that the intent of the ArtScroll editors—beyond the different approaches that individual elucidators might have taken—is to make the Gemara itself "speak" to the reader as a teacher might.[8]

In this respect, it would also be a useful exercise to compare the rhetorical strategies of ArtScroll with the (partial) translation of the Babylonian Talmud into English by the genius Rabbi Adin Steinsaltz. ArtScroll, technically innovative but hermeneutically conservative, strives to present a composite interpretation that draws heavily on the most authoritative medieval commentator, Rashi. Steinsaltz presents his own reading or interpretation. If ArtScroll lets the Gemara be a teacher and seeks anonymity for itself, Steinsaltz speaks more to the reader as a lecturer might. Indeed, his edition is popularly known as "Steinsaltz."[9]

ArtScroll writes about the Gemara as if the Gemara were conducting a dialogue with itself, as is especially clear in passages of elucidation where every move of enunciation in an argument is prefaced with a summary of the rhetorical move taken at and by that moment of enunciation. Thus, in *Chullin* 28a[3], the elucidation introduces each in a sequence of paragraphs with a description of what the Gemara is about to do with words:

> The Gemara's final attempt to resolve the dispute between Rav Nachman and Rav Ada bar Ahava on the basis of a Baraisa: ...
>> Unconvinced by this proof, the Gemara asks ...
>> The Gemara reacts in surprise ...
>> The Gemara voices its reservations with the aforementioned proof ...

"The Gemara finally resolves the dispute...."—admittedly, the Gemara does not, by this device, quite become a spectral teacher.[10] Yet part of my motivation for learning, studying, or reading ArtScroll every morning is to have some way, as an academic without rigorous formal training in rabbinic philology, to enter the conversation about the dynamics of rabbinic discourse. And very occasionally, it does at times allow me to speak as though I really "knew," as when I told a certain well-known academic Talmudist who's been writing for decades about narratives contained in folios 83b–84a in *Bava Metsia* that these narratives have pertinent sequelae also on the subsequent folios, or when I suggested to a doctoral candidate in ancient Mediterranean studies the potential relevance of discussions about blemished firstborns to the question of the continued social status of the Kohanim after the destruction of the Temple. I have suggested here several aspects of the ArtScroll Talmud that are well worthy of further investigation, or—dare I say it?—elucidation:

1. A profound shift in the balance of commentary (for example, adding early modern commentators and deemphasizing the medieval ones) as part and parcel of the translation to English, and what it might bode for the future of Talmud study in Jewish communities and in the academy.
2. The need for close attention to actual patterns of reading, by individuals in both privacy and group study, well beyond the scattered autoethnographic observations I have been able to offer here.
3. Further attention to implicit ideologies as suggested in some of the examples here, without distorting what to me, after a great deal of study, represents a remarkable scholarly effort.

Indeed, I would like to conclude with a strong affirmation of the proposal that the ArtScroll Talmud should be seen as a milestone in the history of the Talmud, especially if, along with the philosopher of Talmud Sergey Dolgopolski, we get in the habit of treating the Talmud as much as a process as a thing, with an unknown but intriguing future as well as an extraordinarily rich past. This is true of all living traditions: the Talmud is not unique in this respect, though it may well be exemplary. The rhetoric of "learning"—both the intense positive affect associated with the term in traditionalist Jewish culture, and the manifold textual, oral, and embodied codes that drive the production of meaning therein—enjoins the learner, as it were, to become the debate. Meanwhile, like a simulated driving lesson, ArtScroll's "elucidation" places the person scanning it inside the text—perhaps we can say the person is in the place of that figure ArtScroll calls "the Gemara." He or she can merely go along for the ride as a reader, but the more actively he or she takes on the roles of interrogator and respondent in the give-and-take of the Talmud, the more he or she will be engaged in that embodied and agonistic rhetoric that Jews call *learning*.

NOTES

I am indebted to Daniel Boyarin and Sergey Dolgopolski for vitally important comments on an earlier draft of this chapter, and to the members of the Scholars' Working Group on the Jewish Book at the Center for Jewish History, where this material was first presented.

1. The word for oaths, *shevuos*, is a homonym for the name of the holiday. The early modern rabbinic scholar known as the Shlah (an acronym for *Shney Luchos Habris* [Two tablets of the law], the name of his masterwork) played on this same homonym in titling the section of that book dealing with the laws of Shevuos, and with the obligation to study Torah thereon and generally (since Shevuos is understood as the "time of the giving of the Torah") *Masekhes Shevuos* (Tractate Shevuos).

2. I use what we might call the "full-size" ArtScroll edition, which is still smaller than many older editions of the Talmud, as opposed to the smaller *daf yomi* edition, which is less expensive and more suitable for carrying to class every day.

3. See, for example, *Avodah Zarah* 19a[4] (page numbers with superscript numbers, like this one, are explained below in the text): "One who studies Torah in a manner calculated to impress others [including himself] rather than to facilitate retention, will not merit long life."

4. The *tsuras hadaf*, or "original" page, is actually not monolingual, containing as it does text in Aramaic, Mishnaic Hebrew, biblical Hebrew, and even (in Rashi's commentary) some medieval French.

5. The "elucidators" for each chapter are listed at the front of the pertinent volume. I will presume, until I learn otherwise, that the footnotes for each chapter may be likewise attributed to that chapter's elucidator.

6. In this case, rather than resisting the modern tendency to make all Hebrew pronunciation conform to the Israeli norm, the ArtScroll editors have effectively Ashkenized—and thus made more legitimate for their project—this reference to a modern Hebrew work.

7. Thus, for example, ArtScroll transcribes this phrase as *u'veho ko mifligi* (and this is what they disagree about)—for example, at *Menachos* 23b[1]—rather than as *u'veho ko mipalgi*. Yitzhak Frank notes that "mifligi" is the common pronunciation of Ashkenazi Jews (51).

8. I say almost nothing here about the use of ArtScroll in group study contexts, because I have little data recorded. On the rare occasions when, formally or informally, I use it in my own instruction, I am careful to "ad lib" rather than read the ArtScroll's elucidation verbatim. Also, on a few occasions I have sat in on a Midwest Orthodox rabbi's *daf yomi shiur*; on the occasions when he resorted to reading an ArtScroll footnote verbatim, I noted my own (unvoiced!) reaction that this was somehow not worthy of a Talmud scholar.

9. See also the first volumes of the new Koren Talmud project, which likewise presents a stark contrast to the ArtScroll approach.

10. Sergey Dolgopolski suggested to me: "Perhaps it becomes a spectral student instead." That is, one might see ArtScroll's figure of "the Gemara" not as a stand-in for a human authoritative guide, but as an idealized version of the reader or student, trying—like the Gemara—to make sense of the Mishna with the help of all the logic and rabbinic dicta at his, her, or its command.

BIBLIOGRAPHY

Boyarin, Jonathan. "Voices around the Text: The Ethnography of Reading at Mesivta Tifereth Jerusalem." In *The Ethnography of Reading*, edited by Jonathan Boyarin, 212–37. Berkeley: University of California Press, 1993.

Dolgopolski, Sergey. *What Is Talmud? The Art of Disagreement*. New York: Fordham University Press, 2009.

Fishman, Talya. *Becoming the People of the Talmud: Oral Torah as Written Tradition in Medieval Jewish Cultures*. Philadelphia: University of Pennsylvania Press, 2011.

Frank, Yitzhak. *Grammar for Gemara and Targum Onkelos*. Jerusalem: United Israel Institutes, 2003.

Reiner, Elchanan. Presentation to the Scholars' Working Group on the Jewish Book, Center for Jewish History, New York City, 3 February 2012.

Schottenstein, Jerome, ed. *Talmud Bavli: The Gemara*. Brooklyn, NY: Mesora, 2005.

Stolow, Jeremy. *Orthodox by Design: Judaism, Print Politics, and the ArtScroll Revolution*. Berkeley: University of California Press, 2010.

14

Of Superheroes and Synecdoche
Holocaust Exceptionalism, Race, and the Rhetoric of Jewishness in America

JENNIFER GLASER

Jewishness as Trope

Angry that her bull's-eye map was receiving some of the blame for the 2011 shooting of Representative Gabrielle Giffords, Sarah Palin issued a scathing statement. By attacking her, she claimed, the media were "manufacturing a blood libel that serves only to incite the very hatred and violence they purport to condemn" (quoted in Dunn, 420). In addition to displacing the responsibility for the shooting from Palin, the use of the term "blood libel" was clearly a calculated attempt by the politician and her speechwriters to claim some of the martyrdom they saw being attached to Giffords and the other victims of the Arizona shooting. To many, what was most shocking about Palin's appropriation of the term to defend herself from charges of complicity in Jared Loughner's violence was that the phrase seemed—in her usage—to be entirely stripped of its original Jewish content. After all, as many pundits angrily pointed out in the days after Palin's statement, the blood libel—the assertion that Jews killed Christian babies in order to make ritual use of their blood—had been used for centuries to justify violence against the Jewish community. The blood libel is central to *The Protocols of the Elders of Zion*, the antisemitic tract that has fueled so much prejudice and violence against Jews around the globe since its publication in the first decade of the twentieth century. How strange was it for Palin to excuse herself from inciting violence against Giffords, a Jewish woman, by invoking a myth that had functioned to incite similar violence against Jews for more than 900 years? Palin's decontextualization of the term, however inappropriate, was nonetheless not the first time that specifically Jewish metaphors or experiences, stripped of their Jewish content, have been used to try to explain American culture in its best and worst incarnations. As I will argue, this sort of substitution has historically functioned not only to negate Jewish experience but also to erase other ethnic histories and evade responsibility for other, uniquely American forms of violence and oppression. In particular, the discourse of Holocaust exceptionalism has often been joined to that of American exceptionalism in ways that simultaneously cement American uniqueness and obscure the history of racialized subjugation in the United States.

Jewishness has long been mobilized as a metaphor for understanding America and Americanness. The rhetoric of American exceptionalism has since its very origins been tied up with Jewishness as discourse. Donald Pease traces the genealogy of the term "exceptionalism" and its centrality in America's understanding of itself. He writes that "the discourse of exceptionalism may be best characterized by its account of the United States' unique place in world history—the 'redeemer nation,' 'conqueror of the world's markets' and, more recently, the 'global security state'" (109). As the historian Deborah Madsen notes in her exploration of the ideological power of American exceptionalism, the nation's earliest Puritan settlers saw themselves not simply as the embodiment of John Winthrop's biblical "city on the hill," but also as the typologically preordained descendants of the Israelites. From this early reading of America's elect status among the nations to the nineteenth-century debates about whether Native Americans might be the remnants of one of the Lost Tribes of Israel, the melding of Jewish and American chosenness has been fundamental to the rhetoric of US uniqueness.

During the twentieth century, the discourses of American and Jewish exceptionalism have been more tightly intertwined, particularly in the figure of the Jewish immigrant as the allegory for the archetypically American experience of immigration. Jonathan Freedman contends that "although Jews constituted a decided minority of the remarkable immigration to the U.S. between 1880 and 1924 (roughly four out of the twenty million or so who made their way to the U.S. during this period), Jewish-specific images, sites, experiences have become broadly representative of that social moment itself—a culturally validated synecdoche, to put it in rhetorical terms, for the experience undergone by all immigrants to America between 1880 and 1924" (7). The particularly Ashkenazi Jewish experience of immigration has become, as Freedman suggests, a stand-in for a host of other groups' experiences of exile and belonging throughout the twentieth and twenty-first centuries.[1] This replacement of a diverse set of lived experiences by Jew-as-allegory is important for a number of reasons—most notable among them that the immigrant experience has itself become a "synecdoche," to use Freedman's term, for the American experience writ large. As Matthew Jacobson points out, Ellis Island has largely replaced Plymouth Rock as the chronotope of American identity, the image of the "tired ... poor ... huddled masses" invoked by Emma Lazarus now central to the nation's overdetermined natal myth of inclusion and incorporation.[2] I would argue, in contrast to Jacobson, that Ellis Island has never entirely displaced Plymouth Rock as America's foundational myth in the national imagination. Instead, in many cases, stories of immigration—particularly Jewish immigration—have been melded into the original image of election that is so central to America's symbolic imaginary as a means of cementing national difference. The primacy of Ellis Island and the idea that the United States, unlike Europe, is a nation bent on a culturally pluralistic acceptance of the others within is central to America's myth of uniqueness. The iconicity of Ellis Island is no less problematic than that of Plymouth Rock was. In recent work such as Karen Yamashita's *I Hotel*, the centrality of Ellis Island—and, by extension, its association with a particular, and particularly Jewish, immigration story—is seen to obscure other experiences, most notably those that emerge out of Angel Island, America's often-brutal Pacific immigration station.[3]

Increasingly, Jewish experience has become a cultural touchstone for our understanding not just of immigration, but of ethnicity more generally. The image of the Jew as the paragon of economic success and radical individualism—"the hardworking entrepreneur with the pushcart or the small candy store" (Freedman, 7)—has also long undergirded ideas about Jewish and American exceptionalism. In America the Jew (alongside the Asian American) became the prototype for the successful model minority—simultaneously exceptional in his or her capacity to acculturate, or melt into the larger national body politic, and exemplary in his or her assimilatory zeal.[4] Central to liberal ideology in America was the idea that the success of model minorities, such as Jews, highlighted the failures of "bad" minorities, most notably African Americans, to succeed on the purportedly level playing field of American capitalism. The discourse of the model minority, as we will see, functioned to absolve the United States of its own failures and obscure the particularities of national racial oppression (including the oppression of the model minorities themselves).

To more fully explore this process of cultural amnesia and the role that Jew-as-trope has played within it, I want to unpack Freedman's assertion that "what seems to be synecdoche, a part standing for a larger whole, rapidly transformed itself into a set of metonymies—of substitutions that work by the fuzzy logic of association—in such a way as to project these [Jewish immigrant] narratives onto other ethnic groups, conflating their quite diverse histories with Jewish American norms and expectations, images and shadows, frequently eliding their own distinctive trajectories and experiences in favor of Jewish ones" (8). Although Freedman is speaking explicitly about Jewish experiences of immigration becoming metonymic for, and thus "eliding," other histories of immigration, I would argue that a similar slippage often occurs when Jewishness is mobilized as a trope for understanding different racial and ethnic experiences in the United States more generally. By suggesting that this "set of metonymies," as Freedman calls them, is ethically problematic, I am not contending that all comparisons between Jews and other others function as a form of erasure.[5] Many critics (including Freedman elsewhere in *Klezmer America*) have persuasively argued otherwise. In her brilliant essay "Fag Hags and Bu-Jews," Naomi Seidman contends that there is something uniquely Jewish in the rejection of one's own difference in favor of other othernesses—the unwillingness to identify as a Jew in the classic sense while still identifying with a variety of marginalized subject positions. Like Seidman, I believe that this secular Jewish form of sympathetic identification provides a powerful position from which to critique social inequities.

I do think, however, that the metonymic function of Jewishness in the American imagination has often obscured difference even as it sought to celebrate it. Kenneth Burke explores metaphor, metonymy, synecdoche, and irony, writing that he is concerned "not with their purely figurative usage, but with their role in the discovery and description of 'the truth'" (503). Metonymy and synecdoche, related tropes that suggest the ambiguous possibilities (both narratively and ethically) of substituting the part for the whole, have tremendous explanatory power for discussions of race and ethnicity, and their mobilization in American rhetoric.[6] In their seminal *The Metaphors We Live By*, George Lakoff and Mark Johnson tease out the continuities and discontinuities between metaphor and metonymy, focusing particularly on synecdoche as a representative metonymic trope. They write:

> Metaphor and metonymy are different *kinds* of processes. Metaphor is principally a way of conceiving of one thing in terms of another, and its primary function is understanding. Metonymy, on the other hand, has primarily a referential function, that is, it allows us to use one entity to stand for another. But metonymy is not merely a referential device. It also serves the function of providing understanding. For example, in the case of the metonymy THE PART FOR THE WHOLE there are many parts that can stand for the whole. Which part we pick out determines which aspect of the whole we are focusing on. (36)

As Lakoff and Johnson say, "metonymy is not merely . . . referential." Instead, "which part we pick out determines which aspect of the whole we are focusing on," an important distinction that highlights the power of synecdochic thinking to evade or erase uncomfortable social realities via its focus on a particular part of a larger whole. Lakoff and Johnson are not alone in noting this aspect of metonymy. For example, in a long note on Kenneth Burke, Hayden White suggests that the tropes through which we organize history into narrative are fundamentally ideological, blinding us to some aspects of the larger historiographic picture (14). I would go even further than White and Lakoff and Johnson to argue that synecdoche is fundamentally a figure of evasion—its focus on the part is a means of avoiding an encounter with a more complicated and diverse whole.

This kind of synecdochic thinking often affects how we approach group identity. Martin Reisigl and Ruth Wodak point out that "the collective singular or 'particularising synecdoche' is typical of stereotypes and prejudiced discourse, in which statements about persons are made in a leveling, generalizing, essentializing and eternalizing manner, in which groups of social actors are presupposed to be homogenous and are selectively ascribed a specific, allegedly shared, either negative or positive feature, trait, mentality, and so on" (63). Examples of the power of synecdoche for understanding (or misunderstanding) racial or ethnic groups are myriad. Think, for instance, of the way the term "urban" has increasingly become synonymous with African American culture and lived experience in public discourse. The figure of the Wandering Jew (the capitalization is intentional) has traditionally been synecdochic for Jewish experience—particularly in antisemitic discourse. Even the word "Jew," stripped of the modifying "wandering" or "eternal," has come to have connotations as an antisemitic slur that stands in for all Jewish experience in some cultures.[7] Reisigl and Wodak assert that "the blatant anti-Semitic abuse of the anthroponym 'Jew' still continues today to have the effect that quite a few, particularly German, non-Jews seem to have problems even to articulate the word 'Jew' or 'Jews' at all. For them, the word is still inseparably associated with massive negative associations and connotations" (63). In a similarly overdetermined manner, the idea of Auschwitz has come to stand in for the entire experience of the Holocaust. The substitutions that operate in this type of synecdochic thinking carry with them the possibility of erasure. As Jennifer Clary-Lemon puts it, "the most obvious problem with substitution is the possibility that when something is substituted for something else, there is a loss involved—a sense of reduction, of oversimplification, of subtraction" (W7).

By dramatizing questions of representation in a dual sense, the trope of synecdoche proves particularly useful in prodding us to critique not only what happens when an idea, word, or characteristic comes to stand in for a whole group or group of experiences, but also what happens when one group comes to stand in for all others in representing a certain aspect of ethnic experience.

Displacement, Disavowal, and the Holocaust in *X-Men: First Class*

Set in 1962, the recent film *X-Men: First Class* rehearses the classic tropes of the Cold War: the bumbling KGB spies, the CIA double agents, the paranoia, the underground bunkers, and the looming possibility of nuclear war.[8] Much of the film is explicitly centered on the arms race that led to the Cuban missile crisis. But despite its Cold War stripes, this superhero flick is a Holocaust movie, situated from its first moments within the generic conventions that have characterized films such as *Schindler's List*. *X-Men: First Class* opens with the backstory of one of the X-Men's central antiheroes, Magneto. In the movie's first scenes, set in 1944, Magneto—or, as he is known at the time, Erik Lensherr—is a small boy, his fragility brought into relief by the pale gray backdrop of a concentration camp in Poland. When he is pulled from his emaciated mother by Nazi guards, his misery allows him to perform a magical feat: bending a metal gate with his mind in order to get to her. For this act—a sign, the viewer soon learns, that he is the possessor of mutant DNA that leaves him with the power to control metal-based substances—Erik is brought before Dr. Klaus Schmidt, a Joseph Mengele figure, for special testing. A eugenicist like many other Nazis, Schmidt is fascinated with the child's mutant status (an allegory for the purported genetic otherness possessed by all Jews) and demands that he perform the trick again—this time by moving a metal coin. When Erik is unable to move the coin, Schmidt brings the child's mother into the room and asks him to make a choice: either show evidence of his superpower or watch his mother die. Borrowing from the generic vocabulary of the Holocaust film, as these scenes do, the movie provokes images of *Sophie's Choice* for the viewer during this tragic moment. When the child cannot will himself to move the coin, his mother is murdered in front of him, setting off a massive reaction in young Erik that kills two guards and destroys the Nazi scientist's laboratory—an unconscious outpouring of his superpower that indicates that the proto-Magneto is not yet fully in control of his gift. Witnessing this display, Schmidt becomes more interested in the boy as a possible subject for his genetic tests. Although the tests Erik undergoes at the hands of Schmidt are left to the viewer's imagination, the film moves—a few scenes later—to Erik eighteen years later, now a young man on a global search for Schmidt, his mother's murderer. Much of the rest of the film centers on this vengeance plot and the "tough Jew," Magneto, who is carrying it out.

Magneto's background was established well before *X-Men: First Class*. Although his Holocaust history was not detailed in early *X-Men* comics, it has been an important aspect of the series since at least 1981.[9] It is not incidental that, although Magneto has been a character in the series since it began in 1963, his Holocaust history only appeared in the 1980s. As Peter Novick points out, it was only in the latter decades of the twentieth century—particularly during the 1970s and 1980s, when both American and Jewish identity were in radical flux, and the celebration of ethnic difference was in vogue—that Holocaust memorialization and representation began in earnest in the United States. *X-Men: Magneto Testament*, a stand-alone graphic novel by Greg Pak that was published in 2008, details Erik's time in a concentration camp and his love for another prisoner, the Gypsy Magda.[10] Pak identifies himself as a self-conscious participant in the discourse of Holocaust representation both in the title of the work (a first-person "testament" being the privileged genre of Holocaust literature) and in his preparation for writing the graphic novel. An article in *Haaretz* states that "to prepare for the admittedly difficult task of telling a Holocaust story in a comic book, Pak has read multiple survivor narratives and histories of the Third Reich and the Final Solution, watched documentaries, and gone back to graphic novels like *Maus*" (Shinefeld).

Despite these previous representations of Magneto's past, it is jarring to see the Holocaust play such a prominent role in *X-Men: First Class*—primarily because the story of the Holocaust seems to stand in for and displace another, even more omnipresent narrative in the *X-Men* universe: that of the civil rights movement and African American identity in the United States. Why is *X-Men: First Class* structured around a Holocaust narrative when it is set, for the most part, not in Europe during or after the Second World War, but in the United States during the 1960s? As Ta-Nehisi Coates puts it, *X-Men: First Class* is "a period piece for our postracial times—in the era of Ella Baker and the Rev. Dr. Martin Luther King Jr., the most powerful adversaries of spectacular apartheid are a team of enlightened white dudes." Despite its temporal and social background, the film manages to make not one explicit mention of the civil rights movement that was beginning to so fundamentally challenge America's own racial landscape during this time period. Instead, the film uses the Holocaust as a trope (mostly divorced from any explicitly Jewish content) that stands in for all racial violence and oppression. As Coates suggests, "*First Class* is not blind to societal evils, so much as it works to hold evil at an ocean's length. The film is rooted in its opposition to the comfortably foreign abomination of Nazism."

X-Men: First Class suggests that it is not only the Jewish-identified experience of immigration that has displaced the experiences of other groups. There are a number of ways in which Jewishness as metaphor has been mobilized to quash the particularity of other others' experiences—most strikingly in this displacement of debates about race and civil rights by conversations about the Holocaust. Although a number of critics have convincingly argued that the Holocaust has come to function as the most powerful and problematic Jewish-identified trope in America, few have noted the way in which the Holocaust has come to stand in for all race-based oppression in a manner that has erased conversations about other forms of racialized violence and inequality. By making this argument, I am not suggesting that the enormity of the Holocaust and its traumatic effects on those who survived it should be ignored as a central framework for understanding postwar Jewish or American identity. After all, the Holocaust has had a powerful effect on a number of discourses. As *X-Men: First Class* indicates, many of our postwar conversations about genetics, for instance, have been framed through the atrocities of the Holocaust and the Nuremberg racial laws that preceded it. By my critique, I am simply suggesting that Holocaust exceptionalism has become married to American exceptionalism in profound ways that require further rhetorical analysis.

Despite having happened on distant shores, the Holocaust has—during the latter decades of the twentieth century—become an American tragedy—and not solely because of the number of Jewish citizens in America or because of national guilt about having not admitted refugees to the country during the war. Instead, I would argue that it has become, in a manner equally problematic for Jews and non-Jews, a means of distancing America from the barbarism of European race-based violence at the same time that it allows the United States to avoid its own vexed racial history—placing evil squarely on "distant shores," as Coates suggests. Not incidentally, the drive to Americanize the Holocaust (and use it as a means of solidifying American difference) was coterminous with a Jewish American quest for ethnic distinctiveness. Alongside an increasing anxiety about the whitening of Jewish identity, the 1960s and 1970s saw the rise of ethnic roots movements and a concomitant revival of interest in white ethnicity.[11] For many American Jews, the Holocaust came to function as a form of ethnic difference—a kind of difference with a difference that served to undergird, rather than threaten, America's sense of itself as a haven for the oppressed.

The importance of the Holocaust to the discourse of American exceptionalism cannot be overstated. In his controversial *The Holocaust in American Life*, Novick points out the way in which America has taken ownership of the Holocaust and its commemoration in recent years.[12] According to Novick, for all Americans "the Holocaust has become a moral reference point. As, over the past generation, ethical and ideological divergence and disarray in the United States advanced to the point where Americans could agree on nothing else, all could join together in deploring the Holocaust—a low moral consensus, but perhaps better than none at all" (13). The centrality of the Holocaust in American life does not simply serve the purpose of creating a "moral reference point," however. It also "is explicitly used for the purpose of national self-congratulation: the 'Americanization' of the Holocaust has involved using it to demonstrate the difference between the Old World and the New, and to celebrate, by showing its negation, the American way of life" (ibid.). There are many ways in which the Holocaust functions to highlight differences between "the Old World and the New" (ibid.). Most strikingly, according to Novick, it harnesses the purported incomparability of the Holocaust in a manner that "promotes *evasion* of moral and historical responsibility. The repeated assertion that whatever the United States has done to blacks, Native Americans, Vietnamese, or others pales in comparison to the Holocaust is true—and evasive. And whereas a serious and sustained encounter with the history of hundreds of years of enslavement and oppression of blacks might imply costly demands on Americans to redress the wrongs of the past, contemplating the Holocaust is virtually cost-free: a few cheap tears" (15). Holocaust rhetoric has become a powerful form of evasion for Americans intent on avoiding their country's own history of racial oppression. The politics of this sort of avoidance are evident in the many competitions about victimhood that have surrounded Holocaust representation in the last several decades—from the controversy about Toni Morrison's epigraph in *Beloved* to the "sixty million and more" who died as a result of the transatlantic slave trade to the battle about whether a museum devoted to African American history and genocide should exist alongside the United States Holocaust Memorial Museum adjacent to the Mall in Washington, D.C.[13] In his famous essay, "Negroes Are Anti-Semitic Because They're Anti-White," James Baldwin manifests a similar anxiety about comparing the experiences of Jews and blacks in America—and the manner in which black suffering gets displaced in such a comparison. In contrast to African Americans, Baldwin asserts, "the Jew can be proud of his suffering, or at least not ashamed of it. His history and his suffering do not begin in America, where black men have been taught to be ashamed of everything, especially their suffering."

Such anxieties about the displacement of America's own racial history via the Holocaust continue in earnest. As Coates has pointed out, the omission of any mention of race in America in *X-Men: First Class* was particularly striking given that *X-Men*—as both a comics and a film franchise—has been largely centered on questions of inequality and (racial) difference. After all, the X-Men are themselves a group of mutants with superpowers, who are hunted and punished for the ways in which their DNA renders them different from the conventional human beings who surround them. Those X-Men who possess not just mutant superpowers but also physical mutations suffer the most because they cannot hide the fact that they are different. Despite the fact that race is never explicitly mentioned in *X-Men: First Class*, much of the rancor within the group of mutants during the film is related to the question of how much the physically marked members of the group should attempt to adapt to look more normative. When Hank, one of the members of the X-Men, creates a serum that can reverse the physical signs of mutant status, he offers to try it on Raven (or Mystique), a mutant who is blue and scaly in her natural state. Raven resists the lure of the serum, saying: "We are different. But we shouldn't be trying to fit into society. Society should aspire to be more like us. Mutant and proud." In response to her assertion, Hank, who also possesses a physical mutation, says, "Well then, it behooves me to tell you that even if we save the world tomorrow, and mutants are accepted into society, that my feet and your natural blue form will never be deemed beautiful." Raven eventually defects from the camp of Charles Xavier (or Professor X) to follow Magneto's more militant form of mutant pride precisely because she resents being told by Xavier that she should hide her physical mutations. The allusion to race, and particularly African American history, is obvious.

Other such references to race in the X-Men universe abound, making their omission in the film particularly glaring. The first *X-Men* comics (known as *The Uncanny X-Men*) were published during the 1960s, and some of the series' earliest creators have acknowledged that race and the civil rights movement provided a powerful backdrop for its construction. In fact, most readers have long believed that Martin Luther King Jr. and Malcolm X—and the conflict between responses to oppression that they came to symbolize—provided the impetus to create the central conflict in the *X-Men* world: the clash between Professor X and Magneto, mutants who have vastly different ideas about the role of violence in the fight for rights and recognition.[14] The films prior to *X-Men: First Class* have often made this comparison explicit. In the last lines of the first film in the series, *X-Men*, an imprisoned Magneto plays chess with his foil, Professor X. Magneto says: "You know this plastic prison of theirs won't hold me forever. The war is still coming, Charles. And I intend to fight it, by any means necessary." This invocation of Malcolm X's famous dictum is unintentionally ironized in a scene in *X-Men: First Class*, when Magneto and Professor X play chess in front of the Lincoln Memorial in Washington, D.C. Sitting in front of a monument to the president who ended slavery (and the site of Martin Luther King Jr.'s "I Have a Dream" speech, given only months before the first issue of *X-Men* appeared, in September 1963), the men play the same game they played at the end of the first *X-Men* film. This time, however, they speak of nothing important: they are playing a game, rather than commenting on the racial politics of the nation they inhabit. Not for the first time in the film, the link between the X-Men's plight and racial strife is minimized.

As Coates points out, 1962, the year in which the film is set, was "the year South Carolina marked the Civil War centennial by returning the Confederate Flag to the State Capitol; the year the University of Mississippi greeted its first black student, James Meredith, with a lethal race riot; the year George Wallace was elected governor of Alabama." Despite the fact that the film is set during this time of official segregation and institutional racism, there is little conversation about the role of the two African American X-men who appear in the film: Darwin and Angel. We are led to believe that, despite this historical context, the world Darwin and Angel inhabit is somehow colorblind. Central to the critique launched by critical race theorists is a suspicion of how the rhetoric of colorblindness, so dear to the liberal nation-state, masks and, at times, propagates the very inequality it purports to erase.[15] The African American characters in the movie hew closely to timeworn cinematic clichés and never get a chance to develop. Darwin is discovered driving a cab in Manhattan. His superpower ability to adapt to whatever environment he is in (becoming a fish when he is underwater, for instance) provides a not-so-subtle commentary on the possibilities and perils of assimilation. Soon after the movie begins, Darwin is killed, leaving him out of the mutants' climactic battle scene or any possible discussion about the repercussions of an African American man being employed by the CIA in 1962 that his character might have introduced. Angel, the other African American character, is a stripper before she joins the mutant group led by Professor X. She is portrayed as hypersexual in the film. In order to manifest her mutation, being able to fly, she has to take her clothing off and unfurl the wings that are kept hidden under a tattoo on her back. She is also utterly cynical and duplicitous, quickly defecting to work with Sebastian Shaw, the film's archvillain, when she is threatened. Disturbingly, it is Shaw, the incarnation of evil in *X-Men: First Class*, who most invokes a politicized racial rhetoric in the film. He convinces Angel to join his group by reminding her of the hatred that nonmutants feel for those who are different from them. He says: "My friends, there's a revolution coming. When mankind discovers who we are, what we can do, each of us will face a choice. Be enslaved or rise up to rule. Choose freely, but know that if you are not with us, then by definition, you are against us. So, you can stay and fight for the people who hate and fear you. Or you can join me, and live like kings and queens." In *X-Men: First Class*, it is the immutably evil Shaw who attempts to keep the mutants from becoming "enslaved." It is also, problematically, Shaw who neutralizes the black voices in the film, killing Darwin and taking Angel from her friends to play a nonspeaking role as his back-up for the rest of the movie.

Despite the facts that Malcolm X and Martin Luther King Jr. haunt the franchise and that the X-Men's own struggle for rights provides an explicit commentary on race, in *X-Men: First Class* "by any means necessary" is replaced by "never again" as the guiding spirit of Magneto's quest. Although much of the film takes place during the Cold War, particularly the Cuban missile crisis, the Holocaust hangs over it from beginning to end. Erik Lensherr's post-traumatic rage is the fuel that ignites the other X-Men and eventually causes the group to split into two opposing camps. The continuity between the Holocaust and the Cold War in the film's universe is also emphasized by the fact that Kevin Bacon plays not just the evil Dr. Klaus Schmidt, the Nazi who torments young Erik, but also the film's other central villain, Sebastian Shaw (whose initials are, not incidentally, "S. S."), a double agents of sorts who seeks to unleash chaos by bringing about war between the Soviet Union and the United States with the help of his own band of mutants. Bacon does not simply play Schmidt and Shaw; the film suggests that they are one and the same person, much as, within the logic of the film, the Nazi and Red menaces become synonymous. The primacy of the Holocaust to *X-Men: First Class* also comes through in the actor chosen to play Magneto. Portrayed by Ian McKellan up to *X-Men: First Class*, in that film Magneto is played by Michael Fassbender, who is associated with another revisionist Holocaust film, Quentin Tarantino's *Inglorious Basterds*.

The fact that the use of the Holocaust trope in American texts has little to do with any actual interest in the lived experiences of the Jews who survived it comes out in the portrayal of Magneto.[16] The film's depiction of this character recycles a variety of Jewish stereotypes. Magneto is one of a series of tough Jews who has found his way into Holocaust representation in recent years. Since at least the time of Adolf Eichmann's trial in Jerusalem, commentators have expressed anxiety about the purported weakness of the Jews murdered during the Holocaust. This anxiety, according to a number of critics, has led to an inordinate focus on the Warsaw Ghetto uprising and other scenes of Jewish rebellion in texts devoted to the Holocaust. In recent years, films such as *Munich*, *Defiance*, and the made-for-television *Uprising* have all highlighted the sort of *Muskel Judentum* once only fantasized about by early Zionist thinkers.[17] Furthermore, the depiction of Magneto (or Erik) as unable to control his superpower is aligned with a number of Jewish stereotypes of excess and uncontrollable affect. For much of the film, Erik can manifest his powers (as he does in the early scene with Dr. Schmidt) only if he is made extremely angry or sad. Erik is the only one of the X-Men who is completely unable to regulate his emotions and his power. In contrast to Erik, the calm, WASP-y Professor X is portrayed as eminently reasonable, his chief superpower being his ability to empathize with others and know their minds better than they do themselves. This feature of Professor X's superpower arsenal is highlighted in his relationship with the hot-headed Erik: Professor X functions as the other mutant's conscience, getting inside his head and cautioning him against using violence in the film's pivotal final scene.

In the end, Erik's emotional response and his desire to avenge his mother's death is too strong, and Professor X loses control over him. Erik murders Schmidt (Shaw) and hangs his body in the sky over the other X-Men with his arms extended, a kind of crucifixion. The fact that the film ends with this sort of Christianization, or sacralization, of post-Holocaust violence is not surprising. The Holocaust has become stripped of its meaning and the experiences it invokes by its deployment in American culture. The semiotic function of the Holocaust in America, like Sarah Palin's mobilization of the blood libel, has rendered it void of its specifically Jewish content.

Instead, the Holocaust is used as a means of solidifying the righteousness of America and congratulating the nation on its own role in geopolitics since the Second World War. In the end, the American government is as dangerous to the X-Men as to any foreign group, being more than willing to fire on the mutants who have helped save their world. Nonetheless, throughout the film, it is clear that Matthew Vaughn, the film's director and one of its screenwriters, has shied away from looking too closely at this danger and the perils facing "mutants" on our own shores. Despite the fact that in America, the Holocaust has been framed as a lesson in tolerance, "the pretense that the Holocaust is an American memory—that Americans, either diffusely, as part of Western civilization, or specifically, as complicit bystanders, share responsibility for the Holocaust—works to devalue the notion of historical responsibility. It leads to the shirking of those responsibilities that *do* belong to Americans as they confront their past, their present, and their future" (Novick 15). It is not by accident that *X Men: First Class* takes place during the height of the Cold War. Although American exceptionalism has been present in one form or another since the nation's inception, it was most clearly codified and articulated during the era immediately following the Second World War. In fact, it was Joseph Stalin himself who first used the term "American exceptionalism" in the manner closest to its present-day meaning.

The sorts of slippages that *X-Men: First Class* trades on—slippages between what America does well (save the world from the Nazis and Communists) and what America does poorly (deal with its own racial problems)—are central to American exceptionalism as it has come to function during the twentieth century. Pease writes that "the relations between U.S. citizens' belief in exceptionalism and the state's production of exceptions to it might be best described in psychological terms as structures of denial. By enabling U.S. citizens to disavow the state's exceptions that threatened their beliefs, the discourse of exceptionalism regulated U.S. citizens' responses to historical events" (110). Examples of this sort of denial abound. Americans pride themselves on having been absent from some of Europe's most violent colonial episodes and expansions so as to avoid conversations about Native American genocide and removal or involvement in the transatlantic slave trade and the legacy of racial prejudice and dysfunction left behind by it. The Cold War was in large part waged to avoid America's problems at home.[18] More recently, politicians have explicitly used the argument of American exceptionalism to suppress anxiety about the fallout from episodes such as the violence at Abu Ghraib prison.

America's cherished belief in itself as a postracial landscape also goes hand in hand with the discourse of national exceptionalism. As Nikhil Singh asserts, "civic myths about the triumph over racial injustice have become central to the resuscitation of a vigorous and strident form of American exceptionalism—the idea of the United States as both a unique and universal nation—once thought mortally wounded by the Vietnam War and the divisive racial politics of the late 1960s" (17). By substituting the Holocaust for racial strife in the 1960s, *X-Men: First Class* participates in just such a postracial sham. Synecdoche is a powerful trope that can allow us to make important transhistorical and transcultural connections between groups and ideas. It can also, when used too blithely, become a means of fostering amnesia and erasure. By becoming aware of how we marshal Jewish-associated metaphors—from the blood libel and the Ashkenazi immigrant experience to the Holocaust—we can avoid some of the blunting effect that such use can have.

NOTES

1. I emphasize that it was the Ashkenazi experience of immigration that has shaped the American imagination of Jewishness because Sephardi Jewish histories have largely been absent from accounts of Jewish culture in the United States. This omission contributes to a problematically monolithic concept of Jewishness and is particularly ironic given that Sephardi Jews were some of the earliest Jews in the United States.

2. The quote is from Emma Lazarus, "The New Colossus." I use the word "chronotope" here to invoke Mikhail Bakhtin's original sense of the term and Paul Gilroy's later deployment of it in his exploration of the trope of the slave ship.

3. After the Chinese Exclusion Act of 1882, many Chinese immigrants attempting to gain entry to the United States were kept in detention at Angel Island for up to three years.

4. In *The Accidental Asian*, written during the height of the 1990s debates about multiculturalism, Eric Liu dubs Asian Americans "the new Jews" for precisely this vaunted ability to acculturate.

5. I borrow the idea of the relationship between Jews and "other others" from Daniel and Jonathan Boyarin's *Jews and Other Differences*. In this volume, the authors call for a Jewish studies that is responsive to comparative work, particularly concerning questions of race and ethnicity.

6. Victor Villanueva points out the use for Burke's four tropes in understanding how we talk about (and don't talk about) race in "The Rhetorics of the New Racism or the Master's Four Tropes."

7. The idea of the *ewige Jude* (eternal Jew) was particularly prevalent in German antisemitic discourse. The idea of Jewishness as being somehow eternal was itself a chronotope of sorts, combining both spatial and temporal stereotypes of the Jew into one convenient term—that is, Jews were essentially Jews in a way that transcended time and place, but they were also eternally nomadic and placeless.

8. The subtext of the film is, in fact, the question of American difference: Are the Americans really so different from the Russians? Do they care any more about the others within—the mutants—than Europe did? This conflict is dramatized in the final scene of the film, when the mutants must protect themselves from the American navy after having defeated the Russian one, and Magneto says that he will "never again" be subject to the whims of men who are "just following orders."

9. Magneto's background as a Holocaust survivor was first explicitly mentioned in *Uncanny X-Men*, in August 1981.

10. There are other reasons why *X-Men* comics might not have dealt with Jewish themes during the early years. Jewishness was often not depicted explicitly in superhero comics in the period immediately after the Second World War. As Andrea Most has pointed out, the doubleness of the superhero, as epitomized in the Clark Kent–Superman split, was cherished by Jewish artists precisely because they were particularly aware of the problems of repressing parts of one's identity. It was not until the more confessional, underground comics of the 1970s that Jewishness became a topic for Jewish comics artists.

11. For more on this process, see Eric Goldstein, *The Price of Whiteness*; Matthew Jacobson, *Roots Too*; Karen Brodkin, *How Jews Became White Folks*.

12. I call Novick's representation of the Holocaust controversial because some of it has been disputed by other historians, most notably by Hasia Diner (*We Remember With Reverence and Love*). Diner takes particular umbrage at Novick's contention that the Holocaust was largely not commemorated in the United States until the latter decades of the twentieth century, as a kind of instrumental memorialization.

13. Emily Budick takes up the issue of Morrison's epigraph in *Blacks and Jews in Literary Conversation*. Michael Rothberg focuses on competitive memory and the Holocaust in *Multidirectional Memory*.

14. In an interview, Michael Fassbender, the actor who plays Magneto in *First Class*, said that Malcolm X and Martin Luther King Jr. have been the inspirations for the portrayal of the Magneto–Professor X dyad in his film, as well (Kaye, "Across the Universe").

15. Krista Ratcliffe's *Rhetorical Listening* focuses on how the often-neglected category of listening can be used to dismantle the liberal rhetoric of sameness that has historically silenced so many women and people of color.

16. By suggesting that the Holocaust might be associated with Jewishness, I do not mean to erase the many other victims of the genocide—from Gypsies and homosexuals to those deemed physically or mentally "defective."

17. Todd Presner's *Muscular Judaism* and Michael Stanislawski's *Zionism and the Fin de Siècle* both provide useful accounts of the discourse surrounding *Muskel Judentum*.

18. Recently, historians (see, for instance, Dudziak) have averred that the Supreme Court's decision in *Brown v. Board of Education* might have been different had Americans not been afraid that segregation was turning attitudes abroad against them and for the Russians.

BIBLIOGRAPHY

Bakhtin, Mikhail. "Forms of Time and Chronotope in the Novel." In Mikhail Bakhtin, *The Dialogic Imagination*, translated by Michael Holquist and Caryl Emerson, 84–258. Austin: University of Texas Press, 1981.

Baldwin, James. "Negroes Are Anti-Semitic Because They're Anti-White." *New York Times*. 9 April 1967.

Boyarin, Daniel, and Jonathan Boyarin. *Jews and Other Differences: The New Jewish Cultural Studies*. Minneapolis: University of Minnesota Press, 1997.

Brodkin, Karen. *How Jews Became White Folks*. New Brunswick, NJ: Rutgers University Press, 1998.

Budick, Emily Miller. *Blacks and Jews in Literary Conversation*. Cambridge: Cambridge University Press, 1998.

Burke, Kenneth. *A Grammar of Motives*. Berkeley: University of California Press, 1969.

Claremont, Chris. "I, Magneto." *Uncanny X-Men*, no. 150. August 1981.

Clary-Lemon, Jennifer. "The Racialization of Composition Studies." *College Composition and Communication* 61, no. 2 (2009): W1–17.

Coates, Ta-Nehisi. "You Left out the Part About . . . ." *New York Times*, 8 June 2011. www.nytimes.com/2011/06/09opinion/09coates.html?_r-0

Diner, Hasia. *We Remember with Reverence and Love: American Jews and the Myth of Silence after the Holocaust, 1945–1962*. New York: New York University Press, 2009.

Dudziak, Mary L. "Desegregation as a Cold War Imperative." *Stanford Law Review* 41 (1988): 61–122.
Dunn, Geoffrey. *The Lies of Sarah Palin*. New York: Macmillan, 2011.
Freedman, Jonathan. *Klezmer America*. New York: Columbia University Press, 2008.
Gilroy, Paul. *The Black Atlantic: Modernity and Double Consciousness*. London: Verso, 1993.
Goldstein, Eric. *The Price of Whiteness: Jews, Race, and American Identity*. Princeton, NJ: Princeton University Press, 2007.
Jacobson, Matthew Frye. *Roots Too: White Ethnic Revival in Post-Civil Rights America*. Cambridge, MA: Harvard University Press, 2008.
Kaye, Don. "Across the Universe: Meet Magneto." MSN Entertainment. http://entertainment.msn.com/news/article.aspx?news=623079. Accessed 26 January 2014.
Lakoff, George, and Mark Johnson. *Metaphors We Live By*. 3rd ed. Chicago: University of Chicago Press, 2003.
Lazarus, Emma. "The New Colossus." In *Emma Lazarus: Selected Poems*, edited by John Hollander, 58. Washington: Library of America, 2005.
Liu, Eric. *The Accidental Asian: Notes of a Native Speaker*. New York: Random House, 1998.
Madsen, Deborah. *American Exceptionalism*. Jackson: University Press of Mississippi, 1998.
Most, Andrea. "Re-Imagining the Jew's Body: From Self-Loathing to 'Grepts.'" In *You Should See Yourself*, edited by Vincent Brook, 19–36. New Brunswick, NJ: Rutgers University Press, 2006.
Novick, Peter. *The Holocaust in American Life*. New York: Mariner, 2000.
Pak, Greg. *X-Men: Magneto Testament*. New York: Marvel, 2008.
Pease, Donald. "Exceptionalism." In *Key Words for American Cultural Studies*, edited by Glenn Hendler and Bruce Burgett, 108–12. New York: New York University Press, 2007.
Presner, Todd. *Muscular Judaism: The Jewish Body and the Politics of Regeneration*. New York: Routledge, 2007.
Ratcliffe, Krista. *Rhetorical Listening: Identification, Gender, Whiteness*. Carbondale: Southern Illinois University Press, 2005.
Reisigl, Martin, and Ruth Wodak. *Discourse and Discrimination: Rhetorics of Racism and Antisemitism*. New York: Routledge, 2001.
Rothberg, Michael. *Multidirectional Memory: Remembering the Holocaust in the Age of Decolonization*. Stanford, CA: Stanford University Press, 2009.
Seidman, Naomi. "Fag Hags and Bu-Jews: To a Vicarious Politics of (Jewish) Identification." In *Insider/Outsider: American Jews and Multiculturalism*, edited by David Biale, Michael Galchinsky, and Susannah Heschel, 254–68. Berkeley: University of California Press, 1998.
Shinefeld, Mordecai. "X-Men Mutant Survives the Holocaust in New Marvel Comics Miniseries." *Haaretz*, 7 June 2008.
Singh, Nikhil Pal. *Black Is a Country: Race and the Unfinished Struggle for Democracy*. Cambridge, MA: Harvard University Press, 2004.
Stanislawski, Michael. *Zionism and the Fin de Siècle*. Berkeley: University of California Press, 2001.
Villanueva, Victor. "The Rhetorics of the New Racism or the Master's Four Tropes." *First-Year Honors Composition* 1 (spring 2006): 1–21.
White, Hayden. *Metahistory*. Baltimore, MD: Johns Hopkins University Press, 1973.
X-Men. Directed by Bryan Singer. Los Angeles, CA: 20th Century Fox, 2000.
X-Men: First Class. Directed by Matthew Vaughn. Los Angeles, CA: 20th Century Fox, 2011.
Yamashita, Karen Tei. *I Hotel*. Minneapolis: Coffee House, 2010.

15

"That Ceremonious Feeling of Growing Up"
The Educational Practice of Bar Mitzvah in the Jewish Children's Folkshul

ELI GOLDBLATT

This essay presents a portrait of an educational practice. Distinguished by its rhetorical emphasis on audience and purpose as well as an emphasis on literacy as personal engagement, the b'nai mitzvah (the collective name for the bar and bat mitzvah) celebrated in the Philadelphia Jewish Children's Folkshul combines a Jewish attachment to words and learning with the fierce commitment to progressive social thought. The Philadelphia Folkshul claims a descent from the *shule* movement and Workmen's Circle organizations that gathered together Jewish immigrants, socialists, unionists, and anarchists starting in the first decades of the twentieth century. This movement formed quite separately from Sherwin Wine's Humanistic Judaism, which emerged from the Jewish Reform synagogue. Wine's Humanistic Judaism promotes religious ritual without divinity and pays little attention to the culture of the shtetl and the ghetto, the Yiddish culture that Eastern European immigrants carried with them to the United States. The Folkshul and similar Jewish secular groups may share Wine's conception of Jewish identity as internationalist, intellectual, and anti-authoritarian (Wine, 98–101), but they explicitly celebrate their roots in the immigrant experience and Jewish history. The Folkshul also emphasizes social justice and progressive political engagement. Today the Folkshul collects disaffected religious Jews, families that have multiple faith traditions, and others in search of a meaningful Jewish cultural experience for their children without the influence of theology or prayer addressed to a deity.

Such a nonreligious formation in a faith tradition seems paradoxical, if not downright self-contradictory. However, the Folkshul's lively history—the Folkshul is sometimes referred to as the Yiddishkeit movement because of its roots among immigrants who spoke Yiddish—reflects Judaism's longstanding identity not only as a religion and as a Zionist nation, but also as a people. Mordecai Kaplan, the founder of modern-day Reconstructionism, defined Judaism as "the evolving religious civilization of the Jewish people" (quoted in Alpert and Staub, 15), and he noted the problem of teaching such an old and complex a tradition: "Judaism is a problem for those who have to teach it, and what Jew is exempt from teaching it?" (Kaplan, xi). The Workmen's Circle tradition avoids the faith aspects, defining Jewish identity in terms of culture and history while emphasizing the commitment to social justice for immigrants and other oppressed people.

Rabbi Rebecca Alpert remarks that "the majority of Jews (in the United States and Israel, the two largest Jewish communities in the world, in that order) aren't part of any religious denomination at all, and for them Judaism is not a religious practice but a kinship network they belong to, often with pride" (5). My purpose in this essay is not to sift through the complexity of identity formation among Jews who don't believe in God (see Wine; Ibry; Seid; Alpert), nor to recount in detail the history of secular Judaism (see Silver; Harris-Shapiro). Instead, I want to focus on a particular cultural practice, the bar or bat mitzvah, in a localized secular Jewish organization called the Jewish Children's Folkshul. The practice at this organization is not unique, and many elements are shared by other secular Jewish, humanist, and even religious congregations. The Folkshul b'nai mitzvah do represent a distinctive version of the Jewish coming-of-age ceremony that can have lasting intellectual, emotional, and developmental effects on a young person. The last half of this essay is devoted to the experience of a single young man named Jacob, who underwent bar mitzvah at the Folkshul more than ten years before our conversation. Jacob cannot be called representative, but his experience both illustrates the process of secular b'nai mitzvah at the Folkshul and demonstrates the possibilities of growth fostered by this educational process.

I see Jacob's Folkshul bar mitzvah and its legacy as resonating with practices embraced by composition and rhetoric pedagogies and with the educational philosophy of John Dewey. For that reason I believe a study of this secular Jewish practice can contribute to our thinking about writing pedagogy in schools and colleges today. Dewey's influence is wide-ranging, and I cannot track many elements of his thought in a short essay. However, he so clearly articulates the human problem of transmitting cultural understandings from adults to children that his thought seems especially pertinent in the case of the learning that is involved with a coming-of-age ritual. The Folkshul bar mitzvah, particularly the way Jacob pursued his project, involves the young person in large-scale questions of history and identity but also gives him or her safe ground, what Dewey calls "luminous familiar spots" (157), on which to explore new and challenging material. In addition, Dewey links educational experience to political practice, a connection that the Folkshul emphasizes throughout its Jewish secular curriculum. It may be an open question whether or not a rhetorical practice beyond the confines of traditional classrooms can model for us possibilities in school, but I believe stepping out of our usual frame gives us an opportunity to imagine new practices even in the narrowest circumstances.

Two crucial terms need to be established before we can turn to the specific issues raised in my conversation with Jacob. The first is secular Judaism, a label often regarded with confusion or suspicion by those who have never heard the oxymoronic-sounding phrase (for a discussion of the distinction between this formulation and Jewish secularism, see Silver, 61). Again, the history of American secular Jews is a complicated story of Jewish immigration from Eastern Europe and elsewhere; the commitments and betrayals swirling around the sectarian struggles among Jewish unionists, anarchists, communists, and socialists; and the overwhelming drive in Jews to assimilate into mainstream American Protestant life while holding onto a modicum of cultural identity. Most of this fascinating story lies outside the scope of this essay, but I will try to summarize some of the threads for the sake of orienting the reader to the issues at stake in the contemporary Folkshul education.

The second pivotal term is bar mitzvah, a concept that is perhaps simpler to explain but is redolent with stereotypes, jokes, and nostalgia. Along with weddings and funerals, the bar mitzvah (and later the bat mitzvah, instituted in America by Kaplan when his daughter, Judith, came of age in 1922) has represented for even the most disaffected Jews a mark of identification with the tradition. Secular Jews, including those who did not adopt alternative rituals to commemorate births and deaths, defined b'nai mitzvah for young people within their families and schools. In many ways, as Jacob's story will indicate, the bar mitzvah encapsulates the values of the culture that adults most wish to preserve, so it is an ideal opportunity to observe beliefs in action and values in concrete manifestation. B'nai mitzvah celebrations in any Jewish tradition are inherently rhetorical as well as deeply embedded in the instructional and literacy practices of the group. For all these reasons b'nai mitzvah are invaluable social practices for composition and rhetoric scholars and researchers to study.

Secular Judaism

In her wide-ranging discussion of progressive Judaism, Alpert refers to the old observation that if two Jews gather, there will be three opinions (1). The history of secular Judaism illustrates the organizational results of the Jewish tradition of questioning authority and formulating ever more opinions. Immigrants, unionists, Zionists, socialists, communists, and anarchists played their roles in this complex drama, alongside those who embraced secularism from inside the Reform movement, as Wine did, or in reaction or response to other Jewish practices. To recount the history briefly is an impossible task. The splits and alliances among the players are too much to follow in a book-length treatment (though Mitchell Silver's *Respecting the Wicked Child* does a respectable job of it, along with his consideration of the deeper philosophical questions), let alone in a brief essay. All I can hope to do here is describe the background for the Jewish Children's Folkshul in Philadelphia at the time of Jacob's bar mitzvah.

According to Paul Shane, a longtime board member of the Folkshul, the school traces its origins from four secular Yiddish schools started in Philadelphia early in the twentieth century: "There were schools run by the Workmen's Circle (an anti-Soviet socialist and anarchist group at the time). Others were run by the Labor Zionists (socialist Zionist) and the Jewish People's Fraternal Order (JPFO) (pro Soviet)" (quoted in Harrar). Gradually these schools shifted from a focus on preserving the Yiddish Eastern European socialist culture to identifying and reinvigorating a Jewish identity that was both progressive and nontheistic. The current Jewish Children's Folkshul, according to Sari Harrar, was the result of a merger in the 1980s of various schools whose populations had dwindled too much for the schools to remain independent. By the 1990s, when Jacob attended the school, it was still teaching Yiddish songs, but the curriculum stressed general themes of Jewish cultural history and highlighted social justice group projects at each grade level. The Folkshul was affiliated with the Congress of Secular Jewish Organizations (CSJO), a broad collection of secular Jewish schools and centers not directly allied to Sherwin Wine's more mainstream Humanist Judaism. Wine's International Institute for Secular Humanistic Judaism says that an "emphasis on progressive social action, secular *Yiddishkeit* (Jewishness) and Jewish history and culture are core elements of [the CSJO's] activities." Compared to the other secular Jewish organizations that the institute describes, CSJO is the most focused on progressive social action and the only one that openly harks back to the Yiddish Eastern European immigrant past.

Reflecting Silver's assertion that progressive politics is essential for secular Judaism (71–72), the Folkshul has long been shaped by members with leftist politics and, more recently, a generalized commitment to liberal and progressive social action projects. Silver suggests that a focus on nature and history can serve spiritual functions just as a belief in God can, but he names history as the approach that secular Judaism takes: "History is another large, albeit metaphysically ungrounded, source of spirituality. Smaller than nature but more germane to the peculiarly human, history can show us our place in the human story. By identifying with historical movements, our personal purposes can merge with past and future purposes. Our ends do not die with our end" (68).

Silver claims that, in order for historical spirituality to establish moral and ethical authority within the community, people must be able to tell a story of continual striving for justice and improvement for others: "Secular Judaism needs progressive politics as part of its tradition: It makes Secular Judaism part of something that is good" (72). This rings true for the Folkshul, where social justice is a constant theme, as the curriculum moves from "Practicing Our Customs" and "Living Our Values" for children in prekindergarten through first grade to "Middle Ages and Democratic Revolutions" and "Modern Times" with ten- to twelve-year olds.

Many members of the Folkshul, at least in the past twenty years, are in interfaith, interracial, gay and lesbian, and otherwise nontraditional families. They simply do not feel at home with American Jewish organized religion. Mindy Blatt, the Folkshul's director, explains: "Our families and adult community members feel disconnected from traditional synagogues but they desire an inclusive, accepting, welcoming atmosphere that nurtures all who wish to identify Jewishly. Our emphasis is on Jewish history, culture and values of social justice and personal responsibility for ourselves and each other" (quoted in Harrar). For those who still wish to identify as Jewish, this alienation from religious worship sharpens the desire to embrace and construct their own meaningful and welcoming Jewish present.

B'nai Mitzvah

The jokes about precocious, confused, or greedy bar or bat mitzvah kids and their extravagant families are legion, but in fact the event marks a profound turning point for most families under any cultural norm. The early bar mitzvah ceremony, thought to have been formalized in the thirteenth century in Germany, involved a thirteen-year-old Jew blessing and reading a portion of the Torah (Hebrew Bible) on a Saturday morning. Here is a description of that early ceremony, provided by a Folkshul student who used the origins of the bar mitzvah as the topic of his own secular bar mitzvah: "The boy was called to the Torah for the first time, usually for the *maftir aliya*, which means he had the additional honor of chanting a portion from the Prophets. When the boy finished, his father would rise up and say, 'Blessed be He who has freed me from this responsibility.' After the service the parents provided a *seudah*, or meal, for relatives and friends in their home. The meal was often followed by a speech by the Bar Mitzvah boy, in which he showed how well he knew the Talmud" (quoted in Seid, 154).

This account contains the essential elements of most b'nai mitzvah today. The idea that the child must learn how to perform publicly, drawing on texts that adults regard as sacred or important, seems central to a variety of religious but also secular or humanistic Jewish b'nai mitzvah. The performance demonstrates the young person's willingness and competence to join the adult community, at least where religious or moral responsibility is concerned. At the same time, parents express relief and joy that the child is taking at least some of the burden of decision making from them. The meal not only indicates the parents' emotional investment but also emphasizes the communal nature of this step, this shifting of obligations onto the young person and his or her new status as a member of the group. The speech represents not only learning but also rhetorical and hermeneutic engagement with valued texts, a requirement that community members must not only formulate opinions but also share them with others as a part of their participatory responsibilities. The account in Judith Seid's book suggests something additional about secular Judaism's approach to b'nai mitzvah. Seid introduces her chapter on this ritual by painting a picture of an extravagant bat mitzvah that she clearly does not approve of. However, she soon focuses on a more important aspect: that young people fully understand the words they speak and the concepts they encounter in their study. Seid says this of the imaginary parent who decides against a traditional bat mitzvah for her daughter: "Ruth wanted Ariella to understand and participate in more than the religious expression of Jewish culture" (156). Secular Jews want their rituals to help them make sense of their lives, and they are repelled by orthoprax customs (emphasizing correct practice) that require the memorization of Hebrew prayers and texts but no deep comprehension of them. Rabbi Peter Schweitzer, the leader of New York City's City Congregation for Humanistic Judaism, says of the parents who consult him about their child's coming-of-age ceremony: "They especially have not wanted to repeat [the] rote memorization and lack of comprehension of their own youth" (Schweitzer). At the same time, they shape their version of b'nai mitzvah as an encounter with important cultural material, however that is construed for the individual or group.[1] Secular Jews seem to prefer the moment in the Folkshul student's account when the medieval thirteen-year-old gives a speech to show the audience that he can talk about what he has learned.[2] But the account above also tells us something specific about the Folkshul. The contemporary young man who studied the practice of bar mitzvah was working in a tradition of studying self-reflexive topics in the Folkshul b'nai mitzvah program. Unlike students at other humanist congregations and schools, who are required to write a series of research papers on topics they choose from a large prescribed list, Folkshul students choose a single topic to research for an entire year, usually one that speaks to a personal interest of the student or to his or her conscious effort to make sense of Jewish history and tradition. The current Folkshul b'nai mitzvah coordinator, Judy Heath, told me: "The topic is chosen by the student and, with the guidance of an adult mentor, the year of study becomes an unfolding of self discovery, as the student is encouraged to think about her own beliefs and understanding of her personal Jewish heritage." The community prizes understanding rather than rote memorization, choice rather than prescription. Teachers are expected to act more as mentors than authority figures in the classroom, and classmates are encouraged to share ideas with each other and reflect on their experiences with social justice projects. The b'nai mitzvah mentors are chosen for their close relationship with the child, and they are meant to work more like a coach or an older friend learning alongside the child than like a teacher. The Folkshul provides an environment outside of regular school to observe how a learning experience in literacy can be structured around a dialogic relationship between a child and adult mentors.

A short list of topics from which students could choose in the Folkshul during the period Jacob attended included:

- Anti-Jewish propaganda in Nazi Germany
- African American and Jewish relations
- Jewish Philadelphia, 1860–1940
- Art created by concentration camp victims
- The use of wine in Jewish tradition
- Klezmer music
- Jewish humor

In each case the student found both a personal note in the study—a family connection, a longtime curiosity about the subject—that sustained him or her through the long process. Every student had a mentor, often an adult family friend who either had expertise in the topic or a strong relationship with the student (or both). My son, for example, did his bar mitzvah on Jewish storytelling with a couple who were family friends and veteran public storytellers. Most b'nai mitzvah in humanist and secular groups—and in an increasing number of religious congregations as well—include a requirement the thirteenth-century Jewish teenager did not have to fulfill: a social justice project. As Silver notes, a commitment to social justice is characteristic of secular Judaism because it contributes to the sense that secular Jews' commitments have value and depth once God is removed from the conversation. In the Folkshul, students at all age levels must take on a social justice project. By the time the child is ready to commit to bar or bat mitvah training, a longtime Folkshul student will have been through at least five or six large projects with her or his class. Every bar or bat mitzvah must include some sort of long-term project that involves helping others or political advocacy, and this often frames the experience, even if the topic isn't itself particularly political. A commitment to the group, to one's place in history, characterizes a Folkshul bar or bat mitzvah as both an event marking a personal passage and a performance for the sake of group membership.

A Conversation with Jacob

At the time I interviewed Jacob, I had known him and his parents for nearly twenty years. My son is two years younger than Jacob, and they played in the same neighborhood baseball league, a league that Jacob's father has long run as a serious avocation. I chose to talk to Jacob because he is articulate, passionate about progressive politics, reflective about his choices as an adult, and willing to revisit his bar mitzvah experience. In 2012 he was working for an organization that supported Philadelphia public-school children in their attempts to advocate for better learning conditions in their school district, and he had also developed a reputation for being a highly political hip-hop poet who had won a number of poetry slams. I know many young people from the Folkshul who fit this general profile of political activity and personal creativity, but I do not claim that Jacob is representative.[3] His story merely serves as an illustration of what a pedagogical and rhetorical practice like the Folkshul bar mitzvah can do for a person in formation. I will leave it to others to do a more methodical assessment of the practice. I mean here to flesh out the details of this secular rite of passage with the testimony of a single participant who underwent a type of Deweyan rhetorical training that was adopted wholeheartedly by a single community built on an ideal of ethical and intentional education.

When I asked Jacob if he had enjoyed his bar mitzvah, he set down his coffee cup, gathered himself together, and said: "It was definitely significant and momentous. I remember . . . that ceremonious feeling of growing up." First, let me offer a brief outline of Jacob's bar mitzvah project and the travels he pursued years later as a result. In 1999 Jacob recounted to an assembled audience of Folkshul regulars, friends, and family members the story of his paternal family's flight from the Nazis as they moved from their home in Yugoslavia to Italy, Switzerland, and eventually the United States. In preparation, Jacob had interviewed his great-aunt, the only living survivor of that journey, and other relatives who knew details about it from family stories. He read historical accounts as well as his aunt's memoir, which had been published privately. At his father's urging, Jacob had also read reports on the civil war and genocide that was taking place in Serbia in 1999. When he was twenty-one, Jacob visited Europe and retraced the route his family had taken as closely as possible. He described his method on that trip simply: "When they took a train, I took a train." In 2009 he returned to Serbia with father and other family members, including the great-aunt who had been the central informant in his bar mitzvah study. This was the first time she had gone back to her homeland and the first time his father had seen the place from which their family had fled. In short, not only did his study reveal to him a family story he had barely known before, but he also used the story and his reconstruction of the journey to bring his family into greater intimacy with the history they had lived through.

Jacob reported that he felt a profound investment in the project while he pursued it. He admitted he was pretty much a regular middle-school boy who would not have completed the work without constant reminders from his parents and regular meetings with his mentor, yet something deeper was taking hold during the process. He told a compelling story when I asked him for an example of his commitment to the bar mitzvah work:

> I remember being in a cafeteria at MHS [his school] in the seventh grade. I won't say his name—I remember who—made a terrible Jew joke. It was right when I was studying for my bar mitzvah and learning about it. I lost it, just broke down crying in the cafeteria. I wanted to go see the counselor, and he was terrible. I do remember him making this joke, it was a Holocaust joke, and me getting very, very upset. So I don't think it was compartmentalized or I was just going through the motions.

The project not only elicited this kind of reaction ("It takes a lot for a middle-school boy to cry in a school cafeteria," Jacob observed), but it led him to make two subsequent trips to Serbia, following up on his family's story.

Perhaps the most impressive element of Jacob's interview was his insistence that his study not only connected him with his family and his Jewish heritage, but that it also tied him to other cultural stories of courage in the face of displacement and loss. Indeed, Jacob explicitly emphasized his sense of connection beyond the Eastern European Jewish story:

> Learning about one's family, or one's history, or one's people . . . can either become a very isolating experience or can be one that allows people to find common connections with lots of different people. I feel really fortunate that learning about my family and learning about my ancestors and the Jewish people in a broader context has given me an affinity and a connectedness to humanity. I don't know if that's a result of [the] Folkshul's humanist leanings or what, but people also engage in that same type of study and become very isolated from other communities.

He was very clear that at the same time he was learning about the particulars of his family's journey, he did not feel their story entitled them to special treatment or set them apart from other families. In fact, he reported just the opposite reaction. He saw himself bound to other, very different populations—African Americans and Palestinians were two of the examples he gave—because he recognized the intensity of his own family's trials and could connect those with the suffering of other people. He returned to this point at least three times in our hour-long interview. He had known other Jews of his age who had used their knowledge of the Holocaust to distance themselves and their culture from other groups, but he rejected what he called the "chest-thumping attitude" that "we survived" as a badge of difference. He asserted that his family's good fortune in surviving tied him more closely to others who had faced atrocities, including those living in Serbia in 1999:

> I think that because I learned about a contemporary genocide happening in the same place where the Holocaust happened, [it] made me look at the Holocaust as a moment in time that's connected to and similar to a lot of other moments in time. By the time I got to college, learning about Pol Pot in Cambodia, and the Rwandan genocide, and mass killings by Pinochet... I kind of felt that [the Jewish slogan] "never forget" was selective and ethnocentric.

He evinced no hostility to organized Judaism, though he expressed reservations about contemporary Zionism. He saw himself as a member equally of a group with a special history and of many groups with various terrible stories to tell.

I asked if he was better able to pay attention to the fortunes and misfortunes of other populations because of his bar mitzvah study. He answered: "Absolutely. Having this knowledge that my existence as a person is due to a lot of luck and privilege... I carry with me, from the point of my bar mitzvah on, that my life was one of very fortunate circumstances." He clearly felt that what he and his family have today is precious, but because there was no God involved in his version of the story, their current state was due to both exceptional good fortune ("a bomb didn't explode, a soldier just happened to look away") and the ethical behavior of others ("Strangers risked their lives for my grandfather. People along the way chose to do the right thing."). His humanistic interpretation of the story seemed tied to his passionate commitment to progressive politics. At the end of our conversation, he emphasized this process of defining himself as part of a community that he had not felt attached to before: "I remember my bar mitzvah as being a deepening of identity, a connection to something bigger than myself." This reminded me of the traditional function of the bar mitzvah: joining the adult congregation, taking on the responsibility for one's own moral choices.

A Rhetorical Practice

The bar mitzvah Jacob describes includes elements of rhetoric and literacy that are familiar to those involved in college writing programs, yet—outside the institution of school and with the benefit of hindsight—the whole seems more alive than anything that could happen in a classroom. Jacob admitted that when he stood up before the audience, he probably wasn't a terribly dynamic speaker. In fact, the only time he remembers breaking his monotone was one instance when he was talking about the Swiss militia, when his voice rose in boyish romance: "At a moment's notice, the troops..." Still, at an age when most kids would prefer to hide behind a computer screen or joke with their friends in the cafeteria, Jacob distilled personally compelling materials into a presentation that he delivered before people he knew and cared for. Not for a grade or the far-off promise of getting into college, he developed his talk from the logic and intensity of the materials themselves, and his purpose stuck with him some thirteen years later. The bar mitzvah, above all, seems to have left him "connected"—to family and Jewish culture, to people who share a similar story of disempowerment, to other rhetors who speak out of a commitment to social justice.

A number of factors in the public performance mark this coming-of-age ceremony enacted by a thirteen-year-old boy:

- A one-time presentation arising from a sustained collaborative effort
- An inquiry process motivated by the personal desire to know
- Multimodal performance incorporating pictures, maps, and audio recordings
- Interview material dramatizing history as a lived reality
- Narrative, scholarly, and critical genres combined and interwoven
- Intergenerational dialogue, especially among great-aunt, father, and son
- A rite of passage attaching a child to the adult community through intellectual inquiry
- Jewish identity located within secular and historical contexts

Readers can recognize most of these threads from the account in the previous section, so I will focus only on a few concluding points that I think run across the threads and weave them together.

Dewey emphasizes from the outset of *Democracy and Education* that all societies of any sort must find ways of transmitting cultural practices from adults to the young. Although formal instruction seems more necessary as a society becomes more complex, much is lost in isolating children from daily activities in which learning has consequence in action: "Sharing in actual pursuit, whether directly or vicariously in play, is at least personal and vital.... Formal instruction, on the contrary, easily becomes remote and dead" (8). The challenge of passing on cultural knowledge about Judaism in a largely Christian culture has always been great, even overwhelming, to many Jews in America. Hebrew or religious school is at a remove even greater than conventional education because it is held after hours or on weekends, when kids would rather be doing almost anything else. The curriculum is strange to their non-Jewish friends and foreign to the secular (but still heavily Protestant) extracurricular activities that constitute American out-of-school life. A bar mitzvah like Jacob's addresses the transmission issue in a very Deweyan way: the learning is informal but deeply ensconced in relationships with others, focused on a subject of the learner's choosing, based on an active attempt at understanding, and intellectually reinterpreted for the benefit of an audience. Dewey emphasizes that students need to be learning in the context of "doing things and in discussing what arises in the course of their doing" (156). "A well-trained mind," Dewey says, "is one that has a maximum of resources behind it, so to speak, and that is accustomed to go over its past experiences to see what they yield" (157). This linkage between action and reflection is at the heart of the progressive education tradition spawned by Dewey's work (sometimes to his dismay), and we can find this approach in the process movement of composition, the widespread use of portfolios in contemporary writing classes, and the strong interest in community-based learning for literacy instruction.

Dewey reminds us that education is ultimately political and moral in character, its practices reflecting explicit or assumed connections between the individual and the social group through the acquisition and generation of knowledge. He advocates an approach in which learners can choose their own active educational experiences, both alone and in groups, guided by teachers who act alongside their students rather than as authorities who loom above them. He hopes for the greatest possible intellectual freedom and "play of diverse gifts and interests" that are encouraged when students choose their own areas of inquiry, and he warns against the "intellectual servility" caused by rote memorization and reproduction of accepted understandings (305). Yet he sees the social setting as crucial for counteracting the tendency for knowledge to isolate the individual: "When knowledge is regarded as originating and developing within an individual, the ties which bind the mental life of one to that of his fellows are ignored and denied" (297). He concludes *Democracy and Education* with the observation that "all education which develops power to share effectively in social life is moral" (360). This morality, in his view, is the basis for a vibrant and constantly renewing democratic process.

Jacob chose his own subject when he determined to track down the story of his family's flight from Serbia, but he was hardly alone in his endeavor. His mentor, a close friend of the family, and his father, whose parents and sister were the subject of the study, were intimately involved but never in charge of the project. They gave Jacob suggestions, helped him look for material and get to his interview appointments on time, but he had to make sense of what he was finding in order to tell others on the day of his bar mitzvah in words and pictures. In one of Dewey's clearest statements of his attitude toward an effective learning environment, he could be describing the path Jacob followed: "A large part of the art of instruction lies in making the difficulty of new problems large enough to challenge thought, and small enough so that, in addition to the confusions naturally attending the novel elements, there shall be luminous familiar spots for which helpful suggestions may spring" (157). When Jacob described his studies alongside adults who cared for him, I could not help but think what a world we might have if every child could have even one learning experience that was so richly nurturing and fundamentally challenging. Family, in this coming-of-age event, becomes something more than a collection of people who share DNA and a common history. The dialogue binds them together in a living relationship that gives meaning over and above birth order and preserved memory. What the child learned for the first time about his great-aunt expressed itself again in the shared experience of the trip they later took back to Serbia, an expression of gratitude and collaborative renewal. It was Jacob's father who suggested that the boy read about contemporary Serbia, and in many ways this made all the difference in the son's ability to see historical tragedy as ongoing and inclusive of others he could not otherwise know. Jacob's father—long unmoved by the Jewish religion and far from his family's history in the American web of work and baseball—wanted to celebrate the bar mitzvah with a roast pig, but Jacob and others dissuaded him. The aunt thought maybe Jacob should have read from the Torah, but he reminded her he really knew nothing about the Torah. They negotiated so that the celebration, the ceremony, and the spoken word could feel genuine to everyone present. I asked Jacob what this event did for his relationship with his family:

> Jacob: I think it made me more appreciative of my grandparents. I remember, like, my parents being behind it, a part of it, and enthusiastic about it. It was definitely like all of us working on it together. It was my bar mitzvah, but it was definitely a group effort.
>
> Me: But you felt like it was *your* project? You didn't feel like you were doing *their* work?
>
> Jacob: No, definitely not. I felt like they were supporting me in my work. And they were excited about the learning, too, which was good. They're not helicopter parents: "You need to get this done because this needs to be a great bar mitzvah and we can't have you embarrassing the family name." It was more like: "This is really cool!"

The family became engrossed in the project and took it on together. Excitement fueled the purpose, legitimating intellectual effort for the group reward of publicly honoring family courage and tragedy. Jacob still felt in charge, still felt ownership of the process, but his mentor, parents, and older relatives joined respectfully in the undertaking as well. School is almost never like this in its ordinary way. The bar mitzvah—when it works in any setting—is a gift for the way it can transfigure learning. A coming-of-age learning experience such as this one demonstrates the power of rhetorical performance to focus and empower inquiry. The boy speaks to his elders out of what he has learned about history and about the way their memories can be his. He speaks in the presence of his peers, who may not regard the performance as sacred but can recognize that something out of the ordinary is happening to their schoolmate. The boy may not speak with a dynamic voice (the way the adult Jacob can rap on a slam stage), but internally the decibels register and the tonalities of violence and exile sink in. The Folkshul director had warned Jacob before the lights went down that he would be signaling the boy about pacing, about slowing down his words. When the lights went up at the end, Jacob felt he hadn't rushed his speech because he hadn't seen any signs from the director. When Jacob asked him about the pacing, the director said, "Didn't you see me waving at you?" No, Jacob had gone at his own speed, curled into his own delivery, and he's still living the effects.

NOTES

1. Humanist Jewish groups in the Wine tradition seem to prescribe a more academic program than the Folkshul requires. For a comparison, see Seid, 156–59.

2. It must be said that there is a strong sentiment in many religious congregations of various types to bring more meaning and understanding to the bar or bat mitzvah celebrations. The work of the organization "B'nai Mitzvah Revolution," sponsored by Reform Judaism, provides an example of efforts along these lines.

3. At least four other former Folkshul students, and one from another secular Jewish school, offered to be interviewed for this study when they heard about it, but I decided to focus on a single person in the hope that the Folkshul might begin collecting retrospective stories itself.

BIBLIOGRAPHY

Alpert, Rebecca. *Whose Torah? A Concise Guide to Progressive Judaism.* New York: New Press, 2008.

Alpert, Rebecca, and Jacob Staub. *Exploring Judaism: A Reconstructionist Approach.* Elkins Park, PA: Reconstructionist Press, 1985.

Dewey, John. *Democracy and Education.* 1916. New York: Free Press, 1944.

Harrar, Sari. "The History of the Jewish Children's Folkshul." 9 September 2012 www.folkshul.org/our-history. Accessed 22 December 2013.

Harris-Shapiro, Carol. *Messianic Judaism: A Rabbi's Journey through Religious Change in America.* Boston: Beacon, 1999.

Ibry, David. *Exodus to Humanism.* Amherst, NY: Prometheus, 1999.

International Institute for Secular Humanistic Judaism. "Organizations." 9 September 2012 http://iishj.org/organizations.html. Accessed 22 December 2013.

Kaplan, Mordecai. *Judaism as a Civilization: Toward a Reconstruction of American-Jewish Life.* 1934. Philadelphia: Jewish Publication Society, 1981.

Schweitzer, Peter. "Bar/Bat Mitzvah." 9 September 2012 www.secularjewishceremonies.net/barbatmitzvah.html. Accessed 22 December 2013.

Seid, Judith. *God-Optional Judaism.* New York: Citadel, 2001.

Silver, Mitchell. *Respecting the Wicked Child.* Amherst: University of Massachusetts Press, 1998.

Wine, Sherman T. Humanistic Judaism. Buffalo, NY: Prometheus, 1978.

ACKNOWLEDGMENTS

The ideas that eventually gave birth to this collection were inspired, influenced, and informed by the important work of many scholars and communities. Although they probably don't realize it, Janice Fernheimer's Talmud teachers at the Pardes Institute for Jewish Studies had a hand in shaping this collection, for it was from sheer frustration with her Talmudic learning that she became curious about the relationship of Jewish pedagogical/rhetorical practice to what is acknowledged as the "Western" or Greco-Roman rhetorical tradition. With this intellectual seed planted, Janice's initial work at the intersections of the history of medieval rhetoric and rabbinic rhetorical practices took shape during a very influential graduate seminar taught by Marjorie (Jorie) Woods at the University of Texas, and she is grateful for Jorie's early encouragement to continue with this line of research.

Both Janice and Michael are indebted to the warm support of scholars in the field of rhetoric, Steve Katz and David Metzger, who worked with Janice to hold the first-ever Rhetoric Society of America Summer Institute Workshop on Jewish Rhetorics in Troy, New York, in 2007, and whose ideas—along with those of David Frank, Susan Handelman, Pat Bizzell, and Eli Goldblatt—served as touchstones. Those scholars, and the participants in that seminar, later went on to help found Klal Rhetorica, the International Society for the Study of Jewish Rhetorics, a wonderful community of curious minds that helped spur the development of the many ideas that eventually became chapters in this collection.

Michael also wishes to thank his colleagues at the Mosse/Weinstein Center for Jewish Studies, who served as mentors for his work in Jewish Studies, and to thank his colleagues in the English department, particularly Morris Young, who encouraged his interest in the relation between Jewish rhetorics and ethnic rhetorics. The volume editors are grateful to the Rhetoric Society of America for supporting a second workshop in 2011 in Denver, Colorado, and for recognizing Klal Rhetorica as an affiliate organization. This institutional support, along with the support of our respective institutions, the University of Kentucky and University of Wisconsin–Madison, fostered and facilitated one of the main intellectual questions at the heart of the collection—How might Jewish studies and rhetoric/composition/writing studies find themselves in productive conversation?

Janice is very grateful to her co-editor, Michael Bernard-Donals, who has been a supreme mentor and wonderful collaborator; she feels fortunate to have the blessing of working with such a gifted teacher and scholar. He helped keep the project (and Janice!) moving forward. Michael sincerely thanks his co-editor, Janice Fernheimer, for her intellectual energy and boundless optimism; her enthusiasm for the project kept it on track, and kept Michael on track as well. We are grateful to each of the contributors for working so hard and so consistently, and for keeping to deadlines to enable this collection to see the light of day in a timely fashion. Much appreciation is owed to Bronwyn Becker for her tireless attention to detail and generous kindness. We are thankful to Brandeis University Press and Phyllis Deutsch for seeing the value of this work and helping to bring it to a much wider audience, and to the two anonymous reviewers who offered constructive feedback to sharpen the volume's focus. Janice is also eternally grateful to her two beloved scaly friends, Electra and Salsa, who took turns basking computer-side to offer her silent but palpable support. Without them, the collection may never have been proofed! And of course, Janice is grateful to her loving husband and life partner, Jim Ridolfo, who supports her in every way imaginable, and some that she couldn't have even imagined. Michael thanks his wife, Hannah, and their three children—Shoshana, Miryam, and Avi—for their love and support, and for helping him keep things in their proper perspective.

ABOUT THE CONTRIBUTORS

Joy Arbor is an assistant professor of communication at Kettering University, where she teaches writing, listening, and ethics.

Michael Bernard-Donals is the Nancy Hoefs Professor of English and Jewish Studies, and the Vice Provost for Faculty and Staff at the University of Wisconsin–Madison.

Patricia Bizzell, Distinguished Professor of English at the College of the Holy Cross, recently earned a master's degree in Jewish studies from Hebrew College in Newton Centre, Massachusetts. Among her publications is *The Rhetorical Tradition: Readings from Classical Times to the Present*, coedited with Bruce Herzberg, which received the National Council of Teachers of English Outstanding Book Award. She has also won the Conference on College Composition and Communication's Exemplar Award.

Jonathan Boyarin is the Leonard and Tobee Kaplan Distinguished Professor of Modern Jewish Thought at the University of North Carolina. An anthropologist and lawyer, he has served as a visiting professor at Wesleyan University and Dartmouth College. He came to North Carolina from the University of Kansas, where he was Distinguished Professor of Modern Jewish Studies. Boyarin received a JD from Yale Law School in 1998 and a PhD in anthropology at the New School for Social Research in 1984.

Davida Charney, a professor of rhetoric and writing at the University of Texas at Austin, has published on the psalms in *Rhetoric Society Quarterly* and *Biblical Interpretation*. Her book, *Persuading God: Rhetorical Studies of First Person Psalms*, is forthcoming.

Janice W. Fernheimer is director of Jewish Studies and an associate professor of writing, rhetoric, and digital studies at the University of Kentucky, where she teaches courses on rhetoric, technology, and pedagogy; digital writing; and Jewish rhetorical studies. Her research focuses on questions of identity, invention, and cross-audience communication. Her publications have appeared in *Rhetoric Society Quarterly*, *College English*, *Argumentation and Advocacy*, *Computers and Composition Online*, the *Journal of Business and Technical Communication*, and *Technical Communication*. She is the author of *Stepping into Zion: Hatzaad Harishon, Black Jews, and the Remaking of Jewish Identity*.

David Frank is dean of the Robert D. Clark Honors College and a professor of rhetoric at the University of Oregon. He writes on rhetorical theory, history, and practice.

Shai Ginsburg is an assistant professor of Hebrew and Israeli culture in the department of Asian and Middle Eastern Studies at Duke University. He writes about Hebrew rhetoric in the context of modern Jewish nationalisms and Israeli cultures. He is the author of

Rhetoric and Nation: The Formation of Hebrew National Culture, 1880–1990, and the translator into Hebrew of Paul de Man's *The Resistance to Theory*.

Jennifer Glaser is an assistant professor of English and an affiliate faculty member in Judaic studies and women's studies at the University of Cincinnati. She is completing a book titled *Exceptional Differences: Race, Chosenness, and the Postwar Jewish American Literary Imagination*. Her work appears in venues such as *PMLA*, *MELUS*, *Safundi*, *Literature Compass*, *ImageText*, and the *New York Times*.

Eli Goldblatt is a professor of English and the director of the First-Year Writing Program at Temple University. His most recent book is *Writing Home: A Literacy Autobiography*.

Susan Handelman, now a professor of English at Bar-Ilan University, taught at the University of Maryland for twenty years. She is the author of *The Slayers of Moses*, *Fragments of Redemption*, and *Make Yourself a Teacher*. She has edited several other books and written many articles on literary theory, Jewish thought, pedagogy, religion, and psychology.

Richard Hidary is an assistant professor of Judaic studies at Yeshiva University. He is the author of *Dispute for the Sake of Heaven: Legal Pluralism in the Talmud* and of articles in *Encyclopedia Judaica*, *Encyclopedia of the Bible and Its Reception*, *AJS Review*, *Dine Israel*, *Oqimta*, and *Conversations*. His next book will analyze Talmudic dialectic and argumentation in the context of the Greco-Roman rhetorical tradition.

Steven B. Katz, the Pearce Professor of Professional Communication at Clemson University, has published several articles exploring the relationships between ancient Greek and Hebrew rhetorics. His work is motivated by the attempt to define Jewish rhetoric, especially the rhetoric of the *alef-bet* in Jewish mysticism.

David Metzger is a professor of English and dean of the Honors College at Old Dominion University.

Hannah S. Pressman is an affiliate faculty member and communications coordinator for the Stroum Center for Jewish Studies at the University of Washington. She received her PhD in modern Hebrew literature from New York University and is a recipient of the Hort Fellowship at YIVO, the Schusterman Israel Scholar Award, and the Cole Fellowship in Jewish Studies at the University of Washington. Her areas of specialization include autobiography, translation studies, Yiddish, and religious-secular dynamics in Israeli culture. She is coeditor of the anthology *Choosing Yiddish: New Frontiers of Language and Culture*. Her writing has appeared in *Lilith*, the *Jewish Daily Forward*, *AJS Perspectives* and online at JewishBookCouncil.org and MyJewishLearning.com. She is working on a book about autobiographical expressions of Jewish identity in Hebrew literature from the middle of the twentieth century.

Jim Ridolfo is an assistant professor of writing, rhetoric, and digital studies at the University of Kentucky. He received his PhD in rhetoric and writing in 2009 from Michigan State University. In 2012 he received a Fulbright Middle East and North Africa Regional Research Fellowship to continue his research with the Samaritans in the West Bank and

Israel. His work has appeared in *Rhetoric Review, Kairos, Enculturation, JAC, Pedagogy,* and *Ariadne.*

Susan Zaeske is a professor of rhetoric, politics, and culture in the Department of Communication Arts and associate dean of arts and humanities in the College of Letters and Science at the University of Wisconsin–Madison. The author of *Signatures of Citizenship: Petitioning, Antislavery, and Women's Political Identity,* she is working on a book about rhetorical appropriations of the Book of Esther.

INDEX

Aaron, 205–6
Abraham, 170–71, 172, 173
Abraham Ibn Ezra, R., 135, 138, 139, 145
Abramowitz-Silverman, H., 193–94
acknowledgment as gift, 206–7
Adelman, R., 148–50, 158
aesthetics: comics, 159; and language, 64, 66, 68, 72
Africa, x, 46, 53, 55n5
African Americans: as "bad" minority, 233; civil rights movement, 238, 241, 242, 247n18; Jews as synecdoche, 238, 240, 245; "urban" term, 235; *X-Men*, 238, 241, 242–43
Agamben, G., 107
Aggadot, 139–40
Ahasuerus, 180, 181, 183, 185, 189–90
Akiva, R., 117, 118, 156
aleph and alpha, 93–109
alphabet: ArtScroll, 222–24; comparison of Greek and Hebrew, 93–109; Hebrew, 73n14
angels, 135, 136–37
anger, 125, 126–27, 206
antisemitism: blood libel, 231; and Cixous' Jewoman identity, 180; modern, 89, 235–36; Perelman, 79, 80–82, 87; stereotypes, 235–36
appropriation rhetoric, 19, 28–33
Arabic language, ix, xxvi
Aramaic language, 73n14, 215, 229n4
Arendt, H., 80
argument: and *baraita*, 99; eliminating, xix; listening as a gift, 205–6; New Rhetoric Project, 79, 86, 87; Psalms, 1–14; Talmud, xviii, 79, 86, 87, 99, 143–44
Aristotle: angels and demons, 137; anger, 126; creation, 141; epideictic function, 87; the mean, 125; medical metaphor, 119–20; New Rhetoric Project, 77–78, 87, 88; *Nofet Zuphim*, 50, 52; self-deception, 118–19; truth, 143
ArtScroll, 215–30
Ashkenazim: ArtScroll, 226; cultural dominance, viii, xxv, 232–33; Gersonides, 48–49, 51; Hebrew poetry, 67; split with Sephardim, xxvii–xxviii n5; transmission of laws to Spain, 137–38; Yiddish development, 58–59

Asian Americans, 233, 246nn3–4
Askénazi, Y. L., 150, 152–53
assimilation, 82, 233–34, 242, 246n4
attentiveness, 200, 201, 204, 205, 209, 210
audience: analyzing, 198, 205; anger, 126–27; epideictic function, 87; hearing and listening, xiv, xxviii n9, 204, 207–9, 210; legal fiction, 22; obedience, 198; Psalms, 2, 12; self-persuasion, 112
Auschwitz, 84, 236
authority: anger, 126–27; ArtScroll, 216, 221; Esther, 183; 15th c. Italy, 47, 48; judicial, 27–28; purity laws, 31–33; secular Judaism, 253; shift from priests to rabbis, 16–36
Averroes, 50
Azazel, 134–36, 145

Baldwin, J., 240
baraita, 99–104, 109n1, 223
bar/bat mitzvah, 249, 251–52, 254–64
Belarus, x
Belgium, 80, 81, 82, 83–85, 87
Benjamin, W., xx–xxi
Bible: allusions in Yizhar, 166–67, 168, 170–73, 174–76; establishment of Israel, 169–70; Esther, 180–96; Genesis, xii, 105–6, 140–41, 148–49, 174–75; Greek translation, xvii; Jonah, 147, 148–50, 153–62; listening, 199, 212n1; *Nofet Zuphim*, 49–50; Psalms, 1–14
biopicture, 151
bitter herbs, 30
black box, 96–97, 108
blood libel, 231
b'nai mitzvah. *See* bar/bat mitzvah
Bokser, B., 33
Bonfil, R., 50–51, 53
Booth, W., 77, 78
both/and approach, 132–37, 139–40, 142–45
Boyarin, D., 98, 141–42, 148, 162n2
bread, 30–31, 40n84, 41n90
Bregman, M., 148, 162n2
brevity, 115
Buber, M., xii
Burke, K., 33–34, 42n114

INDEX

canon: polysystem theory, 74n21; rhetoric, xiii–xv, xxiv
Chanin, M., 204–5
charity, 23, 28, 39n56
Chaver, Y., 61, 71
children and language war, 69, 74n20
choice: and health, 116–17, 119–23, 123–27, 129nn6–7; and learning, 255, 261
Christians: justice, 79; listening and obeying, 212n1; Moses ben Nachman interactions, 142–43; relations in 15th c. Italy, 47–48, 53; Yiddish development, 59
chronotope, 233, 246n2
Chute, H., 151, 157–58
Cicero, xi, 78
circumcision, 149, 156, 163n9
civil rights movement, 238, 241, 242, 247n18
Cixous, H., 180
Cold War, 236, 245, 247n18
comics, Midrash as, 147–50, 153–62
commandments and Moses ben Nachman, 132–37
commitment and the Shema, 200
community: bar mitzvah, 254, 259; dangers of, xxi; in Esther, 186; and memory, xv; and rhetoric, xi, xviii–xx
comparison rhetoric, 19, 20–22, 34
competitive memory, 240, 247n13
Conat, A., 50–51, 55n4, 55–56n6
concealment rhetoric, 46, 51–53, 54
confession, 3–4
conflict resolution, 206
conflict rhetoric in Yizhar, 165–76
Conley, T., 77, 78
consensus, x, xxi
continuity, rhetorical, 167
conversion, xiii
courtiers, 138–39, 142
covenant, reminders of, 4–5
Creation, xii, xx, 140–41, 200
crisis of rhetoric in Yizhar, 173–74
Crosswhite, J., 77–78, 84–85
curses, 7, 10–11

days, terms for, 133–34
Dead Sea Sect, 17, 31
Declaration of Establishment, 169–70, 174, 177n15
Declaration of Independence, 177n15
deliberative function, xi
delivery, rhetorical, 51–53, 54
demons, 135, 136–37
denouncement, 3, 8–11

Derrida, J., xix–xx, xxi
deterritorialization, xix, xxii
Dewey, J., 250–51, 261–62
Diable, K., 3–4
diaspora: apartness, ix, xxi; ethical rhetoric, xix; nationalism, 60–61, 65, 81, 82
digital culture/delivery, 54, 107
Di goldene keyt (journal), 67–70
Diner, H., 247n12
disagreement. *See* argument
Dissoi Logoi, 131–32, 142
Dolgopolski, S., 142–43, 144, 228, 230n10
double fidélité, 77, 79–87, 88, 89

Edelman, S., xxiii, xxvii–xxviii
education: ArtScroll, 220, 222, 227, 228, 230n8; bar mitzvah, 249, 255–62; *havruta*, 201–2, 204, 213n4; *heder*, viii, xxvii n4; interactivity, 216, 217, 218–19; language war, 71, 73n7; listening, 198, 199, 201–2, 204, 208, 210–12; Messer Leon, 48, 49, 53; Socrates, 97, 98; Talmudic argument, 143–44; in Yizhar, 166. *See also* yeshiva
Eleazar, R., 24
Eli, 39n68
Eliezer, R., 25–26
Eliezer ben Yose ha-Gelili, R., 99, 100–101
Elisha Acher, 117, 118
Elper, O., 160–61
emotions and listening, 203–4, 205
engagement: rhetorical canon, xiv–xv, xxii, xxiv; Talmudic argument, xviii
English language: ArtScroll, 215, 220–21, 222–23, 226, 227; Zionism, 177–78n19
Enlightenment and New Rhetoric Project, 78, 79–80, 83, 85–86, 88
enthymeme, 118
epideictic function, xi, 13, 87
equity. *See* justice
erasure, 232, 234, 236, 238, 242, 245
Esther, 180–96
eternal forms, 143
eternal Jew, 235–36, 246n7
ethics: alphabet, 105–6, 107–8; comics, 151; education, 261–62; health, 113, 116–17, 119–23, 129nn6–7, 139; internal rhetoric, 113, 115–16; listening, 199, 207–12; the mean, 123–27; Midrash, 99; modern period, xii, xix–xx; sophists, 138; in Yizhar, 167–76
ethnicity. *See* Jewishness; race
ethos, xii, xiv
Europe: antisemitism, 80–81, 87, 89; cosmopolitanism, xix, 79, 80, 85; Holocaust memorial-

ization, 239–40; origin and spread of rhetoric, x, xiii, xvii–xviii, 46, 53, 55n5; Yiddish development, 59
evil: and American exceptionalism, 239; listener's role in evil speech, 207; Psalms, 5–6, 9–10
exceptionalism, 231–32, 236–38, 239, 244–45, 246n8, 259
exigence, xviii, 3, 14n7
exile: and identity, x; of Jewish women, 180; Jews as stand-in for immigrants, 232–33; lament in Manger, 62–66; Purim story, 184; vulnerability, xxi–xxii; in Yizhar, 173
eyes: in Midrash and comics, 158–61; reading, 221–22

faculty psychology, 113, 116
faith affirmation in Psalms, 3, 12
false accusations: listening, 207–8; Psalms, 8
fanaticism, 86
fasting, 35
feminist interpretations of Esther, 180, 186–94
fertility tropes, 71
Fichman, Y., 58, 62, 66–71, 73n18
fiction, importance of, 188–89
figurative language, rhetoric as, xi
Fine, S., 25
first-fruit offerings, 23, 31, 38n44
Folkshul, 249–51, 252–54, 255–62
food: eating metaphor, 122–23; impurity, 31–33, 41n105; as sacrifice, 23, 24–27, 30–31, 39n56, 40n84, 41n90
footnotes in ArtScroll, 216, 223–24, 227
forensic function, xi
France, 46–47, 83, 87, 89, 138
Freedman, J., 232–33, 234
French language, 229n4
French Revolution, 79, 80
Furley, W., 13–14

Gage, C., 192–93
Garden of Eden imagery in Yizhar, 174–75
Gemara, xv, 227–28, 230n10
gender. *See* women
Gendler, M., 186–87
Genesis: alphabet, 105–6; imagery in Yizhar, 174–75; Leviathan, 148–49; nothingness, 140–41
Germany, 58, 73n7, 177–78n19
Gersonides, 48–49, 50–51, 52
Giffords, G., 231
gift, listening as, 199, 204–7, 210, 212
goat sacrifice, 134–36, 145

God: letters in name, 94, 106–7; Psalms, 1–14
grace, xvii, 174
graphic narrative. *See* comics, Midrash as
Greco-Roman rhetoric: canon, xiii–xv; comparison rhetoric, 20–22, 34; connections to Jewish rhetoric, x, xvi–xvii; defined, x–xi; humor, 141–42; internal rhetoric, 112; justice, 79; legal fiction, 22; Maimonides, 113–14; vs. Midrash, 99–101; Moses ben Nachman, 131–45; New Rhetoric Project, 77–78, 87, 88; *Nofet Zuphim*, 49–50; poetry and hymns, 13–14; principles, xii; transmission, 53, 55n5; visualization, 148. *See also* Plato; Socrates
Greek language, xvii, 93–97, 101–4, 106
Greenbaum, A., viii, xiv

Halkin, H., 60–61
hand washing, 24, 31–32, 41n98
haroset, 30
havruta, 201–2, 204, 213n4
Hawhee, D., xxiii
health: choice, 116–17, 119–27, 129nn6–7; listening, 206
hearing: in Judaism, 198–99; vs. listening, 198, 200, 212n2; rhetorical canon, xiv, xxiv; scholarship focus, xxviii n9; vs. seeing, 152–53
heave offerings, 31, 33, 41n105
Hebrew language: alphabet, 73n14, 93–109; ArtScroll, 215, 222, 229n4; exclusion of Jewish rhetorics, viii–ix, xxvi; first printed book, 49; as inseparable from Jewish rhetoric, 152; Kabbalah, 104–6; Zionist slogans, 177–78n19
Hebrew-Yiddish relations, 58–74
Hecht, B., 203
heder, viii, xxvii n4
Helfer, I. (I. Manger), 58, 62–66, 70–71
hidush (rhetorical canon), xiv–xv, xxii, xxiv
Hillel, R.: *baraita*, 99–100; Sabbath observation, 133–34
Hillel school, xv, 33, 37n22, 79, 133–34, 202–3, 209, 211
Hoffmann, E., 205–6
Holdstein, D., viii, xiv
Holmberg, C., 52
Holocaust: Belgium, xix, 83–85, 87; and exceptionalism, 231, 232, 236–38, 239, 259; *Maus* (Spiegelman), 155, 157–58; memorialization, 237, 239–40, 247n12; need for fiction on, 188–89; New Rhetoric Project, 77, 79, 88; synecdoche, 236–38, 243; Yiddish, viii

Humanistic Judaism, 249, 253, 264n1
humility, 202, 209, 212
humor, 141–42, 150, 155
Hyde, M., 206–7, 209
hymns, Greek, 13–14

identification in Psalms, 12
identity: *double fidélité*, 83; exile, x; intellection, 113, 124–25; Jewishness as marker, vii, xiii; and language, 68–70, 72; New Rhetoric Project, 79
idolatry, 152–53
image-picture distinction, 151–52
immigration: Chinese, 246n3; Jewish Americans, 232–37, 246; Jewish Italians, 46–47, 48
immortality, 18
impermanence in Esther, 181, 183, 185
inheritance, observation and retribution, 171–72, 177n15
innocence: Psalms, 3–4, 5–7, 8; in Yizhar, 172, 173–74
intellection, 113, 114, 124–25
internal rhetoric, 112–29
Internet, 54
intertextuality, 169, 177n11
irony, 33, 34, 35
Isaac, R., 25
Isaiah, 32, 204–5
Ishmael, R., 99–100
Islam, 46, 53, 89
Israel: criticism in Yizhar, 166–76; Declaration of Establishment, 169–70, 174, 177n15; language war, 62; and Perelman, 82
Israelite term, 83, 88
Italy, 46–47

Jacob (bar mitzvah subject), 250, 251, 257–60, 262–64
Jesus, 212n1
Jewish Children's Folkshul, 249–51, 252–54, 255–62
Jewishness: as marker of identity, vii, xiii; New Rhetoric Project, 78; as synecdoche, 231–46; as term, xiii
Jewish rhetoric: canons, xiii–xv, xxiv; history, viii–x, xiii, xvi–xx, xxii–xxiii, xxvii n2; as term, x, xiii; textual modes, xv–xvi; theory and practices, xx–xxvii
Job, 12
Johnson, M., 234–35
Jonah, 147, 148–50, 153–62
Josephus, 18, 40n82

Joshua, 39n68
Joshua, R., 21
judges: listening and ethics, 207–8; priests as, 27–28, 40n71
justice: New Rhetoric Project, 79, 88; Psalms, 2, 7, 8–11, 13; as rhetorical canon, xv, xix, xxiv; secular Judaism, 253; in Yizhar, 169–70, 171, 176

Kabbalah: Creation, xx, 200; letters, 94, 104–6; Maimonides, 139–40; Moses ben Nachman, 131, 133, 138, 139–40; theory of rhetoric, xx–xxi
kairos, xii, xxii, 2, 3–5, 138, 209
Kaplan, L., 121–22, 129n13
Kaplan, M., 251
Kents, O., 201–2
Khirbet Khizeh (Yizhar), 165–76
kindness, 2, 39n56
King, M. L., 241, 247n14
Koren Talmud, 230n9

Ladino, ix, 71
Lakoff, G., 234–35
laments, 4, 62–66
language: ArtScroll, 215–29; development and metaphor, 42n114; divinity of, xii; exclusion of Jewish rhetorics, viii–ix; host and guest, xxi; and Kabbalah, xx; militarism, 167–68; the Shema, 200; war, 60–62, 64–65, 67–70, 73n5, 73n7; Zionism, 177–78n19. *See also individual languages*
laughter, 156
laws: internal rhetoric, 128; reforms by Messer Leon, 48; shift from priests to rabbis, 19, 20, 22–33, 36, 38nn44–45, 40n71
learning: and intellection, 114; as term, 217–18, 219–20. *See also* education
legal fiction and shift from priests to rabbis, 19, 22–24, 34, 38nn44–45
Lesley, A., 46–47, 55n4, 55–56n6
letters. *See* alphabet
Leviathan, 148–50, 153–63
Levinas, E., xii, xix–xx, xxi
Levine, M., 138
LGBT, 192, 253
lies, 207–8
listening: in Judaism, 198–212; rhetorical, 206, 213nn5–6, 247n15
literacy, 20, 38n31, 147, 185, 260
logic, 86, 97–98, 113–14
Lorberbaum, M., 137–38

INDEX

love and listening, 208
lulav, 23–24, 29, 40n82

Maimonides, xii, 112–29, 139–41
Malcolm X, 241, 247n14
Manger, I. (I. Helfer), 58, 62–66, 70–71
Manger, N., 64
Maus (Spiegelman), 155, 157–58
McCloud, S., 159–61
mean and morality, 121, 123–27
medical metaphor, 116–17, 119–23, 129n7, 129n12
Meir, R., 147, 149
memory, xv, xviii–xx, xxiv, 240, 247n13
Messer Leon, Judah, 46–56
metaphor: eating, 122–23; as master trope, 33–34; medical, 116–17, 119–23, 129n12; stage, 42n114; use of Jewish in American culture, 231–32, 238
meta-picture, 151, 154–55
metonymy: Jewish immigration, 234–36; as master trope, 33, 34; shift from priests to rabbis, 34–35; stage, 42n114
middot. See baraita
Midrash: comics as, 147–50, 153–62; eyes in, 158–61; vs. Kabbalah, 104–5; reflected in Esther, 184–85; as rhetoric, ix, xv–xvi; vs. Socrates, 94, 98–101; as term, 150. See also priests, shift to rabbis from
Miletto, G., 47
militarism, 61–62, 70, 73n7, 165–76
Miller, C., 52
minority: acknowledging, xxi; model, 233–34
Mishna: ArtScroll, 223; dissent in, 37n22; as rhetoric, xv; study of, 152–53. See also priests, shift to rabbis from
misperception, 120, 121, 122, 123, 126
Mitchell, W. J. T., 151, 154
Mizrachi traditions, xxv–xxvi
mockery, 6
modeling in Psalms, 3, 12
model minorities, 233–34
modernism, 67, 68
monsters. See Leviathan
morality. See ethics
Mordecai. See Esther
Morrison, T., 240
Morrow, W., 14n7
Moses, 177n15, 205–6
Moses ben Nachman, R. (Nachmanides), 131–45
Moshe ben Maimon (Maimonides), xii, 112–29, 139–41
Muir, D., 177–78n19

multiplicity (rhetorical canon), xv, xxiv
mutants. See *X-Men*

Nachmanides, 131–45
Nagen, Y., 26–27
names, xii, 102, 103, 106–7
nationalism, 60–62, 65, 142–45
New Rhetoric Project, 77–89
Niencamp, J., 112–13
1948 War, 165. See also *Khirbet Khizeh* (Yizhar)
nobility and internal rhetoric, 115
Nofet Zuphim, 46, 49–56
notarikon, 101, 102, 105, 109
Novak, D., 136, 137
Novick, P., 239, 247n12

oaths, 217, 229n1
obedience, 198, 204, 207, 212n1
object-oriented philosophy, 94–96, 108–9
observation, retribution and inheritance, 171–72, 177n16
Olbrechts-Tyteca, L., 84, 89n1. See also Perelman, Chaim
Olson, C., xxiii
openness. See vulnerability
orality: ArtScroll, 225; Rashi, 222; Socrates, 98; Talmud, 215, 216, 222–26, 227; Torah, 18–19
Organon, 114
Ostriker, A., 196n12
"otherness," recognizing, xx, xxi
Oz, A., 74n20

Pak, G., 237–38
Palin, S., 231
Passover, 30–31, 40n84, 41n90
Patrick, D., 3–4
Pease, D., 232
Perelman, Chaim, xix, 77–89
Perelman, F., 82, 83, 84
Perelman, N., 83
perfection, 226–27
performance: bar mitzvah, 254, 256, 260; rhetoric as, 174
persuasion: self, 112–29; shift from priests to rabbis, 16–36, 37n5
Pharisees, 17–18, 31, 33, 41n105
Philo Judaeus, xvii, 40n83
phronesis, 125. See also mean and morality
pictorial turn, 151
Plato, xii, 97, 98, 101–4, 106, 108, 141–42
pluralism and New Rhetoric Project, 86–87, 88

INDEX

poetry, 13, 62–70
Poland, x, 81, 87, 177–78n19
politics: education, 251, 253, 261; and printing press, 50–51; sexual, 186; shift from priests to rabbis, 17–18
polysystem theory, 74n21
positivism, xix, 86
postmodernism and self-signification, 95
praise in Psalms, 11
prayer vs. sacrifice, 21, 22–24, 28
priests, shift to rabbis from: appropriation rhetoric, 19, 28–33; comparison rhetoric, 19, 20–22, 34; history, 16–19, 37n5; legal fiction, 19, 22–24, 34–35, 38nn44–45; purity laws, 19, 20, 28, 31–33, 35, 36, 41n93, 41n98, 41n105; substitution rhetoric, 20, 24–28, 35, 36, 38n37, 39n57
printing press, 49, 50–51, 53, 55–56n6, 222
print rhetoric, ArtScroll, 222–24
progymnasmata, 20
pronunciation, 226, 229n6
prophetic speech, 123–24
prophets, 36n1
The Protocols of the Elders of Zion, 231
Psalms, 1–14
punctuation, 224–25
Purim: exile, 184; memories of, 180, 181, 187, 193, 194; name, 195n3
purity laws, 19, 20, 28, 31–33, 35, 36, 41n93, 41n98, 41n105

rabbis. *See* priests, shift to rabbis from
Rabinowitz, I., 50–51, 55nn3–4
race: conflation with ethnicity, viii; model minorities, 233–34; secular Judaism, 253; synecdoche, 231–46
the Rambam. *See* Maimonides
the Ramban. *See* Nachmanides
rape, 192–93
Rashi: Aggadot, 139–40; ArtScroll, 223–24; effect on discipleship, 222; French language, 229n4; goat sacrifice, 134–36, 145; listening, 205–6
Ratcliffe, K., 203, 213nn5–6, 247n15
rationalism: Maimonides, 117, 129n9, 139; Moses ben Nachman, 137
reading: ArtScroll, 217–18, 219–20, 221–22, 228; comics, 151; in Esther, 184–85, 194
realism, speculative, 96
reason and New Rhetoric Project, 78, 80, 81, 85–86, 88
reciprocity, 8–11
recognition and intellection, 114
redemption, xx, xxi

redress, 3, 5–7
reflection: bar mitzvah, 261; comics, 160; Jonah, 159; metaphor as tool for, 119; repentance, 155; vs. self-persuasion, 129n11
reflective-persuasive communication, 115–16, 128n4
refusal to listen, 208, 209, 211–12
Reisigl, M., 235, 236
relationship (rhetorical canon), xiv
repentance, 135, 136, 154, 155, 159
responsibility: exceptionalism, 232; listening, 208, 209
retribution, observation and inheritance, 171–72, 177n15
revenge, 126
rhetoric: canons, xiii–xv, xxiv; defined, x–xi, xiii; master tropes, 33–34; principles, xii; theory, xx–xxii. *See also* Greco-Roman rhetoric
rhetorical continuity, 167
rhetorical listening, 206, 213nn5–6, 247n15
Rock of Israel, 169–70, 177n15
Roman rhetoric. *See* Greco-Roman rhetoric
Rosen, N., 187–92
Rosh Hashana, 29
Russia, x

Sabbath observation, 132–34
sacrifices: Azazel, 134–36, 145; Greek, 13; shift from priests to rabbis, 17, 19, 21–27, 28, 30–31, 35, 36, 39n56, 40n84, 41n90, 41n105; by women, 182, 191
Sadducees, 17, 19, 38n31, 41n105
Schottenstein Edition. *See* ArtScroll
scrolls and impurity, 32–33, 41n105
secular Judaism and bar mitzvah, 251–64
Sedgwick, E., 181
seeing: comics, 159; vs. hearing, 152–53
Sefer Nofet Zuphim, 46, 49–56
Seid, J., 254–55
self-consciousness in Esther, 181, 182–83
self-cursing, 7
self-deception, 116–19
self-interest, God's, 3, 11
self-persuasion, 112–29
self-reflexivity in Esther, 182–84
self-signification, 95
Seltzer, R., xvii
Sephardim: Ladino, ix, 71; rhetoric, xxv–xxvi; split with Ashkenazim, xxvii–xxviii n5; syllabic accent switch, 67; U.S. immigration, 246n1
Septimus, 139
sexuality in Esther, 186, 187, 190–91, 192–93, 195

INDEX 277

Shahar, D., 73n5
Shamir, M., 176n4
Shammai and Hillel schools, xv, 33, 37n22, 79, 133–34, 202–3, 209, 211
"Shema Yisrael," 198, 199–201
Sheshet, R., 23, 35
Shevuos, 217, 229n1
Shimon, R., 23
shiur, ArtScroll as, 215–29
shofar, 29
shule movement, 249
silence: and listening, 202; Maimonides, 127; and receiving the Torah, 200; in Yizhar, 175–76
Silver, M., 253
Simon, H., 96
Simon II, 17
Simon the Just, 39n68
sin offerings, 134–36
Sirach, 17
skepticism and fanaticism, 86
social justice projects, 256
social networking, 54
Socrates, 93, 97–99, 101–4, 209
Sodom and Gomorrah, 166–67, 168, 170–71, 172–73
Solomon, 207
Solomon ben Isaac. *See* Rashi
sophism, 98, 108, 131–45
soul, 18, 129n6
South America, x
sovereignty, 169, 177n15
Spain, x, 137–38
speaking: intellection, 113, 114, 124–25; interactions with God, 5, 6–7; internal vs. external, 114; listening as gift, 204–5; prophetic speech, 123–24; as redemption, xxi; vulnerability, xii
speculative realism, 96
Spiegelman, A., 147
Stampfer, S., 213n4
Steinsaltz, A., 227
Stemberger, G., 99–101
stereotypes and synecdoche, 235–36, 243–44, 246n7
Strack, H., 99–101
studying vs. learning, 217–18, 219–20
substitution rhetoric, 20, 24–28, 35, 38n37, 39n57. *See also* synecdoche
suicide, 191–92, 195
Sukkoth, 23–24, 25–27, 29, 40n83
Summit, J., 208
superheroes, 231–32, 236–38, 246n10
synagogue: as replacement for Temple, 25, 29, 35, 39n57, 39n59; whale as, 161

synecdoche: Jewishness as, 231–46; as master trope, 33, 34; shift from priests to rabbis, 35; superheroes, 231–32, 236–38

Talmud: access to, viii; argument in, xviii, 79, 86, 87, 99, 143–44; ArtScroll, 215–29; and *baraita*, 99; humor in, 141–42; Koren Talmud, 230n9; letters in, 94; listening, 199, 201–3, 208; as oral tradition, 215, 216, 222–26, 227; pluralism, 86–87, 88; as rhetoric, ix, x, xv, xvii–xviii; Steinsaltz translation, 227; truth, 144
Tanakh. *See* Bible
Tarfon, R., 149
technology, writing as, 183, 185
Temple, and shift to rabbis from priests, 16–18, 20, 21, 22, 24–33, 35, 36n2, 39n57, 39n59, 40n38
teshuvah. See repentance
testimony: Esther, 182–83, 188–89; listening by judges, 207–8; right of redress, 5, 6
testing and redress, 5, 6–7
text as character, 183–84
textual modes, xv–xvi
Thucydides, xi
time: comics, 151, 155–56, 157; repentance, 155; Talmudic argument, xviii, 143, 144
Tirosh-Samuelson, H., 49–50, 55n4
Tompkins, P., 213nn5–6
to-ness (rhetorical canon), xiv, xv, xxiv, xxv, xxvii
to prepon (fitness), 138
Torah: access to, viii; and *baraita*, 99; orality, 18–19; as rhetoric, xv; shift from priests to rabbis, 16, 20–21, 22–24, 27, 39n68; silence, 200
Tosafists, 137–38, 139, 224
translations: ArtScroll, 215–29; Hebrew Bible, xvii; rhetorical acts as, xxi; Steinsaltz Talmud, 227; as work of redemption, xx–xxi
truth: Aristotle, 143; and fanaticism, 86; Moses ben Nachman, 131; sophism, 132, 138, 144; Talmud, 144
Twersky, I., 115, 129n6
tzedek. See justice

Ukraine, x
Understanding Comics (McCloud), 159–61
United States: Declaration of Independence, 177n15; Hebrew, viii–ix; Jewishness as synecdoche, 231–46
universalism, 80

value, rhetoric of, 65–66, 86
Vashti, 183, 184, 187, 190–91, 192, 193–94, 195, 196n12
Vespasian, 18
Vickers, B., 77, 78
Vilna Edition. *See* ArtScroll
visual rhetoric: ArtScroll, 220–27; defined, 162n1; midrash and comics, 147–62
vulnerability: exile, xxi–xxii; listening, 199, 201, 203, 204, 209, 210; of speaking, xii
V'ahavta, 208, 213n7

Walker, J., 13
Wandering Jew, 235–36, 246n7
War of Independence, 165. See also *Khirbet Khizeh* (Yizhar)
washing, 24, 31–32, 41n98
Ways of Wisdom, 201
Weil, S., 87
Weinreich, M., 58–59, 72n3
Western Wall, 193–94, 196n30
whale and visual rhetoric, 148–50, 153–62
Wine, S., 249, 253, 264n1
witnesses. *See* testimony
witness-through-the-imagination, 188–89
Wodak, R., 235, 236
Wolfson, E., 148, 162n2
women: commandments, 133; Esther and Jewish feminists, 180–96; lack of scholarship, xxvi; language war imagery, 64, 65

Women of the Wall, 193–94, 196n30
Workmen's Circle, 249, 250, 252
writing as rhetoric in Esther, 180–96

X-Men, 236–38, 240–45, 246nn8–10

Yavneh, 18, 19, 28
yeshiva: ArtScroll, 216, 222; decline of culture, viii; *havruta*, 213n4; interactivity, 218–19; reforms by Messer Leon, 48, 50, 53; rhetoric in, xxv
Yiddish: ArtScroll, 221, 225–26; decline of, viii; exclusion of Jewish rhetorics, viii–ix; resurgence of, xxvii n3; as subject of rhetoric, 62; Zionist slogans, 177–78n19
Yiddish-Hebrew relations, 58–74
Yiddishkeit movement (Folkshul), 249–51, 252–54, 255–62
Yizhar, S., 165–76
Yoḥanan, R., 24
Yoḥanan ben Zakkai, R., 18, 21, 29, 39n56
Yom Kippur, 154, 156, 163n9

Zhitlovsky, H., 61
Zionism: language war, 60–62, 65; and Perelman, 81, 82; slogans, 175, 177–78n19. See also *Khirbet Khizeh* (Yizhar)
Zulick, M., xiv